D1189798

WHEELS OF MISFORTUNE

WHEELS OF MISFORTUNE

The Rise and Fall of the British Motor Industry

Jonathan Wood

SIDGWICK & JACKSON
LONDON

To David Wood

First published in 1988 by
Sidgwick & Jackson Limited
1 Tavistock Chambers, Bloomsbury Way
London WC1A 2SG

ISBN 0 283 99527 0

Typeset by Hewer Text Composition Services, Edinburgh
Printed by Butler and Tanner Ltd, Frome, Somerset

Contents

Preface

The history of the British motor industry has a fascination all of its own and one with more than its fair share of intriguing byways and diversions. Faced with such a formidable panorama, from 1896 until the present day, I have therefore confined the mainstream contents of this book to the birth and evolution of the Austin, Ford, Morris, Rootes, Standard and Vauxhall companies, in other words the firms that emerged as the Big Six car makers during the 1930s. However, any account of the industry's growth and retrenchment would be incomplete without reference to the firms of Jaguar, Rover and Triumph, which were united when the indigenous motor industry was combined to form the British Leyland Motor Corporation in 1968.

My interest in the industry's history was first fired back in 1962 when, as an enthusiastic seventeen-year-old, I purchased for the princely sum of £15 a derelict 1928 Austin 16, then sitting in the corner of a local farmyard. The Austin's rescue, and subsequent renovation – achieved, I should add, with considerable help from friends and fellow enthusiasts – led to my researching, and then writing about, the industry's history and its personalities.

For this book is first and foremost about people and the cars that they created. I have tried, wherever possible, to tell this extraordinary story through the words of its principal participants, either from their written accounts or from interviews. Over the last quarter-century I have talked to hundreds of past and present industry engineers, executives and employees, many of them for *Thoroughbred and Classic Cars* magazine (now known as *Classic Cars*) during my eight years, from 1973 until 1981, as its features editor. I owe a great debt of gratitude to my then editor, Michael Bowler, and associate editor, Lionel Burrell, for their support and encouragement which permitted me to write with frequency and length on the affairs of the

British motor industry during my time on the journal. My thanks must also go to Tony Dron, the magazine's present editor, for continuing to accept my contributions as a freelance writer and I am grateful for his permission to quote from past articles I have written for that publication.

Of the many individuals I have interviewed, I must single two out for special mention. Hamish Orr-Ewing, as the Ford Motor Company's light car planning manager from 1959 until 1963, was closely involved with the creation of the Mark 1 Cortina and subsequently became a product planner with the Leyland Motor Corporation; while Harry Webster joined the Standard Motor Company in 1932 and went on to become technical director of Standard-Triumph and the Austin Morris division of the British Leyland Motor Corporation. In both instances they were not only able to give me accounts of their respective industry careers but were also able to provide invaluable perspective material.

In addition, my thanks must go to the following for their assistance, by granting me interviews, specifically for this book; David Andrews, finance director Austin Morris, British Leyland Motor Corporation, managing director Leyland International, executive vice chairman BL Ltd and chairman and chief executive Land Rover-Leyland Ltd; John Barber, finance director Ford Motor Company, finance director, managing director and deputy chairman British Leyland Motor Corporation; Sir John Egan, chairman Jaguar Cars; Ray Horrocks, chairman and managing director Austin Morris, chief executive cars BL Cars Group; and Lord Stokes of Leyland, chairman Leyland Motor Corporation and the British Leyland Motor Corporation. My thanks are also due to John Pullen, director of corporate affairs The Rover Group, but in this and all previous instances, I am responsible for any conclusions arising from these conversations.

I trust *Wheels of Misfortune* will provide a unique account of the British motor industry's affairs over the past ninety years and offer some explanations for the decline of this all-important manufacturing sector.

Jonathan Wood
Frensham, Surrey
October 1987

Acknowledgements

The author and publisher gratefully acknowledge the assistance of the following individuals and publishers for permission to reproduce extracts from the following books and magazines: Bob Murray, editor, *Autocar*; Cambridge University Press, for *Dudley Docker* by R. P. T. Davenport-Hines, *The Unbound Prometheus* by David S. Landes; William Collins Sons, for *Back from the Brink* by Michael Edwardes; Croom Helm, for *The Motor Car Industry in Coventry since the 1890s* by David Thoms and Tom Donnelly; Eyre and Spottiswoode, for *Business in Britain*, *The Car Makers* and *The Leyland Papers*, all by Graham Turner; Haynes Publishing, for *Jaguar Project XJ40* by Philip Porter, *Land-Rover* by K. and J. Slavin and G. N. Mackie; David Higham Associates, for *The Castle Diaries 1974–1976* by Barbara Castle; Michael Joseph, for *The Writing on the Wall* by Philip Whitehead, *The Labour Government 1964–1970* and *Final Term* by Harold Wilson; Howard Walker, editor, *Motor*; Christopher Drake, editor, *Motor Industry Management*; Maurice Platt, for *An Addiction to Automobiles* by Maurice Platt; Praeger Publishing, for *Chrysler UK* by Stephen Young and Neil Hood; Queen Anne Press, for *Milestones in a Motoring Life* by Dudley Noble; Patrick Stephens, for *Jaguar: The history of a great British car* by Andrew Whyte; Mike Taylor, for *Troubled Times*; Unwin Hyman, for *The IRC* by Douglas Hague and Geoffrey Wilkinson.

Thanks are also due to the following for photographs and illustrations: Austin Rover – 1·8 litre MGB, Triumph 2000, Morris Marina, Austin Allegro, Triumph TR7, 800 Series Rover and Austin Metro; John Barber – photo of himself; Ford Motor Company – Ford Cortina, Sir Patrick Hennessy and Sir Terence Beckett; Jaguar Cars – Jaguar XJ6, Sir John Egan and Sir William Lyons; Land Rover – the Land-Rover and the Range Rover; National Motor Museum – Sir Herbert Austin, Daimler dog cart, 1912 Rover, 1915 Ford Model T, Morris Cowley, Model Y Ford, Eight of 1935, 10hp Hillman Minx, 1959 Herald, Jaguar 240, Hillman Imp, Renault R16, 1937 Standard 14, Austin Maxi; Press Association – Michael Edwardes; Quadrant Picture Library – William Morris. The remaining photographs are from the author's collection.

The illustration on page 88 is from *Engineering Education: A Social History* by George S. Emmerson (David and Charles, Crane, Russak, 1973).

'In the conditions of modern life the rule is absolute: the race which does not value trained intelligence is doomed. Not all your heroism, not all your social charm, not all your wit, not all your victories on land or at sea, can move back the finger of fate.'[1]

Alfred North Whitehead, 1916

1

From Tricycles to Tin Lizzies

1896–1914

'We are celebrating the birthday of the most wonderful industries that God has ever blessed mankind with ... since the world began ... each large town will have its own manufactories, and Nottingham carriages will vie with Birmingham carriages for lightness, elegance and speed.'[2]

H. J. Lawson, chairman of the Daimler Motor Company,
1 May 1896

'Every family in the United Kingdom has contributed the equivalent of £200 to British Leyland and such a situation cannot continue.'[3]

The prime minister, the Rt. Hon. Margaret Thatcher,
20 February 1986

Almost ninety years separate these two statements. The first, uttered in 1896 in the high summer of Victorian prosperity, was made on the eve of the birth of the country's motor industry and, by the following year, the first British-built motor cars were leaving the Daimler Company's grandly named Motor Mills in Sandy Lane, Coventry. The second statement came from the prime minister of a Conservative government which, having inherited an ailing motor industry, wanted to return this problem child to the private sector. Since nationalization in 1975 it had absorbed £2.2 billion of public funds, and been guaranteed a further £1.6 billion.

Yet it should not be forgotten that Britain had Europe's second-largest motor industry until 1932 when she overtook France and remained in this pole position until 1955. In 1950 Britain moved ahead of America to become the world's largest exporter of motor vehicles and when, in 1968, the indigenous industry combined to form the British Leyland Motor Corporation, it was fifth in world terms behind the American Big Three car makers and Volkswagen. Yet in 1987 we built 1.2 million cars, and slipped to fifth in the European production league behind Germany, France, Italy and Spain. Today the United Kingdom is ninth in the automobile production table and the only significant profits in the motor industry are made by the American-owned Ford Motor Company with Jaguar as the sole viable survivor in the British-owned sector.

So just what has happened during these ninety years to bring about such a spectacular decline? Is it the result of inept, untrained management or bloody-minded trade unions, encouraging their work-shy members to strike at the slightest pretext, or is it simply a case that our competitors produce better cars than we do? Is the demise purely a post-war one or is it the result of a more deep-seated industrial malaise?

This book sets out to answer these questions and our starting point is the creation of the motor car in 1886. It is not a British invention but was born, just over a century ago, in Germany when Carl Benz and Gottlieb Daimler, each working independently of the other, created what we now call automobiles and in doing so also triggered the creation of the world's motor industry. Both drew on bicycle and carriage trades for their cars' chassis, while the rear-mounted, single-cylinder power units were derived from the stationary gas engine which employed the four-stroke cycle, patented by their fellow countryman Nicholas Otto in 1876. Final drive was by belt, though Daimler switched to gears in 1889.

Yet these so-called horseless carriages created little interest in their native land and it was the French who embraced the idea with great enthusiasm. This followed the Parisian firm of Panhard and Levassor, which had hitherto specialized in the production of woodworking machinery, taking up a licence to manufacture a V twin engine that Daimler had patented in 1889. Car production began that year, but in 1891 Emile Levassor, a partner in the firm and, like Panhard, a graduate of the prestigious *Ecole Centrale des Arts et Manufactures,* moved the Daimler engine from the rear to the front of the car, so making the power unit more accessible than had previously been the case. As a trained engineer he no doubt abhorred the vagaries of belt drive, with its slipping, snatching and stretching, for the new alignment permitted him to follow Daimler's example and employ a set of gears, used in conjunction with a clutch, and in line with the engine's crankshaft. Final drive, via a differential, was by chains to both rear wheels. The result was more worthy of the term 'motor car' than 'horseless carriage'.

What Levassor had done (which rather unfairly became known as the *Système Panhard*), was to produce a layout capable of almost infinite development, whereas the rear engine/belt arrangements would, within a few years, represent an archaic backwater. Other manufacturers gradually followed suit though Peugeot, and Panhard's principal rival, which built bicycles prior to diversifying into cars in 1899, did not go front-engined until 1900.

That year France was, by far and away, the world's leading car maker with Paris the undisputed capital of the automobile world; De Dion Bouton was easily its leading manufacturer, followed by Panhard, Peugeot and Renault. In that year the French motor industry produced about 4,800 cars, ahead even of America, which came late to the automobile and built only 4,192. In Europe, Germany was a poor second to its Gallic neighbour with around 800 cars, while Britain was some way behind with about 150.

The British motor industry differed from its continental contemporaries in that it sprang, to a notable extent, from the bicycle industry. No less than five major car companies, Humber, Sunbeam, Singer, Rover and Hillman, all made bicycles before turning to automobiles; and the founder of the British Daimler company, so called because it had purchased the patents of the German Daimler car, was a bicycle mechanic-cum-financier. Therefore, from the very outset, though there were some exceptions, British-built cars leaned heavily on their continental counterparts for design initiatives as the bicycle makers wrestled with the intricacies of the internal combustion engine. Just as Paris had emerged as the main centre of the French motor industry, Coventry became Britain's first motoring city.

Yet, prior to the 1860s, Coventry had little or no engineering tradition. This sprang from the bicycle trade which arrived in Coventry in 1868 and greatly expanded following John Kemp Starley's invention of the Rover Safety bicycle in 1885, the name having been adopted for a new tricycle the previous year because 'it was felt that this machine was ideal for "roving" or "wandering" around the countryside'.[4] Bicycle sales soared, culminating in the bicycle boom of 1893–7; this collapsed, partly as a result of the challenge of the cheap, mass-produced bicycle from America.

Henry (Harry) John Lawson had made a fortune from the bicycle boom and, from 1895, attempted to do the same by floating motor manufacturing companies. The most important of these was Daimler, founded in Coventry in 1896, which began producing Britain's first cars in the following year. These first Daimlers closely followed contemporary Panhard practice and the front-engine/rear-drive layout was to dominate British car design for the next sixty-two years. Eighteen ninety-six was also significant as the despised Locomotives on the Highways Act was amended to permit automobiles to travel at 14mph, instead of 4mph in the country and 2mph in towns, as had hitherto been the case. With the collapse of the bicycle boom, all Lawson's companies were in trouble. He ceased to be Daimler's chairman in 1897, his affairs fell apart and in 1904 he was sentenced to twelve months' penal servitude for fraud.

Although Lawson had been the first person to seize the automotive initiative, and so trigger the birth of the British motor industry, initially his fellow businessmen did not follow his example. Instead it was engineers who set the pace by producing prototype cars which then excited entrepreneurial interest. Two of the most significant pioneers, who both built experimental cars in 1896, were Frederick Lanchester and Herbert Austin. A greater contrast in approach to car design than theirs is difficult to imagine. Lanchester was educated at the Hartley Institute, Southampton, and the Norma School of Mines, and his towering, trained intellect produced cars which were highly original in concept. The largely self-taught Austin, on the other hand, was never slow to ignore any idea, particularly if it belonged to someone else. However, the Lanchester company's independent existence came to an end in 1931, while Austin went on to become one of Britain's leading car makers.

Herbert Austin (1866–1941) was born in Little Missenden, Buckinghamshire. In 1870 the family moved to Wentworth in Yorkshire where Giles, Herbert's father, became farm bailiff to Earl Fitzwilliam. Herbert attended Rotherham Grammar School and he soon developed a passion for freehand drawing. 'The long winter evenings would have been quite awful unless I had been able to indulge my hobby,'[5] he later remembered. After leaving school, Austin spent two years at Brampton Commercial College and, although he was initially bent on an architectural career, his growing interest in engineering resulted in his parents applying, on his behalf, for an apprenticeship with the Great Northern Railway. But before he could take it up, his mother's brother arrived from Australia and his tales of the antipodes so captivated the eighteen-year-old Herbert that he accompanied his uncle on his return there.

In Melbourne Herbert obtained a job and served an apprenticeship with Messrs Richard Parkes and Company, which his uncle managed, and imported Crossley gas engines. Austin remained there for about two years before moving to Langlands Foundry. Although he had mixed feelings about that firm, he later recalled that it was there he 'received a thorough training as a mechanic'.[6] Later, in 1887, he moved to another small engineering company and, the same year, married Helen Dron, whose Scottish parents had emigrated to Australia.

Austin returned to Britain in the winter of 1893, having met Frederick York Wolseley, brother of the Sudan war hero General (later Field Marshal) Viscount Wolseley. In 1876 Frederick Wolseley had patented a sheep-shearing machine and in 1887 had established the Wolseley Sheep Shearing Company to manufacture it, though the design was not perfected and there were plenty of teething troubles. In 1889 the firm's headquarters moved to London and in 1893 Austin was offered the post of general manager.

Once back in Britain, Herbert was faced with the problem of thousands of defective shearing machine parts flooding back from Australia. He recognized that the only satisfactory way of resolving the problem was for Wolseley to manufacture the components itself. He therefore initiated the purchase of a small factory in Broad Street, Birmingham, and, in 1895, these activities were transferred to the larger and appropriately named Sydney Works in Alma Street, Aston, Birmingham. Bicycle parts and machine tools mostly for cotton machine makers, the latter designed by Austin, were also manufactured.

Frederick Wolseley resigned from the company in 1894 and died in 1899, and Austin was unable to get the firm's directors to support his idea to diversify into motor car production. He therefore built an experimental vehicle at his own expense. Austin had already visited Paris and he must have later noted Léon Bollée's single-cylinder *voiturette* tricar, which first appeared in December 1895, for his own first car, completed in 1896, bears a striking similarity to the Bollée, the final drive mechanism being virtually a carbon copy, though the 2hp two-cylinder engine was a great improvement on the original. However, he did not proceed with the design, probably because it infringed the Bollée patents that were snapped up by H. J. Lawson's British Motor Syndicate in May 1896.

By this time the Wolseley management had had a change of heart and, in the spring of 1896, agreed to spend £2,000 on a plant for car manufacture. So the next car Austin built in 1896 was at the company's expense. It was again a three-wheeler, though with a single wheel at the front, and powered by a 3hp single-cylinder engine. An improved 3.5hp version followed in 1897. A four-wheeled Wolseley was completed in time for the Automobile Club of Great Britain and Ireland's 1,000 Mile Trial of 1900 which 'demonstrated to the public that the motor car was not merely the toy of the wealthy *dilettante* . . . but a commercial reality capable of accomplishing long distances day after day'.[7] Of the sixty-five entries, only a handful were British. These were from Daimler, MMC and three firms which entered prototype cars – Lanchester, Napier which was soon to emerge as one of the world's foremost marques, and Wolseley which won a prize awarded by the *Daily Mail* for being first in its class.

However, for all the car's success, the Wolseley directors were still reluctant to commit themselves to car production and Austin succeeded in interesting the mighty Vickers Sons and Maxim armaments concern, which wanted to enter the motor business in view of its military potential, in his ideas. As a result, Vickers formed the Wolseley Tool and Motor Car

5

Company in February 1901. Austin joined the new company as works manager, the Sheep Shearing Company received £12,400 in cash and Vickers also bought some debenture stock. It took up the manufacture of cream separators instead of cars and survives today as the Droitwich-based Wolseley-Hughes Group, which produces central heating and agricultural equipment.

Fortunately Vickers already had a factory suitable for car production at Adderley Park, Birmingham, about 2 miles to the south of the Sheep Shearing Company's Aston works. This was a large 3½-acre establishment that Starley Brothers and Westwood Manufacturing Company had built in expectation of a boom in bicycle sales. Vickers had bought the plant in 1899 and it was sold to the new Wolseley company for £31,545. The firm was quick off the mark issuing its first catalogue of 5hp and 10hp models and, by the end of the year, about 50 cars had been produced. This rose to 270 in 1902, with 341 built in the following year and 850 in 1904, all of which made Wolseley Britain's largest car manufacturers. Despite these outwardly impressive figures, Wolseley was soon in financial difficulties. In 1901 there was a loss of £5,429, and although there were profits of £5,400 and £12,512 in 1902 and 1903, this was achieved on turnovers of £82,247 and £132,456 respectively. In 1904 a loss of £2,579, on a £137,140 turnover, was recorded. This was against a background of the creation of a further £90,000 shares in 1903, and the following year Douglas Vickers made Wolseley a personal loan of £40,000.

One of Wolseley's problems was its general manager. Austin, displaying what was soon to be recognized as a traditional stubbornness, continued to design Wolseley cars with old-fashioned horizontal engines and completely ignored the front-mounted vertical units, as pioneered by Panhard in 1891. In 1902, while delivering a lecture on transmission systems, he also berated the increasingly popular Renault-designed universally jointed propellor shaft, which drove a gear-driven rear axle. The Austin-designed Wolseleys, by contrast, retained old-fashioned chain drive and, though the cars were reliable, this 'backwardness' soon attracted the attention of the Vickers management. It brought in John Davenport Siddeley to design vertically engined models and, in 1905, Herbert Austin, piqued at this action, departed in a huff.

Siddeley lasted until 1909 when he left to join with Captain H. H. P. Deasy to build Siddeley-Deasys. In the meantime the cars from Adderley Park became Wolseley-Siddeleys but, from 1911, reverted to being plain Wolseleys and the firm's best seller was the 3.2-litre 16/20hp. By the outbreak of the First World War this, and a brace of sixes, constituted the model range. Ironically the best-selling Wolseley of the day was not badged as such but sold under the Stellite name. This 1.1-litre light car was

6

made by the Electric and Ordnance and Accessory Company of Aston Road, Birmingham, a Vickers subsidiary, which also produced Timken roller bearings. By 1913 Wolseley was still the country's largest car maker with 3,000 vehicles produced but, with 4,000 employees, it had the doubtful distinction of being one of the country's most unprofitable car makers. Survival was only made possible by the Vickers financial umbrella.

Herbert Austin's sudden exit from Wolseley was to have its own repercussions. On 4 November 1905, four days after his thirty-ninth birthday, Austin and three companions set off in a 7.5ph Wolseley to examine a disused printing works, formerly occupied by the firm of White and Pike Ltd, 7 miles south west of Birmingham and adjacent to a branch of the Midland Railway. The asking price for the factory and land was £10,000 and Austin obviously liked what he saw because the Austin Motor Company was registered in December 1905 on a capital of £50,000, having paid £7750 for Longbridge. There were just two directors, Austin himself and Frank Kayser, whom Herbert had first approached for financial support back in 1899. They were subsequently joined by Harvey du Cros Junior, managing director of the Swift Motor Company, which had been building cars since 1900, and whose father was chairman of Dunlop.

Anxious to obtain the greatest possible publicity for the new Austin marque, Herbert took a stand at the 1905 Motor Show, where he displayed drawings of what was to be the first Austin model, a 23–30hp car with a conventional *vertical* T head four-cylinder engine. Production began at Longbridge in 1906 and Austin cars soon acquired a reputation as well-built if slightly old-fashioned vehicles. The coachwork was made at the factory and outstanding for its quality, elegance and proportion. Here one can detect the artistic sensibilities of Austin himself – his ability as a stylist was his real forte as a motor manufacturer. Mechanically the cars were less adventurous and 'were unashamedly copied from other sources and the similarity of, say, a 1907 Austin to a contemporary Gladiator or Clement is marked . . . On his own cars, with the exception of the 15hp, Austin clung to the practice of using separate cylinders long after most of his contemporaries had abandoned the idea.'[8]

Yet the financial problems that had clouded Austin's spell at Wolseley did not recur once he had full charge of his own affairs. The Austin Motor Company remained firmly in the black during the pre-1914 era and in 1912 attained record profits of £50,533. By the outbreak of the war in 1914, Austin had emerged as a medium-sized firm. It built 545 cars that year, and in February became a public company. Its capital was accordingly increased to £250,000, though Austin revealed subsequently that he had had serious misgivings about this progression. 'The truth is that that was the biggest mistake I have ever made. Had it remained a private concern its development would have been more personal and less spectacular,' he told *The Autocar* in 1929.

In 1908 Longbridge, following a world-wide trend, introduced its first six-cylinder car, a 60hp Austin. Britain's first major contribution to automobile design was the London-based Napier company's initiation of a pioneering 18hp six-cylinder model in October 1903, introduced at the instigation of wily Australian-born S. F. Edge, the firm's energetic publicist, who sold Napiers from a Regent Street showroom. The six's smoothness and flexibility, when compared with the four, was overwhelming, even if the unit had a tendency for torsional vibration. The continentals quickly followed suit: in 1905 Panhard offered its first six, followed by Mercedes, Fiat, Renault and Peugeot. Napier's sales were greatly boosted by the racing activities of Edge who won the influential Gordon Bennett Cup when his three opponents broke down in 1902, though the world would have to wait another twenty-one years for another British grand prix victory. Edge and Napier parted company in 1912 and things were never quite the same again in the face of the formidable Rolls-Royce challenge.

In 1903 Napier built 250 cars and a 16hp model, discreetly but luxuriously finished in the manner of a gentleman's carriage and costing £1,300. At the other end of the market was the American-built £150 Oldsmobile, with virtually no bodywork to speak of, tiller steering and chain drive. In 1903 Oldsmobile built 4,000 examples of what it called its 'Curved Dash' model, making it the most productive car company in the world. The spectre of American mass production was once again challenging the essentially handcrafted products of the British engineering industry. Some bicycle makers had successfully countered the trans-Atlantic challenge by streamlining production methods and cutting prices. Would the nascent motor industry be equally successful?

Mass production is not, of course, a twentieth-century phenomenon. It had already been applied to the American watch, sewing-machine and bicycle industries prior to its adoption by motor manufacturers. The mass production process is almost as old as the USA itself and is rooted in that country's armaments industry. Back in the late eighteenth century the reliability of a frontiersman's musket invariably had spelled survival. If the weapon was damaged, it was essential that its owner could repair it without the help of a skilled gunsmith. The answer was to make the parts so that one would be interchangeable with the next, rather than being crafted to fit just one weapon. Pioneers such as Eli Whitney and Simeon North attempted to achieve this objective with varying degrees of success, and in 1815 'the U.S. government laid down that all hand and shoulder weapons must be made from interchangeable parts'.[9] By the mid-nineteenth century the principle was well established, and the arms trade grew in size and influence during the American Civil War.

More peaceful applications, stimulated by a shortage of skilled labour, followed, one of which was Isaac Singer's production of sewing machines. The firm of Wilcox and Gibbs, in competition with Singer, 'caused him to pass many unhappy hours',[10] and although it initially produced its own machines, in 1858 Brown and Sharpe Ltd of Providence, Rhode Island, took over the work. Previously this company had repaired only watches, clocks and scientific instruments, though in 1850 it began making steel rules. Stimulated by the sewing-machine production, the firm started manufacturing precision machine tools. By the turn of the nineteenth century Brown and Sharpe had acquired a world-wide reputation for outstanding machine tools of the highest quality.

In 1867 came the world's first practical hand micrometer, while the Universal Milling Machine followed in 1862. It proved ideal for cutting twist drills, and in 1874 Joseph Brown, son of the firm's founder, added a cutter which permitted the manufacture of precision gears. This was followed in 1872 by the Universal Grinder, invented by Brown, Richmond Viall and Henry Leland, who joined the firm from the famous Colt armoury in 1872. Leland, destined to be revered as the 'Master of Precision', later acclaimed this grinder as 'Mr Brown's greatest achievement'. Its advantage was that it 'enabled us to harden our work first and then grind it with the utmost accuracy'.[11] Brown and Sharpe was just one of a number of influential American machine tool makers, while the Fellowes gear shaper of 1876, Frederick Taylor's use of tungsten chrome to cut high-speed steels and Charles Norton's heavy precision grinder combined to speed and improve the mass production process. Not surprisingly, when in 1899 a Special Correspondent of *The Times* visited a number of firms in the USA, including Brown and Sharpe, he reported: 'I wish the council of the Institute of Mechanical Engineers would pass a by-law that no one should be admitted to membership until he had visited a certain number of American workshops.'[12]

These machines were, of course, expensive to buy, but provided there was sufficient demand for the product the economies of scale took over. Therefore the more items that were produced, the lower the unit costs. This gave exports a particular importance as the vulnerable British watch and sewing-machine industries, unprotected by tariffs, knew to their cost. The American bicycle industry took up mass production techniques so successfully that, between 1890 and 1897, national output rose from 40,000 to 1 million machines. Before long, some of the more progressive British bicycle manufacturers were importing machine tools from across the Atlantic, and this spurred British machine tool makers into action. One of these was Alfred Herbert in Coventry, formed in 1889 essentially to supply the growing requirements of the bicycle industry.

In America, Henry Leland had decided to leave Brown and Sharpe and, in 1890, he established his firm of Leland, Faulconer and Norton in the city of Detroit, bringing to the venture the passion for precision which had been honed at Rhode Island. The firm produced lathes, milling machines and gear cutters and, in 1899, the mustachioed figure of Ransom Olds appeared in Leland's Trombley Avenue works. He wanted advice on the transmission for a small runabout he was designing. As a result Leland obtained the contract for its two-speed epicyclic gearbox, and in June came a further order for 2,000 single-cylinder engines for what was to emerge in 1901 as the $650 (£133) 'Curved Dash' Oldsmobile. The order was later shared with John and Horace Dodge who opened a Detroit machine shop in 1901. Leland took the initiative and improved the engine, so that instead of developing 5hp, it achieved 9.7hp, though Olds was not interested in improving his car as he could sell as many as he could make. So Henry Leland and his son Wilfred decided to use this engine to enter the motor business on their own account. The result was the Cadillac Automobile Company, named after Le Sieur Antoine de la Mothe Cadillac, the Frenchman who had discovered what became Detroit. Leland lavished the same meticulous approach on car production that he had applied to earlier work. Output began in 1902, and in 1903 Cadillac followed Oldsmobile into Britain, where they were imported by the Anglo-American Motor Car Company.

The American challenge had played its part in the collapse of the British bicycle boom in 1897 and one of the companies that toppled into deficit in 1899 was the Humber Cycle Company promoted by H. J. Lawson, with premises in both Coventry and Beeston. With the bicycle trade in the doldrums, the firm decided to diversify into cars, the transition partially made possible by a bank loan guaranteed by the managing director. The first Humber cars, which appeared in 1898, not surprisingly revealed their bicycle ancestry and motor tricycles and quadricycles were also produced.

In 1900 the firm wisely distanced itself from Lawson and was reconstructed as Humber Ltd. The following year Humber was fortunate to secure the services of twenty-two-year-old Louis Hervé Coatalen, who, although French, was to emerge as one of the outstanding figures of the British motor industry in the pre-First World War years. A graduate of the Parisian *Ecole des Arts et Métiers*, Coatalen spent some time in the Panhard, Clement and De Dion-Bouton drawing offices, before coming to Britain in 1900. After working briefly for Charles T. Crowden at Leamington, who had just built a 5hp horizontally engined car, Coatalen moved to Humber where he was made chief engineer. There he designed a robust four-cylinder 12hp car which was well priced at £300. In 1903 came the small 5hp Humberette, powered by a De Dion-type single-cylinder engine, identical to the French product apart from the fact that it was designed to run in an anti-clockwise direction! The model was greatly improved and enlarged to 6.5hp in 1904 when it emerged as Britain's first popular light car.

In 1904 Humber made only £1,125 profit but, in 1905 the range was reduced to two basic types, a 10/12hp four built at Coventry and Beeston's 16/20hp, the Humberette having been dropped. This rationalization literally paid dividends, for the firm's profits soared to £106,559 in 1906, when a record output of around 1,000 cars put the firm at the top of the British production league. Indeed, the firm's chairman reported that the 10/12 became so popular that 'we were almost driven to assembling the vehicles in the street so great did the demand outstrip our factory capacity'.[13] In view of this, Humber decided to build a massive new works in Folly Lane (later renamed Humber Road) in the Stoke district of Coventry, which would be the largest in the motor industry. The idea was that production could be concentrated in Coventry: Humber's other factories in Beeston and Wolverhampton would be closed when the new works became operative.

By July 1907 one observer noted that 'the size of the factory is simply enormous and already part of it is in occupation'.[14] It was opened early in 1908 and the satellite plants were subsequently closed down. The works, alas, became fully operative in what was to be a depression year and Humber recorded a loss of £23,499 in 1908. There was talk in Coventry of hundreds of unsold Humbers filling back yards, and although most of the industry recovered in 1909, Humber was left with the crippling overheads of a new plant and insufficient car sales to cover them. As if this were not enough, Louis Coatalen had left to join Hillman in 1907.

Humber was facing bankruptcy and was only saved at an extraordinary general meeting, held early in 1909, when Lord Russell, a wealthy shareholder, led a scheme of capital reconstruction of Humber Ltd. In February 1909 this went into voluntary liquidation and was reconstructed as a company of the same name. It was decided to utilize some spare capacity to build aircraft, and Humber offered its own machines and engines along with Bleriot wings at £40 a pair and propellers for £12 12s (£12.60) which were 'guaranteed perfect'. Humber had built motor cycles since 1900 and it also bought the liquidated assets of the Centaur Cycle Company of Stoke which produced similar machines. By late 1911 Humber was still in difficulties and the balance sheet of 1910, which showed a profit of £5,045 for a nineteen-month period, was 'not an inspiring document'.[15] The aircraft department was closed down and Centaur 'did not seem to be a good bargain'.[16]

In 1908 came a move down market with an 8hp twin for £195, perhaps memorable only for its peculiar starting arrangement for, although the engine ran clockwise, it was cranked anti-clockwise apparently to obviate the risk of a backfire. It lasted until 1910, but was too expensive for its class and in 1912 came a 11hp side-valve four with a 1.7-litre engine – a timely arrival in an expanding market which helped Humber to record a £25,670 profit that year. In 1913 the firm revived the Humberette name and offered a lively, but noisy, 8hp air-cooled V twin-powered cycle car for £125. A total of about 2,500 cars, were built that year, making Humber one of Britain's largest car companies. By mid-1914, the year in which water cooling was adopted, there were over 2,000 Humberettes on the road.

At the other extreme Frederick Tasker Burgess, the firm's chief designer, created a team of sophisticated Humbers for the 1914 Tourist Trophy Race powered by 3.3-litre twin overhead-camshaft engines and inspired by the racing Peugeot of the previous year. None of the trio, alas, completed the race, which must have been galling for Burgess who drove one of the cars.

Unlike Humber, Rover waited until 1904 to enter the car market, but it was more financially secure, John Kemp Starley not having succumbed to the blandishments of H. J. Lawson. Starley had produced an electrically powered three-wheeler in 1888, which was probably Coventry's first self-propelled vehicle. In 1899 he imported a few of the motorcycles that Peugeot had just introduced and Rover started producing its own two-wheelers in 1902, a year after Starley died at the tragically early age of forty-six.

His son, John Kemp Starley II, was just fourteen when his father died, though he subsequently became Rover's general manager. Therefore the running of the firm fell to company secretary Harry Smith. He was remembered by a former employee as 'short, choleric, and could hardly say a dozen words without liberally sprinkling in what are today known as four-letter ones. He was a dominating character, one that nobody crossed if they could help it . . .'[17]

Rover's bicycle sales began to fall away after 1902, despite its marketing of the cheap Meteor, and the company decided to diversify into motor cars. The firm succeeded in hiring no less than Daimler's chief engineer, Edmund Lewis, though only on a year's contract, and he departed for Deasy in late 1905 after completing his task. He designed a single-cylinder 8hp model with an unusual backbone chassis which appeared in 1904, and this was joined in 1906 by a 6hp version with a conventional frame. These reliable little cars were much favoured by doctors. The switch to car production was justified by the fact that although Rover recorded a uncharacteristic loss in 1904 through falling bicycles sales, two years later the firm achieved a £16,900 profit, its largest since 1897. A sign that Rover was beginning to downgrade bicycle production came in September 1905 with a change of name from the Rover Cycle Company to the Rover Company Ltd. That year 754 cars were built and 694 sold; only Argyll, Humber and possibly Daimler built more. Four-cylinder models had arrived in 1905 and a 16/20, not dissimilar to the 28-36hp Daimler, which progressively shared the same bore and stroke as the 6hp model, won the 1907 Tourist Trophy race. Its driver, Ernest Courtis, was presented with a gold watch and given an extra week's holiday by the grateful directors. His success helped the firm to produce a record 1,211 cars in 1907. As a result Rover decided to build a new factory for bicycle production so that the car business could expand.

What was clearly needed was an expert in automobile design and engineering to fill the vacuum caused by Edmund Lewis's departure, a question to which the Rover board addressed itself in February 1909, and it was agreed that such an individual should join the firm at board level. While a search for a suitable candidate proceeded, a brace of curious hybrid models were produced in 1910/11 which were fitted respectively with 8hp single and 12hp two-cylinder Daimler sleeve-valve engines. They did not sell well and at least one member of the Rover workforce of the day remembers them as 'a decided flop'.[18]

Rover's salvation came, in September 1910, with the arrival of thirty-two-year-old Owen Clegg as works manager. This Leeds-born engineer had served an apprenticeship with Kitson's locomotive engineers where he rose to be assistant works manager, though his interest in cars had resulted in his moving, in 1904, to Wolseley. He soon came to the attention of the Vickers management, who transferred him to Glasgow to manage one of their companies there, and he joined Rover from that assignment. Clegg was responsible for a new 2.2-litre four-cylinder 12hp, competitively priced at £350. The engine was an up-to-date rendering with its cylinders cast in one piece, rather than in blocks of two, side valves and a chain-driven camshaft instead of expensive and traditional gearing. The 12hp proved an instant success and laid firm foundations for much of the marque's subsequent popularity. A new recruit to the motor trade of the day recalled the 12hp as 'much in demand and second hand fetched very inflated prices'.[19]

Rover had built only 400 cars in 1911 but this figure more than trebled to 1,300 in 1912, was up to 1,800 the following year and reached the 2,000 mark in 1914. During this time the company's finances improved to such an extent that Rover became one of Britain's most profitable car companies, and in 1913 a 40 per cent dividend, the highest in the industry, was paid.

Regrettably for Rover, and the country's motor industry, Owen Clegg departed in March 1912 to take over the running of the British-owned but French-domiciled Darracq factory at Suresnes, Paris. This once front-line firm had been debilitated following a disastrous flirtation with the Henriod rotary-valve engine, though Clegg soon got it back on to an even keel with a new four-cylinder model, available in 2.1- and 2.9-litre forms and clearly inspired by the Rover 12hp; a welcome though rare instance of a British design inspiring a French one.

A surprising entry in the 1907 Tourist Trophy race was a new make, which was entered under the Hillman-Coatalen name. William Hillman was a veteran of the bicycle industry who, following the success of his Auto Machinery and New Premier Bicycle ventures, decided to enter the motor business. He managed to woo Louis Coatalen from Humber and a small factory was established in the grounds of Abingdon House, his home in Folly Road, adjoining the Humber works. The 25hp four-cylinder car was completed in time for the Tourist Trophy when Coatalen took the wheel. Despite putting up the fastest lap, the model retired with a broken spring. The car duly entered production though the make made little impact in the pre-war years. Coatalen, in the meantime, moved to Wolverhampton and the Sunbeam Motor Company, where he was appointed chief engineer in February 1909. This was not, however, before he had married one of Hillman's six daughters.

Although the Sunbeam Motor Company had not been registered until January 1905, car production had begun four years previously. The firm's founder, John Marston, had set up in business in 1859 when, as a young man of twenty-three, he began to manufacture tinned plate and japanned goods. In 1871 Edward Perry, for whom he had originally worked, died. Marston bought the business and moved into his Penn Road works. By this time japanned goods were becoming unfashionable and Marston looked around for another product. The arrival of John Kemp Starley's Safety Bicycle in 1885 had laid the foundations for the bicycle boom and, in 1887, Marston transformed the former Jeddo Works into the Sunbeamland Cycle Factory. The Sunbeam bicycle became 'one of the best finished and best made bicycles on the British market and the "little oil bath" chain case was one of its most endearing features'.[20]

Much of the success of the Sunbeam bicycle was the responsibility of Thomas Cureton, Marston's 'right hand in the cycle business'.[21] It was no doubt the downturn in bicycle sales that resulted in Marston contemplating car manufacture. In 1899 the firm experimented with a 4hp belt-driven car. Following this, in March 1900, Cureton proposed that there was 'a good trade to be done with a good Car. As a go ahead Firm, I think we should not let such a subject so important pass without giving same our

14

serious consideration.'[22] In the face of opposition from his friends and co-directors, Marston agreed. The result was an experimental single-cylinder car, though the first production model of 1901 was De Dion Bouton-engined, designed by a Mr Mabberley-Smith, sold under the Sunbeam-Mabley name and resembled a Victorian 'sociable' settee on wheels. It remained in production until 1904.

In 1902 Thomas Pullinger joined Sunbeam to get motor production on a sounder footing. A victim of H. J. Lawson's plans to build Humbers in France, he had remained in Paris when that particular venture failed and worked first for Darracq and subsequently became works manager for the Teste et Moret company. On arrival in Wolverhampton, Pullinger proposed that Sunbeam buy 'from an established firm a finished "chassis", say of 10/12hp . . .'[23] and some French Bertliets were subsequently imported.Not surprisingly, the 12hp Sunbeams of 1902/5 'were virtually indistinguishable from Berliets'.[24] Sunbeam soon followed Napier with a six-cylinder model in 1904 and Cureton departed for Humber at Beeston in 1905. That year, Angus Shaw, who had been chief draughtsman under Pullinger, emerged as a competent engineer in his own right and produced a robust four-cylinder 16/20hp model which served the company well for the next four years.

Then, in 1909, Louis Coatalen arrived in Wolverhampton and his efforts were to transform the Sunbeam company. That year the firm recorded a modest profit of £5,395, though this soared to £40,998 in 1910/11 which *The Economist* considered 'very satisfactory'.[25] Nineteen thirteen's figure was more than double at £93,409. Coatalen began his transformation of the Wolverhampton company's affairs by first designing a new 12/16hp four-cylinder model which proved to be 'one of the great commercial successes of the pre-war era'.[26] To generate publicity, Coatalen initiated an aggressive racing policy, an approach far more in keeping with continental traditions than British ones. Using the apparently mechanically unadventurous 12/16 as its basis, Coatalen prepared a racing team which achieved a sensational one-two-three success in the *Coupe l'Auto* race at Dieppe in 1912. The firm took up record breaking in 1913 and Sunbeams were campaigned in America the same year.

In the following year Sunbeam introduced its first Grand Prix car and a close copy of the contemporary Peugeot. This occurred because Coatalen, perhaps subversively, obtained a racing Peugeot, had it delivered to Wolverhampton when 'it was driven to the drawing room of [his] then residence, Waverely House on Goldthorn Hill, stripped right down, and the pieces laid out on the floor. Two draughtsmen, Hugh Rose and Ted Hatlands, then set about making detailed drawings of the entire car.'[27] In 1914 one of the resulting Sunbeams was placed fifth in the prestigious

French Grand Prix and won the Tourist Trophy race on the Isle of Man.

Coatalen also turned his attention to Sunbeam's manufacturing base. New factories were built in Upper Villiers Street on land that the firm had prudently purchased earlier 'and his requests for tools and equipment staggered everybody in the firm . . . he was not a man who muddled through doing everything in his head; he was all the time building up a team of reliable subordinates.'[28] The new manufacturing facilities boasted an impressive range of machine tools and Sunbeam had more American Potter and Johnson automatic lathes outside the USA, and outside Renault in France, than any other plant in the world. The way of building Sunbeam cars also differed from the usual British practice in that the chassis was movable rather than static. In the erecting shop there were small gangs of men who were responsible for only one job. When this was completed, the frame was hoisted by a girder tramway suspended from the roof and moved one stage further, the shop being a true assembly area. Production rose from 853 cars built in 1911 to 2,350 the following year, though it dropped back to 1,700 in 1913, which was still over three times the 1910 total, when 515 cars were built. The pre-war years therefore closed with Sunbeam's racing, productive and financial fortunes riding high.

Even before Coatalen arrived at Wolverhampton, French influence was strong at Sunbeam, which was by no means unusual in the British motor industry of the day. With a few exceptions, of which Lanchester was the most significant, practically the whole industry looked across the Channel for most of its design initiatives. One such firm was Royce Ltd, a Manchester-based firm of electrical engineers, which, in 1904, produced three prototype 10hp cars inspired by the two-cylinder Decauville. But to infer that they were nothing more than unthinking copies of a French design does a terrible injustice to their creator, Frederick Henry Royce.

Henry Royce (1863–1933) was a self-taught artist-craftsman of undoubted genius who, after a harrowing childhood, served an apprenticeship with the Great Northern Railway at Peterborough. He subsequently met Ernest Claremont, a doctor's son of about his own age, and in 1884 they founded the firm of F. H. Royce at Cooke Street, Hulme, Manchester. Initially simple household bellsets were produced and the firm progressed to dynamos and electrical cranes. Although the business prospered, Royce continued to drive himself to a state of exhaustion in his quest for mechanical perfection. In an effort to get him to relax, his partner and doctor suggested that he buy a car to enjoy the delights of motoring. As a result Royce bought the aforementioned secondhand Decauville but, dissatisfied with it, decided to produce his own 10hp two-cylinder car.

A 1904 meeting with pioneer motorist the Hon. Charles Rolls, who had opened a London motor agency in 1902, produced an order for nineteen two-cylinder cars and these, along with three-, four- and six-cylinder models, were all called Rolls-Royces. In March 1906 Rolls-Royce Ltd, which took its name from the cars, was formed, though the key appointment was that of managing director Claude Johnson, Rolls's partner since 1903 and later to be known as 'the hyphen in Rolls-Royce'.

In 1906 the firm unveiled a new model, the six-cylinder 40/50hp. It was Henry Royce's masterpiece and more than justified the firm's claim that it was 'the Best Six Cylinder Car in the World'..This model represented the quintessence of Royce's design philosophy for it was not in itself original but was refined to an extraordinary extent to meet its creator's perfectionist standards. The model, later to be known as the Silver Ghost, performed well, was extremely quiet for its day and beautifully finished. It was also large enough to transport wealthy customers, and their retinue, to winter in Cannes or Monte Carlo. Previously they might have bought a Daimler or Napier. After the arrival of the 40/50hp, increasing numbers bought Rolls-Royces.

Rolls-Royce moved from Manchester to a new factory at Derby in 1908, the same year that the 40/50hp became the firm's sole model. This was at a time when practically all car companies offered a wide variety of models. In 1912, for instance, Napier offered no less than eleven.

Then, in 1910, Rolls was killed in a flying accident and Royce's own fragile health broke down. He underwent an operation but, although it was successful, he never returned to Derby. He did, however, continue to design Rolls-Royce cars, spending the summer months on the south coast in England and the winter with his design team on the French Riviera. Royce's enforced exile permitted Claude Johnson to hone and refine the Rolls-Royce image.

Meanwhile, how was Daimler, Rolls-Royce's great rival of the pre-war years, fairing? In 1900 its sales received a welcome fillip when the Prince of Wales ordered a 6hp model, delivered to him in March, after which he was reported to have proclaimed: 'I shall make the motor car a necessity for every Englishman.'[29] It was the start of a long-standing royal association with the marque. In 1901 the firm appointed an American, Percy Martin, educated at Ohio State University, as works manager. But profitability continued to elude the firm and it was reconstructed in 1904, a year in which the famous but unbadged fluted radiator appeared. Under Sir Edward Jenkinson's chairmanship, the firm began to prosper and, in 1906, a substantial profit of £185,785 was recorded.

In 1906 Edward Manville took over the Daimler chairmanship. Educated at University College School, he was a pioneer electrical engineer and a partner in the Westminster-based Kincaird Waller, Manville and Dawson consultancy which advised on tramway construction the world over and on the electrification of the London, Brighton and South Coast Railway. Yet 'he was always to retain other business interests besides Daimler and was to spend more time in London than in Coventry.'[30] Following Manville's appointment, Percy Martin was made Daimler's managing director in 1906.

Four-cylinder models were produced exclusively between 1904 and 1908, and although Daimler was anxious to follow Napier with a six-cylinder model, a weakness of the configuration was its proneness to torsional vibration and crankshaft breakage. In 1909 Daimler had the good sense to appoint Frederick Lanchester as its consulting engineer and technical adviser, a position he held for the next twenty years. Lanchester solved the problem by inventing the torsional vibration damper in 1909 which took the form of a small flywheel mounted on the front of the crankshaft and driven by a multi-disk friction coupling. In the words of Sir Harry Ricardo, Britain's respected expert on engine design: 'It proved completely successful in eliminating torsional vibration and thus laid the ghost that had haunted the six-cylinder engine.'[31] In 1910 Lanchester patented his invention for which he 'received very substantial royalties in Britain.'[32] During the First World War he sold the American rights for around £4,000 to the Warner Company which marketed it as the Warner Crankshaft Damper. Lanchester's invention, still used throughout the world on six-cylinder engines, represents Britain's first major contribution to automobile engine technology.

Until 1909 almost all Daimlers employed the rather old-fashioned chain drive, and that year Lanchester convinced them to change to his efficient and, above all, quieter, worm drive. The same year Daimler, no doubt concerned by the success of the superlative Rolls-Royce 40/50hp, switched from conventional poppet valves to more complex but quieter double-sleeve valves. Lanchester was again called in to make the system work, 'although he never approved of it himself'.[33] Invented in 1905 by Charles Yale Knight, a fellow countryman of Percy Martin, sleeves had the disadvantage that they were more expensive to produce than the usual poppet valves and 'at high speed the risk of seizure was very great . . . the sleeves were also very apt to break away from the lugs which moved them if the engine was incautiously accelerated from cold'.[34] Nevertheless Daimler opted for sleeve valves and was the only front-line British car maker to do so, but the resulting cars were 'quiet, smoke belching, costly, complicated and slow'.[35] Although Daimler had lost £49,286 in the depression year of 1908, the arrival of the sleeve-valve cars in 1909 coincided with a return to profitability and in 1909/10 the company recorded an impressive profit of £98,775. Then, in September 1910, news broke that the firm was to merge with BSA.

BSA's origins reached back to the mid-nineteenth century when a group of local gunsmiths formed an association called the Birmingham Small Arms Trade, formalized, with the blessing of the War Office, as the Birmingham Small Arms Company in 1861. The intention was to mass produce firearms and a 25-acre site was acquired at Small Heath, Birmingham, flanked by the London and Birmingham Railway on one side and the Warwick and Birmingham Canal on the other. An impressive works was built there but, although BSA was given access to drawings from the Royal Small Arms factory at Enfield, the firm was beholden to the British government for arms contracts which ebbed and flowed as the international temperature rose and fell.

Consequently the company realized that diversification into the civilian market was essential. In 1881 BSA started to build the Otto Dicycle and in 1893 began producing components for the booming bicycle trade. A BSA bicycle finally appeared in 1908 and a motorcycle two years later. The company had also begun building cars in 1907. In the previous year it had bought the Royal Small Arms factory in nearby Montgomery Street which was next door to the Lanchester works. The cars were designed by Colonel E. E. Baguley, formerly of the Ryknield Motor Company of Burton-upon-Trent, and were undistinguished four-cylinder models ranging from 2.5 to 5.4 litres capacity. Baguley seems to have been lacking in originality and the top-line model was a straight copy of the Italian Itala that had won the celebrated 1907 Paris to Peking race. This diversification proved disorganized and ill-equipped, and by October 1909 it was found that only sixty-five cars had been built with no fewer than four models on offer.

In 1906 Sir Hallewell Rogers had taken over the BSA chairmanship. A former Lord Mayor of Birmingham, he was also the youngest, having been only thirty-eight years old on his 1902 elevation, and was knighted in the following year. Another 1906 BSA board appointment was that of industrialist and financier Dudley Docker, whose reputation was beginning to outstrip his native Birmingham; in fact, he might have been responsible for Hallewell's appointment. In 1902 Docker was instrumental in merging five railway rolling-stock companies into the Metropolitan Amalgamated Carriage and Wagon Company. He became, in 1909, BSA's deputy chairman and, well aware of the deficiencies of the motor department, turned his attention to Daimler, the country's oldest and most respected car company. He also ran a Daimler car and was acquainted with the firm's management.

In June 1910 the BSA's directors' worst fears were confirmed when a report on BSA cars revealed that 'Baguley has proved incapable of organisation, his only solution for bottlenecks being to employ more staff; he had presided over anarchy not only in design, production and after sales service, but in essential and simple matters like stock taking and the supply of cars.'[36] The Colonel departed, returning to his native Burton-upon-Trent where, in 1911, he introduced the 15/20hp Baguley car, clearly based on a 1910 BSA.

Docker was undoubtedly aiming at repeating the success of his 1902 railway wagon merger but, in the event, little effort was made to rationalize Daimler and BSA's motor departments and he retired from the BSA board in 1912, though he continued to exert influence from behind the scenes. The company paid £600,000 for Daimler and there was an exchange of BSA shares for Daimler ones. Three Daimler directors, chairman Edward Manville, who became BSA's vice chairman on Docker's retirement, majority shareholder Arthur H. E. Wood and managing director Percy Martin joined the BSA board, following confirmation of the merger in October 1910. It was hailed by the *Financial Times* as 'one of the most important ever effected in the motor industry', though the reality was somewhat different. One of the conditions of the alliance was that Daimler should make an annual payment of £100,000 in dividends to BSA, regardless of whether it had the funds. This meant Daimler extending its overdraft which, by February 1912, stood at over £200,000 with the result that the firm was left grievously short of resources to develop new models. Meanwhile, BSA's motor division, by then under the managership of Albert C. Hills, continued at Sparkbrook though, from 1911, the cars used sleeve valves and resembled scaled-down Daimlers.

In 1913 Daimler had built around 1,000 cars while, across the Atlantic in America, Cadillac mass produced 17,284 of them. The divergent manufacturing approaches had been dramatically highlighted in March 1908 when three Cadillacs gave the British motor industry a thought-provoking display of American production methods. The cars were driven to Brooklands track, opened only the previous year, and stripped down to their individual 721 parts. Then 89 items were removed and replaced with new spares. The cars were then reassembled and given a successful 500-mile run around the circuit. British practice, by contrast, was to manufacture parts in small batches and a considerable amount of hand fitting was necessary before components became compatible. Cadillac had shown that 'cheap' did not necessarily mean 'nasty'. For this impressive display the firm was awarded the Royal Automobile Club's revered Dewar Trophy and adopted 'Standard of the World' as its advertising slogan. In America this accolade was just one factor in William Crapo Durant's deciding to add Cadillac in 1909 to Buick and Oldsmobile as a member of his General Motors Company, established in September 1908, though Henry Leland remained at its helm with the brief to 'run [it] exactly as though it were your own'.[37]

The formidable American challenge again manifested itself later in 1908 with the 13 November opening of the Motor Show at Olympia. There the world got its first official view of the Ford Motor Company's new Model T, which went on sale in Britain for £225. Although the *Motor Trade* drily commented that 'visitors interested in American practice should not fail to see the new Ford', this was the car destined to put the world on wheels. Such was its market penetration that by 1919 it was estimated that every other car in the world was a Model T. That year the value-for-money Ford would account for a staggering 41 per cent of British car production.

The Model T, a deceptively frail-looking car, was as tough and wiry as Henry Ford, its creator. A farm boy from Dearborn, Michigan, and an undoubted mechanical genius, he had established his Ford Motor Company in nearby Detroit in 1903. His first car, the single-cylinder Model A, made no great impact, though with the coming of the four-cylinder Model N in 1906, Ford moved ahead of Oldsmobile to become America's top car maker. Then came the R and S models, which were more expensive versions of the N, and these were succeeded in 1908 by the legendary Model T, known throughout the English-speaking world as the 'Tin Lizzie'.

Above all, the Ford Model was the first car in the world specifically designed to reap the benefits of mass production. Behind the handsome brass radiator was a 2.9-litre four-cylinder engine which bristled with revolutionary features. Up until the arrival of the T, practically all manufacturers built their engines by mounting a cast-iron cylinder block, with an integral cylinder head, on an aluminium crankcase. Ford first combined the iron crankcase and block in one piece. But it was still necessary to decarbonize the engine, so the cylinder head was made detachable which considerably simplified the block casting. By 1914 most American manufacturers had copied Ford, with Europe following suit after the First World War.

There was more to come. At this time nearly all car makers mounted their gearboxes separately from the engine, which harked back to 1891 Panhard practice. The 'box, located on its own subframe, was separated from the engine by a short drive shaft. To speed and cheapen the production process, Ford attached the T's two-speed epicyclic gearbox directly to the engine and, at a stroke, dispensed with the cost of the subframe and shaft. In addition, once the engine and gearbox were bolted together, the resulting unit could be easily located in the chassis, dispensing with the necessity for time-consuming alignment of engine and gearbox.

The car's suspension was equally cost-conscious and featured a single transverse spring front and rear, located by tie bars. Although the T weighed only 13 cwt, its apparent frailty was countered by Henry Ford making extensive use of vanadium steel, a strong, light alloy which he introduced to the American motor industry. The high-stepping T – it stood well clear of the ground so that it would not become bogged down on the atrocious American roads of the day – was offered with four standardized body styles, the $850 four-seater open tourer being the most popular option.

In 1909 Ford decided to drop all his other models and concentrate on the T. From 1910, as output rose, he was able to reduce its price as the components were mass produced, so reducing unit costs. By 1913 it was found impossible to make substantial reductions without interfering with the T's design and Ford was adamant that that must remain inviolate. So he and his lieutenants set about altering the way in which the model was made. In the spring of 1913 the firm took the revolutionary decision to use a conveyor belt to assemble the car's flywheel magneto assembly and the time taken to produce the unit fell from twenty minutes to thirteen. Later in the year, a crude experiment was tried: a chassis was pulled through the factory by a rope and windlass and parts were added as it progressed. The results were impressive. With the chassis static, it had taken twelve hours twenty-eight minutes to build a Model T. By moving it, manufacturing time was cut by over half to five hours fifty minutes. Car production by moving track was born. A refined version of the system was introduced into Ford's Highland Park factory early in 1914 and as output soared, so the T's price tumbled, as the following figures show:

Year	Production*	Price ($)
1908	307	850
1909	10,607	950
1910	18,664	780
1911	34,528	690
1912	78,440	600
1913	168,220	550
1914	248,307	490
1915	308,213	440
1916	533,921	360

* Fiscal year, ending in June

Ford cars were available in Britain almost from the arrival of the Model A in 1903, with sales handled by the Central Motor Company in London's Long Acre. This firm existed on somewhat precarious finances and was reconstructed in 1907. However, it was the potential of the Model T that convinced Henry Ford of the wisdom of establishing a permanent British presence. In October 1909 a branch was established in Shaftesbury Avenue where thirty-one-year-old Percival Perry, who had an interest in the earlier venture, was in charge of administration.

Percival Lea Dewhurst Perry (1878–1956) was to be intermittently concerned with Ford's British operations for the next thirty-nine years. Arguably the most able executive of his day in the British motor industry, he not only 'kept the confidence and liking of the two Fords [Henry and his son Edsel]', but also Ford's 'tough minded men [who] made personal inspections in Europe'.[38] Born in Bristol and brought up in Birmingham, Perry won a scholarship to King Edward's School there, and although he had set his heart on a legal career, his parents did not have the money for him to fulfil this ambition. Then, in 1896, he saw a newspaper advertisement for a £1-a-week job with H. J. Lawson in London, so eighteen-year-old Perry sold his stamp collection to buy his train ticket there. He got the job and the following year saw him taking part in Queen Victoria's Jubilee Parade on a truck containing a Coventry Motette (Lawson's version of the Léon Bollée) bearing a notice which proclaimed: 'Even a fool can drive a Bollée'. Perry soon left Lawson to work for his uncle who ran a printing business in Hull. But before long he returned to London where, in 1904, he met up with a young man who had obtained the Ford European franchise for a mere £50 a year! As a result the Central Motor Car Company was established in the same year.

Finance was a recurring problem and, in 1906, Perry and his wife crossed the Atlantic and headed for Detroit where they stayed with the Fords at their Harper Avenue home. His aim was to persuade Henry to establish a proper branch in Britain, but he was unsuccessful. While in North America, however, he visited Gordon McGregor in Canada who, from December 1907, had the rights to sell Ford cars in Britain and the Empire. McGregor generously waived the British rights, saying that the Empire was enough for him.

Back in London, the business was reformed in 1907 as Perry, Thornton and Schreiber. But Perry clashed with his partners, left and took up an agency selling American Reo cars. Then, in 1909, Detroit decided to establish a permanent British presence and Perry was a natural choice to run the business. Model Ts were imported direct from Detroit, complete apart from their hood, wheels and windscreens. The cars were unloaded on the Thames side at Vauxhall, where the missing components were added, and then driven to Shaftesbury Avenue ready for sale.

Business was good. Four hundred Ts were sold in the first year which was sufficient incentive for Ford to establish an assembly plant for the Model T, the first such facility outside North America. Perry began his search for a suitable site in 1910 and found it at the Trafford Park industrial estate in Manchester. There was a 5.5-acre site containing a factory which hitherto had produced bodies for underground trains, while nearby was Scott Brothers, an old-established coachbuilding firm which was contracted to produce British bodies for the Tin Lizzie. A pivotal factor in this location was the proximity of the Manchester Ship Canal, so the minimum of time would be spent transporting the crated Model Ts from the quayside to the works. Yet another factor was the excellent rail facilities enjoyed by Manchester.

With work on the conversion of the premises, for which Perry had paid £2,000 on a long-term lease, proceeding apace, in March 1911 the firm's British branch was transformed into the Ford Motor Company (England) Ltd. The Manchester works began its operations in October 1911 and initially had the capacity to produce 15,000 cars per annum, a modest number by American standards though massive by European ones. (Ford's Detroit facilities were by then capable of producing 250,000 Model Ts a year.)

Trafford Park soon followed Highland Park in introducing a moving-track assembly line, so becoming the first British factory to employ this facility. Soon Scott Brothers found it was unable to mass produce its bodies in the American manner, so Ford took it over. Sales continued to rise. In 1911, 623 cars were sold, though in 1912, by which time British assembly had begun, this rose to 3,081 and almost doubled again in 1913 to 6,139. This made Ford by far and away not only Britain's but also Europe's largest car maker.

A crucial factor in the Model T's success was its astounding value for money, the price of the car falling as American sales soared. In 1912 it sold for $600 (£123) while a British equivalent cost £175. The following Model T British production and sales figures tell their own story:

Year	Production	Price
1909	—	225
1910	400*	220
1911	623*	170
1912	3,187	175
1913	7,310	135
1914	8,352	135

* Sales

European and British manufacturers were at a considerable disadvantage because they could not compete with the Model T on price: Ford was able to benefit from the economies of scale by selling his cars not only on the large American market but also throughout the world. Consequently, in the New World a low-priced car was looked upon as a replacement for the ubiquitous horse and buggy, while in Europe the higher-priced automobile was considered as a substitute for the gentlemen's exclusive and more expensive carriage.

The first European response to the Model T was the cycle car, born in

Paris in 1909, a year after the Ford had received an enthusiastic reception at the Paris salon. There Robert Bourbeau and Henri Devaux produced the Bedelia (the name was phonetically derived from the capital letters of their respective surnames) which was crude and difficult to drive but was cheap, had a narrow wooden chassis, was belt-driven, had tandem seating and a single-cylinder air-cooled engine. The cheapest 3.5hp version sold for only 56 guineas in Britain, though a 'luxurious' two-cylinder model cost 96 guineas. Almost simultaneously Ron Godfrey and Archie Frazer Nash produced the G.N. cycle car after building a prototype in the grounds of the latter's mother's house in Hendon, Middlesex. Production began in 1911, the same year in which the Malvern-based Morgan Motor Company started building its three-wheeler. Designed by H. F. S. Morgan, the sliding-pillar independent front suspension was an advanced and unusual feature. By 1911, Britain boasted 'less than a dozen different makes of cycle cars'[39] and there were about the same number in France. The movement gained momentum with the staging of the Cycle and Motorcycle Show at Olympia in 1912 when the newly launched magazine, *The Cyclecar*, sold over a 100,000 copies on its first issue. By 1914 there were 'well over 100 different makers of cycle car'[40] in both France and Britain and the epidemic even spread to America.

For all its cheapness the cycle car, with its lack of weather protection, its noise and unpredictable handling, was a half-way house between the motorcycle and the car. What was really needed was a scaled-down version of a large car that could compete with the Model T on price and this finally appeared in Germany in 1911 and spread to France in the following year. It was the first vehicle to be demonstrably European in concept and thus marked the first divergence between the motor industries of the Old and New World. The concept reached Britain in 1913 when what was called the light car appeared.

Like the Bedelia, the light car had French origins. The concept was triggered by the arrival of the world depression late in 1907. In this chilly economic climate, 'Everyone was saying,' declared a contemporary, 'that the industry could only be saved by the voiturette which, if produced at a low enough figure, would sell in such considerable numbers as to fully compensate the trade for such a sudden drop for more expensive vehicles.'[41]

In 1905 the French motoring magazine, *l'Auto*, had initiated a new trophy, the *Coupe des Voiturettes*, intended to cater for smaller racing cars, and the events run from 1905 to 1907 were for vehicles with one- or two-cylinder engines. For the 1908 race, however, four-cylinder cars were permitted for the first time though 'the promoters apparently thought that the voiturette of the future was hardly likely to be equipped with a four-cylinder engine but it appears that there are quite a number of firms *who believe that the small vehicle should possess all the refinements of a big car* [my italics].'[42] The engine's bore size was set at 65mm, which came in for plenty of contemporary criticism as it was believed at the time that 75mm was the smallest practical figure. Then the Automobile Club of France, the ruling body of the sport, reduced the permitted size again, to 62mm. Although there were plenty of one- and two-cylinder cars, only six firms entered for the new four-cylinder class in the 1908 event, of which the most important was the 62 × 100mm 1208cc Isotta Fraschini FE from Italy. It was the first four-cylinder car to finish, in eighth place, though its impact would go far beyond the confines of the race's Dieppe circuit.

There seems little doubt that Ettore Bugatti, that extraordinary artist-engineer, closely based his 1910 1327cc Type 13 on the little Italian car. Then, in 1911, Bugatti designed an even smaller four-cylinder model, which he intended to sell to another manufacturer. He first approached the German Wanderer company, though its own design was already well advanced and emerged in 1911 as the four-cylinder 1150cc Puppchen (Doll). Bugatti had better luck with Peugeot, which purchased the design, and the result was the Bébé, with a diminutive 855cc four-cylinder engine, which entered production in 1912. 'With this automobile Peugeot became a leader, along with Clement Bayard and others, in the trend to small cars in those years just before the First World War.'[43] The Bébé helped Peugeot to oust Renault as France's largest car maker in 1913.

The concept did not take long to cross the English Channel and in 1913 saw the appearance of a positive rash of light cars, so defined as having an engine of less than 10hp. The arrival of the light car produced the first really significant vehicle from bicycle manufacturer Singer and Company, this Coventry firm having diversified into car making in 1905. Initially Singer built cars under licence from Lea-Francis, which had temporarily given up car manufacture to concentrate on motorcycles. These were produced until 1907 when Singer introduced its own White and Poppe and Aster-engined cars. Yet the firm's best seller was the 1.1-litre Ten of 1912 which cost £185. It was to prove 'one of the best light cars of the period'[44] and survived, in essence, until 1926.

Yet the smallest-capacity (at 1018cc) light car of its day was the Morris Oxford of 1913. Designed by William Richard Morris, who had previously sold cars and bicycles in Oxford, it was also the cheapest, selling at £175. Morris (1877–1963), eleven years younger than Herbert Austin, his great rival and contemporary, also came from farming stock. Even though he is associated with the city of Oxford and his family hailed from there, he was, in fact, born in Comer Gardens, Worcester, where his father Frederick was apprenticed to a draper. When William was three, the family returned to Oxford as Morris Senior became farm bailiff to his blind father-in-law, who farmed at Headington Quarry. Subsequently Frederick Morris developed asthma and was unable to continue with farm work so, with family fortunes at a low ebb, it fell to young William to get a job. Morris therefore left St James Church of England School at Cowley at the age of fifteen to find work.

He decided to pursue a natural talent for mechanics and, in 1893, he got a job at an Oxford bicycle shop. This proved short-lived when the proprietor refused his young recruit's request for a 4 shilling (20p) pay rise. Morris therefore decided to start his own bicycle business 'because I felt that no one else would pay me as well as W.R.'[45] This began in a brick building at the back of his parent's house in James Street, Cowley St John. He started by repairing bicycles and selling accessories, though soon gravitated to making his own machines. This is not such a monumental step as it might seem because all he had to do was to order the parts from specialist suppliers and then assemble the bicycles in his back-garden workshop.

By 1902 Morris's business had grown to a sufficient extent that he entered a short-lived partnership with a local cycle dealer and, in the following year, he became works manager for the Oxford Automobile and Cycle Agency which had grandiose plans for selling cars and building motorcycles and bicycles. But the business was bankrupted within a year and Morris reverted to selling cars and marketing bicycles at 48 High Street, Oxford. A repair facility was established at nearby Longwall under The Oxford Garage name which was changed, in 1910, to The Morris Garage.

These experiences were to sharpen Morris's commercial acumen and he was able to study the design of cars he was selling, gauge how the public responded to them and compare their prices. In addition he began to familiarize himself with the many Midlands firms serving the bicycle and motor industry. It was an awareness that was to stand him in good stead in the future for, as early as 1904/5, William Morris was determined to become a car maker in his own right.

By 1910 he was seriously investigating how he could obtain the parts he required as 'I became convinced that there was going to be a big demand for a popularly priced car.'[46] At this time most manufacturers made as much of their cars as possible in their own factories but Morris's approach was diametrically opposed to this approach: 'The best way for the small concern to manufacture . . . was to get specialists on every separate unit of the job. The work is better and more cheaply done, while the cost and worry of more plant is avoided.' What he was doing was applying to automobile manufacture the same techniques that he had employed in his days as a bicycle maker.

Inevitably his problem was one of finance but help came from an unexpected source in the shape of the Earl of Macclesfield, whom Morris had met in 1905 when the young peer was an undergraduate. He contributed £4,000 to Morris's business, which was registered in October 1912 as W.R.M. Motors Ltd.

With his finances assured, Morris could now approach his suppliers. He knew the proprietory engine manufacturer, White and Poppe Ltd, of Coventry, through the carburettors it marketed. The firm contributed the four-cylinder power unit with the gearbox mounted progressively in unit with the engine in the manner of the Model T Ford. The T head 8.9hp four was, by contrast, a little old-fashioned in design as a side-valve L head would have reflected current design trends, and been cheaper, because it required only one camshaft rather than two. A German Bosch magneto and sparking plugs were fitted. Power was transmitted, via a torque tube, to the rear axle, showing Morris's influence by the American Hupmobile, for which he was an agent. Axles came from E. G. Wrigley and Company of Birmingham, though Morris went to a Belgian firm for the chassis frame. The delightful 'bullnose' radiator came from closer to home and was made by Doherty Motor Components of Coventry. Steel artillery wheels came from Joseph Sankey and Sons of Hadley, Shropshire, and Morris shared the £720 that it cost to make the die with Cecil Bayliss of bicycle component makers Perry and Company of Tyseley, Birmingham, who had designed an 8hp two-cylinder car. Thus the Perry and Morris Oxford have interchangeable wheels.[47] For his bodywork Morris went to the Oxford firm of Charles Raworth.

All Morris now needed was somewhere to build his car. Fortunately, there were empty buildings at Temple Cowley that served his purpose. They had been vacant for twenty-one years but, by a pleasant coincidence, had once housed Hurst's Grammar School where his father had been educated. The more recent extensions were used for car assembly while the older former school buildings served as offices. At the same time Morris, and his wife whom he had married in 1904, moved into the adjacent manor house. Thus Morris could be on hand for the first crucial phase of his business enterprise.

Morris had hoped to have his car ready for the 1912 Motor Show but White and Poppe had not completed the engine in time. It was only later that he heard the truth: a freelance draughtsman had accidentally drawn the unit half-size and the finished block had been cast by Willans and Robinson of Rugby, looking more like a motor cycle unit than a car engine! Nevertheless Morris took the initiative and, armed with a set of blueprints of the Morris Oxford, visited London. He succeeded in convincing Gordon Stewart, of motor agents Stewart and Ardern, of his credibility for the firm ordered 400 cars.

The first Morris car was completed on 29 March 1913, but at £175 was £25 more expensive than the Ford Model T which Morris was attempting to challenge. In addition to this price differential, the 8hp car from Cowley was available only in two-seater form, while the four-seater T tourer had proved very popular with the family motorist. Despite this drawback, Morris assembled 393 cars during 1913. In 1914, which was the first full year of production, 907 Oxfords left the Cowley works, making Morris one of the country's leading car makers. Austin, by contrast, built only 545 cars, though Rover, with about 2,000, was still well behind Wolseley, the industry leader, with 3,000. Yet at Trafford Park, Manchester, Ford produced no less than 8,352 Model Ts, which was by far and away the largest production figure in Europe and about double that of Renault, its nearest rival, which built 4,206.

By 1913 there were 175,300 cars on Britain's roads – more than in any other European country. France was next with 88,300, while Germany was third with about 70,000. Yet the French motor industry was still Europe's largest, with about 45,000 cars built in 1913. Britain was next with 26,238, Germany third with 17,162 and Italy fourth with approximately 8,000. Europe's performance was, however, completely overshadowed by America's. It had moved ahead of France in 1904 to become the world's largest car producer and in 1913 it manufactured 461,500 automobiles, a staggering 44 per cent of this total being contributed by the Model T. It was a year in which Ford's profits stood at a record $25 million.

The same year Morris's profits reached £5,400 though these rose to £15,000 in 1914. The most profitable company in the British motor industry at this time was BSA, which recorded a figure of £187,921 in 1913, though its interests embraced bicycles, motorcycles and armaments production as well as cars. Similarly Rover built bicycles and motorcycles in addition to cars, and the success of Owen Clegg's 12hp model was reflected in profits of £117,624 for the same period. Not far behind was Sunbeam with £93,409 which, *The Economist* opined, was 'good testimony to the value of racing and record breaking as a means of advertisement'. Humber had improved its financial position, with profits of £50,091.

Significantly, all these companies produced cars, typified by the Rover 12 and Sunbeam 12/16, for the affluent upper and middle classes. They would never again enjoy such prosperity as the success of Henry Ford's Model T had inspired both Herbert Austin and William Morris to ape his manufacturing methods and mass produce cheaper cars that would then be within reach of a far wider public. The production engineer, then little known outside his native America, was soon to make his presence felt in the British motor industry.

2

Wheels of Fortune

1915–29

'Until the worker goes to his factory by car, I shall not believe that we have touched more than the fringe of the home market.'[1]
William Richard Morris, governing director Morris Motors,
February 1924

'I look back upon 1922 as [a year] that marks an important milestone in my life, for it was then that I introduced the now famous Seven which has made motoring possible for thousands who could have not otherwise enjoyed its advantages.'[2]
Sir Herbert Austin, chairman Austin Motor Company,
September 1929

When the First World War broke out in August 1914, the British motor industry was a mere eighteen years old and was just starting to think in terms of quantity production. However, when hostilities ended in November 1918, practically all the car makers had been involved in some form of war work, usually in the production of munitions or the manufacture of aero engines. In most instances this resulted in the spectacular growth of factories which were then filled with the latest machine tools, often imported from America, to mass produce the weapons of retribution. Consequently when car production restarted after the war, most car makers turned their minds for the first time to emulating Henry Ford and offering motoring for the masses by perpetuating the manufacturing processes learnt during hostilities. By 1929, as a result of adopting these new production techniques, three firms, Morris, Austin and to a lesser extent Singer, accounted for about three quarters of the British car market.

These were just three of forty-one makes of British car then available on the market, but seven years previously there had been ninety-one. Some, such as Bean, Angus-Sanderson, Ruston-Hornsby and Cubitt, attempted to ape Henry Ford and adopted his one-model, mass-production policy. By the end of the decade all had perished in the attempt. Of the new makes to appear during the decade – eighty-six were created between 1919 and 1925 alone – only two of any significance, Armstrong Siddeley and Alvis, survived into the post-war years.

Cars were changing in appearance. In 1919 the typical British four-seater was an open vehicle with a flapping hood and celluloid sidescreens. Yet, by the end of the decade, Britain had followed America's example and saloons outnumbered open cars, a transition made easier by the arrival, in 1927, of the mass-produced all-steel body. Cars were also getting smaller. Vehicles in the 12hp class, exemplified by the Morris Cowley, had dominated the market place between 1924 and 1928, though in 1929 the 8hp sector, spearheaded by the Austin Seven, moved into pole position with a 25 per cent market share.

During the 1920s British automobile production more than doubled from 71,396 in 1923, the first year cars were separately listed in the Census of Production, to 182,347 in 1929, though it was still second to that of France which continued as Europe's leading automobile manufacturer with 193,000 cars produced in the latter year. However, the continent's combined output of around 530,000 in 1929 was still dwarfed by that of the USA which produced a record 4.4 million cars.

The First World War was to have another far-reaching effect on the British motor industry. Until 1915 Britain had espoused the doctrine of Free Trade, whereby imports paid no duty. With the outbreak of the war, when France, Europe's largest car maker, was deeply embroiled in hostilities, the American manufacturers saw their chance to increase sales on the British market for, as a neutral country, its wares could be shipped across the Atlantic unimpeded by the U-boat menace. In August 1915, with the publication of the Board of Trade's import figures for 1914, the car makers appealed to the government to stem the flood. The response came in September 1915, when Chancellor of the Exchequer Reginald McKenna introduced his first war-time budget, which included a 33⅓ per cent duty on specific imports, including cars, thus effecting the first breach of the Free Trade bastion. These so-called McKenna Duties protected the British motor industry from the full effects of foreign competition for the next fifty-seven years for, apart from a brief period in 1924 and 1925, they remained in force at this level until 1967.

The imposition of the McKenna Duties in 1915 affected not only the Americans but also William Morris at Cowley, who in April had introduced his new Morris Cowley made with American rather than British-made components. It had been in 1913 that Morris, having successfully launched his White and Poppe-engined Oxford, realized that he had made a serious error in its conception. He recognized that if he was successfully to challenge the Model T Ford in Britain he would have to offer a four-seater car instead of one with only two seats. But this would require a larger-capacity engine than the 1018cc unit under the Oxford's bonnet. Morris planned a four-seater Oxford for the 1915 season with an enlarged 1.1-litre engine, but this would put the car's price up and he knew that if he were to challenge the value-for-money Model T he would have to reduce the price of his component parts. He then took the major step of deciding to go to the USA to see for himself what was then known as the American System of Manufacture, or what we know now as mass production. Late in 1913, accompanied by White and Poppe's chief draughtsman, Hans Landstad, Morris sailed for America and headed for the motor city of Detroit. There he visited the Continental Motor Manufacturing Company which had been building proprietory engines since 1904. The firm provided Morris with drawings of a 1.5-litre four-cylinder engine, but such was the sophistication of American production methods that it quoted $85 (£17 9s 3d/£17.46) per unit, while Morris was paying £50 for the White and Poppe engine and gearbox. Even when shipping costs were added, the saving was an appreciable one. The pair returned to Britain and, in Coventry, Peter Poppe confirmed that although he could build the engine to Continental's drawings, there was no way his firm could match the American company's price. Landstad suggested to Poppe that the only answer was for him to return to Detroit to gain first-hand experience of American production methods.

Morris readily agreed to this proposal, Landstad was given six months' leave of absence and, at Morris's suggestion, took his drawing board with him. On 18 April 1914 he and Morris left Liverpool on the *Mauretania* for America. Although Morris travelled first class and the Norwegian second, on their first day at sea Morris went down to Landstad's cabin, and the pair began planning the design of what was to be the best-selling British car of the 1920s: the Morris Cowley. Morris was a good sailor but Landstad suffered from seasickness and the atmosphere was not improved by the motor manufacturer's addiction to cigarettes.

On arrival in Detroit, the pair found a cheap hotel and the work continued. Components from local suppliers were delivered there and taken to their hotel room, which did double duty as an office, for inspection, and Morris later remembered that the room 'was so blue with tobacco smoke that one could not see across it'.[3] Contact was once again made with the Continental company and Morris placed an order for 3,000 examples of its U Type Red Seal engine. The three-speed gearbox, which cost £8 6s 2d, (£8.31) came from the Detroit Gear and Machine Company, while the front and back axles and steering box also amounted to £8 6s 2d and freight and insurance cost £6 10s (£6.50). Morris remained at Detroit for about three weeks though Landstad obtained a job with Continental and continued to work on the design of the Cowley in the evenings. He spent his weekends visiting manufacturing plants in the city, including the massive Ford factory at Highland Park. He remained in America until the end of 1914 and returned to Britain well versed in mass production methods. Morris had suggested that he leave White and Poppe and he joined W.R.M. Motors as works manager.

The first sample engine from America arrived at Cowley late in 1914 and supplies built up so that Morris was able to announce his 158 guinea (£165) two-seater Cowley in April 1915. Significantly it was £41 cheaper than the smaller Oxford, while the all-important four-seater cost £194, though it was still £59 more than the Ford. The car's American origins were only obvious when the bonnet was raised for, like the Model T, the cylinder head was detachable and the gearbox in unit with the engine. It was also fitted with a dipstick, a considerable novelty for its day. Yet another trans-Atlantic feature was the centrally mounted gear change, introduced on the American Reo car in 1913 and almost universally accepted there. Practically all British cars of the day were fitted with right-hand gear change, a convenient but more expensive mechanism. The American-made rear axle also featured a helically cut crown wheel and pinion at a time when almost all British cars were fitted with noisier straight-cut teeth.

Production began in September, but that very month American imports were subjected to the McKenna Duties and in October the price of the two-seater Cowley rose to £194 and the four-seater to £222. Then, in March 1916, such imports were banned altogether so that shipping space could be devoted to essential supplies. Despite this, Morris had sufficient parts to continue building the Cowley throughout the war. In 1916 he produced 684 examples, 125 in 1917 and 198 in the following year. His mainstream activities were, however, associated with the war effort and the production of hand grenades and bomb cases.

More significantly, mine sinkers were mass produced from interchangeable parts using principles learnt by Landstad in Detroit. At Morris's suggestion, rather than one factory making them, parts would be made by 'scores of . . . small works up and down the country, each producing one unit only and assembling the mine sinkers at Cowley'.[4] Initially the Admiralty had been paying £40 to £50 for its sinkers, but by adopting Morris's idea the cost 'worked out roughly at £30. Approximately we produced 45,000 mine sinkers; as our production outstripped the Navy's we had to take the Crystal Palace to store them in!'[5] He was to apply these same methods, with devastating effectiveness, when he resumed car production after the war.

Morris's Cowley works was greatly enlarged during hostilities, but by the end of the war the Austin Motor Company's Longbridge factory had expanded to such an extent that it was soon transformed into the largest car manufacturing plant in the country. In 1914 Austin employed between 2,000 and 3,000 workers, though with the ending of hostilities the figure had spiralled to 20,000. Factory space had expanded enormously, the original plant having grown to a 41.5-acre complex. (In 1906 it had covered just 2.5 acres.) This was joined in 1916 by yet another plant built by the Ministry of Munitions; divided as it was from the existing premises by the London Midland Scottish Railway, it became the North Works, while the original plant was named the South Works. In 1917 came the West Works on the other side of the Bristol Road, another munitions factory. Covering a 43.75-acre site, this was the largest of the three.

War-time output was concentrated on the production of shells, and all-aluminium V8 Arab and V12 Sunbeam Coatalen aero engines were built along with ambulances and armoured cars. Forty-eight examples of the latter, based on the 50hp car chassis with steering at each end, were delivered to Tsarist Russia from 1914 and six of the survivors regularly appear in May Day parades in the Russian capital.

Tragedy came to Austin early in the war when, in January 1915, his only son, Vernon James, was cut down by a sniper's bullet at La Bassée, France, while serving as a second lieutenant in the Royal Field Artillery. With the coming of peace and without an heir to inherit his business, Sir Herbert, as he became in 1917, was something of a reluctant motor magnate and, as will emerge, made a number of fruitless efforts to sell the Austin Motor Company.

It was during the war that Austin began to formulate a new model strategy. In 1914 his firm had manufactured five models of which the best seller was a 1.6-litre 10hp car. Instead of perpetuating this theme, he decided to discontinue his pre-war range entirely, follow in Henry Ford's footsteps and adopt a single-model policy. (An inscribed photograph of Henry Ford, whom he came to know, was one of the few decorative features of Austin's spartan Longbridge office.) The 3.6-litre 20hp model, which entered production in 1919, was intended, like the Model T, for world markets and Austin closely followed the dimensions of its engine, the 20hp sharing the T's 95mm bore though its stroke was increased by 1 inch to 127mm. Like the Ford, the 20hp also had a detachable cylinder head, while the unit construction gearbox, with its centrally located gear change and hand throttle control labelled 'Gas' were borrowed from the

American Hudson Super Six, Austin having run an example during the war.

Despite the enormous growth of Austin's Longbridge factory, car production had effectively ceased by 1917, though lorries and ambulances were in constant demand. Yet 70 miles to the north at the Ford factory at Trafford Park, Manchester, Model T output was soaring and peaked in 1916 when 16,204 vehicles were built, nearly double the 1914 figure. They were produced not only in car form but as ambulances and lorries as well, while an ingenious independent variant was the Hucks starter designed by Benjamin Hucks, who was the first Englishman to loop the loop – this was used for starting large aero engines. By 1916 Trafford Park was making over half the parts used in the Model T. There were two reasons for this: shipping was being continually subjected to U-boat attacks and those components that got through were subjected to the 33⅓ per cent McKenna Duties.

Although Percival Perry continued to run Ford's British operations, he felt limited by the Trafford Park site. In 1914 he submitted a plan to Henry Ford for a great new factory at Southampton to serve the needs of Europe and the British Empire. For this he bought the Ridgeway Estate in 1915 for £5,000 on Ford's behalf, while a further £20,000 purchased the Milbrook Estate in 1916. Ford, by contrast, preferred Ireland: his paternal grandfather had emigrated from County Cork to America in 1847. Perry considered the location as 'remote' for the purpose but, with the outbreak of the First World War, his efforts were concentrated on stepping up Model T production at Manchester. In 1916, however, he was seconded by the government for the Food Production Department where he served in the Implements and Machinery Section.

With U-boat attacks concentrating the government's attention on food production, Prime Minister David Lloyd George suggested to Henry Ford that Ireland might be a suitable site for a factory to build a tractor that Ford had been developing. The latter responded positively while Perry did not object because such a presence would not affect his dream for a Southampton factory.

Perry was in Ireland in November 1916 and chose a site on the south bank of the River Lee that he and Ford had selected during a visit early in 1913. As it incorporated the city's park and race track – municipal land – an Act of Parliament had to be passed to enable this change of use. Henry Ford and Son Ltd, with its headquarters in Cork, was registered in April 1917, but Perry soon realized that the factory would not be ready to start tractor production until 1918. Then plans were made to build it in Britain, but the government decided that aero engines must have priority so Sir Percival, as Perry became in 1917, was given authority to order 6,000 tractors from America. Ford's Cork operations were not to be significant until the 1920s.

At the other end of the market, Sunbeam, Napier and Rolls-Royce had been commissioned by the government first to manufacture French aero engines and then to initiate their own designs. Napier and Rolls-Royce perpetuated the practice into the years of peace, and the former ceased building cars in 1924. Although the Derby company continue to manufacture them, by 1935 'Rolls-Royce was primarily an aero engine firm'.[6]

With the ending of the war in November 1918, William Morris was already thinking in terms of the needs of the family motorist who would probably be buying a car for the first time. He was in a strong position to restart car production at Cowley. Above all, he had an up-to-date, reliable car in the shape of the Cowley but there was a fly in the ointment when Continental announced that it was going to discontinue production of its U type Red Seal engine because it was too small for the American market. Morris then approached White and Poppe, which had submitted designs for a new side-valve four-cylinder engine in 1914, but director Alfred White was against supplying it as the firm wanted to produce its own car and was also negotiating with Dennis, which took it over in November 1919. So Morris decided to buy the production rights of his existing power unit from Continental, as it had already proved its worth, and had been designed with mass production in mind. He then looked around for a British manufacturer to build it for him. He tried Oldhams of Coventry but the latter could not agree to Morris's price while Landstad was not satisfied by the sample engines produced by Dormans of Stafford which also required a £40,000 deposit. The New Pick Motor Company of Stafford was interested but lacked the capacity. Time was of the essence but, in the late spring of 1919, Morris received a visit from American Laurence Benet, managing director of the French Hotchkiss Company, two Frenchmen and Henry (Harry) Ainsworth, works manager of a Coventry factory established by Hotchkiss in 1915 when it feared that its own works at St Denis, Paris, might be overrun. This Gosford Street works had manufactured Hotchkiss machine guns during the war but was urgently in need of work. The visit to Cowley had been prompted by Benet's suggestion that they contact the local Labour Exchange which, fortuitously, had heard that Morris was looking for an engine contractor.

Hotchkiss was quite prepared to build engines to Morris's specifications and at less than £50 apiece, although Ainsworth cautioned that initially they might cost £100 but the price would drop as output rose. But would Hotchkiss require a deposit? 'Benet . . . was on the point of suggesting a sum when Ainsworth interposed and said that no deposit was required, as they had sufficient financial resources.'[7] Morris took the opportunity to make a few changes to the design. The engine's stroke was increased from 100 to 102mm, which raised the capacity from 1495 to 1548cc, but the main modification was the introduction of a cork-faced, oil-filled clutch, because the Continental engine anyway leaked lubricant on to the clutch face! The modification was suggested by Morris himself and was one of the few contributions he made to the detail design of his cars.

Morris took this opportunity to commission new suppliers. Rubery Owen took over the manufacture of the chassis, while Fisher and Ludlow was responsible for the radiator case and rear axle housing. Doherty Radiator of Coventry was contracted to supply radiators but when it could not cope with the demand, Morris bought a former roller skating rink in Osberton Road, Oxford, and then helped Harold Ryder and A. L. Davies, two foremen transferred from the Coventry firm, to buy the business. Bodywork presented something of a problem. Before the war Morris had relied on Charles Raworth in Oxford, and the Coventry company of Hollick and Pratt had supplied bodies for the Continental-engined Cowley, but, as neither firm was able to cope with the expected demand, they built low-production saloon and coupé bodies. Morris therefore established his own bodyshop at Cowley in 1919, under the direction of Lancelot Pratt of Hollick and Pratt, to produce mainstream touring bodies.

Morris also restructured his corporate affairs in 1919. In July W.R.M. Motors was wound up to invalidate a contract he had made with W. H. M. Burgess, giving them sales rights for the south of England and export markets, while H. W. Cranham had the northern agency for Morris cars. Morris needed more than two distributors and control of export markets for the sort of targets he had in mind, so the renamed Morris Motors was born to enter into new distribution and sales agreements.

Morris offered two models from 1919. There was the popular Cowley, and he decided to re-introduce the Oxford name, which had been dormant since 1917, for the more expensive option. He was, incidentally, well ahead of his time in giving his cars model names; most car makers specified only horsepower ratings at this time. Hotchkiss delivered sample engines in July 1919 and production proper began in September. Total car deliveries for the year amounted to 360 cars, though the firm was still using up its supply of American engines and these lasted until January 1920. That year Morris built 1,932 cars at a time when demand was outstripping supply but, along with those of other motor manufacturers, his car prices rose as labour costs soared. In October 1920, for example, the price of the four-seater Oxford went up £45, from £450 to £495. That month Morris's overdraft stood at £57,625. By that time the post-war boom had collapsed and 1921 proved to be 'the worst year for depression since the industrial revolution'.[7]

Business was so bad that, by January 1921, Morris had a factory full of unsold cars. His overdraft had risen to £84,315 and he even spoke of emigrating and re-establishing his business in Australia. The factory was geared to produce about 60 cars a week, though only 68 cars were sold that month. As cars were sold for cash and suppliers paid on specified dates after delivery, the effects of the shortfall were felt immediately.

He took the momentous decision to make substantial cuts in the prices of his range, the announcement being made on 9 February. The most dramatic cut fell on the popular four-seater Cowley, which was reduced by £100 to £425, while the price of the two-seater came down by £90 to £375. Oxford prices also fell but by only £25. Sales immediately responded and rose to 244 in February and to 377 and 376 in March and April respectively. Thereafter demand began to fall away again. In October 191 cars were produced, compared with 288 the previous year. Morris therefore cut his prices yet again on the eve of the Motor Show. The four-seater Cowley was down by £84 to £341 while the price of the two-seater fell to £229. Sales rose to 234 in November while December's figure was 208. By the end of 1921 Morris had built 3,077 cars. In a year of terrible depression he had succeeded in swimming against the financial current and selling more cars than in 1920. Of the main-line car producers, only Rover and briefly Wolseley achieved similar results.

Market conditions improved in 1922 and production doubled to 6,956 cars; in 1923 output soared to 20,024, giving Morris 28 per cent of British car production. The following year Morris overtook Ford as the country's largest car maker. In 1925 he built 54,151 Cowleys and Oxfords which represented 41 per cent of the country's car production, the highest market share ever attained by Morris and a British-owned car company in the inter-war years. The famous 'Bullnose' models were discontinued in 1926; but these best-selling British cars of the 1920s were Yankees at heart.

The Cowley and Oxford model names were perpetuated for 1927 but the charming 'Bullnose' radiator was replaced by a flat-fronted one which Morris 'likened to a gravestone when he saw the prototype and insisted that it be made two inches narrower'.[8] In 1929 Morris Motors built a record 63,522 cars, while profits stood at £1.5 million, the highest in the industry. The previous year Morris had been made a baronet, which underlined his position as Britain's leading car maker.

This success produced its own problems because, from 1922 onwards, Morris's suppliers found it impossible to keep pace with demand. He responded by buying the principal ones. This meant that, unlike Austin and Ford, which each had one factory, by the end of the decade, Morris had no less than seven plants scattered around the Oxford area and the industrial Midlands. This piecemeal growth, which was unique to a major European manufacturer at the time, was to present Morris Motors, and its successors, with considerable operating problems but these would not be apparent until after the Second World War.

The first acquisition occurred almost by accident when, on 1 August 1922, the Hollick and Pratt body factory in Quinton Road, Coventry, was destroyed by fire. Lancelot Pratt pointed out that there was little point in his rebuilding it as Morris Motors was his only customer, so Morris bought it. Next, in January 1923, came Osberton Radiators which he acquired for £15,000.

By far the most significant purchase was Hotchkiss's Coventry factory because, in the autumn of 1922, as demand for his cars rose, Morris asked the plant to increase its output to 500–600 engines per week. However, 'Hotchkiss . . . said that they could not produce more than 300 engines.'[9] The firm, with the Hollick and Pratt precedent no doubt in mind, suggested that Morris buy the works and he did so by May 1923 at a cost of £349,423, when the business's name was changed to Morris Engines. Frank Woollard, formerly chief draughtsman of E. G. Wrigley, was appointed works manager at the Gosford Street works. Educated at Birbeck College, where he obtained a BSc degree in engineering, Woollard had served an apprenticeship with the London and South Western Railway prior to joining Wrigley in 1910.

Woollard completely reorganized the Coventry works, so that Morris could claim, in February 1924, that 'we have produced 600 engines a week out of the identical cubic space'.[10] Plans were immediately put in hand to extend the plant so that, by December 1924, a weekly output of 1,200 engines was achieved, making Gosford Street by far and away the most productive engine factory in Britain and rivalling the giants of America in its sophistication. In June 1925 the Coventry factory produced its half-millionth engine and Morris, as a regular smoker, was presented with a gold cigarette case, appropriately engraved with an illustration of an 11.9hp engine. Woollard's endeavours were recognized in 1926, when he was made a director of Morris Motors.

Other firms were purchased. In December 1923 Morris bought Woollard's old firm of E. G. Wrigley, then in receivership, for £213,044 and moved into the Foundry Lane premises in Soho, Birmingham, on New Year's Day 1924. That year he began making commercial vehicles which were built at the former Wrigley works. The last components business Morris acquired was the S.U. Carburettor Company of Kentish Town, London, for which he paid £100,000 in December 1926.

Until 1926 Morris Motors had been a private company, but in June of that year it became a public one. Its name was accordingly changed to Morris Motors (1926) Ltd, though this suffix was discontinued in August 1929. Morris retained all the £2 millions' worth of ordinary shares, though the £3 million preference shares were offered for public subscription when the issue was oversubscribed.

In 1926 Morris was instrumental in establishing the Pressed Steel Company near his own Cowley works. During the 1920s Morris, like practically all British car companies, built bodies in the traditional way. A wooden frame was clad with either aluminium or steel panels and the work was labour-intensive and highly skilled. In America the Budd Manufacturing Company of Philadelphia had pioneered pressed-steel body construction, the first all-steel body having appeared on the 1916 Dodge. The concept had been introduced to Europe, under Budd patents, in 1925 by André Citroen, the continent's leading car maker. Morris decided to visit Budd in 1925 and the outcome was the Pressed Steel Company, which was granted the production rights of the Budd patents and set up with finances from Morris Motors, merchant bankers J. Henry Shroeder, and Budd itself, which held the controlling interest in the new business.

When established at Cowley, Pressed Steel was the largest body plant in Europe. The first Morris car produced with all-steel bodywork was the Light Six, introduced in 1927. To operate economically Pressed Steel required contracts from other car makers, but Morris's involvement in the business was sufficient deterrent for other manufacturers not to deal with it for fear that their competitor might become aware of their future plans. In 1930, therefore, Morris withdrew his interest in the company and his two nominated directors resigned. Pressed Steel was thus demonstrably free to take work from rival car makers and the body for the 1931 Hillman Wizard was the first outside contract it received. Thereafter Pressed Steel continued to grow and, by 1939, its floor space had more than doubled. By this time the firm had become wholly British-owned, having gone public in 1935 when Budd withdrew its interest in the firm.

Until 1924 the Morris car was the sole Morris Motors product, but that year the MG marque made its appearance. In Oxford, Morris had maintained the retail arm of his business that had preceded his debut as a car maker. Called The Morris Garages, in 1921 it appointed a new sales manager named Cecil Kimber, educated at Southport Grammar School and Manchester Technical School. Before joining Morris he had worked for Sheffield-Simplex, A.C. Cars and Martinsyde Aircraft but, at the end of the First World War, he moved to Birmingham and joined E. G. Wrigley as an 'organization expert' and he came to Oxford from that assignment. In 1922 Kimber took over as Morris Garages' general manager. The following year, no doubt frustrated at having to sell Humbers, Singers and Wolseleys as well as Morris cars, he had the idea of producing a sporting version of the Cowley. The result was the Morris Chummy, with an open two-seater body by Carbodies of Coventry and finished in distinctive pastel shades.

This led, in 1924, to a 13.9hp closed model which, significantly, was publicized as 'the M.G. [for Morris Garages] vee-front saloon'. It was advertised in the March 1924 issue of *The Morris Owner*, and in the May issue displayed for the famous MG octagonal badge designed by Edmund (Ted) Lee, MG's cost accountant, who had flair for drawing. Lee recalls that, after seeing the badge, Morris said to him that it 'was the best thing to come out of the company', adding, 'and it will never go out of it'.[11]

MG output grew with the decade and, after being shunted around various premises in the city, the firm moved in September 1927 into a purpose-built factory in Edmund Road. The arrival of the 18/80 Super Sports in 1928 marked the first of the sports cars with which the marque is forever identified. Like practically all MGs, it was based on a production car, in this case the contemporary Morris Six and Isis. The company was again outgrowing its premises and The M.G. Car Company, as it became in 1928, moved in the winter of 1929/30 to a permanent home at a disused part of the Pavlova Leather Works at Abingdon-on-Thames, conveniently located only 6 miles from the Morris Motors' headquarters at Cowley.

In February 1927 Morris's growth was further accelerated by his buying, for £730,000, Wolseley Motors, a firm that had maintained its pre-war momentum of producing large numbers of cars while simultaneously absorbing considerable sums of money. In 1919 Wolseley, while keeping its Adderley Park works, extended car production to a 65-acre factory at Drews Lane, Ward End, Birmingham, built in 1914 by the Electric and Ordnance Accessories Company which, like Wolseley, was a Vickers subsidiary. When the first post-war 10 and 15hp Wolseleys arrived in 1920, they both featured expensive overhead-camshaft engines echoing the V8 Hispano-Suiza aero engines that the firm had made during the war. Curiously these models employed cost-cutting front and rear quarter elliptic springs. There was also a 3.9-litre side-valve six, with old-fashioned two-pot cylinders, which endured in a variety of capacities until 1927. In short, Wolseley's affairs smacked of ineffective management which failed to control overheads of two large and well equipped factories where, unlike the Morris approach, as much of the car as possible was made on the premises. However, the firm embarked on the construction of the £250,000 Wolseley House in Piccadilly, 'which introduced the fashion of luxury motor showrooms in the West End of London'.[12]

Initially sales went well in the post-war boom and in 1921 Wolseley built an impressive 12,000 cars, a figure only bettered by Ford. It was a case of 1913 all over again when the firm 'had become the largest, if one of the most unprofitable, British car manufacturers'.[13] Bernard Caillard, son of Sir Vincent Caillard, the Vickers chairman, was in charge of the firm at Vickers House and was found to be 'quite incapable of running any business'.[14] A more cost-conscious 7hp model arrived in 1922 but did little for the firm's dismal financial performance. In 1923 its Vickers parent wrote off £250,000 on its car subsidiary and Wolseley's managing director, Arthur McCormack, resigned. He was replaced by a committee of management headed by M. B. U. Dewar, yet he was unable to staunch the haemorrhage and, in 1924, Wolseley swallowed another £200,000. During the years from 1923 to 1925, the Wolseley Tool and Motor Car Company absorbed a total of £841,000 so that it began to threaten Vickers's very existence. Consequentially, in 1925, a committee of inquiry was set up to consider the crisis. This reported in December and resulted in Wolseley being allowed to go to the wall. The spring of 1926 saw the firm's life-giving overdraft standing at about £650,000 but, by October, Wolseley was unable to pay interest on its debentures and their holders 'put in receivers, whose task was to find a buyer'.[15]

It did not prove to be a problem for the sale generated considerable interest within the motor industry, mainly because of the potential of Wolseley's two large, well-equipped Birmingham factories. In due course the number of interested parties was reduced to three: William Morris, Sir Herbert Austin and possibly General Motors Corporation. The American firm subsequently dropped out, leaving the British bidders. Austin, who had begun his career with the firm, had commercial and sentimental reasons for wanting Wolseley, though Morris was stronger financially at this time and told Austin's finance director, Ernest Payton: 'I am going just a bit further than you.'[16] Austin decided not to match Morris's eventual bid of £730,000 and Wolseley was his.

Morris wasted little time in consolidating his purchase. A portion of the Adderley Park factory was sold off, while some of Morris's commercial vehicle activities were transferred there from the former Wrigley works at Soho. Both plants continued in operation until the Foundry Lane premises were sold in 1932 and Adderley Park became Morris's sole commercial vehicle factory. Wolseley's car operations were, in the meantime, concentrated on Ward End.

If the 1920s were Morris's decade, the same could not be said for Ford, the market leader until 1923. Where Ford had been fortunate was that it was able to continue building the Model T, just as it had been doing during the war, with no lengthy delays as the works switched from war- to peace-time production. Therefore it built 9,293 Ts in 1918 and the Ford was easily Britain's best-selling car, with the figure spiralling to an impressive 46,362 from October 1919 to the end of 1920. Austin was a long way behind, with 4,319 cars, in second place. Not surprisingly, Ford's British operations made a record profit of £852,652 for the fifteen months ending December 1920. Yet, by 1926, Ford's output had sunk to 24,900 cars and trucks and Trafford Park had dropped into third position behind Morris and Austin. There were two main reasons for this decline: the effects of the 1921 horsepower tax, which penalized big-bored American cars, and Sir Percival Perry's departure from Ford's British operations in 1919.

Back in 1906 the Royal Automobile Club had set down its RAC rating formula so that the public might 'arrive at the approximate power of any given engine in comparison with others', though, the club cautioned, it was 'not to be considered as an accurate or scientific calculation of actual horsepower'.[17] The RAC rating formula was defined as $D^2N/2.5$. D represented the bore of the engine and N the number of cylinders, while 2.5 was arbitrarily arrived at 'and will be found reasonable and sufficiently accurate for comparative purposes'.[18] When, in 1909, a new graduated Road Fund licence was introduced, it used RAC rating as its basis, so a 12hp car, for instance, paid £12 and a 60hp £21.

After the war, with Ford sales riding high, the system was changed again to the detriment of American imports. At this time a Ford owner would have paid 6 guineas a year to tax his car, but after the introduction of the Finance Act in 1921 this rose to £23. This was because the Model T Ford had a 22.5hp RAC horsepower rating as the new tax was implemented at the rate of £1 per horsepower. (RAC rating was based on the engine's bore, and American engines were larger than British ones because petrol was substantially cheaper there). In contrast, the T's Morris Cowley-owning next-door neighbour paid only £12 a year to tax his car as it was rated at only 11.9hp. In view of this, British car makers of the inter-war years stressed the RAC rating of their engines (Austin Seven, Morris Eight, Singer Nine and so on) as this had a direct relation to the price of the Road Fund licence. But the existence of the tax was an incentive for British car makers to build low-capacity, small-bored engines which were ideal for the home market but not a world one.

The second blow to Ford's British operations came in May 1919 when Sir Percival Perry resigned. Following the war he had been anxious to press ahead with his plans for a new Ford plant at Southampton and suggested to Ford that the resulting company embody a 40 per cent British sharehold-ing. Ford decisively rejected this last proposal. Perry was physically exhausted from his war-time endeavours and he also clashed with Detroit about the way he was running the British company. Fortunately, he had other irons in the fire. In 1919 and 1920 he headed a group which bought war surplus British and American cars; this subsequently purchased the Slough Motor Company's Buckinghamshire depot and from it sprang the Slough Trading Company which was reorganized as Slough Estates in 1926, so creating a trading estate in the manner of the Manchester Trafford

Park facility with which Perry was so familiar. By 1922 Perry had resigned as chairman and managing director, though he continued as a director. The previous August, while cruising in his yacht in the Channel Islands, he visited the Island of Herm and was obviously struck by it for he took over the lease of a 300-acre house and estate there from the novelist Compton Mackenzie. Perry spent some of his time writing poetry and prose and, in 1926, published a book about Herm which he called *The Island of Enchantment*. Trafford Park must have seemed a long way away.

None of Perry's replacements was of his calibre and, in 1923, when William Klann, head of production at Detroit, visited Trafford Park to see manager Charles Gould, 'there he was with his feet on the top of the desk, drinking tea and reading the morning paper'.[19] Meanwhile the plant was faced with a new problem. In 1919 Ford's Cork factory had produced its first tractor, though it soon became apparent that another product would be necessary to make the business viable. So Cork began making engines and axles for Manchester and spare parts for Ford's European operations. Then, in 1923, a problem arose following the creation of the Irish Free State the previous year which established its own customs system. Parts imported to Manchester would now be subject to an unacceptable 22$\frac{2}{9}$ per cent tariff. Although Trafford Park already made some of its own parts, the Irish situation resulted in a corporate rethink in Detroit. There it was recognized that Model T component production in Ireland must cease, although tractor production would continue. All Model T manufacture would have to be concentrated in Britain. Manchester was unsuitable as a new site of about 100 acres would be required with good rail communications and, above all, a river frontage. How Ford removed its British operations from Trafford Park to the marshes of Dagenham, Essex, is told in the next chapter.

In 1929 Ford had fallen to fourth place behind Morris, Austin and Singer, and although Morris Motors was profitable from 1920 until 1929, despite the crisis of 1921, his great contemporary Sir Herbert Austin had been passing through the industrial fire at Longbridge. Austin, it will be recalled, had decided to follow in Henry Ford's wheeltracks and market just one model, a 20hp car, intended for the world as well as the home market. Production began in 1919 when around 200 were built as the works was being reorganized. Output in the following year stood at 4,319 cars, which was only 200 less than Longbridge's entire production between 1906 and 1914. The strategy seemed to be paying off, but in the autumn of 1920 came the onset of depression, which was compounded by the arrival of the horsepower tax in 1921. Because the 20hp's engine dimensions closely followed those of the Model T, an Austin owner had to pay the same £22 Road Fund licence as someone who had bought a Ford.

Inevitably, 20hp production slumped by almost half to 2,246 cars in 1921. The falling sales contributed to a deterioration in the firm's already strained finances and, in April of that year, Arthur Whinney was appointed receiver on behalf of the Midland Bank and the Eagle Star Insurance company, which were the firm's principal creditors.

Sir Herbert wasted little time in resolving the situation. Just as he had scaled down a 30hp model to produce a 20hp one in pre-war days, so he did the same with the new 20 and produced the 12hp with a 1.6-litre engine of approximately the same capacity as the best-selling earlier 10hp. But he was thwarted in his attempt to get the new car into production by the receiver who would not sanction the necessary expenditure. However, Austin realized that the 12hp was essential for the company's survival so it was financed by the sale of unwanted plant and stock. The model entered production in 1922 and a great success it proved to be, overtaking sales of the overstrong 20hp in 1923. It was a popular, reliable, if slightly pedestrian car and remained in production until 1935 while the quaint but proven taxi version endured until 1939.

Austin's next model was even more audacious and was undertaken in the face of considerable opposition from his co-directors. After his experience with the 20hp, Sir Herbert decided that what the firm wanted was a really small car that was more tailored to the economic climate. In view of the unfavourable response of his board, he decided to finance the project from his own pocket.

As was his way, Austin was all for copying an existing design and his starting point was an 8hp two-cylinder air-cooled Rover, made by a firm that had outproduced Austin in 1921. His chief cashier, Arthur Day, ran such a model and Sir Herbert borrowed it and made detailed drawings of the design. As this was his own project, Austin needed the help of someone who was familiar with contemporary design and was technically and theoretically competent. He found him in his own drawing office in the shape of an eighteen-year-old draughtsman named Stanley Edge. Sir Herbert had made his acquaintance because young Edge used to arrive at work an hour ahead of his colleagues as he caught the only available train from Halesowen. The only other person around at that hour was Sir Herbert Austin. The two soon got talking, and when Austin decided to proceed with his small car project, he asked, in the autumn of 1921, that Edge be relieved from his day-to-day duties and work with him at Lickey Grange, his nearby home.

On arrival, Edge found Austin keen to proceed with his two-cylinder car. Despite his youth, Stanley, who had a sound knowledge of most British and continental car and motorcycle design, registered his opposition to fifty-five-year-old Austin's producing what he considered to be a crude two-cylinder car. After Sir Herbert eventually conceded this point, 'he wanted three cylinders and we studied this from all possible viewpoints'.[20] Edge was able to convince Austin that what was required was a small *four*-cylinder engine, which followed established continental practice and would result in a more refined model, effectively a large car in miniature. But, above all, 'I was responsible for sticking to the view that a small four could be made as cheaply as any engine having less cylinders.'[21] The car that particularly inspired Edge was the French 698cc Peugeot Quadrilette of 1920, a spiritual successor to the Bugatti-designed Bébé of 1912. For the lower half of the engine, he drew on the Belgian FN four-cylinder motorcycle engine with its two roller bearing crankshaft and splash lubrication. However, the FN was an air-cooled unit, with overhead valves, so the rest of the engine followed traditional Austin practice in that the tiny cast-iron side-valve cylinder block was mounted on the aluminium crankcase.

For the car's triangular-shaped chassis, Austin drew on that of an American Gray truck of which there was an example at Longbridge. Suspension followed Quadrilette practice and used a transverse spring at the front, itself courtesy of the Model T Ford, and cost-conscious quarter elliptic springs at the rear. Four wheel brakes, revolutionary for a British car at this time, also featured. Work on the project was completed by Easter of 1922 and the Seven was announced in July, though the engine's capacity was increased from 696 to 748cc in March 1923. Despite this the £225 Austin Seven was Britain's smallest-capacity four-cylinder car throughout its production life. It spelt death not only to the cycle cars which had survived the war but also to two-cylinder models, notably the Rover 8hp which ceased production in 1925!

In 1926 the Seven moved ahead of the 12hp to become Austin's best-selling model and remained so for the next six years when it was overtaken by the firm's newly introduced 10hp car. Annual production, at 27,280, did not peak until 1935. When the Seven ceased in 1939, this lion-hearted little model had established itself as Britain's top-selling car of the inter-war years, providing transport for thousands of people who might otherwise have gone by train. It was built under licence by the German Dixi company which produced a mirror image of the Seven from 1927 and that company was taken over by BMW in 1928. It was also made in Paris by Lucien Rosengart, while in America it was marketed, between 1930 and 1934, as the Austin Bantam.

As Austin had personally financed the project, he no doubt felt justified in getting his board to ratify payment to him of a 2 guineas royalty for every Seven made. His steadfastness and foresight were therefore well rewarded.

By 1922 Austin could consider himself back on course and the receiver was discharged in March. But, at the insistence of the Midland Bank, two appointments were made to the Austin board intended to remedy Sir Herbert's all-too-obvious shortcomings in the areas of production and finance. As a result Carl Englebach joined the company as works director with responsibility for car manufacture. A production engineer, Englebach had spent much of his working life in the highly mechanized arms trade which, as we have seen, was the forcing house on mass production methods. He began his career at the Royal Arsenal at Woolwich and then moved to Armstrong Mitchel and Company at Newcastle-upon-Tyne where he served a three-year apprenticeship.

Englebach gained experience of car manufacture when he was appointed to take charge of Armstrong Whitworth's motor department. During the First World War he ran the howitzer department of the Coventry Ordnance Works and moved from there to take up his position at Longbridge, though Austin is said to have described him as 'that bloody interloper'[22] on his arrival in 1921 and relegated him to a modest office. Englebach responded by installing himself in a larger and more suitable room at the front of the building opposite Sir Herbert's own office. From 1924 Englebach embarked on a radical restructuring of Longbridge's manufacturing facilities, although this streamlining in production methods represented a dramatic contrast to the highly traditional cars produced.

Yet another significant appointment was that of Ernest Payton, who joined the board in the role of finance director. He became deputy chairman in 1928 and chairman following Austin's death in 1941. This triumvirate of Austin, Payton and Englebach was to run Longbridge for most of the inter-war years.

For all the firm's success after the 1921/2 financial debacle, and its record profits of £1.2 million in 1929, there is considerable evidence to suggest that, with no male heir to inherit the business, Sir Herbert Austin would have liked to sell the company that bore his name. There were talks with General Motors, in 1920, about a possible takeover, but at that time the American corporation was facing its own financial problems. The dialogue was re-activated in 1924. In the following year, James Mooney, vice president of the corporation's export committee, visited Britain and the Longbridge works and reported in favour of its purchase. Austin was all for the deal but was vetoed by his fellow directors. 'Well, her dowry was quite substantial, but my relations didn't like her and therefore the engagement was broken off,'[23] he later told a gathering of Austin agents. General Motors' president, Alfred Sloan, was 'actually relieved to hear the news . . . [Austin's] physical plant was then in poor condition and its management weak. And I still had doubts that our own management was strong enough to make up for Austin's deficiencies.'[24]

Austin had the small car market to itself with the Seven until 1927, when Singer responded with its 8hp Junior. It was an appropriate challenge from a firm that enjoyed considerable growth during the 1920s. During the decade Singer's expansion was largely a result of the 'dictatorial guidance of William Bullock, whose methods were in keeping with his name'.[25] Bullock, born in Birmingham in 1877, had begun his career at the age of fourteen as a toolmaker's assistant with the Handsworth firm of Dennison and Wigley. He left to join an electrical engineering company, though returned to his old employer and the newly formed Wigley-Mulliner Engineering Company. It had produced arms during the Boer War, subsequently moved from Birmingham to Coventry, and was transformed in 1905 into the Coventry Ordnance Works where Bullock was appointed manager. In 1908 he moved down the road to Singer at Canterbury Street where he became works manager.

The arrival of the Singer Ten in 1912 was a landmark in the firm's affairs. This light car sold strongly before and after the war and was the company's only model until 1922 when it was joined by a 15hp Six, well ahead of its contemporaries. By 1924 Singer offered this model with a Weymann fabric body, another trend-setting feature. Bullock again set the pace in 1923 when the Ten received overhead valves which were unusual in a cheap car, even though old-fashioned exposed pushrods were employed. But the big event of the decade was the arrival of the £148 Junior in 1927. The significant aspects of the design were that the car was a genuine four-seater and powered by a single overhead camshaft engine, a costly feature usually reserved for more potent, sporting makes. Yet the Junior was a great success. Annual sales never dropped below the 6,000 mark during its six-year production life, while its engine was the ancestor of all Singer models made up until 1956.

As Singer prospered and production rose (it paid dividends throughout the decade), it was continually running out of factory space, a problem experienced by many Coventry car companies. In 1920 it bought the Coventry Premier Company, which had begun building cars in 1914 and possessed a 3-acre factory which Singer absorbed. Next, in 1922, came the Coventry Repetition Company, and three years later Singer took over the Sparkbrook Manufacturing Company, which had built the Sparkbrook motorcycle. The factory in nearby Paynes Lane was used for burgeoning car production. In 1927 Singer made its last major takeover by buying Calcott, a Coventry car maker since 1913. Its works in Far Gosford Street became the Singer spares and service department. Singer's London depot, acquired in 1928, was in Wembley and formerly the home of the Aster car, though the business was taken over by Arrol-Johnson in 1927 and transferred to Dumfries. Yet, despite these additional facilities, by 1928 Singer was building about 300 cars a week and was so short of space that when a representative of *The Autocar* visited the Canterbury Street headquarters, he found that 'the panel beaters . . . were so close together that one man was in danger of beating the next man's panel'.[26]

What Singer desperately wanted was a new, large factory and in 1927 Bullock found it on the Coventry Road at Sparkbrook, Birmingham. It had been built by BSA during the First World War for small arms manufacture and was near to its own works, but was considered 'something of a "white elephant" until [Bullock's] organizing ability converted it into a means of prosperity',[27] noted a correspondent in 1930. This six-storey building with 34 acres of floor space should have represented the start of a new era for Singer. As will emerge, it was a contributory factor in its subsequent downfall.

If Morris, Austin and Singer represented the success stories of the British motor industry in the 1920s, what of Rover, one of the most profitable firms of the pre-war era? Its reputation was based almost solely on the 12hp which was updated, with a detachable cylinder head, and continued in production until 1924. As the mass market was the order of the day, Rover spent £400,000 on tooling up to produce an 8hp two-cylinder air-cooled model, designed by Jack Sangster. Only twenty-two years old when he arrived at Rover in 1918, Sangster left in 1921 to join the family business, which included Ariel motorcycles, where he became joint managing director. As Rover had no room for expansion in its works in West Orchard, Coventry, the 8hp car was built in a new factory 12 miles away at Hay Hall Street, Tyseley, Birmingham, where, during the First World War, the government-directed Component Munitions Ltd had made fuses. Although 8hp sales of 3,021 were impressive in the depression year of 1921 and demand rose in 1922, the arrival of the Austin Seven that year proved a formidable challenger. 'This, with a four-cylinder water-cooled engine was, according to Rover dealers, something the public thought much superior to a twin cylinder,' recalled Dudley Noble, Rover's publicity manager during the 1920s.[28] The 8hp lasted until 1925, by which time some 17,000 had been built.

In February 1923 Harry Smith stepped down as Rover's managing director, a year in which the firm had recorded a loss of £36,752, its first deficit since 1908. His place was taken, in February 1923, by John Kemp Starley who had the crucial task of replacing the successful but by then dated Twelve. It lasted until 1924 and was followed by the 14/45 of 1925 which proved a costly blunder. Designed by Peter Poppe, late of White and Poppe, it had a four-cylinder 2.1-litre engine and boasted a single overhead camshaft which actuated inclined valves in hemispherical combustion chambers, via no less than two rocker shafts and a horizontal cross pushrod arrangement. Not only was it expensive to make but 'sounded as if a big end had gone . . . and it gave the service department one long nightmare, trying to cure the gear noise from the engine'.[29] The arrival of an enlarged 16/50 version in 1926 simply compounded the error. By this time Rover's finances had deteriorated to such an extent that the firm had a loss of £123,450 in 1924/5, though this was cut to £77,945 in the following year. Perhaps to make amends, Poppe designed a more straightforward 2-litre overhead-valve Six which appeared in 1928 and served the company until 1934.

Rover had paid no dividends since 1924 and matters came to a head in April 1928, when Colonel W. F. Wyley, the Rover chairman since 1909, resigned. John Kemp Starley left for a visit to Australia, ostensibly to investigate an alleged breach of contract by a Melbourne dealer. He officially stepped down as managing director in February 1929 and was replaced, in his absence, by a former Tank Corps colonel, Frank Searle, despite the fact that he had no motor industry experience. With a view to bringing body building in house, Searle acquired a lease from English Electric on a 12.75-acre site in Helen Street, Coventry, and it was subsequently purchased for £30,000. He initiated the Scarab project, a rear-engined, air-cooled car intended to sell for £85, and although a prototype was built at his home at Braunston House, Braunston, near Rugby, he departed in late 1931, like Starley before him, to the antipodes and journeyed to New Zealand to dispose of a subsidiary he had established there. He never returned to Rover, but he was responsible for the appointment, in September 1929, of Spencer Bernau Wilks, to whom he was related by marriage and who was joint managing director of Hillman, as general manager.

Spencer Wilks (1891–1971), on the face of it, seems an unlikely candidate for the motor industry. Educated at Charterhouse, he appeared destined for a career in the law and entered a legal practice in 1909, though this was interrupted by the outbreak of the First World War. After military service, in which he rose to the rank of captain, he decided to enter the motor industry and, at the age of twenty-six, joined the Hillman Motor Company. This was still being run by its founder, William Hillman, who died in 1926. By this time Wilks had married one of his employer's daughters and was managing director, a post he shared with another captain who had also studied law in pre-First World War days and, like Wilks, also married a Miss Hillman. Although the two were brothers-in-law, there the resemblance ended.

John Paul Black (1895–1965), a controversial figure to say the least, was successful, ruthless and dictatorial. A former assistant, and later deputy, summed up his personality thus: 'No one hit it off [with him] really, and this is nothing against him. He was an individualist. You either hated him, or loved him . . . and I alternated between the two fairly often!'[30] Wilks, by contrast, 'was kind, courteous and considerate almost to a fault . . . having had a legal training earlier in his life and possessed of a finely honed analytic intellect, he never seemed to lose his impressive calm in any crisis'.[31]

This unlikely duo managed to run Hillman during the 1920s with a successful pre-war Nine carried over, though from 1926 until 1928 the only model available was the straightforward, though rather dull, 1.9-litre 14 which culminated in the ambitious Rootes brothers taking the firm over in 1928. Spencer Wilks went to Rover in 1929, while in the same year John Black joined Standard.

Standard had begun life in Much Park Street, Coventry, in 1903 but in 1915 Reginald Maudslay, its founder, had the good sense to buy a 30-acre site from Lord Leigh at Canley, on the western outskirts of the city. In mid-1918, Maudslay acquired a further 300 acres to cater for further expansion – to the envy of Coventry's other car makers which were always cramped for space. The firm introduced its first post-war model, the 13.9hp overhead-valve SLO 4 which sold for £375 in 1924, a year in which Standard built around 10,000 cars, putting it on a par with Austin. Yet this promise was not maintained and a 2.2-litre overhead-valve 20/25 Six attracted few buyers. For Maudslay 'was a gentlemanly engineer [he was Marlborough-educated] of the old school who found it difficult to adjust his ideas to the post-1918 motor industry'.[32] No dividend was paid from 1927, and by 1929 losses amounted to £123,698. Had it not been for Barclays Bank (and in Coventry rumour was rife that William Morris, as a friend of Maudslay's had threatened to withdraw his own substantial funds to prevent Standard's bankruptcy), it seems likely that the firm would have succumbed to the blandishments of the increasingly influential Rootes brothers.

In 1927 a new chief engineer was appointed in the shape of thirty-eight-year-old Alfred Wilde, from Morris Engines in Coventry, where he was chief designer. A graduate of Manchester University, Wilde immediately got to work and the result was the ultra-reliable Nine, which appeared in 1928 and marked the start of the firm's recovery. Just one of the innovations introduced by Wilde, who was much in advance of his time, was to 'display prototype parts . . . on long tables, just as soon as they became available from the experimental shops; there they were examined by production engineers who were encouraged to suggest any design changes that might be expected to facilitate manufacture'.[33] This approach, coupled with the introduction of a rigorous day-and-night testing programme between Coventry and the Bwlch-y-Groes mountain passes in North Wales, won Wilde the respect of his colleagues. Yet an appointment to the Standard board failed to materialize and, in 1930, Wilde accepted an offer to join Rootes but fell ill and died in December 1931, aged only forty-one. Captain Black (he used this fashionable 'handle' throughout the inter-war years) was able to build on the foundations that Wilde had laid, so that, in the following decade, Standard emerged as one of Britain's Big Six car makers.

The firm in which William and Reginald Rootes took a controlling interest in 1928 was Humber. Although it had a chequered financial history, in 1913 Humber was second only to Wolseley in output with around 2,500 cars produced. The Humberette light car was discontinued after the war and the firm moved up market with a range of beautifully made and appointed if slightly old-fashioned cars, which proved increasingly expensive to build as the decade progressed. During this period Humber's managing director was Lieutenant-Colonel John Albert Cole, 'a dear old boy who had a wonderful knack of making a sonorous speech that was both impressive and carried extremely well'.[34] He had come to the fore in Humber's affairs as an articulate speaker at a shareholders' meeting during the firm's 1910 troubles, which resulted in the loss-making aircraft department being closed down.

In 1923 Humber introduced quiet, efficient but costly overhead-inlet/side-exhaust-valve engines to its car range which consolidated the firm's reputation for sound engineering; a Humber apprenticeship was highly valued within the industry. Yet Humber cars, like Colonel Cole, were conservative in the extreme and, by 1928, were still being built with such Edwardian features as separate gearboxes and cone clutches. Front-wheel brakes did not arrive until 1925, two years behind the rest of the industry. This was because Colonel Cole regarded them as 'a costly and possibly dangerous mechanism'.[35] He even threatened to stop advertising in *The Motor* magazine if Maurice Platt, its technical editor, did not stop inciting its readers to demand them. Cole eventually succumbed, but the foot-operated transmission brake, a pre-First World War anachronism, persisted. But Cole, whose 'guiding principles seemed too respectable for the cut and thrust of the motor industry',[36] saw the firm's finances deteriorate: no dividend was paid in 1928, the first such lapse since 1917, which was when the Rootes brothers stepped in.

Having effectively taken over Humber, the pair looked around for another firm with which to merge. They mentioned their plans to A. C. Armstrong, editor of *The Motor*, who 'suggested the Hillman car company [which] adjoined the Humber factory'.[37] The Rootes duo wasted little time and, in December 1928, the Humber share capital was increased to effect the Hillman purchase. For his role in the takeover Armstrong was presented by the brothers with a gold Asprey cigarette case. Later, in 1934/5, the old-established Talbot and Sunbeam companies would come within the Rootes' expansive orbit – the Rootes story is told in detail in the next chapter.

Sunbeam had put up a sparkling performance in pre-war days, but Louis Coatalen, the architect of its revival, returned to his native France after the First World War and, although he continued as the firm's chief engineer, he was no longer Wolverhampton-based. In June 1920 it was announced that Sunbeam was to merge with A. Darracq and Company. That firm, its coffers swelled by war-time arms contracts, had, in October 1919, taken over Clement-Talbot, which had been building cars in the London suburb of Ladbroke Grove since 1903. Sunbeam therefore became embroiled in what was to prove the unwieldy Anglo-French STD [Sunbeam-Talbot-Darracq] Motors. When car production restarted in 1919, the traditional Sunbeam quality was maintained and the successful pre-war 12/16 revived, renamed the 16 and updated. In 1925 came the Super Sports, with a 3-litre twin-overhead-camshaft engine, the only British production car to offer this facility. From 1927 only sixes were on offer, though in 1929 the firm introduced a top-line straight eight for £1975. But without Coatalen's dynamic presence, and as a result of the effects of the mis-managed STD combine, 'by 1927 the rise of Sunbeam can be said to have finished'.[38] In 1929 the firm's profits tumbled to a mere £14,362.

In one area, however, Sunbeam had emerged triumphant. Coatalen's enthusiasm for motor racing was as strong as ever in the post-war era, and at the 1923 French Grand Prix Henry Segrave drove his Sunbeam to victory, giving Britain its first major racing victory since S. F. Edge and his Napier had triumphed in the 1902 Gordon Bennett race. Segrave won again at the Spanish Grand Prix of 1924, but it would be another thirty-three years before a British car would once more take the chequered flag in a front-line event. Although Segrave's car carried the Sunbeam name, there were justifiable jibes that it was a 'Fiat in green paint' because Coatalen had recruited two Italian engineers, Bertarione and Becchia, from the outstanding Fiat racing team to design the car, which, not surprisingly, bore a striking resemblance to the 1922 Fiat 404.

Racing cars contined to be built until 1926 but that year, in the wake of a fall in STD profits, Coatalen and Segrave decided on a change of strategy which would continue to give Sunbeam valuable publicity but at a fraction of the cost of running a grand prix team. This followed Kenelm Lee Guiness and Malcolm Campbell, in special cars powered by Sunbeam aero engines, holding the World Land Speed Record in 1922 and 1925 respectively. So the firm began its own record-breaking activities and, with

Segrave successively at the wheel of three purpose-built Sunbeams, held the record in 1926, 1927 and 1929, reassuring a generation of schoolboys that an Old Etonian and an Englishman (Segrave actually had an Irish father and American mother) was the Fastest Man on Earth. But the costly racing programme left a deadly legacy of £500,000 worth of 8 per cent Guaranteed Notes, issued by STD Motors in 1924 and redeemable ten years later.

When the STD combine was created in 1920, its aim was to emulate the American General Motors Corporation, as it became in 1917, with its bevy of makes and component manufacturers. William Durant, its founder, his position imperilled by a financial crisis in late 1920, had stepped down from the corporate presidency to be subsequently replaced, in 1923, by Alfred Pritchard Sloan Junior. A graduate of the prestigious Massachusetts Institute of Technology, Sloan immediately recognized that one man was incapable of running such a huge conglomerate. In instigating a decentralized management structure, in which the separate divisions became autonomous units though operating within the corporate framework, he created the blueprint for the modern corporation.

With General Motors back in profit again in 1922, and the Chevrolet make in use for the corporate assault on the Model T's supremacy, Sloan decided to follow Ford's example and establish European presences at a time when the continent's principal industrial countries were operating protective tariffs. An attempt to buy the newly founded French Citroen company in 1919 had fallen through, so Sloan turned his attention to Britain. There American imports were subjected to the 33⅓ per cent McKenna Duties, so there were powerful arguments for buying an existing manufacturer and creating a presence behind the tariff-wall. At some stage General Motors tried to buy Morris Motors, as did Ford in 1923. Morris refused both offers and said of the General Motors approach: 'I should have been selling my country to another country and that I refuse to do. I should have felt a traitor.'[39] Although Sir Herbert Austin suffered no such qualms, he was overruled by his fellow directors. After this rebuff, in December 1925 General Motors purchased the small Vauxhall company, which that year had built just 1,398 cars compared with Austin's 16,429. Sloan subsequently recalled; 'It was in no sense a substitute for Austin; indeed I looked on it only as a kind of experiment in overseas manufacture.'[40]

Established in 1857 at the Vauxhall Iron Works, the firm took its name from the South London suburb in which it was located. There it manufactured marine engines, though in 1903 Vauxhall diversified into car production, while 1905 saw a move to Luton, Bedfordshire. A pivotal appointment in the firm's affairs came in 1912 when twenty-nine-year-old

Laurence Pomeroy was made chief engineer. His 1908 20hp model 'put Vauxhall in the forefront of advanced thinking'[41] and established a design strategy that was to endure until 1921. Pomeroy pursued a racing programme, though with considerably less success than Coatalen's at Sunbeam, and in 1913 Vauxhall introduced its legendary 30/98 sports car which endured, in updated form, until 1927.

Pomeroy departed for America in 1919 and in 1922 came the cheaper 2.3-litre M type, though at a £750 chassis price there were few takers and that year Vauxhall built only 650 cars. 'The post-1918 programme was extravagantly ambitious and demanded an investment in money and manpower which was far beyond the resources of the organization, and they had lost Pomeroy, the realist, who would have had a restraining influence.'[42] The firm had paid no dividends from 1920 and the General Motors purchase, which cost 'only' $2,575,291 (£543,310), produced an outcry from the public. 'One result of this clamour was that the General Motors connection was never mentioned in Vauxhall's advertising . . . for many years afterwards.'[43]

The Vauxhall managing directorship had been jointly shared from 1907 by Eton-educated Leslie Walton and Percy Kidner, and while the 'more adaptable and well-balanced Walton'[44] remained at Luton, Kidner departed. He was 'a robust extrovert and motor car enthusiast, but he was also opinionated, inflexible and not particularly intelligent'.[45] The first effects of the General Motors takeover were not felt until the arrival, in 1928, of the R type. It was the first model to betray the firm's new ownership, and was powered by a 2.8-litre overhead-valve six-cylinder engine, while it visually resembled a scaled-down Buick. But in 1929 Vauxhall's sales amounted to a mere 1,668 cars.

Across the Atlantic in October of that year, American confidence was shattered by arrival of the Wall Street financial crash. As the country reeled from the effects of depression, car output slumped from a record 4.4 million units in 1929 to 1.1 million in 1932 and the 1929 highpoint was not to be bettered until 1949. Would the British motor industry be similarly devastated?

3

Six of the Best?

1930–9

'The concentration of interests in the hands of the Big Six [Morris, Austin, Ford, Standard, Rootes, Vauxhall] made it difficult for individual manufacturers of new cars to enter the industry, and particularly for anyone who wished to make a cheap priced car.'[1]

Although America was devastated by the effects of the depression, the British motor industry suffered only a temporary setback in production. Output dipped in 1930 and 1931 while, the following year, Britain surpassed France as Europe's largest car maker, a position it maintained until 1955. In 1933 Britain overtook its own 1929 record year and output continued to rise until it peaked in 1937 when 379,310 cars were built, a high that was not overtaken until 1949.

Automobiles therefore became one of the growth industries of the 1930s in a decade which saw the emergence of the Big Six motor manufacturers, so setting a pattern for the post-war years. This was not only the result of a growing market when motoring established itself as a mainstream middle-class pursuit, but the combined effects of a fall in world commodity prices and the full benefits of mass production, which saw a drop in car prices. An Austin Seven saloon cost £135 in 1929 but ten years later what was effectively the same car cost £13 less at £122. In addition, Morris and Austin watched their respective market shares decline as Ford, Standard, Rootes and Vauxhall, in market order, filled the void. Singer, by contrast, failed to maintain the momentum it had established in the previous decade.

The saloon car continued to tighten its hold on the market and, although firms offered convertibles, the open car became largely the preserve of the low-production sports car sector. The 8hp class continued to dominate the market place until 1933, when it was overtaken by the 10hp one as such cars as the Austin Ten and Hillman Minx had become strong sellers; however, the 8hp car, exemplified by the Ford and Morris Eights, re-asserted itself in 1935 and 1938.

The motor industry, prior to 1936, had operated within a *laissez-faire* environment and government intervention was confined to the protective effects of the horsepower tax. That year Stanley Baldwin's coalition government asked the industry to participate in what was called a Shadow Factory scheme which recognized that war with Germany was inevitable. The exchequer would pay for the creation of new factories, which would be administered by the car makers, in the first instance for the manufacture of Bristol aero engines. The motor industry overcame its initial reluctance and, after some teething troubles, the arrangement worked well enough. But the partnership between government and industry marked the beginning of a new era for both institutions; one would never again operate independently of the other.

So how was it that Morris Motors' share of British car production fell by nearly half, from 51 per cent in 1929 to close on 27 per cent in 1938, even though the market's growth ensured that output rose from 63,522 to about 95,000 over the same period? Also in 1933 and 1934, for the first time, Morris's Austin rival built more cars. At the root of the problem was what Morris's biographers tactfully refer to as 'uncertainty in management'.[2] Sir Herbert Austin's cash crisis of 1921 had highlighted his limitations and there is little doubt that the Austin Motor Company was all the better for the arrival of financier Ernest Payton and production engineer Carl Englebach. Yet there was no such triumvirate at Cowley and Morris ran his scattered business empire empirically, just as he had his first bicycle shop, despite the arrival of greater competition and an increasingly complex market place.

Morris Motors was crying out for strong, professional direction and it is true to say that Sir William did inherit a range of managerial skills following his takeovers of the 1920s. His first deputy was Lancelot Pratt, of Hollick and Pratt, who died in 1924 from cancer, aged only forty-four. Morris's senior executive was Whitworth Scholar and production expert Arthur Rowse, 'a man of great intellect who wrung more value out of component suppliers, by organizing their production methods, than has ever been recognized'.[3] He was passed over for the post of deputy governing director by general sales manager Hugh Wordsworth Grey. Morris soon thought that Grey 'was losing his grip'[4] and in 1926, again ignoring Rowse, he appointed as his deputy Edgar Blake, who came from Dunlop where he had been sales manager.

Then, from 1927 onwards, Morris, who had always enjoyed sea voyages, began to absent himself from his factory by taking long cruises to

Australia. Accompanied by his friend, company secretary and accountant Wilfred Hobbs, he delighted in playing endless games of deck tennis, a game in which he excelled, but his corporate affairs drifted and profits tumbled from £1.5 million in 1929 to £844,000 in 1933. It was from that year, observed Miles Thomas, then general sales manager and director, that Morris 'took a decreasing part in the functional running of his companies'.[5] Although Blake was ostensibly in charge during Morris's absences, the reality was that his employer would reverse any decision to which he had not been a party. Sir William clashed with Frank Woollard, his production genius, who departed in 1931. He was followed in April 1933 by Arthur Rowse and in June by Edgar Blake 'who had toiled unremittingly at Cowley to be an administrative buffer between the volatile, mercurial and at times so irritable Morris and his second echelon executives'.[6] The reason for the departure of the latter two managers was the arrival at Cowley, in April 1933, of the thrusting, aggressive thirty-six-year-old Leonard Lord whose rise in the Morris Motors hierarchy is directly related to the firm's muddled model car programme of the late 1920s and early 1930s.

In 1928 Sir William had followed the lead taken by Austin and Singer and made his bid for the small-car market sector. The arrival of the 847cc Minor followed Singer in that it was powered by an expensive overhead-camshaft engine, though Cowley used a Wolseley design which was simultaneously and more suitably employed in the contemporary in-house MG Midget. Morris cars had an excellent reliability record prior to the Minor's arrival but, despite its nippy performance, it was difficult to maintain after it had gone off tune and there were dynamo problems as its armature did double duty as the camshaft drive. It cost £135 in saloon form, which was the same price as the rival Austin Seven, but it was consistently outsold by the more reliable, side-valve-engined Longbridge baby.

Morris realized his mistake and decided that the Minor must be replaced by a cheaper and simpler car that was offered, in addition to the two-door saloon, in no-frills two-seater form and seductively priced, at Miles Thomas's suggestion, at £100. Speedily introduced in February 1931, the revised Minor was soon outselling its more complex brother which remained in production until 1932, while the side-valve car endured until 1934. The Wolseley engineer responsible for this important new model was Leonard Lord. 'The swiftness with which . . . Lord had got the new Morris Minor side-valve engine into production at Wolseley's had impressed [Morris]. He decided that he be transferred to Cowley,'[7] recalled Thomas.

Leonard Percy Lord (1896–1967) was destined to dominate the affairs of Morris, Austin and, finally, the British Motor Corporation until his retirement in 1961. His maxim, 'If the door isn't open then you kick it open', probably says more about him than my words may be able to convey. Although Miles Thomas, on their first meeting, made the not uncommon mistake of describing him as a 'ginger-haired Yorkshire lad',[8] he was in fact born in Coventry and both his parents were natives of the city. He succeeded in obtaining a place at Coventry's old-established Bablake public school and, on leaving, joined the local Courtaulds works at Foleshill. A quick-witted, hot-tempered youth, Lord had a natural flair for solving mechanical problems. Deeply devoted to his mother, he used to teach at the local technical college in the evenings to provide her with little luxuries. It was during one of these classes that Lord learnt to control his temper, 'because he very nearly got into trouble for throwing the wooden backed blackboard scrubber at a pupil who got on his nerves'.[9]

During the First World War, Lord moved to the nearby Coventry Ordnance Works, where one of the managers was Carl Englebach, who later became Austin's production engineer. After a spell there, Lord moved to Daimler and finally to Hotchkiss which had just obtained the contract to make a copy of the U Type Continental Red Seal engine for William Morris. One of the problems that the works faced was that, being a French plant, it was equipped only with metric tool heads but, so that garages could cope with them, Leonard Lord came up with the suggestion that the metric threads be retained, so saving substantial retooling costs, but externally the nuts be fitted with Whitworth flats which would fit British spanners. It was a typical Lord response; a cheap and simple solution sparked by an intuitive flash of brilliance. Lord soon made his mark on Gosford Street and rose to be machine tool engineer, a post that was specially created for him. There he was responsible for the purchase of the all-important transfer machines, 'and when the machine could not be bought it fell to his lot to produce appropriate new designs'.[10]

Leonard Lord's undoubted abilities had come to William Morris's notice and, following his purchase of Wolseley in 1927, he decided that its machine shops would benefit from Lord's attention. There he worked more or less in tandem with Wolseley's Oliver Bowden though, perhaps inevitably, 'there were from time to time distinct signs of differences between them'.[11] Lord once again impressed Morris when he so speedily produced the Minor's side-valve engine but, on being made the offer to move to Cowley, Lord said that 'he was going . . . with full management control or he would prefer to stay where he was'.[12] Fortunately Edgar Blake offered to stand aside at this point and Lord arrived at Cowley with full executive control. He immediately embarked on a £300,000 investment plan which included laying down a moving-track assembly line, something that most major manufacturers had possessed since the 1920s. A new half-mile-long paintshop was built and, by 1936, expenditure had soared to £500,000, an additional 125 acres of buildings having been erected. With an annual capacity to produce 100,000 cars, Lord had transformed Cowley into one of the most modern car factories in the country.

'LP', as he was known by his immediate colleagues, galvanized Cowley into activity, though his bluntness and cutting tongue came as a revelation to most of the workforce. Miles Thomas, who had the opportunity of observing Lord at first hand, recalled that 'everyone admired his methods if not his manners. . . . He walked roughly over the toes of anyone who got in his way,' while LP's habit of keeping 'a lighted cigarette in a corner of his mouth blowing off the ash without taking it from his lips'[13] obviously rankled.

In addition to modernizing Cowley, Lord immediately set about stream-lining the Morris range which, in 1933, had consisted of an undisciplined seven models. Morris Motors had been caught off balance by Ford's new Model Y of 1932 and Lord responded with traditional speed and resource-fulness. The result was the Morris Eight of 1934, visually inspired by its Dagenham counterpart, while its engine also bore a striking resemblance to that of the Ford. It was created at Morris Engines by chief draughtsman Claude Baily who recalled: 'I was asked to draw it up from dimensions supplied by the Inspection Department, who had a Ford Eight engine, took it to pieces, and measured it up!'[14]

When the Morris Eight appeared it was, in effect, a Ford Eight with frills; the Model T-inspired transverse leaf suspension was replaced by more substantial half-elliptics, while Lockheed hydraulic brakes, an excellent feature of the Morris range since 1927, took the place of the Dagenham car's rods. The Morris Eight proved an instant success and remained in production until 1938, by which time 230,000 had been built, making it the best-selling British car of the decade.

Lord also brought greater order to Morris's company and in 1935 and 1936 the Wolseley, MG, Morris Commercial Cars, Morris Industries Exports and SU Carburettors subsidiaries, hitherto owned by Lord Nuffield, as Morris became in 1934, were bought by Morris Motors. The result of Lord's frenetic activity had a dramatic effect on Morris's profits, which stood at £844,000 in 1933 on his arrival and had soared to a record £2.1 million by 1936. There had been some casualties. Miles Thomas took the initiative in 1935 and moved to Wolseley at Birmingham, after Lord had 'muttered something about "big as it was Cowley wasn't big enough for both of us" '.[15]

Against such an impressive achievement Lord went to Nuffield. 'His ideas, quite bluntly, were that the person who recognizably made a business profitable should have a fair share of those profits . . . Lord Nuffield was taken aback – stunned.'[16] While Nuffield stonewalled, Lord and his family (he had married in 1921 and had three daughters) went off for a holiday on the Isle of Wight. As Nuffield contemplated his next move, his friend Wilfred Hobbs motored between Oxford and the island as the two exchanged messages. However, they were unable to agree and in August 1936 Leonard Lord resigned as managing director of Morris Motors. So 'LP' joined Woollard, Rowse and Blake as managers who had clashed with Nuffield though the implications for Morris Motors and the British motor industry were far more serious.

Although Lord agreed to administer a scheme for distressed industrial areas Nuffield had initiated in 1936, a production engineer of his talent was unlikely to remain unemployed for long. The dynamic Roy Fedden, chief engineer of the Bristol Aeroplane Company, who was steeped in the demanding disciplines of the aircraft industry, considered Lord 'as one of the best men in the country on modern machine shop work'.[17]

At about this time Miles Thomas at Wolseley received a visit from Lord. He remembered: 'His rupture with Nuffield . . . hurt him deeply . . . the strain and anger of the split were still heavy on him and suddenly, blowing the ash off the inevitable cigarette between his lips, [he] said, "Tommy, I'm going to take that business at Cowley apart brick by bloody brick." '[18] In 1937 Miles Thomas took over LP's old job as managing director of Morris Motors and returned to Cowley. The following year Lord accepted an offer from Nuffield's arch rival, the Austin Motor Company, as works director. At forty-one and at the height of his powers, Leonard Lord became Lord Austin's heir apparent.

Although Longbridge had not experienced the upheavals that had characterized Lord's three-year tenure at Cowley, its share of British car production fell from 37 to 24 per cent in the years between 1929 and 1938. Austin began the decade well, in 1932 getting a 1125cc Family Ten into production before Hillman and Morris, even though the former's Minx appeared at the 1931 Motor Show. It followed the established Longbridge formula of being a well-built, unadventurous design but offering sound, reliable transport. The Ten became the best-selling Austin of the 1930s, was updated in 1937 and 1939 and soldiered on, literally because of war-time production, until 1947.

Like Morris, Austin began to suffer from a proliferation of its car range: in 1934 the firm offered no less than fifty models when all the variants on the Seven, Ten, the new Light 12/4, the Heavy 12/4, and no less than five six-cylinder models between 1496 and 3400cc are taken into account. Although this number was subsequently reduced, new managerial talent was clearly needed for, in 1937, Lord Austin (as he had become in 1936) was seventy-one, Payton was ten years younger, and sixty-one-year-old Carl Englebach was nearly blind. Englebach stepped down as works director and Leonard Lord took over his job.

Lord soon convinced Austin that chief designer A. J. Hancock and production manager John Hannay, whose service with Austin reached back to the 'Old Man's' days at Wolseley, should be pensioned off and he subsequently quipped: 'You'll need a couple of coaches to take them away by the time I've finished.'[19] Visitors to a Longbridge washroom were not surprised to find that a wit had written on the wall: 'Oh Lord, give us our Engel bach.'[20]

Just one outcome of Lord's arrival was the appearance of an 8hp model in 1939, as Austin had ignored that vital market until then. Lord had also not failed to notice the growth of Bedford, Vauxhall's successful commercial vehicle offshoot, and immediately initiated a range of Austin lorries. For its engine, Lord applied his customary approach and copied the 25hp Bedford unit. Introduced in 1939, the commercial vehicles, which ranged from 30cwt to a 3 ton, were all powered by the first Austin engine to employ overhead valves. Longbridge had espoused simpler but less efficient side valves and in this lagged behind the opposition just as it had regarding the use of independent front suspension and hydraulic brakes. It was not to benefit from such features until after the Second World War.

Austin was therefore poised for expansion when the Second World War broke out in 1939, though Morris was still by far and away the country's largest car producer with about 95,000 cars built in that year compared with Austin's 57,367. In 1938 Morris Motors made its last major purchase when Lord Nuffield bought Riley Motors which had been building cars since 1898. In 1926 this Coventry company had introduced its famous Monaco, a handsome fabric-bodied saloon which followed the 1922 Lancia Lambda by offering the then unusual facility of a boot. Under the bonnet was Percy Riley's ingenious engine, with two high-mounted camshafts operating inclined valves, via pushrods, in hemispherical combustion chambers which offered the performance advantages of twin overhead camshafts but without their cost or complication. It was to form the basis of all Riley engines until 1957. Although the firm faired well enough in the early 1930s, the model range grew in size and variety and by 1937 Riley was heading for a deficit. The appointment of £500-per-month Canadian Lewis Ord from Humber as general manager failed to produce economies which were complicated by the firm's decision to produce an abortive 2.8-litre V8-engined model built by its Autovia Cars subsidiary. Riley made a substantial loss in 1937, Ord having lasted only nine months in the job, and although there were talks of a merger with Triumph, this failed to materialize and a receiver was appointed in February 1938. In September, Riley (Coventry) Ltd was bought by Lord Nuffield for £143,000 following a direct appeal to him by Victor Riley whom he had known since pre-First World War days. A new company, Riley (Coventry) Successors Ltd, was immediately resold to Morris Motors for a nominal £100 and Victor Riley continued as managing director. Morris therefore acquired another Coventry factory, at Durbar Avenue, Foleshill, and Riley car production was maintained.

The same year Morris opened a new and larger engine plant at Courthouse Green, Coventry, and production was transferred there from Gosford Street, which had provided power units for the whole of Morris Motors after Wolseley engine production was moved there following Leonard Lord's 1934/5 rationalization. A foundry was also opened and the Cowley facility closed. Gosford Street was retained and was once again working for the War Office by manufacturing Bofors guns.

In 1939 came the final Morris factory of the pre-war years when Morris Pressings was established at Common Lane, Birmingham, near the Drews Lane plant. Its foundation was prompted by the need to reduce the high proportion of pressings bought out by Morris Motors. This brought the number of large plants operated by Lord Nuffield to ten.

Ford's approach was, by contrast, diametrically opposed to that of Morris Motors for, in 1931, it had opened its only but highly integrated Thames-side plant at Dagenham, Essex, modelled on its American Rouge River works, with capacity to produce 200,000 cars a year. The decision to move from Manchester dated back to 1923 when, on 23 July, Edward Grace, the manager of Ford's British operations reported to his American headquarters: 'After thoroughly investigating England . . . the most suitable place is in the London district – somewhere in the neighbourhood of Dagenham.'[21] Although the site was over 200 miles south east of the Midlands, where most of the motor industry was located, it had excellent deep-water docking facilities, good rail and road communications with the rest of the country and there was plenty of room for expansion. Its proximity to London was yet another important factor. The purchase of a 310-acre site for £167,695 was effected in 1924, though it was not until April 1928 that Henry Ford himself visited the desolate marshland area which had hitherto served as a tip for London's rubbish.

What Ford now needed was someone to direct his British operations and he consulted Sir William Letts of Crossley, who suggested Sir Herbert Austin. Instead Ford decided to patch up his differences with Sir Percival Perry, whom he met on 1 May on board his ship at Southampton on the day before he returned to America. Perry subsequently crossed the Atlantic in October for a two-week discussion at Detroit where he heard details of Ford's '1928 Plan'.

This set down that Ford car production would be concentrated on three main centres: Michigan, USA.; Ontario, Canada; and England. Detroit would look after the American market; Ford's Canadian factory at

Walkerville, Ontario, would be responsible for the British Empire; while Dagenham would produce vehicles for sale in Europe, Turkey, the Middle East and Africa north of Rhodesia. Ford's British operations would require restructuring and, on the advice of Sir William Letts, who no doubt had in mind the public outcry that had greeted General Motors' purchase of Vauxhall, Ford decided that 40 per cent of the shares in the Ford Motor Company, of December 1928, would be offered to British investors to counter any anti-American prejudices, a precedent he followed when establishing his other European subsidiaries.

Perry immediately began recruiting his management team. His second-in-command and general manager was A. Rowland Smith, an expert in production methods and an able administrator. He had begun his career with Humber in 1904 and had joined Ford's Manchester operations in 1924. When his hopes for the post of assistant manager were dashed, he left and joined Standard as works manager and Perry recruited him from there. He also appointed Anthony Hall as head of sales and Roland Philip for the all-important role of purchasing officer, both having worked for him during his 1909–19 stewardship of Ford's English affairs. This coterie formed the basis of the influential 'Perry Group' within the company.

Work on the Dagenham factory began on 16 May 1929 when Ford's son Edsel dug the first sod. His silver spade bent, despite the marshy ground which was to prove a major problem: costs soared when 22,000 47-foot-long concrete piles had to be sunk in the ground. A concrete raft was then applied and the factory built on top of that. As the walls and chimneys of the new plant rose above the bleak Essex marshland, the industrialized world was thrown off balance by the effects of the world depression. Work on the £2 million plant continued apace however, As it aped American practice, the works was highly integrated and possessed its own blast furnace to produce steel on site, and docking facilities, though a power station constructed to serve the needs of the factory did not become operational until 1934, by which time it was a familiar Dagenham landmark. Further land was purchased, bringing Ford's holding to 501 acres, but as Perry believed no more than 112 would be required, he proposed creating an industrial estate on the site, using his experiences at Slough as a model. Dagenham possessed no body shop so the Briggs Manufacturing Company, which built bodies for Ford in America, was encouraged to form a British subsidiary and establish a body plant adjacent to the new works. Similarly Kelsey-Hayes, another American company, built a factory to manufacture wheels for Ford cars.

At 2pm on 31 October 1931 the first vehicle, a Model AA Ford, left Dagenham. It was not until the summer of 1932, however, that the works became fully operational. Trafford Park was shut down at the end of 1931, even though the aim had originally been to retain it for assembly purposes. Dagenham had a terrible problem in that it had very little to build. It was intended to mass produce the Model A which had replaced the long-running Model T in 1928. Even though the smaller-bored 14.9hp AF version was produced, because of the horsepower tax its Road Fund licence cost £15 a year. Of the 4,574 vehicles that left Dagenham in 1931 all but five were trucks. In 1932 more AAs than cars were again built – 13,651 compared with 11,920 – but by this time Ford had introduced the 8hp Model Y, which was specially designed for the needs of the European market.

As early as 1928 Henry Ford had shown Sir Percival Perry the designs for a small car, but the latter was unenthusiastic about the project on cost grounds and he believed that the AF would fit the bill. Yet by October 1931 Perry realized that Dagenham would face financial ruin unless it had the right car to build. It would have to be a small car, which would be cheap to run and tax. Detroit responded positively. 'This job was done pretty darn quick,'[22] remembered chief engineer Laurence Sheldrick, for the car was a reality by January 1932. It received a rapturous reception at the special Ford Exhibition at the Royal Albert Hall in February (the company had to stage its own annual event because its fickle owner would not join the Society of Motor Manufacturers and Traders and was thus unable to appear at the Motor Show) and went into production, in improved form, in the nick of time in August. But such was the precarious nature of the firm's finances that wages and salaries were cut by 10 per cent. Ford-Holland made its British opposite number a £1 million loan and Dagenham, after pleading with Dearborn to reduce its £158,391 bill for designing the Model Y, had this cut to £62,130. Despite these savings, Ford recorded a loss of £681,828 in 1932.

Fortunately, the Model Y proved an instant success, Ford became profitable and would not record another deficit until 1971. It was undoubtedly the best-looking small British saloon of the 1930s, and Ford stylist and former yacht designer Eugene Turenne Gregorie scaled the lines up for the 1933 generation of American Fords. The Y was powered by a sturdy 7.9hp 933cc four-cylinder engine and therefore cost £8 a year to tax. The cost-conscious single transverse leaf suspension was inherited from the Model T and this two-door saloon was competitively priced at £120. By 1934 the Model Y held a massive 54 per cent of the 8hp market and gave Ford a renewed grip of the British market which it holds to this day.

At Cowley, Leonard Lord responded with the Model Y-inspired £118 Morris Eight, while Dagenham's newly introduced 10hp Model C took sales from the smaller car. Ford was now faced with a new set of problems. Although the original 200,000 output figure had been reduced to 120,000 cars per annum, in 1934 Dagenham's blast furnaces, coke ovens and foundry began work but with such low production 'they were white elephants'.[23] A body shop would have been a far better investment. The only answer was to sell the pig iron produced to other manufacturers, and purchasing manager Patrick Hennessy took on the task. He even sold to Austin, and that part of Ford's business soon became profitable.

In the meantime, Rowland Smith initiated a range of manufacturing economies at Dagenham and Patrick Hennessy tackled the difficult task of getting suppliers to reduce their prices. Hitherto bargaining between the two usually resulted in the supplier getting his way. Under the new regime, the component in question was scrupulously assessed, its price was evaluated and then compared with the one asked. Hennessy visited the supplier, examined his production methods and suggested economies. American purchasing methods were thus used for the first time in Britain.

Once savings had been effected, F. S. Thornhill Cooper, who had responsibility for European sales, had the idea of taking a leaf out of Morris's book by producing a £100 version of the Model Y. Significantly, however, there would be no reduction in quality and it would be a proper four-seater, rather than a two-seater. It was announced in October 1935, and the following year would see a dramatic rise in Ford's total output. This rose from 48,551 cars in 1935 to 74,988 in 1936, reaching an inter-war record of 77,830 in the industry's boom year of 1937.

The Model Y endured until 1937 when it was replaced by a rebodied 8hp model which Dagenham initiated itself in the teeth of opposition from Detroit, no doubt wanting to save having to foot another large development bill. The car appeared, along with a 10hp version which replaced the CX, though this developed in 1938 into the long-wheelbase Prefect, while the 8hp was mildly modified and renamed the Anglia for 1940. These closely related models, along with the low-production V8-91, constituted Ford's entire British range in 1939.

In 1937 and 1938 Ford moved ahead of Morris to become the largest vehicle producer in Britain when commercial vehicles and tractors were included in the calculations, Ford holding a near monopoly in the latter instance, though Cowley was back in pole position in 1939. That year only Morris and Austin were producing more cars and Ford's pre-tax profits of £1.7 million were only about £140,000 behind Morris's and around three times those of Austin. It was an impressive endorsement not only of Sir Percival Perry's stewardship of Ford's affairs but also of his flair for appointing talented subordinates. Patrick Hennessy, in particular, would be a man to watch.

If Ford's renaissance during the 1930s had been remarkable, then the performance of the British motor industry's other American arm, the

General Motors-owned Vauxhall Motors, was even more impressive. In 1930 the Luton company built only 1,277 cars or about 1 per cent of British car production, yet by 1938 this had spiralled to 60,111 or just over 11 per cent of total output. Alfred Sloan's 'experiment in overseas manufacture' seemed to be bearing fruit. Back in 1929 the R type, which had grown to 3.3 litres by the time that it was discontinued in 1932, had failed to catch on. 'It was clear by 1929 that we either had to build up Vauxhall or else give up the British market,'[24] Sloan decided. The outcome was the smaller and cheaper (at £280) 2-litre Cadet for 1931. Its pushrod overhead-valve engine echoed in-house Chevrolet practice, but was an unusual feature for a cheap British car. In 1932 the Cadet also became the country's first car to employ synchromesh, which greatly eased gear changing. There was again a corporate precedent: in 1929 Cadillac had introduced the feature to the American market.

Leslie Walton continued as Vauxhall's chairman but, in 1930, Charles Bartlett was appointed managing director. It was rumoured at the time that when Alfred Sloan asked James Mooney, chairman of GM's overseas committee, 'to pick an Englishman to run Vauxhall, he replied "Well, I guess it had better be Charlie Bartlett; he's about as English as they come." '[25]

Charles John Bartlett (1889–1955) was born in Bibury, Gloucestershire, and, after local schooling, completed his education at Bath Technical College. Following war service, Bartlett, who had developed a formidable flair for figures, obtained a job as a clerk at General Motors' depot in the North London suburb of Hendon. In the post-war years this business was responsible for importing Buick chassis from Canada (as it was part of the Empire, the duty was reduced), trimming them and then distributing them in Britain. Bartlett's fiscal flair was coupled with an administrative ability and, in 1926, he became managing director of the business, the year after General Motors bought Vauxhall.

In September 1929 Bartlett moved to Luton as managing director and would remain at Vauxhall until he retired as chairman in 1954. Bartlett, or 'CJB' as he was known, had a broad-based intellect – he once maintained 'everything is found interesting'.[26] His attitude to his shopfloor employees was notable. A former colleague summed him up thus: 'Despite subsequent promotions, he never lost his simple and sturdily democratic approach to industrial management. This robust attitude went well with a determined character, a strong, stocky physique and a sense of humour that leavened what could otherwise have been too paternal an outlook towards the Vauxhall workforce.'[27]

The author of these words is Maurice Platt, who left his job as technical editor of *The Motor* magazine in 1937 to join Vauxhall's engineering department. Although he was earning £1,200 a year as a journalist, Platt took a £400 salary cut because he was keen to start afresh in engineering. 'Later on, I was to discover a curious inconsistency between Bartlett's penny-pinching policy with regard to staff salaries and the generous piecework rates he ungrudgingly accorded to the men on the shop floor; he seemed to have an innate respect for sheer physical toil and a complementary lack of appreciation for the brain worker.'[28]

Vauxhall built only 9,949 cars in 1933, though in the following year this more than doubled to 20,227, after the boxy Cadet was dropped and replaced by two Light Sixes of 12 and 14hp. There was also the increasingly popular Bedford commercial vehicle range, introduced in 1930. In 1935 the cheapest of the Sixes could be bought for £195, and was offered with Dubonnet 'knee action' independent front suspension, introduced in the USA the previous year and yet another first for a cheap British car. In the following year Vauxhall achieved a record £1.1 million profit, which was easily the best in the industry, with the notable exception of Morris's.

The innovative climate was again maintained in 1938 with the arrival of the Ten, the first four-cylinder Vauxhall of the decade but, more significantly, the first British car to feature unitary body construction, so dispensing with the traditional chassis, though front and rear subframes were retained. The advantages of the system were that it was lighter than an equivalent car with a conventional chassis and a far more rigid body structure than had hitherto had been the case was possible. This was a particular advantage with the growing popularity of independent front suspension. On the debit side, tooling costs were greatly increased and long production runs were vital in order for a car maker to recoup expenditure. The body pressings were produced at a new £200,000 press and die shop at Luton, giving Vauxhall an advantage over its competitors which did not enjoy such in-house facilities. Vauxhall was following in the wheeltracks of the 1935 Opel Olympia, Europe's first mass-produced unitary construction car, General Motors having bought Germany's largest car maker in 1929. Yet by 1939 cars were still jockeying with commercial vehicles for popularity at Luton. Between 1931 and 1938 Bedford production stood at 170,812, compared with 148,572 Vauxhall cars built over the same period.

The British company that probably came closest to General Motors in concept was the Rootes Group, established in 1933. At the start of the decade the Rootes brothers already owned Humber and Hillman, which were followed by the Karrier commercial vehicle firm, though a far greater prize came with the Talbot and Sunbeam companies, purchased from the moribund STD Motors. In each instance the pattern was the same. A financially vulnerable established name was acquired and its production facilities were radically updated, while engines and components were rationalized and costs saved.

The Group's driving force was the stocky, dynamic William (Billy) Edward Rootes, 'an active, restless man, friendly yet with an uncanny ability to read people at a glance, a formidable character with more than a touch of ruthlessness'.[29] The Rootes story has it origins not in the industrial Midlands but in the more tranquil environment of Station Road, Hawkhurst, Kent. It was there that William Rootes established a modest general engineering business which branched out into bicycle sales and, with the coming of the automobile, motor car repairs. That was in 1896 and two years later Rootes became a motor agent.

By 1913 the business had grown sufficiently for Rootes to open a branch in the nearby town of Maidstone. This was run by nineteen-year-old Billy, his eldest son. The younger William Rootes was educated at Cranbook, 'though was not a shining success at school and so, at the age of fifteen, he went off to Coventry as an apprentice to Singers'.[30] This episode was also of short duration for, after a year, he was back in Kent, having convinced his father to take a Singer agency. The Maidstone business was virtually shut down during the war years because, in 1915, Billy joined the Royal Naval Volunteer Reserve as a pupil engineer though he transferred to the flying section of the Royal Naval Air Service in 1917.

During the war Billy Rootes decided to extend his horizons beyond his native Kent. He succeeded in convincing his younger brother, Reginald Claude (1896–1977), to leave his civil service post at the Admiralty and join him. Although as brothers Billy and Reggie were both physically and temperamentally different, they proved to be complementary opposites and 'a perfect pair in the business sense – Billy seeing the visions on the horizon and striding towards them in, so to speak, seven league boots; Reggie surveying the intervening ground with his keen and calculating eye and making sure that no loose ends in whatever project was afoot were left untied'.[31] It was to prove a highly successful combination and, as Billy Rootes often quipped, 'I am the engine and Reginald is the steering and brakes of the business.'

William Rootes Senior presented each of his sons with £1,200 and, with their friend and colleague Joe Chaldecott, they established Rootes Ltd at Maidstone in 1917. The brothers were well placed to benefit from the post-war boom and, after weathering the financial storms of 1921, in 1923 they formed Rootes Distributors and that year obtained an important contract by becoming Austin distributors for London and the Home Counties. By a policy of expansion and acquisition, the Rootes brothers were, by 1926, the largest distributors in the country. They had grown from their south-east England base by taking an interest in the Birmingham garage chain of George Heath (in 1924), which was followed by Warwick Wright in London and Tom Garner's Manchester-based garages. In 1925 Rootes purchased their first motor business by buying the old-established Thrupp and Maberly coachbuilding company of Cricklewood, founded in 1790. Rootes showrooms were opened in London's Long Acre, along with small but fashionable showrooms at 141 New Bond Street.

Then, in 1926, Rootes moved to a new impressive headquarters in London's newest and most prestigious office block at Devonshire House, Piccadilly, opposite the Ritz Hotel. This move, as *The Motor* put it, 'rather staggered the retail motor trade'[32] and many wondered whether the brothers (Billy was only thirty-two at the time and Reggie was thirty) had over-reached themselves.

They had not, of course, but they were now in a position to embark on the next phase of their plan: to enter the motor-manufacturing business and then distribute the cars produced through their wholesale and retail outlets. Billy Rootes had made his first visit to America in 1919 and he became such a regular trans-Atlantic traveller that his voice betrayed the time he spent in the USA. There he noticed the progress being made by General Motors' Buick, Cadillac, Chevrolet and Oldsmobile makes, each with their distinct market sector, against the singular but weakening Ford marque.

For all its success, Rootes Distribution did not possess sufficient resources to embark on car manufacture. These came from the Prudential Assurance Company, for Rootes had succeeded in convincing its secretary, Sir George May, of the viability of his scheme. Rather than establishing a Rootes car, the brothers had decided to buy existing firms that were in financial difficulties, streamline production and, again using the American industry as a model, develop a strong export market to spread manufacturing costs. The first move towards this objective came in 1927 when Rootes Distributors announced that it would thereafter concentrate exclusively on British-built cars. Rootes handled the voluminous products of the financially precarious Clyno company and attempted to take it over but were rebuffed. Billy Rootes had bought Standard stock in 1920 and, with that company in difficulties, the brothers tried again. Although they failed, their 1928 bid for a financial interest in Humber succeeded.

Lieutenant Colonel John Cole became chairman, a post he kept until 1943 when he retired at the age of seventy-five, but Humber became the first make to be used as a vehicle for the Rootes' manufacturing philosophy. In 1927 Humber had introduced its first six-cylinder car of the post-war years: the 3-litre 22/55. Its engine was enlarged to 3.5 litres and the model, renamed Snipe, was redirected to the overseas market. However, Rootes was unsuccessful in its attempt to woo colonials away from their robust, value-for-money Chevrolets and Buicks. In 1931 Rootes tried again with the Hillman Wizard, another six though with cheaper side valves, which was offered with two engine sizes, the 20.9hp 2.8-litre version being available for overseas use while a 15.7hp 2-litre version was specified for the home market. Alas, this 'Car of the Moderns' proved little more successful than the Snipe, but its use of pressed steel bodywork was notable as Hillman was the first British firm after Morris to employ the facility, following Morris Motors' distancing itself from the Cowley-based business in 1930.

Far more successful was the 1.1-litre Minx, introduced for 1932 and destined to remain a Hillman model name until 1970. It was nearly called the Witch though fortunately Minx won the day, and was launched at the 1931 Paris Motor Show. This £155 archetypal 10hp family saloon became an immediate best seller and 10,000 were sold with ten months of its introduction. The model acquired an all-synchromesh gearbox in 1935, though this was abandoned in 1939 for cost reasons. By 1938/9 Minx annual production exceeded 55,000 cars.

Yet the early 1930s were years of depression for the entire industry and this was reflected in Humber's financial performance. Hillman and subsequent firms within the Rootes Group became Humber's subsidiaries, the firm recording losses of £48,779 and £107,785 in 1931 and 1932 respectively. It was not until 1933 that profits – of £132,846 – were recorded. That year Rootes Ltd changed its name to Rootes Securities and, with Hillman Minx sales riding high, in 1934 it acquired Karrier Motors of Huddersfield, Yorkshire, and merged it with Commer Cars which Humber had bought in 1926 at Luton. Then, in 1935, came an even greater prize in the shape of the prestigious Talbot and Sunbeam companies.

Rootes was able to make its bids because STD Motors had defaulted on the ten-year Guaranteed Notes, due for payment on 30 September 1934. Ironically Talbot, based in Barlby Road, West London, had been one of the consistently profitable elements of the combine, following the arrival of the 14/45 model in 1926. It was the work of Georges Roesch, Talbot's Swiss-born chief engineer, who had come to Britain in 1914 to work as a designer for Daimler and had transferred to Clement Talbot in 1916. In 1926 he had initiated a one-model policy and staked all on the lively 14/45 tourer, powered by a potent, small, high-revving, 1.6-litre, six-cylinder, pushrod, overhead-valve engine, with a clean external finish that was to be found in all his subsequent work. It can be justly regarded as the ancestor of the modern production engine. During the next nine years Roesch developed this theme and also produced a generation of highly distinctive sports models, the 90, 105, and 110, all of which possessed a watch-like reliability coupled with superlative road holding. It was the success of the

'Invincible Talbot' that no doubt attracted the attention of the Rootes brothers: Reggie ran a 105 saloon, somewhat ostentatiously adorned with gold-plated interior fittings.

Rootes bought Clement Talbot Ltd in January 1935. Although Talbot's Barlby Road factory was maintained, inevitably Roesch's finely engineered models were discontinued, though the final expression of the theme, the 3.3-litre 110, survived until 1937 as spare parts were used up. Like many great artist engineers, Roesch, 'a supreme egotist, incapable of making any concession that threatened the integrity of his concepts',[33] was mortified by his fine cars suffering such an ignominious end. Following the outbreak of war in 1939 he became chief engineer of David Brown Tractors, subsequently joined jet pioneers Power Jets during hostilities, and then became chief mechanical engineer for the Ministry of Supply's National Gas Turbine Establishment. He never returned to the motor industry. Meanwhile, it did not take long for Rootes to rationalize the range, and in 1936 the Talbot 10, 'a Hillman Minx in a party frock',[34] made its appearance.

William Rootes also had his eye on Sunbeam, the other British arm of STD Motors. He bought Sunbeam's trolleybus business, merged it with Karrier's similar facility and formed Sunbeam Commercial Vehicles in November 1934. This Wolverhampton business would remain in Rootes ownership until 1944, and it was subsequently sold to Guy Motors in 1948. Rootes was also indirectly financing Sunbeam car production, such as it was, though it was not until July 1935 that Motor Industries Ltd, a Rootes subsidiary, bought the business. Car manufacture, which had suffered from years of underfunding, was wound up and production ceased in 1937.

There is a fascinating postscript to the story because a new Sunbeam was revealed at the 1936 Motor Show, powered by a Roesch-designed 4.5-litre eight-cylinder engine in the manner of his Talbot units. This Sunbeam was Billy Rootes's tribute to Edward VIII, with whom he had become friendly when the latter was Prince of Wales. Rootes recognized that as king, Edward, who was already a Humber owner, would require an even larger car and the Sunbeam was his response. Whether the model would have entered production had the king not abdicated in December 1936 is a moot question for Bernard Winter, Rootes' 'practical cost-conscious' chief engineer, 'produced such an unfavourable report'[35] on its production costs that the project was abandoned. What Rootes did do was to combine the names of its most recent purchases and the result, in August 1938, was the creation the new Sunbeam-Talbot make, with production concentrated on the former Talbot works at Barlby Road.

In 1937 Rootes made its last major purchase of the pre-war years by buying British Light Steel Pressings in Warple Way, Acton, only 2 miles away from the Sunbeam-Talbot works in Ladbroke Grove. Founded in 1930, the firm had hitherto manufactured a variety of pressings for every industry other than the motor one. Initially it produced Sunbeam-Talbot bodywork, though petrol tanks and other similar pressings were also made.

The 1930s were, to a great extent, Billy Rootes's decade. The revitalized Hillman, Humber and Sunbeam-Talbot makes were essentially his creations, and if a minority of the public mourned the inevitable standardization that followed a Rootes takeover, the Group's busy factories in Humber Road, Coventry, bore witness to the popularity of its products. William Edward Rootes was, after all, not an engineer but 'a supersalesman *par excellence* ... with that gift of "persuading anyone he met that that was the person he had been waiting to see all day" '.[36] Apart from establishing the Rootes Group as a viable force within the British motor industry, Billy Rootes also threw his not inconsiderable weight behind what was to be called the Shadow Factory scheme, initiated by the British government in 1936.

It was in September 1935 that, during a visit to the Air Ministry, Bristol's chief engineer Roy Fedden was informed by Air Marshall Sir Hugh Dowding, Air Member for Research and Development, that 'the Air Staff have come to the conclusion that we are going to have a war with Germany.'[37] This would mean an inevitable increase in demand for aero engines. What the Ministry had decided to do was to choose an established manufacturer and then try to create a replica of its production process elsewhere. 'We have called the technique Shadowing because its aim is to create a second image of the original,'[38] Dowding explained. Bristol had been chosen because its sleeve-valve engines were of relatively simple design and were already in production, under licensing agreements, the world over.

The government would build and equip these Shadow Factories but their running and recruitment would be the responsibility of the motor industry, some members of which had experience of aero-engine production during the First World War. The first engine chosen for this shadowing treatment was the 25-litre nine-cylinder Bristol Mercury radial unit. A meeting was subsequently held at Bristol attended by Lord Nuffield, Sir Herbert Austin, Geoffrey Burton of Daimler, a firm with long experience of building sleeve-valve car engines, the Rootes brothers and Spencer Wilks of the revitalized Rover company.

Nuffield soon distanced himself from the project and his place was taken by Standard's John Black. The manufacturers had their misgivings about the plan, despite being paid a £50,000 per annum management fee and £75 per engine. 'They were unimpressed with the scheme as a business venture and showed no enthusiasm for taking part. There was one outstanding exception . . . and that was Billy Rootes,'[39] Fedden was later to recall, and his commitment broke the *impasse*. Work on the first Shadow Factories began in May 1936 at Coften Hackett, which adjoined Austin's Long-bridge works. Lord Austin himself took over the chairmanship of the Shadow Factories Committee, a position he held until 1940, when his place was taken by Standard's John Black.

This first generation of factories, with one exception, adjoined the car company's own works. The Daimler Shadow was at Capmartin Road, Radford, behind its own factory, as was the Rootes one at Aldermoor Lane, Stoke. Similarly the Standard Shadow was at Canley, and it was only Rover, hemmed in at Helen Street, Coventry, that coped with managing a Shadow about 20 miles away at Acocks Green, Birmingham. After some teething troubles, the first shadow-built engines ran in December 1938, by which time the scheme had been extended to include complete aircraft, and Rootes was responsible for a new plant at Speke, Liverpool, where Blenheim bombers were produced.

As the prospect of world war loomed, it soon became obvious that the original plants would be unable to cope with the Ministry of Aircraft Production's requirements. A second generation of Shadow Factories was therefore planned, though a requirement was that they would have to be distanced from the first plants in view of the risk of bombing. Therefore Daimler's number two Shadow was at Browns Lane, Allesley, on the city's western outskirts, while the second Rootes plant was on a 60-acre site on the Coventry-to-Banbury Road at the village of Ryton-on-Dunsmore, about 4 miles from the city centre. Coventry's largest Shadow Factory was a 1-million-square-foot complex at Banner Lane, managed by Standard. Again Rover's second Shadow Plant, which became operational in January 1940, was outside the city and 16 miles away on a 65-acre site at Lode Lane, Solihull. The motor industry would make good use of these new spacious factories in the post-war years when the climate was for growth, exports and expansion.

The inclusion of Standard in the Shadow Factory scheme was a public recognition of a revival of the firm that had flirted with bankruptcy in 1927/8. In 1930 Standard had built only around 7,000 cars, but this rose to 21,000 in 1933; by 1937 the figure stood at 34,000, while the firm built a record 50,700 cars in the 1938/9 financial year, about half that of Morris, the market leader, but none the less impressive.

As already noted, in 1929 John Black had joined Standard, and the following year, at the age of thirty-five, he became general manager with a seat on the board. Black wasted little time in reorganizing the Canley production facilities and, by December 1931, 'the whole of the assembly shops . . . had been reorganized and mechanized to facilitate mass production, with 10 complete cars leaving the assembly line every working hour'.[40] In September 1933 John Black became Standard's joint managing director with Reginald Maudslay and, following the latter's death in 1934, he became the sole occupant of the office.

John Black's achievement in bringing Standard to the forefront of Britain's car industry is unquestionable, but within the company his approach was essentially a dictatorial one: 'Many of his fellow directors were plainly terrified by his whims and the records show a procession of men promoted, driven too hard and resigning, at times with their health broken.'[41] When Alick Dick, who would eventually succeed him, arrived at Canley in 1933, he was immediately struck by the 'great dominance of the managing director [Black]. His word was all powerful and he was feared.'[42] At least one visitor to Standard was alarmed to find, when he was conveyed to Black's 'holy of holies' that 'the large, de luxe office was, I imagine, similar to Mussolini's in his heyday'[43] and was in stark contrast to the sparsely furnished, modest rooms from which Lords Austin and Nuffield ran their businesses. Yet there were other facets of his character. The improvement of the company's finances in the late 1930s resulted in Standard introducing paid holidays for its workforce in 1937 which, the directors maintained, was 'something in the way of distribution of part of the profits to the work people'.[44] Harry Webster, who joined Standard in 1932 and became the firm's technical supremo in the post-war years, still has pleasant memories of towing winter sports enthusiast Black on a pair of skis behind a car around the firm's golf course after the first sprinkling of winter snow.[45]

Standard's success began with the timely 9hp models of the early 1930s, while the 1.3-litre 10hp of 1934 proved a best seller. In 1936 came the first of the Flying Standards which featured the still-novel boot and a distinctive fastback look. There was first a 12hp, followed by a 16hp and top-line 20hp. In 1937 Standard introduced its contribution to the all-important 8hp market: a two-door saloon, with independent front suspension, for £129, the first British small car to offer this facility. Somewhat less successful was the firm's 2.7-litre V8 of the same year, though this engine subsequently found its way under the bonnet of the short-lived Raymond Mays sports car of 1938/9.

Meanwhile, how was John Black's brother-in-law, Spencer Wilks, fairing at Rover? The decade began badly for the firm. Managing director Colonel Frank Searle had departed for New Zealand, and had refused to resign, despite the fact that his contract was terminated by the board in April 1932. Indeed, that year it looked as though the firm might go into liquidation. In 1931 the loss for the year stood at £80,000 and by December Rover was losing between £2,000 and £3,000 a week. As a result the

Coventry branch of Lloyds Bank pegged its overdraft at £235,000. The firm was at this point at the mercy of the bank and its creditors, the two main ones being Lucas and Pressed Steel. It was they who suggested, in January 1932, that H. Howe Graham, partner in the Birmingham accountancy firm of Messrs Gibson and Ashford, be appointed Rover's finance director. Graham succeeded in obtaining three months' extended credit from the two firms, made around £50,000 worth of saving and proposed that works manager Spencer Wilks be given a seat on the board. He became managing director in 1933. At the beginning of March, Graham succeeded in getting Lloyds to increase Rover's overdraft facility to £270,000. Car production was being progressively transferred from Queen Victoria Road to Helen Street, which was renamed the New Meteor Works, with the Tyseley plant as its subsidiary.

Then on 20 May came a bombshell when Lloyds informed the company that it was not prepared to increase the overdraft 'above £150,000 despite their agreement to the higher limit in March'[46] which prompted offers of resignation from the Rover directors if this would help to get finance to keep the company going. Triumph showed some interest in merging, but this would have required the bank's co-operation, and it had withdrawn by June. That month Lloyds relented and the overdraft was set at £220,000. The terms were the same as the original agreement, though 'a weekly statement of orders, production and sales were to go to the bank'.[47] The terrible financial year of 1931/2 culminated in a loss of £279,000. In 1933, with the worst of the depression behind it, Rover recorded a modest profit of £7,511. The corner had been turned.

That year showed the first effects of Spencer Wilks's husbandry of Rover's affairs with the arrival of new 10 and 12hp models, the result of a more cost-conscious approach to design in that both engines shared a common 100mm stroke, the capacity being achieved by varying the size of the bore, while the overhead valves were perpetuated. These cars, designated P1, had been conceived by Wilks's younger brother Maurice. Educated at Malvern College, he had spent two years, from 1926 until 1928, with General Motors in America before joining Hillman as a planning engineer. In 1930 he moved to Rover as technical engineer.

The next phase of the programme came for the 1937 season with the arrival of the P2 range, distinguished by new well-proportioned though restrained bodywork. The 10 and 12hp engines were continued and new 16 and 20hp six-cylinder developments of the 100mm engine family also appeared. In the space of nine years the Wilks brothers had transformed the company's products by making cars in their own image which catered for the top end of the middle-class market and appealed to the professional man who wanted a car as transport for his family but one which would also not look out of place in the car park of his local golf club. In 1933 Rover had built 4,960 cars and made a £7,511 profit; six years later production stood at 11,103 and profits were at a record £205,957. It was an impressive achievement by a firm which, in 1932, had nearly gone out of business.

Just over a mile away to the north of the New Meteor Works, at Swallow Road, Foleshill, Coventry's newest car company had produced a record 5378 cars, a cause of some satisfaction to William Lyons, its thirty-eight-year-old chairman and managing director. For SS Cars had only been in the motor-manufacturing business since 1931 but its products had already gained an enviable reputation for combining magnificent styling and performance at a sensationally low price. Unlike many Coventry car companies, SS's founders hailed not from the Industrial Midlands but the unlikely location of the seaside town of Blackpool. This was because William Lyons's Irish-born musican father had come to the town with an orchestra, had married a local girl and settled there, whereupon he set up Lyons Music and Pianoforte Warehouse. William (1901–85), the eldest of two children, was educated at the local Poulton-le-Fylde Grammar School and later at Arnold House private school at South Shore, Blackpool. He had already developed a strong interest in engineering and studied the subject at Manchester Technical College, then worked briefly for the local Crossley company followed by the Blackpool firms of Jackson Brothers and Brown and Mallalieu, where he sold cars.

Then, in the middle of 1921, a house in nearby King Edward Avenue was bought by Thomas Walmsley, a prosperous Stockport coal merchant, who had decided to retire to the seaside. His son, William, had already built up a small business making stylish Zeppelin-shaped motorcycle sidecars. Lyons, already a keen motorcyclist, and possessing strong artistic sensibilities, bought one and then proposed that the pair should go into business manufacturing them.

The result was the creation of the Swallow Sidecar Company, founded in 1922 on a capital of £1,000. The business started in the upper storey of a small factory in Bloomfield Road, Blackpool, and clumsily expanded into three different locations until 1926, when Walmsley's father bought a larger works in Cocker Street and leased it to what was soon to become the Swallow Sidecar and Coachbuilding Company: Lyons had decided to expand into the production of car bodywork, which he would design. In 1924 he had married and, soon afterwards, bought a two-year-old Austin Seven. 'The conception of this car had a strong appeal,' he said, 'except that the body was a very stark affair, albeit very practical. I believed that it would also appeal to a lot of people if it had a more luxurious and attractive body.'[48]

The result, in May 1927, was the open two-seater Austin-Swallow, with

77

a distinctive rounded radiator, which was followed in 1928 by a curvaceous saloon with two-colour cream and crimson bodywork in the Alvis manner. It sold for £187, which was £37 more than the standard saloon. Lyons took this to London and Henlys Ltd, which he remembered as 'a new, forward thinking and quickly growing business',[49] and returned to Blackpool with an order for 500 cars. Walmsley told him that 'he must be mad' as it meant producing 20 Swallows a week. With Seven chassis streaming into Blackpool's Talbot Street Station, the Cocker Street factory could not cope. 'The station master was raising hell. There was nothing for it but to get into larger premises.'[50]

If this meant a new factory, Lyons was determined to move to Coventry, the capital of the motor industry, where there would be an ample supply of specialist labour. In November 1928 the business moved into a former shell-filling factory off Holbrook Lane at Whitmore Park, Foleshill, which was about five times the size of the Blackpool premises. The firm had already produced a Swallow-bodied version of the Morris Cowley and, following the move to Coventry, the distinctive coachwork was offered during 1929 on the Fiat 509A chassis and was followed, in 1930, by that ornithological-sounding hybrid, the Swift-Swallow. In the same year came the Standard-Swallow.

By 1930 William Lyons realized that, although he could go on producing these special-bodied cars, 'a great deal of body designs we had used were dictated by chassis design and, therefore, I badly wanted to produce a chassis which did not inhibit body design to such a degree'.[51] In other words, Lyons had decided that the Swallow Coachbuilding Company, as the firm was by then known, would join the ranks of Britain's car makers.

Lyons then visited Reginald Maudslay at Standard and obtained his agreement for the supply of 16 and 20hp six-cylinder engines. These would be fitted to a specially designed Rubery Owen-built chassis to which Standard springs and front and rear axles would be added at Canley, and then delivered to Foleshill where the bodywork would be fitted. Maudslay and his new general manager, John Black, had a long argument with Lyons about what the new car was going to be called. 'This resulted from my determination to establish a marque of our own,' recalled Lyons. The Canley duo would undoubtedly have liked the Standard name in the new car's title, while Lyons was equally insistent that Swallow be incorporated. The result was a compromise, which followed the MG precedent for the use of initials, and the SS name was finally agreed. Lyons subsequently reflected that 'there was much speculation as to whether SS stood for Standard Swallow or Swallow Special – it was never resolved'.[53]

The first car, the SS1, made its debut at the 1931 Motor Show at the near nadir of the world depression. Lyons had designed a low sleek coupé, which clearly followed current French trends though its radiator grille was borrowed from the American Cord. Harold Pemberton in the *Daily Express* caught the mood when he wrote of the SS1 as 'the £1,000 look for £310'. Here was style and a low price; the only absent ingredient was not so much top speed, which was around 70mph plus, but acceleration and refinement that did not reflect the car's appearance.

This was basically because the Standard engines were side-valve units designed for saloon cars, and when, in 1935, Lyons introduced the SS90, which was his first sports car, it was still side-valve powered. He was the first to recognize that what he needed was more performance and even contemplated fitting an American Studebaker eight-cylinder engine, as Henlys had just acquired a British concession for the make. A supercharged version of the six was also contemplated and likewise rejected. The answer came when tuning expert Harry Weslake arrived at Foleshill and informed Lyons: 'Your car reminds me of an overdressed lady with no brains – there's nothing under the bonnet!'[54] After this slightly unorthodox beginning, Lyons asked him how he would achieve the 90bhp he needed. Weslake immediately responded: 'Put the valves upstairs.'[55] He subsequently signed a contract with SS for overhead-valve conversions of the Standard engines, of which the 20hp version set down a pass-out figure of 95bhp. The trouble was that at that stage SS did not even possess a machine shop. So Lyons approached John Black at Standard who agreed 'to put in the new plant, to make the new head and supply the engines complete'.[56]

What Lyons urgently wanted was an engineering department and, in April 1935, William Munger Heynes joined SS. He was later to become chief engineer, a position he held with great distinction. The appointment was made only 'after a number of interviews (and I know now, meticulous deliberation of the pros and cons),'[57] Heynes later recalled. His first assignment, on which he had the help of one draughtsman, was to design a replacement chassis for a new body Lyons had designed to herald the arrival of the overhead-valve cars. He also decided that the new models would require a new name. 'I asked our publicity people to let me have a list of names of animals, fish and birds. I immediately pounced on Jaguar as it had an exciting sound to me.'[58] It also revived memories that a friend had worked on Jaguar Armstrong Siddeley aero engines during the First World War.

The result was a new range of SS Jaguars which appeared for 1936 and now had not only outstanding looks but also performance to match, the 102bhp 2.6-litre version boasting a top speed of 85mph. The popular four-door saloon cost only £375, which was around £400 less than its appearance suggested, and in 1938 the long-suffering 20hp Standard block was stretched from 2.6 to 3.5 litres and all-steel bodywork was adopted.

The sports car line was also perpetuated, the lovely 100 arriving in 1936. In 1939 SS Cars made a profit of £60,461, which was around double the previous year's figure. That year Lyons made a bid to gain self-sufficiency in the all-important bodybuilding field by buying Motor Panels (Coventry) Ltd. This had supplied him with pressings since 1931 and was conveniently located at nearby Burnaby Road, but, financially stretched in 1944, he sold it to Rubery Owen. In 1935 Walmsley announced that he wanted to retire and this was a good opportunity for SS Cars to become a public company, the issue yielding £85,000. Walmsley took the cash for his shares but Lyons retained his 50 per cent holding and later acquired additional shares to obtain a majority holding. However, the small board of directors 'rarely met and only then as a formality to satisfy legal requirements – the real business was conducted by Lyons himself on a day-to-day basis, in consultation with key members of his small staff'.[59]

William Lyons combined a formidable battery of talents, ranging from financial sagacity to the ability to appoint talented executives, but he was, above all, an outstanding stylist in his own right. Whereas many chief executives, from Sir Herbert Austin to John Black, dabbled to a greater or lesser extent in the styling of their cars, none of them possessed Lyons's eye for line and proportion. Like many stylists, he drew extensively on continental themes, but such were his abilities that, with very few exceptions, his pre-war SS cars and later Jaguars possessed their own utterly distinctive visual persona. Lyons was to use his abilities to maximum financial effect because the lines of his cars were sufficiently assured and progressive for him to plan long production runs and this, together with the efforts of the redoubtable Arthur Whittaker as purchasing manager, was how he was able to achieve his highly competitive prices.

If SS Cars represented a Coventry success story, the demise of Singer was a reminder of the increasingly competitive nature of the motor industry during the decade. Although the firm's plant in Canterbury Street, Coventry, was maintained, the new large six-storey Birmingham factory considerably added to the firm's overheads. There was also the fact that, in an era when rationalization was a prime requirement, in 1932 Singer 'listed six models, of which two were side valves, two pushrod operated overhead valves and the two smallest chain driven overhead camshafts'.[60] As if this were not enough, in 1933 Singer decided to enter the sports-car market with the Nine four-seater. It was later available in Le Mans Speed Special guise, but there was little profit in such a low-production diversification, despite a record 2,000 cars being sold in 1934. In 1935 Singer introduced what can be regarded as its last gamble, the Bantam, a Morris Eight lookalike, but with an overhead camshaft engine, rather than side valves. The firm had unwisely ignored the buoyant 10hp market sector and introduced its 1.5-litre Eleven in 1936. Singer recorded a £200,000 loss in 1935 and would probably have gone out of business altogether had not the unsecured creditors agreed to a ten-month moratorium on debt payments. William Bullock suggested a merger with Rover and, although Spencer Wilks was enthusiastic, in August 1936 the Rover board turned the idea down as it would have meant investing £100,000 in Singer.

So Bullock resigned as chairman and managing director and, in December of that year, Singer and Company was restructured as Singer Motors. The new chairman was chairman of the London County Council's finance committee Charles Latham from G. Latham and Company, a London-based accountancy business. A. E. Hunt, his managing director, was also an accountant and this more cost-conscious approach to car manufacture was reflected by the pruning of the Singer range from seven to three models in 1939. The cars, although reasonably priced, were lacking flair, for what spark there had been was extinguished with Bullock's departure. The war prolonged the firm's existence; the reality was that Singer had come to the end of the road.

A Coventry car company that did go into receivership – only three months before the Second World War broke out in September 1939 – was Triumph. Originally an offshoot of the successful Triumph motorcycle business, it began production at a plant in Clay Lane, Stoke, in 1923. In 1927 Triumph followed Austin into the small-car market with the Super Seven, which had the distinction of being the first British car to be fitted with hydraulic brakes. It was succeeded by the Super Eight in 1932 and, with around 17,000 built between 1927 and 1934, they were the best-selling Triumphs of the inter-war years. Instead of perpetuating this theme, Lieutenant-Colonel Claude Holbrook, who had been running the business since the mid-1920s, decided to take the firm up market with the Gloria range in 1933. This took Triumph into Rover and SS territory, but Holbrook was no Spencer Wilks or William Lyons and Triumph lacked pedigree, having been previously known for its cheap small saloons.

The firm lost a record £168,705 in 1933, though this was cut to £55,000 in 1934. That year, although Holbrook remained as chairman, in came accountants T. Dudley Cocke and H. Howe Graham as board members. It was Graham, it will be recalled, who had been largely responsible for pulling Rover back from the brink in 1932. The board decided to stake everything on the Gloria, the 'Queen of Cars', transfer production to a larger factory and sell off the profitable motorcycle division. In April 1935 Triumph bought the former White and Poppe engine factory in Holbrook Lane, Foleshill, which was renamed the Gloria Works, and was sufficiently close to SS Cars so that the 'more curious could climb chimney stacks and peer at each other'.[61]

Although Triumph made only a modest loss of £16,000 in 1935, the overall deficit amounted to £90,000 and total indebtness reached £250,000. Finances were not helped by the arrival of the Dolomite sports car, an extravagant copy of the contemporary Alfa Romeo 8C 2300, but at £1,225 there were no takers. Again there were thoughts of selling the Priory Street, Coventry, motorcycle division. This prompted an approach from Jack Sangster of Ariel Motors (JS) Ltd, which he had recently purchased from Components Ltd, its holding company, that had collapsed in 1932, and he secured Triumph Engineering in January 1936. Sangster made engineer Edward Turner general manager and he was responsible for the fabled Speed Twin of 1937 which proved such a success that Triumph did not get around to producing a new design until the Trident model of 1969.

In October 1936, despite the sale of the motorcycle business, Triumph's losses stood at a horrific £212,104. In 1937 the Gloria was replaced by the Dolomite range, which had no connection with the 1935 folly, and although an inexpensive 1.5-litre 12hp car arrived in March 1939, by June Lloyds Bank had had enough and Howe Graham's firm of Gibson and Ashford was appointed the Triumph Company's receivers. The Holbrook Lane factory was sold to the government for the manufacture of Claudel Hobson aircraft carburettors. For the time being, the 'Smartest Cars in the Land' were no more.

That Coventry institution, Daimler, was in the meantime surviving, shielded from commercial realism by the flabby protection of the BSA company. The firm had, it will be recalled, introduced the quiet but costly sleeve-valve engine in 1908 and it persisted with this obsolete concept until 1933 when more conventional poppet valves gradually took over. Under American Percy Martin, who was managing director until 1929, there was little attempt to rationalize production, and in 1927 alone Daimler produced no less than twenty-three separate models – this figure was *exclusive* of the body styles available, five engine types and twelve different chassis.

In 1928 Daimler's chairman, Sir Edward Manville, became chairman of the BSA group, yet the car company continued in its old ways, encapsulated by its 1935 performance when sales peaked at £176,031 yet a loss of £2,864 was recorded. E. M. Griffith, a BSA director until 1921, had little doubt of the reason for this state of affairs. 'The old style Board of Directors is out of date; it has had its trial since the war and has been found wanting,'[62] he informed Percy Martin in 1931. 'The unfortunate system of appointing Directors having no knowledge of the business has been tolerated too long in this country, and a Director serving on multiple companies is a great source of weakness.'[63]

Like many other businesses, BSA was badly hit by the depression but

Daimler had moved into deficit in 1928, following a sharp decline in sales in the face of sure-footed opposition from Rolls-Royce. BSA commissioned a report into Daimler's affairs, which revealed a chronic lack of investment: only £70,000 had been spent on machine tools in the ten years prior to 1929. That year, in a spate of staff cuts, Frederick Lanchester lost his job. The Daimler body shop was also closed, though this left the firm with £40,000 of unusable coachwork.

BSA decided to broaden the Daimler appeal and, in January 1931, bought the Lanchester company located in nearby Montgomery Street. The idea was that the respected Lanchester name could be applied to a new range of smaller Daimlers, aimed at the middle-class market. The takeover was effected at a time when the Lanchester company's overdraft had reached a modest £38,000 and was falling after having 'varied between £40,000 and £50,000'.[64] Daimler paid £26,000 for Lanchester and production was transferred to its Coventry works, while the Burton Griffiths Machine Tool Company, a BSA subsidiary, occupied the old Lanchester factory. Because of the speed in which the takeover was enacted, the board was given only a fortnight to amalgamate or go bankrupt, and 'there must be a suspicion that the extensive influence of the BSA directors was behind the bank's decision to recall the loan and trigger the Lanchester cash crisis . . . but nothing definite is known'.[65]

Despite this takeover, Daimler car production ceased for a time in the spring of 1931 and the firm concentrated on commercial vehicle and aero-engine work. Not surprisingly, that year BSA recorded a loss of £112,944 which soared to £688,646 in 1932, and when Sir Alexander Roger, a director of the Midland Bank, took over the firm's chairmanship in December, he was the fourth holder of the post in five years. Percy Martin retired as managing director in December 1933 and his place was taken by Geoffrey Burton, who had built up a good reputation as manager of the Metropolitan and Finance Company in 1927–30. BSA was back in the black in 1933 as bicycle, motorcycle and arms production increased, and profits reached £555,594 in 1937. That year Daimler furnished its parent with its largest profits of the decade but they amounted to only a little over £10,000.

Despite its problems, Daimler did make a major contribution to automobile technology under the auspices of Laurence Pomeroy, who returned to Britain and became the firm's chief engineer. In 1930 Daimler introduced a fluid flywheel in conjunction with a pre-selector gearbox to its model range. The flywheel was a scaled-down version of the Vulcan-Fottinger hydro-kinetic coupling then used for transmitting power in diesel-engined shops. When it was transferred to Daimler cars, all the driver had to do was to depress the accelerator and the car would move off; however, the system was not fully automatic because the next gear had to be selected manually and would be engaged only when the 'clutch' pedal was depressed. The arrangement was of such interest to Ernest Seaholm, Cadillac's chief engineer, that he shipped a Daimler back to America after seeing the system introduced at the 1930 Motor Show. It took another ten years, $8 million and the incomparable resources of General Motors to develop the two-pedal Hydra-Matic automatic transmission which first appeared in the 1940 Oldsmobile range. However, Daimler persisted with its original arrangement until 1956, when its automatic transmission first cousin became an option, though the old system was perpetuated on the firm's buses.

The 1930s ended with the British motor industry in an outwardly robust state. The Big Six had emerged as the country's principal manufacturers, though this was a greater number of groupings than in any European country. France had the Big Three of Renault, Citroen, and Peugeot; in Germany Opel, Auto Union, Mercedes-Benz and Ford dominated the field; while Fiat *was* the Italian motor industry. Although Britain led Europe, by 1939 Opel had emerged as the continent's largest car maker, followed by Morris, Renault, Austin and Fiat. Germany was asserting itself not only militarily but also on the automotive front.

The import and export trade played little part in the affairs of the British motor industry between the wars. Foreign car sales peaked in 1925, when the McKenna Duties were briefly repealed, and 31,781 cars worth £5.9 million were imported, which represented a record penetration for the inter-war years. Exports hit a high in 1937 when British cars worth £20.9 million were sold abroad. Australia was by far and away the largest market, accounting for 37.9 per cent of the total, followed by New Zealand, Eire, South Africa, Denmark, India, Malaya, Sweden and Ceylon. Inevitably countries of the British Empire figured prominently because British cars benefited from the Imperial Preference tariff concession. Dudley Noble, who worked for both Rover and Rootes, summed up the attitude of the British car makers to overseas sales at this time when he wrote, 'Exports were not favourably regarded by members of the British industry; selling abroad was a damned nuisance.'[66]

Although there were incentives for the motor manufacturers to export their products, and so spread manufacturing costs in the manner of the American car makers, the presence of the horsepower tax meant that firms had to develop purpose-built models to sell abroad and these were rarely successful. Billy Rootes, who tried with the Humber Snipe and Hillman Wizard, summed up the problem thus: 'If the basis of our taxation could be altered so as to encourage a larger or at least more powerful car, we could then build the one car for home and export.'[67] That was the price the British motor industry paid for such a protectionist measure, but what would the post-war years bring?

4

A Backward Business

'Austin and Morris . . . had made their reputation . . . by the construction of sound, reliable cars . . . designed by successive generations of engineers who must have had a common sympathy with the sentiment expressed by the Duke of Cambridge: "All change, at any time and for any purpose, is utterly to be deprecated."'[1]

Laurence Pomeroy Junior

The outbreak of the Second World War in 1939 marks a convenient point to pause and consider the state of the British motor industry, then the largest in Europe, after the first forty or so years of its existence. How did its structure and products compare with those of our continental neighbours and were there any telltale signs that, within thirty years of the end of hostilities, Britain's automobile industry would be bankrupted and nationalized?

As will have been apparent, the British motor industry relied heavily on France for its design initiatives during its first twenty or so years. After the First World War, America, as the home of mass production, exercised a considerable influence on the European car makers. Mechanical simplicity, the car with a front-mounted water-cooled side-valve four- or six-cylinder engine, was the norm and there is very little to choose between the mechanical specifications of, for instance, a British Morris Cowley, a Citroen B14 from France, an Italian Fiat 514 or German Opel 9/14.

With the coming of the depression in the USA, which savaged the motor industry in that country, trans-Atlantic influence waned somewhat, though independent front suspension and unitary body construction were adopted by General Motors' Opel and Vauxhall subsidiaries. This influence apart, the British, with very few exceptions, perpetuated the traditional front engine/rear drive configuration of the 1920s, but when innovations did appear they had invariably been first adopted by a foreign car maker. By the end of the decade the industry was manufacturing the most technologically backward cars in Europe.

The most obvious outward difference between British products and those of their counterparts in continental Europe was that aerodynamic considerations were becoming increasingly apparent on German and Italian cars from the mid-1930s onwards, stimulated by the purpose-built *Autobahns* and *autostradas*. In France, Citroen introduced its celebrated Traction Avant front-wheel-drive model in 1934 and this, along with the popular German DWK, meant that by the outbreak of the war, one in four continental cars were driven by their front wheels. In Britain, Alvis briefly and later BSA offered front-wheel-drive cars, but these models had little impact on the public and other manufacturers.

In Central Europe and Germany, the backbone chassis, which evolved into the platform, rather than the more conventional perimeter frame, began to gain favour from the early 1930s, along with the cheaply located rear-mounted air-cooled engine of which the most famous example is the German KdF-Wagen of 1938 or what we know today as the Volkswagen Beetle, which also featured independent suspension on all four wheels. A party from the Institution of Automobile Engineers in Britain visited Germany in 1937 and noted wistfully that on the country's four best-selling models 'independent front suspension is adopted throughout, and with one one exception, independent rear wheel suspension also'. No cheap British car from the Big Six at that time, with the exception of the 12hp model from the American-owned Vauxhall company, offered this facility.

Germany also initiated the diesel-powered car. The diesel-engined commercial vehicle had been pioneered by the German Benz company in 1923 and in 1936 Daimler-Benz introduced its 260 D private car, the first passenger model to run on this fuel. Citroen followed in 1937 with its 11UD diesel, ironically with an engine developed by Ricardo Engineering, a British company. It would not be until 1954 that the Standard Vanguard emerged as the first British diesel-powered car.

On the sporting front, advances in aerodynamic research stimulated the creation of the sports racing coupé from the mid-1930s, essentially a continental conception. It sprang from a recognition that a closed body is more aerodynamically efficient than an open one, and the resulting car is therefore faster than its open equivalent. Alfa Romeo, BMW and Fiat were

William Morris (1877–1963) was Britain's leading car maker of the inter-war years. This contemporary photomontage from *The Autocar* magazine shows Lord Nuffield, as Morris became in 1934, surrounded by the cars that made him famous with his 1913 Oxford, extreme left, and a Series E Eight of 1939, in the far right foreground.

Sir Herbert Austin (1866–1941), who became Lord Austin in 1936 and was universally known as 'The Old Man' at his Longbridge factory, is pictured in the 1930s.

Sir Percival Perry (1878–1956), Lord Perry from 1938, who as chairman ably directed Ford's British operations from 1928 until 1948.

Birth of the industry: a 4hp two-cylinder Daimler dog cart, modelled on the contemporary Panhard from France, outside the British company's Coventry Motor Mills in 1897.

(*Above*) Firm foundations: the Rover company's reputation for sound, reliable cars was built on the 2.2-litre 12hp model of 1912, designed by Owen Clegg. It survived until 1924.

(*Below*) Britain's best-selling car from 1910 until 1923 was the 2.9-litre 22hp Ford Model T. Between 1911 and 1928 it was produced at Trafford Park, Manchester. This is a 1915 example.

The 11.9hp Morris Cowley replaced the Model T as Britain's best-selling car of the 1920s. Introduced in 1919, it lasted until 1926.

(*Above*) The 1932 8hp Model Y Ford, created for the European market and designed by Ford in America, is pictured at the company's Dearborn headquarters. It proved to be the British Ford company's salvation.

(*Below*) Morris's, or more correctly Leonard Lord's, response to the Ford Y – the Eight of 1935 – was to be the best-selling British car of the decade and it lasted until 1938.

The Rootes brothers' expansion in the 1930s was based on the 10hp Hillman Minx, introduced in 1932. This 1936 example was competitively priced at £159.

(*Above*) Sir John Black pictured in Wales in 1947 while testing a prototype Standard Vanguard, intended for world markets. Standard was alone within the motor industry in responding to the government's one model policy.

(*Below*) British ingenuity 1: the Land-Rover, inspired by the Willys Jeep. Introduced in 1948, this export-orientated cross-country vehicle is still in production at Solihull, its home since its inception.

The much-loved Morris Minor, the British Motor Corporation's most popular car of the 1950s, was produced in this distinctive wooden-framed Traveller form from 1953.

(*Above*) Italian lines 1: BMC's first corporate car, the Pinin Farina-styled A40 of 1958, which dramatically anticipated the current two-box look by its apparent absence of a boot.

(*Below*) Italian lines 2: the Michelotti-styled Herald of 1959, which successfully relaunched the Triumph marque. It featured a backbone chassis, dictated by its body panels being produced in separate locations.

Alec Issigonis' revolutionary front-wheel-drive/transverse-engined Mini was drastically underpriced on its 1959 launch. This Morris Mini-Minor *de luxe* cost £537 and its Austin Seven stablemate, £496.

(*Above*) Jaguar's top seller of the 1950s and 1960s was introduced in 1955, updated in Mark 11 form in 1959, and lasted until 1969. It is shown here in its final 240 form.

(*Below*) Rootes' unsuccessful bid for the small car market, the Linwood-built Hillman Imp, with rear-mounted Coventry Climax derived 875cc aluminium engine. It lasted until 1976.

A triumph of product planning, Ford's 1962 Mark 1 Cortina was the fastest-selling car in the history of the British motor industry. Over a million were built in four years.

(*Above*) BMC's best-selling performance car, the 1.8-litre MGB, was introduced in 1962 and destined to remain in production until 1980. The majority were sold in America.

(*Below*) Britain's most popular car of the 1960s, the Mini-derived front-wheel-drive 1100/1300, styled by Pininfarina. Produced between 1962 and 1974, a total of 1.1 million were built.

Sir William (Billy) Rootes (1894–1964), who became Lord Rootes in 1959, and his brother Sir Reginald (*right*), aboard the Queen Elizabeth in 1946, after returning from one of their many American trips.

Leonard Lord, pictured in 1950. As chairman and managing director of the British Motor Corporation from its 1952 inception, he dominated the affairs of the indigenous motor industry until his retirement in 1961.

Sir Patrick Hennessy (1898–1981), the outstanding British motor industry executive of his generation, pictured in 1963. He was managing director from 1948 and chairman of the Ford Motor Company from 1956 until his retirement in 1968.

in the vanguard of these developments, while Britain stood on the sidelines and remained faithful to the concept of the traditional and visually impressive open two-seater. In 1938 Fiat introduced its 508C MM, the first series production aerodynamic sports coupé in the world. It was prophetically greeted by the British magazine, *The Motor* with the words: 'A 1950 model comes to town.'

What does this demonstrably conservative attitude to car design, where imitation rather than innovation was the order of the day, tell us about the motor magnates and the engineers they employed? To answer this question, we must briefly return to 1851, the year of the Great Exhibition, because the character and structure of the British motor industry is essentially a nineteenth-century inheritance. In the years following that high summer of Victorian enterprise, British engineers would 'never again . . . command so much esteem and affection; never again would the profession stand so high'.[2] The first half-century had seen Britain attain the industrial supremacy of the world, though much of this strength had been built on 'industrial tinkerers – on a barber like Arkwright, clergymen like Cartright, an instrument maker like Watt, a professional 'amateur inventor' like Bessemer and thousands of nameless mechanics who suggested and effected the kinds of small improvements to machines and furnaces and tools that add up eventually to an industrial revolution'.[3] But commercial success also sowed seeds of an anti-industrial culture, propagated by a spectrum of opinion ranging from Fredrick Engels to Charles Dickens, and an artist-craftsman and idealistic socialist whose namesake had brought mobility to every man: William Morris.

The period between about 1860 and 1900 saw a relative decline in the country's industrial power in the face of sure-footed opposition from America and Germany. One of the weapons in the German armoury was that, by the turn of the century, that country possessed the finest system of technical education in the world, providing Germany with the engineers and managers to overhaul Britain's engineering lead. It was a system which took little account of a student's personal circumstances. An engine driver's widow from Karlsruhe was able to send her son to a local gymnasium, or grammar school, and then on to the town's polytechnic. His name was Carl Benz. Gottlieb Daimler, a baker's son from Schorndorf, was similarly educated and at the Stuttgart Polytechnic learned physics, chemistry, general and specialized engine design, engineering, economics and English. The theoretical instruction they both received instilled in them the scientific disciplines which are the cornerstone in repetitious research and experiment. Each, working independently of the other, was to create a motor car in 1886 which was in turn to give birth to the world's automobile industry.

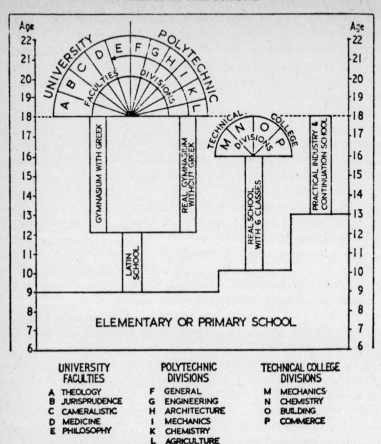

UNIVERSITY FACULTIES		POLYTECHNIC DIVISIONS		TECHNICAL COLLEGE DIVISIONS	
A	THEOLOGY	F	GENERAL	M	MECHANICS
B	JURISPRUDENCE	G	ENGINEERING	N	CHEMISTRY
C	CAMERALISTIC	H	ARCHITECTURE	O	BUILDING
D	MEDICINE	I	MECHANICS	P	COMMERCE
E	PHILOSOPHY	K	CHEMISTRY		
		L	AGRICULTURE		

Bavarian education in the 1880s. The German states' response to Britain's industrial supremacy in the 19th century was a programme of scientific and technical education which, by the 1900s, was the finest in the world. The polytechnics, known as 'technische hochschulen' (technical high schools), offered their students a Dipl Ing (Diploma of Engineering) though, in 1899, Kaiser Wilhelm II enhanced Prussian practice by permitting them to award Dr Ing (Doctor of Engineering) degrees, a precedent soon adopted by other German provinces though, to this day, such a status is not accorded to British engineers.

What Germany had done was to elevate engineering to the status that the classics enjoyed in the British public schools which had been growing in number and influence in the second half of the nineteenth century. Then, as now, they set the social pace and were another source of a deep-seated hostility to trade in general and industry in particular, the very institutions that had created so much of the country's wealth. It was a 'bias . . . derived from the Platonic tradition which regarded money and mechanical labour as vulgar and degrading'.[4] This prejudice rippled through the upper reaches of British society to members of the aspiring middle classes rather in the way that waves radiate from a pebble thrown into a pool of water. In short, engineering was not a proper occupation for a gentleman and the British engineer has consequently never received the social status accorded to his continental counterpart. The armed services, the church or civil service were considered far more acceptable careers for the ex-public schoolboy. Although they were to be found amongst the higher echelons of the motor industry, those who swam against the social current and pursued an engineering career often did so in the face of intense opposition from parents and school masters alike.

Just this happened to Roy Fedden, designer of Straker-Squire cars of pre-First World War days, and the Bristol Aeroplane Company's distinguished chief engineer between the wars. Fedden's father was a prosperous Bristol sugar merchant and, in 1895, Roy was sent to Clifton College, established in 1862. His parents were keen for him to enter the navy but he was rejected on medical grounds and so sat the army examination for Sandhurst. However, he was beginning to experience strong doubts about the wisdom of a service career. His family had purchased a secondhand Decauville car and Fedden had much enjoyed repairing it, imagining himself 'to be a fully qualified engineer. The more he thought about it, the more such a career appealed to him.'[5] Not knowing the way young Fedden's mind was working, in February 1904 his headmaster, Canon Glazebrook, wrote to his father, 'informing him what a good candidate his son would make for Sandhurst'.[6] By this time Roy had made up his mind to become an engineer and informed his father of his decision. A terrible family row then ensued. Fedden's father 'knew his younger son too well to think that he had turned "yellow" and lacked the guts to make a career in uniform. But engineering! It was socially quite unacceptable, being regarded as little better than casual labouring. Was he not letting the side down very badly?'[7] Eventually Fedden's family and school accepted his decision.

But there was worse to come. A friend of the family was one Mrs Crew 'who had three strikingly beautiful daughters'. One of them, Norah, was a good friend of Roy's and, as a fourteen-year-old, Fedden had solemnly informed her that he wanted to marry her. Norah's mother was delighted. When news of young Fedden's decision to become an engineer reached her, however, she was horrified. 'In Roy's own words, pronounced over seventy years later, "She was convinced that I was going to be some kind of plumber, dirty and brutish. She no longer wanted me in her house and suggested that, if I did come, presumably I should go round to the *back* door."'[8]

Other leading members of the motor industry who were ex-public schoolboys were to suffer similarly. When Miles Thomas, one of the outstanding managers in the British motor industry of the inter-war years, announced his intention to go into engineering, he experienced similar parental opposition. He was a pupil of Bromsgrove School when he informed his widowed mother of his decision. She responded that she 'wanted me to go into something which she called respectable . . . she was thinking in terms of the church, law, or particularly medicine. I was thinking in terms of something more dynamic, of movement or of metal.'[9] Like Fedden, he got his way, though unlike Roy he received encouragement from R. G. Routh, his enlightened headmaster. He obtained a premium apprenticeship with the Birmingham engineering firm of Bellis and Morcom.

Another Thomas who decided to go into engineering was John Godfrey Parry, a pupil at Oswestry public school and the second son of the Revd J. W. Thomas, vicar of the Montgomery village of Bwlch-y-Cibau. His mother, however, 'disapproved of his wanting to take up engineering as a career and felt that the army or the church was a more suitable calling for a son of hers'.[10] In fairness to the 'imperious' Mrs Thomas, she later did nothing to curb her son's enthusiasm and, as 'Godfrey was her special favourite',[11] she supported him financially after he had left school. Parry Thomas went on to become chief engineer of Leyland Motors and creator of the fabled Leyland Eight, though he died tragically in 1926 while making an attempt on the World Land Speed Record.

Those public schoolboys with the determination to bridge the social divide and enter the motor industry were often extremely successful in their chosen career. Percival Perry, perhaps the most able motor industry executive of the inter-war years, had won a scholarship to King Edward's School, Birmingham, and was considered by his friend, John Moore-Brabazon, later Lord Brabazon of Tara, as 'by far and away the most cultured, intelligent and attractive personality'[12] of the industry's founding fathers. But Perry only entered the industry by chance. Initially he had wanted to pursue a legal career; however, he was unable to do so because of his parent's limited financial resources. Spencer Wilks, who played such a pivotal role in rescuing the ailing Rover company from bankruptcy, was Charterhouse-educated though, significantly, he had studied law on leaving school.

Inevitably, the vast majority of the industry's recruits in the pre-First World War years came from the bicycle trade and the working or lower middle classes who had little or no formal education, let alone a technical one. During the nineteenth century Britain espoused a *laissez-faire* doctrine which looked to a self-regulating economy and the minimum of government intervention. The continental challenge was a factor in the introduction of compulsory primary education in 1882, though secondary schooling did not attain similar status until 1902 and, without such a facility, technical education cannot operate satisfactorily. This also became subject to state funding with the passing of the Technical Instruction Act in 1889, but technical institutes and universities were often short of funds.

When Henry John Lanchester, architect father of Frederick, visited the Hartley Institute in Southampton in the 1880s prior to his son attending there, the hard-pressed authorities passed off a stove pipe, viewed through a locked glass door, as a drive shaft as evidence that it taught mechanical engineering. By 1901 there were 7,130 engineering students in Germany compared with 1,433 in British universities. Although British government grants were stepped up during the early part of the century, and the quality of the education offered was often on a par with that available on the continent, 'few engineers received a theoretical education, an apprenticeship was the almost invariable starting point even for boys from wealthy families, and a remarkable number served them in the highly traditional atmosphere of railway workshops'.

Laurence Pomeroy, who later went on to become Vauxhall's chief engineer, was exceptional because, although he began his apprenticeship at the age of sixteen in the workshops of the North London Locomotive Works at Bow, he simultaneously undertook a four-year engineering course at evening classes at the East London Technical College. In the three years from 1900 to 1903 'he sat for 22 examination papers, gaining 15 seconds, 5 firsts, and 2 Honours . . . and passed out 16th out of 30 Whitworth Exhibitioners for 1903'.[13] But when Pomeroy sought work he found that 'his academic qualifications were considered of little account, and it was not until he mentioned that he was capable of working in the shops if necessary that he found himself acceptable'.[14] Pomeroy developed into one of the country's outstanding automobile engineers and Vauxhall became one of the few British companies to undertake grand prix racing having entered a team, albeit unsuccessfully, in the 1914 French Grand Prix where German Mercedes cars took the first three places.

During these pre-First World War days 'trained engineers were very thin on the ground'[15] in the motor industry. In 1908 there were only 385 members of the Institution of Automobile Engineers at a time when 'there were some 81 British concerns putting their individual names to makes of motorcar'[16] and that excluded the requirements of the components industry. Little wonder that many firms simply copied the nearest French car they could find. It also meant that Britain played virtually no part in the technically demanding field of grand prix racing for the first fifty years of this century. The first occasion on which a British-designed car had won an international event was S. F. Edge's win, by default, at the wheel of a Napier in the 1902 Gordon Bennett race, while Henry Segrave's victories in 1923 and 1924 were in Italian-designed Sunbeams which were Fiats in all but name and Louis Coatalen, his firm's driving force, was French. A British car did not win a front-line international motor race until 1957 when Stirling Moss, in a Vanwall, took the chequered flag in the European Grand Prix.

While Germany, Italy and France were battling it out on the motor-racing circuits of Europe, Britain looked instead for prestige by attempts on the World Land Speed Record, an activity that was largely ignored by the continentals in the inter-war years. The cars used by the 'speed kings' were powered by aero engines, usually of First World War ancestry, and although the bodywork invariably showed the results of aerodynamic research, the chassis and suspension were often crude because, as the cars ran in a straight line, there was little need to develop sophisticated suspension systems for them. It was, nevertheless, reassuring to know that an Englishman was often the 'fastest man on earth'.

The reason for the traditional nature of British car design in the inter-war years now becomes more apparent because, prior to the Second World War, the design in particular of engines for road cars had 'with a few exceptions, such as Lanchester [and] Pomeroy . . . been in the hands of cycle makers, superb mechanics well versed in the art of light mechanical design but abysmally ignorant of thermo-dynamics, or of the many other factors upon which the performance of their engines depended'.[17] So wrote Sir Harry Ricardo who, after education at Rugby, and Cambridge, where he read mechanical sciences, in 1917 established what became Ricardo Engineering, a research business which concentrated on many aspects of engine design.

One of the main strands of Ricardo's activities related to his work on the universally popular side-valve engine which, although cheap to manufacture, was notoriously prone to knock at compression ratios above 4:1, resulting in low power and efficiency. Ricardo succeeded in providing the side-valve unit with the high turbulent characteristic of the overhead-valve one, thus making it less liable to knock. This meant that its compression ratio could be raised to 5:1 with a 20 per cent increase in output and economy. Ricardo's research had world-wide influence and it thus represents one of the few British contributions to engine design between the wars. His work was, in fact, widely pirated and, at the suggestion of Percy Kidner, whose 14/40 Vauxhall used Ricardo's high turbulent head, the firm successfully instituted a test case against Rootes when Ricardo claimed that the engine of its Hillman Wizard infringed his patents. Thereafter car companies were under greater pressure to pay a royalty to

Ricardo. His Shoreham-by-Sea company is still very much in business, and remains a lasting tribute to the lively, enquiring and, above all, informed mind of Harry Ralph Ricardo.

The innate conservatism of British car design, typified by the products of the Austin and Morris companies, was already discernible by the 1920s. There were, however, strong arguments for mass producing straight-forward, no-nonsense cars in the Ford idiom. Innovation was all very well, but had not Citroen's revolutionary front-wheel drive car bankrupted his company? The reality was that British cars were technically backward not for positive reasons but for the negative one of fear of change through lack of knowledge. This contrasts with the achievement of the Italian Fiat company which, of all the European car makers, showed the most measured approach to innovation at this time. This automotive Janus chose to retain the best of the past in its cars by perpetuating the traditional front engine/rear drive layout while incorporating technically advanced features within this proven framework.

'The British firms go on building not what is wanted but what they think *ought* to be wanted, i.e. what they have always made,'[18] Robert Vansittart, head of the Foreign Office, complained of the car companies in 1927. This approach was little more than a direct reflection of the personalities and backgrounds of William Morris, 'by nature a garage proprietor',[19] and Herbert Austin, 'a mechanic, nothing more nor less'.[20] Both were farmers' sons and essentially self-taught men, in the spirit of the mechanics and tinkerers who had created so much of British industry in the first half of the nineteenth century. Cast in the Victorian mould, they might have stepped straight out of the pages of Samuel Smiles's *Self-Help*, having triumphed by drive, intuition and sheer hard work but possessing little more than a superficial technical knowledge.

Both consequently adopted a cautious approach to car design and had few qualms about copying rival concepts. It is no accident that the two most popular Morris engines of the inter-war years, those of the 'Bullnose' and the 8hp car, were cribbed from American designs. Significantly, the Morris Minor, one of the most outstanding British cars of the post-1945 years, was developed during the war without Lord Nuffield's knowledge, and when he eventually saw it he expressed his extreme displeasure. Austin's imitative approach has already been noted and the fact that such policies enjoyed short-term success meant that there was little incentive for either firm to initiate what they considered to be costly research and development programmes. However, it should be remembered that the British motor industry was largely insulated from the effects of foreign imports by the 33⅓ per cent McKenna Duties that protected the home market from European competition.

Yet another prejudice shared by both Morris and Austin was their hostility to university-educated managers and engineers, reflecting the attitudes of an industry which fostered a disproportionate respect for the benefits of practical experience. In 1930 Sir Herbert Austin proclaimed, 'The university mind is a hindrance rather than a help,'[21] a sentiment also shared by Morris, who even went as far as positively to discriminate against graduates, as is sometimes the way with self-made men. When Morris accepted an invitation from a college to debate the motion, 'Oxford-educated men are useless in the motor industry', an executive who accompanied him revealed, in the heat of argument, that he held a Cambridge engineering degree, a fact of which Morris was unaware. 'Slumbering suspicions about the man were aroused. He watched him work and began to fault him. Before long Morris convinced himself that the sooner they parted company, the better for his organization.'[22] Having disposed of this graduate, Morris began investigating the background of two more of his employees who were found to be degree holders. Although they 'had been giving satisfaction [they] found themselves out of jobs without knowing the real reason'.

A few firms within the industry – Daimler and Riley were two examples – did encourage graduate engineers. It is to his eternal credit that Ernest Hives, head of Rolls-Royce's experimental department, did so from the early 1920s. It was a policy which benefited not only the firm's car division but also, more significantly, its all-important aero-engine department. As in so many aspects of engineering, the Rolls-Royce approach was very much the exception to the rule.

In fairness to Britain's motoring magnates, their parallels could be found, to a limited extent, in the other car-manufacturing countries. In America, Ford, run by another farmer's son, typified this approach. Henry Ford's dictatorial running of his business, his obstinacy and reluctance to change brought the firm to the brink of ruin. Success in the post-war years would go to those car companies which quickly rid themselves of such intuitive, homespun sentiments.

5

Two into One Won't Go

1940–58

'We expect keen competition, but we have a few shillings in the bank and friends who will lend us money. We are feeling pretty comfort-able.'[1]

Sir Leonard Lord, chairman British Motor Corporation,
September 1954

During the post-war years, the motor industry maintained the momentum it had displayed in the 1930s. The 1937 highpoint of 379,310 cars was passed in 1949, and although output dipped in 1951, 1952, 1956 and 1957, in 1958 the industry broke the 1 million-car barrier for the first time. However, in 1956 Britain ceded its place as Europe's largest car manufac-turer to West Germany. In 1955 that country also wrested the position of world's leading car exporter from Britain, an accolade it had held it since 1949.

The Big Six car makers, their productive resources greatly expanded during the war years, remained structurally unchanged until 1952, when the two largest, Austin and Morris, combined to form the British Motor Corporation in the face of the growing strength of the American-owned Ford and Vauxhall companies. BMC was, in sales terms, the fourth-largest car company in the world outside the American Big Three of General Motors, Ford and Chrysler. Rootes also grew modestly by acquisition, taking over the ailing Singer company in 1956.

On the debit side, BSA cars did not survive the war and Lanchester, another BSA marque, ceased production in 1956. A further casualty was the old-established Jowett company. This had bravely attempted to break

95

into the mass market with its advanced Javelin saloon, which ceased production in 1954, while Lea-Francis, with a generation of financial upheavals behind it, stopped building cars in 1953. But there were also some new recruits to the ranks of the car makers: the Warwick-built Healey arrived in 1946 (it became the Austin Healey in 1953), there was the German BMW-derived Bristol of 1947; while in 1953, twenty-five-year-old Colin Chapman began selling his Lotus sports cars from the unlikely surroundings of a former stable block behind his father's public house in Tottenham, North London.

The days of the car makers buying coach builders were largely over, but with the arrival of unitary construction, the bodybuilding firms became prime takeover targets. In 1953 Ford purchased Briggs Motor Bodies which had provided its hulls since 1932, while BMC quickly snapped up Fisher and Ludlow of Birmingham in the same year. BSA wasted little time in following suit by buying Carbodies of Coventry in 1954. But it was BMC's purchase of Fisher and Ludlow that presented problems for Standard, which depended on the firm for much of its bodywork requirements. It responded, in 1954, by forging closer links with Mulliners Ltd of Birmingham, the largest of the small bodymakers, which it absorbed in 1958. Standard's original liaison with Mulliners almost put Alvis out of the car business because the Bordesley Green company built its bodies, and it also resulted in Aston Martin, which was in a similar position, buying the Tickford body company of Newport Pagnell in 1955.

Before the Second World War, the motor industry was largely left to its own devices, but with the Labour landslide of July 1945 the government became markedly more interventionist. This took the form of directing the motor industry to export its products in numbers that would have been unimaginable in pre-war days. A beneficial side effect of this policy was the abolition of the despised horsepower tax and the introduction of a flat-rate system. Yet a further governmental stricture was that the car makers were prevented from expanding at their own works but were instead directed to areas of high unemployment. This policy was perpetuated by Conservative governments from 1951 onwards which, like their predecessor, were pledged to a policy of full employment. However, export quotas were eased to the benefit of the home market. Less desirable was the government's use of the industry as an economic regulator, for although the 1950s are often stereotyped as the 'you've never had it so good' era, they were also the 'stop-go' years.

During the post-war years the industry also began to suffer from the labour disputes that were to plague it for the next 40 or so years. Although the motor industry had, almost from the outset, invariably paid good wages, it represented strictly seasonal employment with work in the autumn, winter and spring and layoffs in the summer, jobs once again becoming available in the early autumn, prior to the Motor Show in October. All the car factories had been unionized by 1945, following war-time legislation, though the post-war years brought round-the-year jobs. Then the Conservative government's economic policies of the 1950s had their effects on employment and in 1956, a poor year for the industry, BMC was forced to lay off one worker in eight, with no redundancy pay. The record 300,000 days lost in strikes during that year were a pointer to the increasing strife of the 1960s.

Clement Attlee's government was faced with an economy bankrupted by war, for by 1941 practically all the country's economic reserves had been exhausted. There was a loss of income from overseas as exports markets had disappeared, while import costs had soared. A buoyant balance-of-payments programme therefore became a cornerstone of the government's economic policy and this meant 'a relentless concentration on the export trade'.[2]

As the motor industry had made virtually no contribution to the country's balance of payments in the pre-war years, it was not included in the government's initial plans for its export drive which concentrated instead on the traditional industries, such as textiles and shipbuilding. The task of exhorting the car makers to turn their attention to export markets fell to the president of the Board of Trade, Sir Stafford Cripps, who was in some respects ideally equipped for the job, having had first-hand industrial experience. He had successfully worked as an assistant superintendent of a Queensferry explosives factory during the First World War and, although a brilliant chemist, had followed his father to the bar and by 1927 was the youngest KC in the country. Cripps joined the Labour Party in 1929, became a leading light in the militant Socialist League and his increasingly extremist posture culminated in his expulsion from the Labour Party in 1939. With the outbreak of the Second World War, he served a stint as British ambassador in Moscow and, in 1942, returned to Britain to become Minister of Aircraft Production, to which he was well suited. It was probably this success that prompted Attlee to offer him the trade appointment. Cripps's knowledge of industry and production methods was an undoubted advantage in his dealings with the car makers, though his intellectual socialism and past extremism did not bode well for his dealings with the Conservative and fiercely independent motor magnates, 'a more highly individualist set of individuals than can be found in any other law abiding trade',[3] a fellow MP Ian Mikardo observed. As the author of a Fabian pamphlet 'The Second Five Years' published in 1948, Mikardo advocated that the motor industry be nationalized to make possible 'a degree of standardization of design and manufacturing methods which could not be achieved under private ownership', though this never became Labour policy.

Sir Stafford spelt out his strategy at the Society of Motor Manufacturers and Traders' (SMMT) dinner in November 1945. 'We must provide a cheap, tough, good-looking car of decent size – not the sort of car we have hitherto produced for smooth roads and short journeys in this country – and we must produce them in sufficient quantities to get the benefits of mass production,'[4] he told his audience. With no doubt the multifarious range of cars offered by most manufacturers in pre-war days in mind, Cripps declared: 'we cannot succeed in getting the volume of exports we must have if we disperse our efforts over numberless types and makes.'[5] Moving on to the all-important export quota, Sir Stafford revealed that the lowest possible figure to be considered was 50 per cent of output, which produced 'an unfavourable reception'.[6] This took the form of boos and shouts of 'No!' and 'Tripe!' to which Cripps responded: 'I have often wondered whether you thought that Great Britain was here to support the motor industry, or the industry was here to support Great Britain. I gather from your cries that you think it is the former.'[7]

A stumbling block to Cripps's objective was the perpetuation of the reviled horsepower tax. Talks between the SMMT and the government had taken place during the war and it was decided that the tax would be abolished in December 1946 after a twenty-five-year life. As a united recommendation from the manufacturers was still awaited, an interim system, in which the tax would still be graduated in 100cc steps and thus geared to engine capacity rather than horsepower, would be introduced for new cars.

By the time that Chancellor of the Exchequer Hugh Dalton made his budget statement in April 1947, he was able to announce that a flat rate of £10 per car would be introduced from 1 January 1948. But there was a sting in the tail because it was recognized that the new system would deprive the government of revenue from the larger higher-horsepower cars. As a result, those models costing more than £1,000 were to be subjected to a 66⅔ per cent rate of purchase tax, double the levy of 33⅓ per cent introduced on motor cars in 1940.

In September 1947 the government was again urging the manufacturers to build a single model. This was largely ignored and in 1948 Austin was offering the largest range of cars in Europe. In the immediate post-war years the Morris family was producing 'ten different engines of three different valve configurations, nine distinct and different chassis and nine body types'.[8] It was only Rover, with its Land-Rover of 1948 and the Standard-built Ferguson tractor, that came closest to the spirit of these exhortations. Of all the car makers, only Standard heeded the governmental overtures with its 1948 Vanguard. The type of car which Cripps had so graphically described in his SMMT address was being built not in Britain but Germany where the pre-war KdF-Wagen had been renamed the Volkswagen, production having started, ironically, under British army auspices in 1945. A decade later the millionth VW left the Wolfsburg production line, a figure that was far in excess of the output of any comparable British car. In France the recently nationalized Renault company was building its rear-engined 4CV car and the 500,000 figure was reached by 1954.

Export performance was geared to steel allocation, the government being in the position to maintain war-time controls, though this had the effect of keeping uncompetitive firms in business. It is unlikely that Singer, for example, would have survived until 1955 had it not been for the export drive.

The target was raised to 60 per cent for 1947 but, in July, sterling was made convertible which had the effect of allowing potential buyers in the sterling area to buy the traditional American cars with hitherto scarce dollars. Morris, for one, lost a £1 million export order at this time. Convertibility was suspended in August and the export target upped to 75 per cent in 1949 but only 53 per cent of British car production went abroad. However, the devaluation of the pound, in September of that year, made British cars more competitive and in 1950 no less than 66 per cent of British car production was exported, the highest ever percentage attained by the industry.

Where did the cars go? The pre-war Imperial Preference markets were maintained and, in 1947, the top six foreign customers were Australia, Belgium, New Zealand, India, South Africa and Switzerland. Although in 1949 Britain had become the world's leading exporter of motor cars, the reality was that much of this success was achieved in the face of little initial competition from America, which was fully absorbed in coping with demand from the home market, while Germany, France and Italy were rebuilding their motor industries after they had been decimated by war.

Many British cars, which were often of pre-war design, were found to be totally unsuited to a foreign environment and, in 1949, one Canadian observer commented: 'The product of the British motor industry, with its narrow tracks, small luggage space and reputed inability to stand up to bad roads had been criticised to the point of monotony.'[9] In addition, many British companies had no proper export department, so that spares and servicing were often poor, a state of affairs that blighted the reputation of British cars for many years.

One surprising but none the less gratifying spinoff from the government's export drive was the growing popularity, particularly in America, of the British sports car. As the American motor industry between the wars was geared to the mass-production process, it had virtually ignored the concept of the low-production open two-seater so beloved of the British. In pre-war days MG had been Europe's largest sports car manufacturer and, in 1945, the Abingdon factory mildly updated its pre-war visually delightful but mechanically archaic TB, renaming it the TC. Exports did not begin in earnest until 1947, when 1,656 cars were sold abroad, and a further six, for the first time, were dispatched to America. Although only 20 per cent of total TC production, which amounted to just 2,001 cars, were subsequently exported to the United States, they had an impact out of all proportion to the relatively small numbers involved and effectively opened the trans-Atlantic market to the open two-seater. The TC paved the way for the similar but updated TD of 1950 and 80 per cent, that is to say 23,488 of a total of 29,664 cars, went to American owners.

The TC's impact had not escaped the attention of other British car makers and its success spawned a new generation of sports cars as the potential of the American market made the manufacture of the open two-seater a viable proposition. In 1948 Jaguar introduced its superlative XK120, while 1952 saw the arrival of the Austin Healey 100 and Triumph TR series. Rootes' Sunbeam Alpine did not appear until 1959. All were aimed at a trans-Atlantic clientèle. Not surprisingly, in 1956 America overtook Australia as Britain's principal export market, a position it held until 1972.

The election of a Conservative government in 1951 saw export quotas initially maintained, but there were growing demands from the home market which did not become fully satisfied until the early 1960s. This, coupled with a less interventionist approach, resulted in a relaxation of targets. Despite this, exports approximately doubled between 1949 and 1958, when 451,261 cars were sent abroad, and although sports models were in the majority, the percentage of total output fell from 53 to 41. Germany, by contrast, increased its exports from 13 to 48 per cent over the same period, which amounted in 1958 to 630,515 cars.

Yet another benefit of government intervention, albeit a pre-war one, was the presence of the Shadow Factories, many of which had been built adjoining the manufacturers' existing plants. Even before the war had ended, in February 1945, the Board of Trade announced that Standard and Rover were to lease the plants that they had managed during the war for car production. Standard therefore had increased manufacturing facilities though even Sir John Black, as he had become during the war, must have wondered what he would do with the 1 million-square-foot Banner Lane plant he also took over. For Rover, its number two Shadow at Solihull was a godsend as its Helen Street works in Coventry had been damaged by bombing during the war and there was, in any case, no room for expansion. Consequently the firm took the precaution of buying an additional 200 acres of adjoining farmland when Lode Lane, Solihull, officially became its headquarters.

In June 1945 Rootes revealed that it was taking over its Shadow Factory at Stoke, its existing works, and the one it had managed at nearby Ryton-on-Dunsmore. Daimler did likewise with its plants at Radford and Allesley, though Austin waited until 1950 to take up an option on its Cofton Hackett extension. However, Dunlop was rather quicker off the mark and took over the Rootes-managed plant at Speke, Liverpool. Fisher and Ludlow moved into a former Spitfire factory at Castle Browmich which was soon converted for body production. The industry was thus able to expand into spacious, modern factories and so enjoyed an enormous advantage over its European contemporaries at a crucial time.

As British car production soared – it doubled between 1949 and 1957 – and existing production facilities were absorbed, the car makers found that their requests for planning permission for new factories were refused because they could not obtain the necessary Industrial Development Certificate. This all-important document, introduced by the Attlee government in 1947, was intended to direct firms to expand into areas of high unemployment. It was a development of the policy, initiated in 1934, which identified the Distressed Areas of the country as Scotland, South Wales, West Cumberland and Tyneside. These were cosmetically renamed Special Areas by the House of Lords but the £2 million made available for the creation of trading estates, and assisting firms which wanted to move there, did not go far and had little impact.

The post-war development of the scheme was given teeth because the government could refuse firms permission to expand in areas of their choice, usually adjoining their own works which, by their very nature, were in areas of low unemployment, even if land was available. There were considerable inducements for manufacturers to expand in the Special Areas but the resulting fragmentation of the industry would not become apparent until the 1960s.

The dominating event of the 1950s was Austin's effective takeover of the Morris family of companies which, since 1940, had been known as the Nuffield Organization. The resulting British Motor Corporation of 1952 united the Austin, Morris, MG, Wolseley and Riley marques under the same corporate umbrella. Less desirably, although Austin possessed one factory site at Longbridge, the Nuffield part of the union embraced sixteen different plants, whereas Ford, Vauxhall and Standard had one each and Rootes three.

During the war years Leonard Lord began strengthening his hold on the Austin Motor Company. Following Lord Austin's death in 1941, Ernest Payton became chairman and Lord moved up as technical director. Then, in 1942, Lord consolidated his rise in the Austin Motor Company hierarchy by becoming, with Payton, joint managing director and also deputy chairman. Payton stepped down as chairman in November 1945 and forty-nine-year-old Leonard Lord took over. He had wasted little time in getting new Austin cars back on to Britain's roads. In September 1944, even before the war had ended, the firm announced its 'new' post-war model, the 16, which was the 1940 12 with a new 2.2-litre four-cylinder engine derived from the pre-war six-cylinder commercial vehicle unit. It was significant for being the first Austin car to be fitted with an overhead-valve engine. On 10 July 1945 Lord scored a public relations success when an Austin 10 (the model had been in production throughout the war) became the first British car to be exported to America since VE Day. It set the tone for the export-orientated early post-war years.

The pre-war range of 8, 10 and 12hp cars was perpetuated until 1947, when a new generation of Austins was unveiled. First came the big Sheerline and Princess saloons, both powered by the same 4-litre six-cylinder truck engine, while independent front suspension made its appearance for the first time on an Austin car. This was a curious duplication of models and the more expensive Princess had bodywork by the London firm of Vanden Plas, which Austin had bought, following an approach from Lord, in June 1946. The works in Kingsbury Road, North London, became Longbridge's first satellite plant.

In October 1947 Austin unveiled the A40, which replaced all the existing Austin models with the exception of the 16. The model was Longbridge's first attempt at modern full-width bodywork and was an odd amalgam of 1930s Austin and 1940 Chevrolet. Far more significantly, under its bonnet was a new 1.2-litre four-cylinder overhead-valve engine, which was to survive, in essence, until 1980. The independent front suspension perpetuated the practice established with the big saloons. The A40 proved Austin's, and Britain's, best-selling model of the day, with an impressive 273,958 sold by the time production ceased in 1952. Most of these went for export to the antipodes and America. Of the 30,000 cars built up until July 1948, only 1,000 were retained for the home market. The A40 theme was applied less successfully to the larger A70 range, while the visually startling A90 Atlantic, designed specifically for America, was a flop.

It was largely the success of the A40 that was responsible for Austin pulling ahead of Morris to become Britain's largest car maker in 1949, so usurping a position that the Cowley company had held, more or less continuously, since 1924. Lord was spending lavishly at Longbridge, just as he had done at Morris Motors in the 1930s, to update Austin manufacturing facilities. The centrepiece was the new Car Assembly Building, better known by its CAB acronym, capable of producing 100,000 cars a year. It opened in 1951 and was claimed to be the most modern factory of its type in the world. The new 60,000-square-foot plant was fed by components drawn from other parts of the Longbridge facility from three conveyors concealed in a 1,000-foot-long tunnel.

These improved facilities represented a direct challenge to Cowley which had been fairing less well than Austin in the early post-war years for Morris Motors was, once again, in the grip of management upheavals. In March 1940 Oliver Bowden, vice chairman and managing director of Morris Motors, had died suddenly and Lord Nuffield appointed Miles Thomas as his deputy. Thomas recalled: 'It took me a long time to pick up all the threads of what I was proposing to call the Nuffield Organisation.'[10] By the time that the war came to an end, the number of factories within the Morris orbit had grown yet again. SU Carburettors had moved to new larger premises at Wood Lane, Erdington, Birmingham, while in 1942 at nearby Coventry, Nuffield Tools and Gauges opened for business in Mile Lane.

In 1939 the Oxford-based Radiators Branch took over the manufacture of radiators for Rolls-Royce Merlin aero engines, but demand for these and other similar components led to the establishment of a new factory on a site at Llanelli, South Wales, which after the war continued to make radiators for cars produced by the Nuffield Organization.

With the coming of peace, Sir Miles Thomas, as he became in 1943, buckled down to getting Cowley back on to a peace-time footing. A brief diversion occurred when he received an invitation from Ernest Payton to move to Austin and run it in tandem with Leonard Lord, but Thomas declined the offer. Another potentially crucial liaison could have developed from a meeting between Lord Nuffield and Harry Ferguson, arranged by Sir Miles in 1945. Ferguson had developed a lightweight tractor and was looking for a British car maker to build it for him.

This eloquent, colourful character, born in Dromore, Northern Ireland, had built his own plane in 1909, entered the motor trade and become the Austin distributor for Belfast. Ferguson had long been interested in tractor design and invented what he called the Ferguson System, an ingenious hydraulic device which raised and lowered implements attached to a tractor with the minimum of human effort. In 1933 Ferguson was building a prototype tractor, which incorporated his system while production was entrusted to the Craven Wagon Company. The project interested David Brown, whose father's Huddersfield Gear Company had made parts for Ferguson, and he agreed to take the project over as by this time neither

Ferguson or Craven was happy about the original arrangement. Although the tractor entered production at Park Works, Huddersfield, difficulties arose and in 1938 'Ferguson said that the partnership must be dissolved'.[11] It was, but Brown decided that there was a future in tractors and the first of many David Brown machines was unveiled in June 1939.

Plans were made for Standard to manufacture the tractor but these plans were sidelined when Ferguson travelled to America where he interested Henry Ford in his project. The two HFs made a verbal agreement that Ford would build the tractor and Ferguson would market it the world over. Production of the Ford-Ferguson tractor began in 1939 and it continued to be built throughout the war, though numbers were small and losses considerable. After Henry Ford II, Henry Ford's grandson, took over the running of the firm in September 1945, one of his many money-saving acts was to shelve the project, which was terminated on 11 November 1946, though this occurred after the Ferguson/Nuffield dialogue.

In Britain, Ford's own tractor production gave it a near-monopoly and an agreement with Ferguson would have opened up this increasingly important market sector to the Nuffield Organization. Nuffield and Ferguson met in the latter's suite àt Claridge's but the conversation was not a success. Nuffield 'was not exactly rude to Ferguson', but, Thomas remembered, when the Ulsterman left the room to answer the telephone, 'Nuffield said to me that he had seen enough of this wild Irishman's ideas'.[12] For his part Sir Miles was convinced that a great opportunity had been missed. As will emerge, Ferguson soon afterwards sold his tractor project to Sir John Black. It proved a considerable success and was to transform Standard's finances in the post-war years.

Thomas was becoming increasingly exasperated with his chairman but, early in 1946, sixty-nine-year-old Nuffield assured him: 'I'm going to step aside completely and leave the running of the whole business to you and the younger men.'[13] Yet when Sir Miles followed his chief's advice and used his 'own judgement' in December 1946, issuing the Organization's annual report in Nuffield's absence in Australia, 'he was very upset and indeed petulantly angry'.[14] Despite his assurance, Nuffield continued to persist 'in exercising what was inappropriately, if undeniably, his right of destructive criticism'.[15] In addition Nuffield disliked the all-important new models then under development. 'The unhappy atmosphere at the executive top permeated not only the Board but the staff, and a feeling of indecision was rife throughout,'[16] recalled Thomas. The engineering staff were equally demoralized. 'There was no urgency, because it was known that the old man did not want changes made.'[17]

By the early autumn of 1947 Thomas admitted that 'I was in a psychological turmoil' and 'I should have been by now deaf as well as blind that if I could not have seen that all was not well between the Chairman and myself.'[18] In November at one of his regular meetings with Nuffield, he brought matters to a head and resigned from his £20,000-a-year post. At fifty years old, Sir Miles Thomas, the Nuffield Organization's vice chairman and questionably its most able executive, was out of a job. He was already a director of the Colonial Development Corporation and was to continue a successful business career as chairman of the British Overseas Airways Corporation from 1949. He also held a similar office with the British subsidiary of the American Monsanto Chemicals. He was made a life peer in 1971. But Sir Miles's departure was a grievous loss for the British motor industry and if it is possible to chart a turning point in the fortunes of the Morris marque, which disappeared in 1983, then that November day at Cowley in 1947 must be strong contender. Austin's able chairman, Ernest Payton, had told Thomas that he considered him 'the best commercial man in the business' and Leonard Lord 'the best production man'.[19] If the two had been able to work in tandem in what became the British Motor Corporation, it might have fared considerably better than it did; though if the period 1933/5, when the pair were together at Cowley, is anything to go by, such a combination would have been impossible.

Thomas's place was taken by Reginald Hanks, who had worked for Morris since 1922 and had headed Nuffield Exports from 1945. Nuffield followed Sir Miles's departure by sacking eight long-standing directors, which reduced the number of board members to nine. Nineteen forty-eight saw a restructuring in the Oxford area, with Wolseley output centred on Cowley while Riley car manufacture was based at the MG factory at nearby Abingdon. This left Ward End to become Morris Motors' machining centre, which was renamed the Tractors and Transmissions branch in 1948 after the firm had belatedly decided to produce the M series Nuffield tractor there. The former Riley works became an extension to the Court House Green engine factory, while sales and service operations were also streamlined.

In October 1948 the Nuffield Organization and Austin announced that they had 'had a series of talks whereby there will be a constant interchange of information on production costs, purchases, design and research . . . which would be likely to result in manufacturing economies. The object is to effect maximum standardization.'[20] This dialogue followed preliminary discussions between the two firms as a result of the Ministry of Supply urging the motor industry to establish a Standardization Committee. The Committee met for the first time at Longbridge in November 1948, and initially looked at ways of reducing the considerable variety of electrical components then available.

The talks between Austin and Nuffield continued into 1949, but what the official announcement did not say was that Lord Nuffield and Leonard Lord were still barely on speaking terms as a result of their 1936 rift. In July 1949 the two firms issued a statement which revealed that, although they would continue with the standardization of components, 'the exchange of confidential information has now ceased'.[21] For the time being, any thoughts of a merger had evaporated.

One beneficial effect of the managerial upheavals at Cowley was that Reginald Hanks accelerated development of a car originally coded as the Mosquito but which we now know as the Morris Minor. This made its debut at the 1948 Motor Show and went on to be the first British car to sell, by 1961, 1 million examples. Yet if it had been left to Lord Nuffield, it is unlikely that the Minor would have ever entered production.

The Mosquito was the brainchild of a 'shy, reserved young man named Alec Issigonis'.[22] Alexander Arnold Constantine Issigonis was born in Smyrna, Turkey, in 1906. Constantine, his father, was a naturalized British subject of Greek descent, who had married Hulda, the daughter of a wealthy Bavarian brewer with premises in Smyrna. Issigonis Senior, along with his brother, ran a marine engineering business in Smyrna and young Alec soon developed a passion for anything mechanical, though he never went to school and was instead taught at home by a succession of tutors. The outbreak of the First World War produced problems for the family which were compounded by Issigonis Senior refusing to undertake repairs on German naval vessels for Turkey's German allies and the upheavals that followed the ending of the war culminated in the British community, including as it did the Issigonis family, being evacuated by the Royal Navy in 1922. Tragically, Alec's father died in Malta and he and his mother arrived in Britain almost penniless.

Young Issigonis had already displayed his prowess at freehand drawing, and although his mother wanted to send him to art school, her son had decided that he wanted to pursue an engineering career. He therefore completed a three-year mechanical engineering course at Battersea Polytechnic, and in 1928 obtained a job as a draughtsman-cum-salesman with Edward Gillett, who was developing a type of semi-automatic transmission in London's Victoria Street. Its refinement and demonstration involved Issigonis in travelling to the industrial Midlands, though the adoption by Vauxhall of synchromesh in 1932 rendered the idea obsolete, so when he was offered a job as a junior draughtsman in the Humber drawing office Alec accepted. There he worked on the Even Keel independent front suspension which appeared in 1936. He was in Coventry for only about two years when Robert Boyle, chief engineer of Morris Motors, offered him a job with Morris at Cowley. There he designed an independent front suspension and rack and pinion steering system for the Series M Morris Eight, though it eventually appeared on the 1947 MG Y Type saloon.

Issigonis had made suspension very much his forte and in experiments he undertook at this time, 'I found that cars ran much straighter and were more directionally stable if I put a couple of sandbags on the front bumper.'[23] He kept this in mind when he began work on his war-time small-car project 'in which the engine was outrageously far forward' ahead of the front wheels.

When war broke out in 1939, Issigonis was able to pursue his idea with the official encouragement of Miles Thomas who gave the project its Mosquito code name. Issigonis was also fortunate to have the blessing of Vic Oak, who had replaced Boyle as chief engineer in 1938. The entire team consisted of Issigonis and two draughtsman, Jack Daniels and Reg Job, who interpreted his freehand drawings. By 1942 Issigonis had completed a scale model which bore a striking similarity to the finished product. He was responsible for the entire car, 'even the little knob that opens the glove box, and the door handles',[24] and has readily acknowledged that he was passing through his 'American phase' at the time, so the front wing line incorporated in the door pressing, along with the distinctive concealed sills, reflect the 1941 Packard Clipper. This influence, however, does nothing to detract from the car's pleasing and highly individual profile. The Mosquito's 14-inch wheels were unique for their day; at this time 17-inch ones were the norm.

The strong unitary construction hull featured torsion bar independent front suspension and rack and pinion steering, and although Issigonis and Daniels designed an 1100cc water-cooled flat-four side-valve engine, which was built by Morris Engines at Coventry, it was never fitted to a production car.

A prototype Minor was running in 1947, which was when Lord Nuffield saw the car for the first time, and although he was not present Issigonis soon heard about the chairman's reaction. 'He was furious. He called it a poached egg, and everything under the sun, and walked out. I wasn't there at the meeting, in fact I only met him twice in my life. The second time was eleven years later, when we'd made a million Morris Minors. Then he had the grace to thank me.'[25]

Despite Nuffield's antipathy – he was particularly irked by the fact that the car did not have a traditional radiator – Hanks pressed ahead and the Minor, and its scaled-up Oxford and Six stable mates, made their debut at the 1948 Motor Show. But this was not before Issigonis had deemed that the Minor be widened, purely for aesthetic reasons, by 4 inches. This, however, was after the body tooling had been completed and a ridge in the bonnet and the front bumper, which contained a necessary distance piece, were the only giveaways. In the interests of time and money, the flat-four engine was dropped and replaced by the 918cc side-valve four-cylinder unit from the Morris Series E.

Morris Motors unquestionably had the finest small car in the world with the Minor for, apart from its visual appeal, it was one of the first vehicles in its class to handle well, a combination of Issigonis's deliberately locating the engine as far forward as possible and by making the front suspension 'softer' than the rear. Yet there is little evidence to suggest that the Nuffield Organization appreciated the quality of their talented designer's work, and although the car proved popular on the home market, the export one was never fully exploited.

Another factor was that, with the 1952 creation of the British Motor Corporation, Austin rather than Morris engineering policy dominated corporate thought, and it was for this reason that Issigonis took Reginald Hanks's advice and left Cowley – he had in any case 'always hated mergers'.[26] He did not remain unemployed for long as Donald Healey told him that Alvis was thinking of building a V8-engined model. Issigonis applied for this assignment and was soon established in Coventry.

The British Motor Corporation was nearly born in 1950 when, on 10 October, Leonard Lord, in an attempt to break the stalemate, telephoned Lord Nuffield to wish him a happy seventieth birthday. With Nuffield's secretary, Carl Kingerlee, acting as an intermediary, Lord and Nuffield subsequently met, though the Morris board, led by Hanks, turned the merger idea down. Lord responded by informing Kingerlee that Austin had decided to proceed with the A30, a Minor competitor, entailing a duplication of resources which in many ways encapsulated the need for a merger. A year later, however, it was Nuffield who made the running, approaching Lord without the knowledge of his board, and a deal was struck.

News of the liaison became public in November 1951 and the British Motor Corporation came into being in February 1952. On the face of it BMC was a straight merger between the Austin and Morris firms with a management team drawn evenly from the two companies: Nuffield was chairman, Lord deputy chairman and managing director, with Reginald Hanks from Morris and George Harriman, Austin's deputy managing director, as directors. The reality, however, was quite different. Nuffield remained as chairman only until December when he retired and took the honorary position of president. He thereafter played no part in corporate affairs and, when he died in 1963, he was better remembered for his £30 million benefactions than as Britain's leading car maker. Today William Morris is barely known outside enthusiast circles. It is the reputation of his artist/craftsman namesake, a fierce critic of mass production, which survives. Leonard Lord then became chairman and managing director and Harriman his deputy. It was an effective takeover of Morris by Austin with the corporate headquarters firmly established at Longbridge. A triumphant Lord was particularly hostile to those Morris directors who had opposed the merger and 'did a great deal to humiliate Hanks in particular and freely criticised Morris Motors and all its works on public occasions'.[27]

Not that Lord restricted his venom to Morris employees. A rising talent at Longbridge was Joe Edwards, who had joined Austin in 1928 and worked his way up to works director in 1954 and BMC's director of manufacturing in the following year. One day in 1956, when he and Lord were having a pre-lunch drink, Lord asked Edwards to take over corporate labour relations. 'Edwards was not enthusiastic: "Count me out on that one, Len," he said. "Well," replied Lord, "if you don't like it you can push off." '[28] Lord subsequently accused Edwards of wanting to take his own job and Harriman was soon instructed to 'pay him off and get him off the grounds today'.[29] BMC thus lost one of its best executives who received fourteen job offers within ten days of his departure and became managing director of Pressed Steel, just across the road from BMC at Cowley. Edwards had some cause subsequently to maintain that Lord had 'set back the full integration of the two companies by a decade'.

When the British Motor Corporation was founded in 1952, it was by far and away the country's largest car maker and the 235,777 cars it manufactured in its first year represented 39 per cent of British car production. Yet six years previously, in 1946, the combined output of the Austin and Nuffield companies accounted for 46 per cent of output, most of the erosion in its market coming from Ford, whose share rose from 14 to 21 per cent over the same period. Thus BMC represented a combination to counter the effects of the American-owned Ford and Vauxhall companies; a record 85,219 cars had been produced at Luton in 1951. By 1960, however, although BMC's output passed the half-million mark for the first time with 585,096 cars built, its share of overall production had dropped to 36 per cent and Ford was catching up fast with 30 per cent.

The fusion of the two companies gave BMC five marque names: Austin, MG, Morris, Riley and Wolseley. It was joined by a sixth, Austin Healey, in 1953, which became the corporate sports car, even though BMC already had MG. Donald Mitchell Healey, a motoring enthusiast from his schooldays, had won the Monte Carlo Rally in a 4.5-litre Invicta in 1931. In 1933 he moved from his native Cornwall to Coventry and Riley, but switched the same year to Triumph. After that company was liquidated in 1939, Healey made an unsuccessful attempt to buy it from Thomas Ward, the Sheffield-based steel company, which owned it. (Sir John Black eventually became Triumph's new owner.) Healey and his associates initially had in mind a car in the Rover or Sunbeam-Talbot tradition but, after losing Triumph, Healey turned his thoughts to a 100mph sports car in the spirit of the Invicta which had given him his Monte Carlo success.

In 1945, on a capital of around £20,000 supplied by Donald and his father, the Donald Healey Motor Company was established in a former concrete-mixer factory at The Cape, Warwick. The Riley-engined Healey appeared in 1946, though it was expensive and Healey was hit by the double purchase tax payable on cars which cost over £1,000. These were difficult years for the specialist producer and by 1951 Healey recognized that he would have to alter his model strategy if he wanted to remain in business. 'I realized that we required a faster, lighter, cheaper car. Money was always tight and I could see us folding up if we didn't produce a new model.'[30]

The outcome was the Healey 100, which appeared at the 1952 Motor Show, powered by the 1.6-litre four-cylinder engine previously used in Austin's ill-fated Atlantic. One visitor enormously impressed by car was Leonard Lord of BMC who 'immediately suggested that we go to his hotel and talk about the car'.[31] When he had conceived it, Healey had envisaged the new model being built at the rate of about twenty cars a week. But Lord proposed that BMC rename it the *Austin* Healey, mass produce it, reduce its price by £100 and sell it on the American market. Healey still retains a great regard for Leonard Lord: 'He was a motor industry man to his finger tips. . . . He had a great sense of humour. Whenever I used to go to Longbridge he used to say, "Here comes Healey – better sew up your pockets!" '[32]

The four-cylinder Austin Healey lasted until 1956, by which time 14,662 had been built. It was replaced by the six-cylinder 100/6 powered by the Corporation's 2.6-litre C Series engine, though Healey always preferred the four-cylinder model, the heavier six being 'much more of a BMC creation'.[33] Enlarged to 3 litres in 1959, it was renamed the 3000 and remained in production until 1967.

In 1956 Lord proposed to Healey that the firm produce a cheap sports car powered by BMC's A Series engine, and Healey's son Geoffrey came up with the Sprite of 1958 with its cheeky 'frogeye' headlamps. 'It was that feature that gave the car all its personality,'[34] says Healey, but the feature was not perpetuated for the 1961 Mark II version. A badge engineered MG Midget version appeared simultaneously.

From 1957, Austin Healeys were produced at the MG factory at Abingdon and the demands of the American market were reflected in the fact that a massive 88.8 per cent of the cars built from then until the Big Healey ceased production in 1967 were exported to America. Only 5.9

were retained for the home market and the remaining 5.3 were allotted to the rest of the world.

MG itself had to continue building its archaic T Series cars until 1955 when it was able to introduce its BMC B Series-engined MGA, which had been waiting in the wings since 1952. It was to prove the most popular sports car in the world of its day with over 100,000 built, and was to pave the way for the even more successful MGB in 1962.

When BMC was created in 1952, Lord made no attempt to rationalize the corporate marques' names and, instead of reducing them to a tidier Austin and Morris duo, it was decided to retain all these makes. The Nuffield and Austin outlets therefore continued as before, united only by the display of the BMC corporate rosette. It was hoped that customer marque loyalty could be maintained in an increasingly competitive decade.

At the time of the merger, BMC was manufacturing no fewer than fourteen models – nine Nuffield and five Austin – and a total of nine different engines. In this area Lord did immediately initiate a three-year rationalization plan. All the Morris power units were phased out and replaced by existing Austin engines. The small pushrod four, which powered the A30 in 1951, became the BMC A Series unit and its descendants remain in production at the time of writing (1987). The 1.2-litre four, introduced in the 1947 A40, was enlarged and improved to become the B Series unit, while Morris Engines at Coventry was responsible for designing a new six-cylinder C Series unit of 2.6 litres in 1954. Gearboxes and rear axles received similar treatment.

Lord then turned his attention to rationalizing bodywork, which represents the most expensive part of a car. In 1955 the French Peugeot company had commissioned the Italian Turin-based Pinin Farina company to style its 403 family saloon, which was destined to sell 1.1 million examples during the following eleven years. BMC followed suit. The A30 had become the A35 in 1956 and Farina was commissioned to design its A40 successor which would be the first corporate car since the merger.

Farina worked rapidly: a studio study had been completed by October 1956 and the new A40 was announced in September 1958. At this time practically all cars conformed to the 'three box' look. What Farina did was combine the looks of the increasingly popular estate car on a short wheelbase, thus dramatically anticipating the current 'two box' look with increased carrying capacity achieved by folding down the rear seats. *Design* magazine was delighted: 'it is certainly the first BMC product which has undeniable "style",' it opined. The A35's engine and running gear were carried over. In 1962 came an improved version with a more powerful engine and increased space for rear passengers, while the Countryman model featured an opening tailgate in the manner of the modern hatchback.

The A40 only appeared as an Austin, but in December 1958 came the Wolseley 6/99 which embodied the second phase of Lord's rationalization plan. This was another Pinin Farina design, though visually it was far less successful than the pioneering A40 and the four-door saloon turned the scales at a substantial 1.2 tons. It also featured then-fashionable tailfins, which soon imbued it with a rather dated appearance. This hull was to carry all the BMC marque names, with minor variations in interior and exterior trim, and the B and C Series engines. The era of 'badge engineering' had arrived.

In 1958 BMC built 447,717 cars, its then highest figure, and achieved record profits of £21 million. Yet labour disputes were becoming increasingly common. 'There can be few industrial organizations which have more labour troubles than BMC,' noted *The Economist* in 1959, and pointed out that the Corporation was 'short of good personnel men to whom the top management could leave the handling of negotiations'[35] to counter the growing power of the shop stewards. Not one of BMC's factories had been closed since the merger. Also, although profits were the largest ever, Ford's, for five years out of seven, were greater at £24.7 million.

Ford, like the Nuffield Organization, had grown during the Second World War, but it closed most of the satellite plants it had managed during hostilities. The firm had built a works at Urmston, Manchester, which produced the Rolls-Royce Merlin engine under licence between 1941 and 1945, and this was shut along with plants at Wigan and Cramlington. However, Lord Perry, as he had become in 1938, retained a foundry opened at Leamington which had produced tracks for Bren gun carriers. During the conflict no less than three of the firm's top managers, Rowland Smith, Stanford Cooper and Patrick Hennessy, had been knighted for services to the war effort. It was an impressive endorsement of Perry's managerial team. Perry himself would step down from the Ford chairmanship in 1948, having reached the age of seventy and although he was replaced by Lord Airedale, 'the Americans looked particularly to Sir Patrick Hennessy . . . whose energy and resourcefulness matched even Perry's'.[36] He became managing director in 1948 and also assumed the Ford chairmanship in 1956, a position he held until 1968.

Patrick Hennessy (1898–1981) had worked for Ford since 1920. Born in Middleton, County Cork, Ireland, he had run away from home as a youngster to join the British army, finally being commissioned in the Royal Inniskilling Fusiliers. Ford had opened its factory in Cork in 1919 and Hennessy later quipped that he had joined the company because he was keen on sport and wanted to work in a factory to build himself up for confrontation on the rugger field! He soon made his mark and was made service manager. When in 1925 H. S. Jenkins, manager of Ford's Trafford

Park factory, visited Cork, he reported that Hennessy was 'a promising young man . . . very well informed . . . of good personality and one that I would say would have good prospects with the Company'.[37] In 1929 Ford's squad of 'yougos', Brubaker, Hoffman and Harrington, arrived in Cork to discharge 145 men, which is how they acquired their nickname. Their task accomplished, they cabled America: 'Hennesy [sic] service manager appears most likely candidate for development should visit Detroit January first.'[38] Patrick Hennessy was on his way.

In 1931 Hennessy moved to Dagenham where he soon showed his mettle as purchasing manager. In passing, it is worth recording that no fewer than three post-war Ford chairmen held this demanding office: Hennessy himself, his predecessor Sir Rowland Smith (1950–6) and Sir Leonard Crossland who succeeded him in 1968.

Like Percival Perry, Hennessy established a good rapport with the Fords, father and son, and his Irish brogue may have reminded Henry of his own Irish origins. Following his success as purchasing manager, the arrival of the £100 Model Y and his spirited sale of unwanted pig iron, in 1939 Hennessy was made general manager at Dagenham. In the dark days of 1940 the redoubtable Lord Beaverbrook was appointed Minister of Aircraft Production and was looking for industrialists to work alongside him in setting up his new ministry. Arthur Greenwood, a Labour minister without portfolio in Churchill's war-time cabinet, suggested Hennessy to deal with materials. The Irishman was initially reluctant, as the Ford management had already been depleted by Rowland Smith's departure to run the Manchester aero-engine factory, but Perry was insistent and Hennessy accepted the post. He soon emerged as Beaverbrook's 'right hand', although he later recalled that the two used to 'fight like tigers'.[39] In 1941 Hennessy was knighted for his services to the war effort.

With the ending of the war in 1945, Sir Patrick was once more in corporate harness. Across the Atlantic, Ford was an ailing giant haemorrhaging $10 million a month. Edsel Ford had died in 1943 and eighty-year-old Henry took over the company presidency, remaining in office until his grandson Henry Ford II, aged only twenty-eight, took over the corporate reins in September 1945. Aided by Ernest Breech, recruited from General Motors in 1946, and the top management 'whizz kids', Ford introduced a sweeping range of much needed corporate reforms. One of the first of these, which was a policy of graduate recruitment, reached Britain in 1948. As will have already been apparent, this was a revolutionary feature for its day.

In 1950, when Ford's policy was merely two years old, it attracted the attention of twenty-seven-year-old Terence (Terry) Norman Beckett. After education at Wolverhampton Municipal Secondary School, Beckett decided that he wanted to be an economist, but this ambition was thwarted by the outbreak of the war. Instead he took an engineering course at the Wolverhampton and South Stafford Technical College. After the war and national service, he then pursued his original career objective and entered the London School of Economics, leaving in 1950 with a BSc (Econ.) degree. But when he looked around for a job in engineering he found himself, if anything, overqualified, as he was both an engineer *and* an economist. He recalled: 'I started going through the companies who were offering management training schemes where I could use my qualifications and there weren't many. When I'm asked, "Why did you join Ford?" I'm a bit like the girl who married a chap and, when people wondered why, she responded, "Well, nobody else asked me . . ." But having joined, I've never regretted it.'[40]

On arrival at Dagenham, Beckett began an eighteenth-month management training scheme, 'which, thank heavens, was cut short to just over twelve months'[41] for, in 1951, he became Sir Patrick Hennessy's personal assistant. For the next three years Beckett kept an eye on the product and engineering side of the Ford business for Hennessy, and in 1954 was made Ford's styling manager. But the 'really big leg up' came in 1955 when Terry Beckett was put in charge of the company's new product planning department. 'It was a very big move. I was a divisional manager at thirty-two and many of my staff were twenty to twenty-five years older.'[42]

Beckett's task was a formidable one. In 1953, in the face of considerable opposition from his engineering staff, Hennessy had introduced product planning to Dagenham, and Ford was alone within the British motor industry in applying the concept. Product planning, an American creation, had been introduced by the parent Ford company as one of its much needed management reforms. It was born of a recognition that a chief executive, by a combination of hunch and whim, could no longer be responsible for the creation of one or two models but, in the more complex post-war world, as many as six. This became all the more important as development and production costs soared. As Beckett later put it, 'We cannot afford to make mistakes.'[43]

When Ford introduced product planning in 1953, its first manager was Martin Tustin who had joined Ford in 1933 and had previously been head of the firm's parts division. Tustin remained until the end of 1954 when he left to join Standard and Beckett took over from him. On arrival, he established three departments, concerned respectively with small, medium and large cars, though the reality was that product planning would not begin to make a real impact at Dagenham until the following decade and the arrival, in 1962, of the Ford Cortina.

Yet another pointer to the future came in 1955 when John Barber joined Ford from the Ministry of Supply, where he had been Principal of the Central Finance Department. He remembered:

When I joined Ford it was a fairly old-fashioned company and the finance department was full of little men in green eyeshades. At the time we virtually had no graduates. There were about five or six in the company: Terry Beckett was one. I decided that we needed to move from having little more than a recording function to making a positive contribution to running the company. I set up the analytical functions in Ford and we hired a lot of high-calibre people. One year I think we recruited about 100. Then people began to perceive that the financial function was beginning to become dominant, we got better people, and then others starting hiring graduates. Then we set up a formal graduate training scheme. They were young financial analysts in their late twenties who formed the new philosophy in Ford.[44]

In 1962 John Barber was made Ford's finance director, though he left in 1965 to join the AEI electrical company in a similar capacity.

The creation, in particular, of a product planning department at Dagenham was a recognition by the parent company of the British firm's need to manage its own affairs. For, following a visit by Henry Ford II in 1948, the appointment of a chief engineer and body and styling engineers was sanctioned. It also marked the end of the once much vaunted 1928 Plan as Dagenham's control over Ford's other European companies ceased at this time. British Ford was also now free to export its products the world over, even to America. By 1957 Ford was the British motor industry's leading exporter to the United States.

Ford's British production facilities were also expanding. In 1947 Ford took over the Dagenham-based Kelsey-Hayes wheel company and, in 1948, it leased a former aircraft factory at Langley, Buckinghamshire, for commercial vehicle production. In 1951 Ford received funds, via America, from the sale of its holding company's investments in the European and Egyptian companies, which helped Hennessy to achieve his greatest prize with the purchase of Briggs Motor Bodies in 1953. What worried Hennessy was Briggs's parent company in Detroit and what would happen when Walter O. Briggs, its founder, died. He was convinced that Chrysler, its largest customer, would buy it 'and would then control our body supply'.[45] Between 1951 and 1953 he made numerous attempts to purchase Briggs's British operations, but the two were unable to agree a price. Then, early in 1953, the negotiations were successfully concluded, over the telephone, though in the face of a ban on the export of precious dollars. 'I got an option for some weeks,' said Hennessy, 'and undertook to supply dollars in the belief that there was some way of doing this despite the rigid government control at that time.'[46] Fortunately, with government approval, he got his dollars. Ford paid £3.2 million, or almost $9 million, for Briggs and this gave Hennessy not only the Dagenham plant but also the factories it had acquired at Romford, Doncaster and Southampton. Just as Hennessy had expected, Chrysler did indeed buy Briggs's American operations later in 1953 for $75 million. Not surprisingly, he 'later spoke of the purchase of as one of the most important events in Ford-England's post-war history'.[47] Quite incidentally, Hennessy's action reduced Ford-America's holding in its British company from 59 to 54 per cent.

With the Briggs purchase effected, Hennessy then set about in improving Dagenham's production facilities, aimed at increasing floor space by half as much again. Announced in 1954, this £75 million expansion plan culminated in the opening of a new paint, trim and assembly building in 1959. Finance came from internal funding as Ford retained far more of its earnings than its BMC rivals. In the nine years between 1947 and 1956 it kept 79 per cent of its profits, compared with the British company's 68 per cent.

These new facilities were the result of a rapidly growing demand for Ford models. In 1945 Dagenham had built only 2,324 cars; by 1958 the figure stood at a record 284,081. After the war Ford continued to produce its pre-war 8hp Anglia and closely related 10hp Prefect. This, along with the briefly revived V8, represented the Ford range until 1950, when a new family of post-war cars made its appearance. It is difficult to think of a greater contrast between the two generations of models. The Anglia and Prefect were spiritual heirs to the Model T Ford, with its transverse-leaf suspension, separate chassis, simple side-valve engines, 6-volt electrics and vacuum windscreen wipers of legendary inefficiency.

The four-cylinder 1.5-litre Consul and its 2.2-litre six-cylinder Zephyr stablemate were modern offerings, with new full-width body, unitary construction hulls and MacPherson strut independent front suspension, designed by Earle S. MacPherson, Ford-America's vice president of engineering. The engines were also new overhead-valve units and they reflected the repeal of the horsepower tax by their oversquare characteristics, in that the bore was greater than the stroke. There was maximum interchangeability between the two models: they shared, for instance, the same 79×76mm bore and stroke, to speed and cheapen the production process. Both cars proved strong sellers, though Mark II versions of the Consul and Zephyr, which appeared in 1956, were even more successful with respectively 350,000 and 221,000 built, compared with Mark I production of 231,481 and 152,677.

In 1953 the Consul/Zephyr theme was applied to the small-car range. The Anglia and Prefect names were transferred to this new 100E model and, with its updated 997cc side-valve engine, it lasted, with considerable success, until 1959. Not that the arrival of the 100E range spelt the end of the old pre-war-based cars. From 1953 the 10hp Prefect engine was fitted in the Anglia two-door body and the result was the Popular, which at an introductory price of £390 was the cheapest car on the British market and echoed both the name and appeal of its famous 1936 forebear. By the time that production ceased in 1959, 155,350 had been built.

If Ford represented a motor industry success story, in Coventry Standard saw a decline in its share of British car production from 11 per cent in 1946 to 8 per cent in 1960 while it also recorded the smallest profits in the industry over the same period. It was for this reason that, from 1954 onwards, Alick Dick, who took over the managerial reins, felt the need for Standard to merge with another company.

The firm had expanded rapidly during the war and, in 1940, John Black was appointed chairman of the Joint Aero Engine Committee, in charge of Shadow Factories (in 1943 he was knighted for this work). He was soon contemplating the post-war years and, in 1944, purchased the moribund Triumph company from the Thomas Ward Group which had owned it since 1939. However, H. Howe Graham, the receiver, first approached William Lyons to see whether he was interested in buying the firm. Lyons examined Triumph's accounts but 'realized that, without jeopardizing our resources, we would be unable to restore the company to a profit-earning basis and it would be better to concentrate on our own successful company'.[48]

Sir John then approached Lyons and told him that he was thinking of buying Triumph but, recalled Lyons, 'he would not do so if I would change my mind and join forces with him. I told him that I would not change my mind, whereupon he said that he would buy Triumph and go into competition with us.'[49]

This is precisely what happened. Black had made his first approaches in October 1944 and Standard formally took over Triumph in November. The price was £77,000 and Black sold off the Clay Lane factory, that had been bomb-damaged during the war, to the B. O. Morris Group in 1946. Triumph car production would thereafter be centred at the Standard factory at Canley, Coventry.

Despite his brave words, Sir John's attempt to establish a distinct persona for Triumph in the early post-war years was a failure. There was the curious 1800 Roadster of 1946, which was the last series-production

British car to be fitted with a dickey seat, and its razor-edge saloon stablemate, while the smaller Mayflower saloon of 1950 on similar lines made little impact on the American market for which it was intended. This contrasted sharply with the initial success of the Standard Vanguard which, from 1948 until 1953, was the sole representative of the marque. Of the Big Six car makers, only Standard responded to Sir Stafford Cripps's exhortations for a one-model policy with a car aimed foursquare at export markets.

What became the Vanguard was sanctioned in 1945, by which time the all-too-obvious trans-Atlantic lines had been set down by Walter Belgrove, Sir John's hard-working stylist. Inspired by the American Plymouth, 'the actual sketching was done from Belgrove's own car in London's Grosvenor Square, under the eyes of American embassy patrols'.[50] There would be no carry over from previous designs, so a new four-cylinder engine, inspired by the Traction Avant Citroen, was designed and accordingly fitted with wet cylinder liners for ease of production. Although the Vanguard was announced in mid-1947 in 1.8-litre guise, by the time that it appeared in 1948 the power unit had been enlarged to its familiar 2088cc. The choice of the Vanguard name reflected Sir John's interest in nautical matters – he was a member of the Royal Welsh Yacht Club – and one of the prototypes was accordingly photographed alongside HMS *Vanguard*, Britain's last and largest battleship. Although the prototypes had been tested over the demanding gradients and rough tracks of the Welsh mountains, once the cars were exported, shortcomings soon emerged. Just across the English Channel in Belguim the *pavé* wrought havoc with the car's suspension and 'the fractures in the chassis had to be seen to be believed';[51] and there were similar problems for African customers, who were used to the rugged durability of American cars. Despite these troubles, around 185,000 examples of this Phase 1 Vanguard were built in the car-hungry years of 1948 to 1952.

The model's rugged but economical four-cylinder engine was extended to the Triumph range in 1949 but, more significantly, it was also used in the highly successful Ferguson tractor, which Standard began building in 1946. Such was the demand for this lightweight machine, which cost only £343, that in the 1947/8 financial year, Standard built more tractors than cars: 47,209 compared with 37,023. Although these totals were subsequently reversed, tractor manufacture played a pivotal role in the firm's finances to the extent that Standard's survival for so long 'was due to the profits it earned from tractors'.[52]

Chance played a role in Sir John Black's obtaining this lucrative contract. When Harry Ferguson established himself in London's Claridge's Hotel in 1945, one of his associates, Trevor V. Knox, later to be his home sales manager, was staying at the Farmers' Club in Whitehall Court. There he met a director of the Distillers Company and this individual, who was a regular commuter, happened to mention to a fellow passenger that Ferguson was looking for a manufacturer to take on the production of his tractor. By coincidence, his travelling companion handled the Standard publicity account and so the news reached Sir John Black. On the face of it, these two tricky, erratic individuals seemed unlikely business companions and one of Black's first actions was to despatch Harry Webster, his engineering troubleshooter, on a fruitless trip to America to examine the patents of the Ferguson System to see if it could be pirated. When the negotiations got under way, Black used journalist Dudley Noble as his intermediary. Once at Claridge's, he conveyed Sir John's wishes to Ferguson: 'Harry would discuss these with Mrs F and eventually daughter would be told to get her typewriter out and put down on paper what the *Famille* Ferguson had in mind.'[53]

The deal had an enormous appeal to Black. Not only could the massive 1-million-square-foot Banner Lane former Shadow Factory be used for tractor production, but the vehicle could also be powered by a version of the Vanguard engine, then under development, so spreading manufacturing costs. The final agreement was set down on the back of a Claridge's menu which read: 'A marriage has been arranged this day between John and Harry, witnessed by Oliver and Henry.'[54] 'Oliver' was Lucas, of the electrical equipment giant, who had encouraged Black to take the job, while 'Henry' was Henry Tiarks, Schroeder merchant bank's representative on the Lucas board. Sir John duly reported this 'gentleman's agreement' to the Standard board on 28 August 1945.

There were the inevitable upheavals before the first tractor left Banner Lane in July 1946. Earlier that year Black threatened to withdraw from the entire scheme though, in 1947, he was talking of stopping car manufacture altogether to concentrate on tractor production! A problem then arose about the tractor's engine. The Vanguard's power unit did not go into full production until 1948, so Continental engines had to be imported from America. Government approval was therefore required to spend precious dollars for these and associated trans-Atlantic machine tools. Luckily Chancellor of the Exchequer Hugh Dalton and President of the Board of Trade Sir Stafford Cripps 'proved particularly helpful'[55] in this respect.

The wet liner engine had yet another application which did much to establish the credibility of the Triumph marque. The success of the MG TD and the Jaguar XK120 convinced Sir John of the need to produce a sports car to slot in between them and compete in the growing American market. He first attempted to take over the Morgan company, for which Standard had supplied engines since 1939. The offer was rebuffed, so Black went in house for his sports car and the outcome was an open two-seater, retrospectively titled TR1 ('TR' for Triumph Roadster), which appeared at the 1952 Motor Show. It was only after chief tester Ken Richardson and Harry Webster ironed out many of its shortcomings that the TR2, the progenitor of a long and distinguished line, appeared in 1953. In 1954 an example won the RAC International Rally, which was the first of many competition successes.

By this time Standard had a new managing director in the shape of thirty-seven-year-old Alick Dick, who was distantly related to Black by marriage (his uncle had married yet another of the Misses Hillman) and was Sir John's personal assistant for eight years. In November 1953 Black was involved in an accident while travelling as a passenger in the prototype TR-engined Swallow Doretti, which collided with a pick-up truck outside the Banner Lane works. Within a week he announced that he had 'been given a clean bill of health by the hospital authorities',[56] yet when he returned to Canley it was obvious that he had not fully recovered from the incident.

The firm's Christmas party was an occasion for Sir John to vent his black humour because invariably he would remark that there were too many managers present. 'The next day he named those who he thought should get the sack.'[57] Amongst those whom he decided to dismiss was Edward (Ted) Grinham, Standard's engineering director who had joined the firm in 1930. During the 1950s 'his ambitions were aimed directly at Sir John Black's chair'.[58]

For the majority of the Standard board, this was the last straw, particularly as, on 16 December, Black had taken over the company's chairmanship from seventy-nine-year-old solicitor Charles Band, who had held the post since 1934. This gave Sir John supreme control at Canley. On New Year's Day 1954 most of the Standard board met at Alick Dick's house at Hill Wootton, near Kenilworth. 'Black, they decided, must be ousted . . . Dick's wife typed out the letter which Black was asked to sign and the directors (only one member of the board was absent) then drove the four miles to Black's home at Bubbenhall.' There they were ushered into the drawing room. '"Sir John," said the butler, "the Board of the Standard-Triumph." '[59]

Black asked why they were there and they told him they had come for his resignation. ' "Why?" asked Black. "If you think, Sir John," replied Dick, "you'll know why." ' Black subsequently signed the prepared letter, dated 4 January 1954, which stated: 'As a result of consultations with my doctor today, I am not considered fit enough to return to the enormous responsibilities of managing director of our very important company and I am recommended to go away for an extended period to overcome the effects of a very serious accident which I recently received.'[60] So, after twenty-nine years as Standard's managing director, Black was out at the age of fifty-eight. He received £30,000, a Bentley and Triumph Mayflower and the use of the company bungalow in Wales for five years at £50 a year. He died in 1965.

Alick Dick took over as managing director, at thirty-seven the youngest in the industry, with Ted Grinham as his deputy, until he retired in 1956. Charles Band briefly returned to the Standard chairmanship, though in June 1954 his place was taken by a Marshal of the Royal Air Force, Lord Tedder.

With Black's departure, Alick Dick got down to the business of trying to find a suitable partner for Standard. He was soon contacted by Rover's Spencer Wilks, to whom he was related, and talks began in earnest in February. The two firms got as far as discussing United Motors Corporation or Consolidated Motors as names for a possible holding company but then problems arose, just one of which was Rover's concern about Standard's profits forecast. By July the talks had been called off. In the spring of 1955 discussions began with the Rootes Group and these dragged on for about eighteen months before, in April 1957, Dick reported their failure. The stumbling block was that the resulting company would have contained a heavily Rootes-orientated board of directors. So that was the end of R and S Holdings.

In the meantime, a dialogue had been established between Standard and Massey-Ferguson. This was the firm that had resulted from the merger of Harry Ferguson Ltd with the Canadian Massey-Harris company in September 1953. In October Sir John Black had signed a new twelve-year agreement with the new company which guaranteed tractor production until 1965. Dick began talks with them late in 1956 and, after the breakdown of the Rootes discussions, negotiations began in earnest. Massey-Ferguson had meanwhile been quietly buying Standard shares and owned under 20 per cent of its equity. Then, in 1957, tractors had a bad year and Massey's profits suffered accordingly. The outcome was that Massey offered to buy the tractor business outright. Standard accepted, the deal was completed in August 1959, and it received £12 million. Much of this would have been used in creating Allied Motors with Rover which had again appeared on the scene but, once again, negotiations foundered.

While these time-consuming merger talks were under way, Dick had another pressing problem: how to contend with the British Motor Corporation's purchase, in August 1953, of Fisher and Ludlow which produced Standard's bodies from a plant in Tile Hill, Coventry, near the Canley works. Although Fisher and Ludlow had guaranteed existing contracts, BMC's Leonard Lord told Dick, in no uncertain terms, to 'push off'. Luckily for Standard, in September 1953 the Vanguard was joined by a new model, the utilitarian Eight, intended as a competitor for BMC's Austin A30 and Morris Minor. It was the firm's first unitary construction model and boasted a new overhead-valve engine which shared its 803cc and 58 × 76mm bore and stroke with the BMC A Series engine! Fisher and Ludlow would build its body until it ceased production. But what of its successor? Pressed Steel, the only independent bodybuilder in the country, was fully occupied. In 1954 Standard therefore strengthened its links with Mulliners Ltd of Birmingham and obtained exclusive rights for its entire body output.

This was the problem that faced Harry Webster, who in 1955 had become Standard's chief engineer: 'We had to devise a car which was designed in such a way that its body components could be produced in various locations and then come together like parts of a jigsaw.'[61] In April 1956 the Triumph board agreed to proceed with the Eight's replacement, for a projected 1958 launch. The new car was coded Zobo, 'a Tibetan pack animal of indeterminate sex, a cross between a bull and a cow'.[62] In view of its unusual body construction – instead of having a unitary hull, it had a backbone chassis – the Standard team decided right from the start of the project that the car should have all-independent suspension, which was a revolutionary feature for a cheap car. Then there was the steering gear. A rack and pinion layout was chosen, then 'one night about five of us went up to Alick Dick's house to have a brainstorming session. It was then that Martin Tustin, our general manager, said, "Wouldn't it be marvellous if it would turn like a London taxi?" '[63] From thereon a 25-foot turning circle became one of Zobo's inviolate specifications.

In 1955 the Eight was joined by a Ten stablemate and its 948cc engine was to be used for the new car. Webster was the first to recognize that the heavier Zobo really required a larger-capacity engine. The limitation was Standard's boring and honing equipment. One day Webster found a way round the problem and he realized that it would be possible to increase the engine's capacity to 1300 cc. 'Alick Dick decided to go halfway, to 1147cc, though the car was initially 948cc, and keep 1300cc up our sleeves.'[64]

With Zobo's unconventional mechanics virtually resolved, it was essential that the body lines were equally distinctive. Here Standard had a problem because, in 1955, Walter Belgrove, who had styled most of Standard's projects for close on thirty years, slammed out of Canley in the wake of a long-standing feud with technical director Ted Grinham. Following his departure, the Banner Lane styling studio struggled to come up with an acceptable body but the results, to say the least, fell far short of expectations.

Then, in the spring of 1957, Webster received a visitor named Captain Raymond Flower, who wanted to buy some Standard Eight chassis running gear for the Frisky micro car he was designing for Henry Meadows Ltd. He did not yet know what the car would look like but assured Webster that he could get a prototype body produced within three months. He would not reveal where. Intrigued, Harry later chose a design from a selection of sketches, provided Flower with a TR3 chassis and, three months later, a sensational rebodied car was returned to Canley. It had cost the firm only £3,000. Only just before they received it did Standard discover that the work had been undertaken by Vignale in Turin to the designs of a young Italian stylist named Giovanni Michelotti.

Standard immediately placed him on a £3,000 a year retainer and the first fruit of the liaison was the Vignale Vanguard of 1959, created to arrest the pioneering model's fast-fading fortunes. In September 1957 Michelotti was commissioned to style the Zobo range of coupé, saloon, estate car and convertible, and the first of these, a black and metallic silver coupé, arrived at Canley three months later just before the works was shutting for Christmas. 'We got it into the styling studio and put it on the turntable. Then Alick Dick and the rest of the board turned up. Everyone thought it was superb. Afterwards we all went down to the canteen and got gloriously drunk!'[65] remembers Webster.

With Zobo's styling at last resolved, Dick had now to consolidate his body supplies. In 1958 Standard purchased Mulliners Ltd, which was to be responsible for the bulk of the car's body pressings; it had already absorbed the Forward Radiator company in the preceding year. In 1959 Standard paid £2 million for another pressings supplier, Hall Engineering of Liverpool, which also owned the Auto Body Dies tooling concern. The same year Alford and Alder, which produced front suspension and steering gear, joined the growing Standard group. The remainder of Zobo's body sections came from Sankey at Wellingborough and Pressed Steel's Swindon factory. The resulting bodies would be painted and trimmed at the former Fisher and Ludlow plant at Tile Hill, which Standard bought from BMC. Most of these purchases were paid for with the money the firm received from Massey-Ferguson and were aimed at pushing Standard's capacity up to 200,000 vehicles a year.

What the new car now wanted was a name. In June 1958 the Standard board decided on Triumph Torch but, fortunately, soon afterwards Alick Dick announced: 'I've been on my boat over the weekend. It's called the *Herald*. We'll call the new car that.'[66]

Standard's pre-tax profits for 1957/8 were the second highest ever at £2.3 million. Disposing of the profitable tractor enterprise meant that everything would depend on the success of the Herald which, significantly, would be marketed not as a Standard but under the Triumph name.

Standard output did not break the 100,000 barrier until 1959 and although Rootes, its Coventry neighbour, attained this figure in 1955, it was 'quite apparent that both firms failed to obtain anything like the economies of scale necessary for efficient production'.[67] This was the problem which faced Sir William Rootes, as he had become in 1942. During 1940/1 Coventry suffered forty air raids of which the worst came on the night of 14/15 November 1940 when two thirds of the medieval city was destroyed. Billy Rootes played a leading role in the city's rebirth by his chairmanship of the Coventry Industrial Reconstruction and Co-ordinating Committee though, ironically, it was the results of the conflict that permitted Rootes to expand its production facilities by taking over its former Shadow Factory at Ryton-on-Dunsmore when the war ended. The Group moved swiftly to rationalize production and, in May 1946, the last car left the old Talbot works in London's Barlby Road and Rootes Acceptances, the group's distributing division, was transferred there.

Sir William had been a long-standing critic of the horsepower tax and, with its repeal at the end of 1946, Rootes once again looked to foreign sales to boost output and so spread manufacturing costs. The Group led the British motor industry with the establishment of an Australian plant in 1946, while Rootes Motors Inc. and Rootes Motor (Canada) Ltd followed in 1947. Sir William was the instigator of the first British Car Exhibition to be held in New York in 1950 and, in the following year, he became chairman of the new Dollar Export Board which was intended to encourage manufacturers to look to world rather than home markets.

The pre-war policy of acquisition was perpetuated in 1950 when Rootes acquired Tillings-Stevens, commercial vehicle makers since 1911, which in 1938 had absorbed the Vulcan concern. Both names lasted until 1953, by which time the Maidstone plant was concentrating on the production of a new three-cylinder two-stroke diesel commercial vehicle engine. Commer and Karrier output was stepped up and transferred to a new Dunstable factory in 1954.

In 1955 the Rootes Group purchased the ailing Singer concern for which it paid £235,000. Singer's decline had been rapid in the decade that followed the end of the war. Lord Latham, as the firm's pre-war chairman became in 1940, was made head of London Transport and A. E. Hunt took over his post. The range consisted of the pre-war Nine, Ten and Twelve. These were replaced in 1948 by the pricey and uninspiring SM1500 and, although an improved Hunter derivative appeared in 1954, the reality was that once the post-war demand for cars had evaporated, Singer was in trouble. In April 1954 Maurice Curtis was made director and general manager, but the appointment did little to arrest Singer's slide and by August 1955 production had fallen to forty cars a week. From September talks began with Rootes, which prompted Curtis's resignation, but the deal went through in December against the background of a £140,177 loss in 1954/5.[68]

Sir William made much of his Singer apprenticeship and became chairman while Hunt was briefly his deputy. Hunter production lasted until 1956, though the Ryton-built Gazelle, and up-market version of the Hillman Minx, which retained the distinctive Singer overhead-camshaft engine, replaced it and lasted until 1958; thereafter a Rootes pushrod four was fitted. Car production had ceased at Birmingham in 1956 when the never-satisfactory six-storey premises became the Rootes parts depot.

As in pre-war days, Hillman remained the group's mainstay with just one model, the Minx, on offer. The unitary construction Mark I was effectively the 1940 model year car, though independent front suspension did not arrive until 1949 and it was not until 1954 that the long-running side-valve engine, which dated back to 1932, was replaced by a new 1.3-litre overhead-valve unit. The Group was, in the meantime, moving towards a corporate body shell, which arrived in May 1956, and shared commonized components with the in-house Sunbeam Rapier, introduced the previous year. The Minx was aimed at the middle-class motorist who wanted a comfortable, well-equipped car, would not yet contemplate buying a Ford and wished for something better than his next-door neighbour's Austin A40. This Minx shape endured until 1967, by which time its engine had been enlarged to 1.7 litres, but what had been acceptable enough in 1956 was, eleven years later, a dated, heavy car which had been largely overtaken by the opposition.

Rootes was to perpetuate the Sunbeam-Talbot sporting theme into the post-war years with the arrival of the stylish 80 and 90 saloons in 1948. The underpowered 80 was discontinued in 1950 though a Mark II version of the 90 arrived in 1951 and in the following year Rootes was to benefit from the model's success in the Alpine Trial when the team was awarded three Coupes des Alps and the Manufacturer's team prize. This inspired the Sunbeam Alpine two-seater of 1953, in which the Talbot suffix was discontinued, and the Sunbeam name was perpetuated on the Mark III saloon of 1954 which lasted until 1956. By this time it had been replaced by the Sunbeam Rapier, the best-selling Sunbeam ever, with 68,809 built. The Series II version of 1958 was distinguished by well-proportioned fins but, like the Minx, the Rapier also had to soldier on until 1967.

The Humber range fared less well during the decade. The top-line Super Snipe did not acquire overhead valves until 1952 and its styling lacked the flair of the smaller cars: it was too conservative and rather gloomy, though the quality of the interior trim and fittings could not be questioned. The difficulty was that the Hawk and its Super Snipe stablemate were respectively selling against the Rover P4 range and Jaguar Mark V11/V111 and could not approach them for refinement and performance.

In 1958 Sir William Rootes, in his sixty-fourth year, remained firmly in the driving seat as chairman of Rootes Motors with his brother Sir Reginald, knighted in 1946, as his deputy. Meanwhile the next generation of the family was moving up the executive ladder. Sir William's son Geoffrey became Humber's managing director in 1949 and deputy chairman in 1955 as he was groomed for the Rootes Motors chairmanship. Brian, his younger brother, set up the American Rootes Inc. and, on his return to Britain, became managing director of Rootes Ltd. Although Rootes' share of production had held up, it was nearly 11 per cent in 1946 and 10.5 per cent in 1960. In the difficult financial year of 1956/7, Rootes alone in the British-owned sector recorded a loss – of £600,000. It was a pointer to troubles ahead.

The only other member of the Big Six to record a deficit in 1957 was the American-owned Vauxhall company, though it was in the middle of a £36 million expansion plan. Like Ford, it managed to increase its productive share though, less spectacularly, from 9 per cent in 1946 to 11 per cent in 1960. Sir Charles Bartlett, knighted in 1944, stepped down as Vauxhall's managing director in 1953 at the age of sixty-four after twenty-three years. When he joined the firm in 1930, it built 1,277 cars, though such was its growth, and General Motors' resources, that it joined the ranks of the Big Six car makers and, in 1953, the year of Bartlett's retirement, Vauxhall produced a record 61,606 cars. A pioneer in industrial relations, in 1941 Bartlett set up his Management Advisory Committee, consisting of management and workers' representatives, which played an important role in Vauxhall's remaining almost strike-free for the two decades following the war.

Sir Charles was replaced by the English-born, American-educated Walter Ewart Hill, who had joined General Motors in 1922 and had briefly worked at Vauxhall in 1949/50 as director of forward planning. Maurice Platt, who was appointed Vauxhall's chief engineer in 1953, had mixed views about Bartlett's departure: 'I felt sympathy for his democratic views. . . . On the other hand it had become increasingly obvious that Vauxhall needed a shakeup. . . . Leslie Walton [Vauxhall's chairman until 1947] perhaps the only man from whom our obstinate managing director would sometimes take advice . . . [had] left a gap which even his diplomatic and talented successor, G N. Vansittart, was unable to fill.'[69]

Hill was destined to remain in his post for only two years, for in May 1955, at the age of fifty-seven, 'he quietly announced that, due to considerations of health he would be resigning . . . to take indefinite leave of absence'.[70] To the Vauxhall board this was a 'bolt from the blue' and, Platt believed, 'few people could have handled so adroitly the difficulties inherent in succeeding a man so well known and respected as Sir Charles Bartlett'.[71] Sudden changes of managing director were, alas, to be a feature of this General Motors' subsidiary in the post-war years. In the twenty-three years from 1930 until 1953 Vauxhall had just one managing director in the shape of Bartlett. In the next twenty-three years, to 1976, it had no less than five. This starkly contrasted with Opel, GM's successful German subsidiary, where Ed Zdunek was managing director for thirteen years, from 1948 to 1961. During this period Vauxhall had no less than three chief executives.

Hill's place was taken by Philip Copelin, an American, who had previously run the corporation's Belgian subsidiary. He remained at the helm for five and a half years and left in April 1961 to head General Motors' New York office: 'The reasons behind the top level decision were not disclosed.'[72]

Like Ford, Vauxhall had a single car factory with an integral body plant and, in 1948, the firm initiated a £14 million expansion plan, but this was 'too small [for Vauxhall] to remain a significant force within the car industry'.[73] So, in 1954, a more ambitious four-year £36 million investment was initiated. Luton got a new production building and, in 1955, it became exclusively a car plant when Bedford truck manufacture was transferred to an enlarged war-time factory the firm had established at nearby Dunstable.

When car production restarted in 1945, the pre-war 10 and 12 were perpetuated, but the former was discontinued in 1947 with the disappearance of the horsepower tax. The 1.7-litre six-cylinder 14 was also perpetuated. David Jones, Vauxhall's stylist, cleverly updated the existing four-cylinder body shell with a new bonnet and boot for what was to become the Wyvern in 1948. Then O. E. Hunt, GM's executive vice president, suggested that the six-cylinder engine, which had been enlarged to 2.2 litres, should be shoehorned into the new model. This eleventh-hour fitment meant that the Velox became the first European car not to enjoy the facility of a starting handle because there was no access for one. In a time-honoured American tradition, the four- and six-cylinder engines shared the same bore. These were stop-gap models and, in 1951, Vauxhall introduced its new E Series cars. The trans-Atlantic influence was all too obvious as they closely resembled scaled-down 1949 Chevrolets, while the overall dimensions were shared with the contemporary Holden, the product of GM's Australian subsidiary. Both power units were fitted in a common body shell because of limitations in the size of Vauxhall's body shop. New four- and six-cylinder oversquare short-stroke engines, with a commonized bore and stroke, followed in 1952. The Cresta, an up-market version of the Velox, arrived for 1955. By the time that production ceased in 1957, a total of 341,626 E Series cars had been built.

With expansion at Luton under way, GM's influential Detroit-based Overseas Policy Group agreed that the E Series cars could be replaced by two models: the 1.5 F Type Victor in 1957 with the 2.2-litre six-cylinder PA Cresta following in 1958. The Victor's 1957 launch date in reality proved overambitious. The blatantly trans-Atlantic styling and distinctive wrap-around windscreen were controversial, to say the least, but the model also suffered from difficulties with its door seals and, later on, there were more serious rusting problems. The Victor soon became Britain's number one export model as it was sold in America by Pontiac dealers where its lines probably raised fewer eyebrows. In view of this, 100,000 Victors were made within fifteen months of its announcement and Luton built a record 119,177 cars in 1958.

Perhaps the most striking feature of Vauxhall at this time was the essential simplicity of its model range which was initially constrained by lack of manufacturing facilities. Only three body styles were produced between 1951 and 1958 with the maximum interchangeability between engines. In 1956 Vauxhall's profit per vehicle was the highest in the industry at £80, which compared with Ford's £45, BMC's £35 and Standard's £30. However, it should be remembered that at this stage Vauxhall produced no small car (the Victor had a 1.5-litre engine), in 1956 Bedford truck production actually outstripped that of cars and there was a higher proportional profit margin on medium-sized cars and commercial vehicles. Yet at the time Britain was the only country in the world where Ford cars outsold General Motors ones; an endorsement of Sir Patrick Hennessy's twenty-year stewardship which ensured that Dagenham benefited from a far greater degree of independence than Luton ever enjoyed.

On the face of it there would not appear to be any connection between Vauxhall and the Rover company, based from 1945 onwards at Solihull. The common denominator is that during the war both firms worked on Frank Whittle's pioneering jet engine. Vauxhall made much of the original W2B unit of 1940/1, while Rover also struggled with production and development work until 1943 when Rolls-Royce's Ernest Hives suggested to Spencer Wilks that his firm take over this pioneering turbine development. In return Rover would receive the manufacturing rights of the Rolls-Royce Meteor tank engine derived from the Merlin aero engine. Wilks agreed and this contributed to Rolls-Royce's world lead in gas turbine technology which would take it into the jet age, while Rover received a profitable power unit which, in reality, did not come into its own until the post-war years.

Rover's Coventry factory was damaged by bombing during the war and, although repairs were effected, there were powerful arguments for disposing of the property as there was no room for expansion in the city and plenty at Solihull. Machine-tool maker Alfred Herbert bought the Helen Street works and Rover concentrated on transforming the former Shadow Factory at Solihull into a car plant which was officially opened by Sir Stafford Cripps in February 1946. The trade minister again took the opportunity to stress the importance of the export drive and the need for manufacturers to adopt a one-model policy. He also revealed that the first car he ever owned was a single-cylinder Rover. The firm was at this time producing its closely related pre-war 10, 12, 14 and 16hp range. Wilks calculated that Rover might be able to produce around 15,000 of these a year (in 1939 a record 11,103 had been built), yet the large Solihull plant could absorb far more vehicles than that. A. B. Smith, at the time Rover's buyer and stores controller, recalled Spencer Wilks saying to his brother Maurice: 'We shall never be able to use a million square feet in our lives! We shall have to let it out.'[74] (Recounted in *Land-Rover, The Unbeatable 4×4*, Haynes 1984.)

Spencer Wilks estimated that at this stage it would be possible to produce 20,000 vehicles a year. But what of the 5,000 shortfall? Initially it was intended to produce a completely new car, the 699cc 6hp M1 ('M' standing for miniature), which had been designed at the end of the war and, in view of a shortage of sheet steel, was conceived with a platform chassis made of Birmabright aluminium alloy. A prototype was running by 1946, yet the model never went into production because it had little export potential and would have been expensive to tool up as there were no carry overs from earlier models. So the M1 was dropped, but before long the Wilks brothers came up with another vehicle, one which was tailor-made for those austere, export-conscious days and in the same spirit as the Ferguson tractors which were by then pouring out of Standard's former Shadow Factory.

Maurice Wilks owned an estate on the island of Anglesey which consisted of 250 acres of farmland, woods and sand dunes. After the war Wilks got to work tidying up his property and for this purpose he acquired an ex-War Department Ford V8-engined half-track truck. The truck proved too unwieldy for its role, so Wilks replaced it with one of the many war-surplus Jeeps then available. Its great advantage was that four-wheel drive could be optionally engaged, making it ideal for cross-country work and coping with muddy rutted tracks which are to be found the world over. It was far from reliable and was constantly being brought to the factory for repairs. 'I well recall Maurice saying . . . that if he couldn't make a better, more reliable vehicle he shouldn't be in business,' recalled Smith. Subsequently, while visiting his brother in Anglesey, Spencer asked him what he'd do when the battered old Jeep finally gave out. 'Buy another one, I suppose,' answered Maurice. *'There isn't anything else.'*[76]

So the Land-Rover, as Maurice Wilks immediately christened it, was born. A Jeep-based prototype was built, though the masterstroke of the concept was the use of Birmabright bodywork, and simple, functional lines were adopted to keep tooling costs to a minimum. On 4 September 1947, Spencer Wilks received board approval for the production of 'an all-purpose vehicle on the lines of the Willys-Overland Jeep'.[77] The Land-Rover was announced in July 1948, but not before Sir Stafford Cripps had visited Solihull to examine some pilot vehicles. 'He accepted the recommendations we made to him that here was something new for the British motor industry which had a future not only for exports but agriculture. He gave it his full support and indeed when he became Chancellor of the Exchequer [in November 1947] he specifically exempted Land-Rovers from purchase tax.'[78]

The vehicle therefore sold for £450 and, in 1949, Land-Rover production overtook car output. This doughty workhorse, with its optional four-wheel drive and unique appeal, had ensured Rover's survival in the post-war world though, ironically, it soon outstripped the confines of the Solihull factory. As government policy prevented expansion there, the firm had to take over small factories in the Birmingham area which became responsible for individual components, the chassis and transmission production being devolved first. In 1952 Rover acquired a works at Perry Barr with another following at Percy Road in 1954 and the 100,000th Land-Rover was built the same year. At this time exports were accounting for around 75 per cent of output and Rover was to claim subsequently that it had supplied vehicles to every country in the world except North Vietnam and Albania!

The Land-Rover was in fact intended as a stop-gap to absorb capacity before the company's new post-war car range was ready. This arrived in 1949 in the shape of the six-cylinder 2.2-litre 75 which offered the traditional Rover formula of sound engineering and comfort with a discreet, well-finished interior. It was intended to appeal to the discriminating professional man who could not yet afford a Mark VI Bentley and regarded a Jaguar as too flashy. Designated P4 in company parlance, further variations followed and what was affectionately known as the 'Auntie' range endured until 1964.

In 1957 Spencer Wilks took over the Rover chairmanship from Howe Graham and Maurice Wilks moved up to become joint managing director with George Farmer. Although it was a public company, the Wilks had made Rover a 'family business' in the very best sense of the word. Yet the record pre-tax profits of £2.4 million in 1955 would not be bettered until 1960.

If it had not been for the Land-Rover, Rover car production would have been about the same as that of Jaguar Cars, as SS became in 1945. The change of name was made because, as Lyons with wry understatement later put it, 'the SS initials [had] acquired a tarnished image . . . a reminder of the SS German troops, a sector of the community which was not highly regarded'.[79] The pre-war range of 1.5-, 2.5-, and 3.5-litre models was perpetuated until 1948 when the XK 120, a new Jaguar sports car, was announced. Under its bonnet was a 3.4-litre twin-overhead-camshaft six-cylinder engine which was to power every Jaguar from 1951 until 1975. But, remembered Lyons, 'had we taken the advice of the respected authorities, we would not have gone ahead' with the engine.

Paradoxically, the XK engine had not been designed as a sports-car unit but had been conceived during the war, under Lyons's direction, by chief engineer William Heynes with Walter Hassan and Claude Baily 'to be capable of propelling a full-sized *saloon* [my italics] at a genuine 100mph in standard form and without special tuning'.[80]

This demanded a twin-overhead-camshaft layout but hitherto such a configuration had been confined to racing machinery and low-production sports cars. On its 1948 introduction, no other car company in the world, with the exception of Alfa Romeo and Salmson, was offering such a layout. Such a unit also met yet another of Lyons's requirements that it should also look good, while Heynes believed that it would 'convey to the layman some idea of the thought and care which had been expended on such a design'.[81] For the XK 120's lines Lyons drew on the styling of a special-bodied 328 BMW built for the 1940 Mille Miglia race which had been brought to Britain after the war by H.J. Aldington, the pre-war importer of BMW cars. Jaguar had the car for a time, which gave Lyons the opportunity to study it at first hand. The XK 120 was the starting point of the post-war Jaguar sports-car line though, as ever, William Lyons's main preoccupation was mainstream saloon production.

The Mark VII, the 100mph saloon for which the XK engine had been conceived, was ready in 1951, a year in which Jaguar exported 96 per cent of its output, an all-time record for a British manufacturer. It was in that year, when 5,805 cars were built, that Jaguar overtook its 1939 record of 5,378 cars produced. The Mark VII lines were to last until 1965 after a fifteen-year production run.

Although the Foleshill premises had expanded during the war, the firm's growing output meant that Jaguar urgently needed more space. By 1950 Lyons had 600,000 square feet at his disposal and he applied for planning permission to increase floor space by a further 50 per cent. Although there was plenty of room between the works and Beake Avenue, government policy prevented new buildings being erected in Coventry. As luck would have it, Daimler's number two Shadow Factory at Browns Lane on Coventry's outskirts, between the villages of Allesley and Brownshill Green, was becoming surplus to requirements. In 1951 Lyons leased and eventually bought the plant from the Ministry of Supply and the move was completed by the following year.

The XK 120 sports car and big Mark VII were essentially low-production models but, in 1955, Jaguar unveiled its smaller 2.4-litre saloon. Not only was it the firm's first unitary construction car but it also gave Jaguar a model that could be built in quantity. What was to develop into a range 'accounted for a substantial increase, not only in our volume of production, but also in our profits, which rose five-fold between 1955 and 1968',[82] was how Lyons put it. Over 37,000 examples were built in the first four years of production and the usual Jaguar formula of looks and performance (particularly with the larger-capacity 3.4 and 3.8 models from 1959) at a highly competitive price ensured that the design was to survive for thirteen years, until 1969.

Jaguar saloon sales were undoubtedly aided by the firm's success in the Le Mans 24-hour race and, after a works-prepared but privately entered XK 120 was placed third in the 1950 event, Lyons believed that 'in a car more suitable for the race, the XK engine could win the greatest of all events'.[83] The publicity incentive was enormous and the result was the sports racing C-type which won in 1951, giving Britain its first win at the French circuit since 1935. Jaguar was to prove victorious again in 1953, and with the fabled D-type in 1955, 1956 and 1957, though the last success was achieved by the Edinburgh-based Ecurie Ecosse racing team. These five victories were to give Jaguar a racing pedigree and allure that has never left it. What had begun in the 1930s as a Standard-engined special had emerged, two decades later, as one of Britain's greatest marques.

Jaguar's move to Browns Lane highlighted the plight of Daimler which was descending into disorganization and deficit. In 1940 Sir Alexander Roger, chairman of the BSA parent company, was seconded to the Tank Board, so Dudley Docker's son Bernard took over his post while also serving as managing director in the absence of Geoffrey Burton, who was on secondment to the Ministry of Supply. In June 1944, a few days before Dudley Docker's death, Burton was summoned to his Amersham mansion where he was informed that 'quite plainly he had to go. One reason given was that Bernard should be made managing director of [the] entire group.'[84]

Sir Bernard's mother died in 1947 and two years later the Old Harrovian, who had spent 'over twenty-five years of business life in his father's shadow',[85] married for a second time. His bride was Norah Collins, a former dancing girl; Docker was her third millionaire husband and the couple's extravagant lifestyle was soon extended to the BSA directors who were equipped with a fleet of luxurious Daimler limousines. In the meantime, the post-war Daimler range had been revamped, though the 5.5-litre straight eight, which lasted until 1953, was in any case a pre-war anachronism. It did, however, form the basis of some of the legendary Docker Daimlers, the first of which appeared in 1951. Although the six-cylinder Consort saloon sold about 4,250 examples, there was a bewildering range of other sixes which sold in penny numbers.

Sir Bernard, meanwhile, took to charging his wife's 'gems and clothes to the company on the pretext that [her] glamorous reputation was an asset to the BSA group'.[86] Matters boiled over at a board meeting on 2 May 1956 when Sir Bernard attempted to appoint R.E. Smith, who was his wife's brother-in-law, to the board and the proposition was only passed by Docker's casting vote. It was a Pyrrhic victory, because chief accountant John Rowe had succeeded in persuading the Prudential Assurance Company, an institutional shareholder, to take sides. Sir Bernard was ousted at a meeting on 31 May, a decision that was confirmed by shareholders' meeting on 1 August, whereupon he and his wife each bought themselves a Rolls-Royce.

Docker's place as chairman was taken by Jack Sangster, who had led the revolt against Docker and had joined the BSA board after the firm had paid £2.4 million for his Triumph and Ariel motorcycle concerns. Sangster made the brilliant but dictatorial Edward Turner head of BSA's newly named Automotive Division. The Daimler range was rationalized, automatic transmission was offered for the first time and the low-production Lanchesters were discontinued in 1956.

The front engine and rear-wheel drive of the Victorian Daimler, Britain's oldest marque, had been widely and thereafter almost exclusively copied by the rest of the British motor industry. Then, in 1959, the British Motor Corporation switched to a front-wheel drive design of such a radical and ingenious concept that it changed not only the face of the British motor industry but also the course of car design the world over. The consequences of the Mini's arrival are considered in the next chapter.

6

Mini Cars Make Mini Profits*

1959–67

'"*It was new; it was singular; it was simple.*"
Admiral Lord Nelson on the tactical
plan prepared before Trafalgar

'*History records how he completely achieved his aim on 21 October 1805; posterity will in turn regard 26 August 1959 as a landmark in the development of the popular car. For it will be generally agreed that the end product of a small design and development team led by Alec Issigonis during the past two years marks a real breakthrough in automobile engineering. . . . It is the production of a 10-foot-long car capable of exceeding 70 mph . . . [which] has variable-rate all-independent rubber suspension and yet is one of the lowest priced cars in the world.*'

British Motor Corporation's press release on the
occasion of the launch of the Mini Minor, August 1959

Until the early 1960s, the car makers were operating in a sellers' market. Car ownership not only increased amongst the middle classes but was also extended for the first time to blue-collar workers. A cartoon that appeared after the Conservative election victory of 1959 showed Harold Macmillan thanking his 'colleagues' – a car, a television set and a vacuum cleaner – for the part they played in the Tory triumph. However, after 1960, the market became increasingly competitive and triggered a series of mergers that dominated the industry throughout the decade. In 1960 Jaguar took over Daimler and the following year Standard-Triumph at last found the

* Post-1959 motor industry aphorism

partner it had been searching for when it was bought by the Lancashire-based Leyland commercial vehicle company. The British Motor Corporation, having embraced the concept of front-wheel drive, saw output soar, yet underpricing and lack of forward planning contributed to a fall in profits which resulted, in 1966, in its merging with Jaguar. Then, in 1968, came its takeover by the Leyland Motor Corporation. These were years in which Ford tightened its hold on the British market, though the creation of Ford of Europe in 1967 was to see an eventual integration of its successful British operations with the company's German division. American involvement in the industry was extended in 1964 when the Chrysler Corporation took a stake in the ailing Rootes Group which was consolidated by a complete takeover in 1967.

In productive terms, the industry enjoyed switchback fortunes. Britain produced a record 1,352,728 cars in 1960 which in 1961 plunged to 1,003,967, the worst figure since 1957. Nineteen-sixty-one was also the year in which France overtook Britain to become second to Germany in the European manufacturing league. Britain was back in second place from 1962 when the industry embarked on a three-year boom, though from 1965 until 1967, as the Labour Party tried to resist devaluing the pound by initiating a credit squeeze, car production fell in each successive year and, in 1966, France again overtook Britain to be number two in Europe and has remained ahead ever since.

This was a time when both Conservative and Labour governments took a markedly more interventionist approach to the motor industry. When, in 1960, all the principal car makers announced expansion plans, these were significantly located in areas of high unemployment, such as Merseyside and Scotland. The Industrial Reorganization Corporation, set up in 1966 by the Labour government, played a leading role in the merger of the British Motor Corporation with Leyland. Although British entry to the Common Market was vetoed by the French in 1962 and 1967, tariffs on imported cars fell from 33⅓ per cent, where they had stood since 1915, to 30 per cent in 1962 and dropped again to 17 per cent in 1969. Imports, that in the 1945/58 era had peaked in 1955 at a mere 11,131 cars, gathered momentum in the 1960s and stood at 92,731 in 1967 or 9 per cent of new car registrations. Labour troubles continued to plague the industry, with strikes accelerating after 1965 when stoppages more than doubled from 2.7 million hours lost in 1964 to over 8 million.

The most important event of these years was the British Motor Corporation's announcement, in August 1959, of the front-wheel drive Mini Minor, the most technically significant car in the history of the British motor industry. The chain of events that culminated in the Mini's launch began in 1955 when the Morris Minor was by far and away BMC's most successful car. However, Alec Issigonis, its designer, was at the time working for Alvis in Coventry. So, at the end of 1955, he recalled, 'Sir Leonard Lord rang me one day . . . and said, "Come back to Longbridge." '[1] As it happened, Alvis had decided not to proceed with the car Issigonis had designed because tooling costs for its body had proved prohibitively expensive.

On Issigonis's arrival at Longbridge, he was immediately rejoined by Jack Daniels, his old associate from Minor days, and he brought with him Chris Kingham, with whom he had established a good working rapport at Alvis. This small team immediately set to work on what might have been a successor for the big BMC Farina models. Coded XC 9000, it was a 1.5-litre rear-wheel-drive model, though Issigonis did not like it. 'I thought it was driven at the wrong end,'[2] he said. Then, in September 1956, Egypt nationalized the Suez Canal and in the resulting war the Arabs blew up the Syrian pipeline that provided Britain with 20 per cent of its petrol supplies. In addition the canal was blocked which meant that oil tankers from the Middle East then had to make the longer journey around South Africa. There was an almost immediate petrol shortage and it rose in price to a record 3s 6d (18p) per gallon. In December 1956 the government introduced rationing, which lasted until May 1957.

British car sales slumped and registrations in the 900–1000cc class soared from 25,971 in 1956 to lead the market with 108,879 in 1957. Some of these were motorcycle-engined 'Bubble Cars', often of German origin, and their appearance in growing numbers on Britain's roads produced a furious response from Sir Leonard Lord. In March 1957 he informed Issigonis: 'God damn these bloody awful Bubble Cars. We must drive them off the streets by designing a proper miniature car.'[3] This impulsive, intuitive remark was the first in a series of events that culminated in BMC's takeover by Leyland in 1968. Issigonis therefore set aside project XC 9000 for the time being and began work on XC 9003 – which was to become the Mini.

Issigonis was delighted. 'I was really weaned on the Austin Seven, so it is perhaps natural that in my professional work I dislike designing big cars.'[4] His experiences with the Morris Minor had told him that for the best possible directional stability a small car must have as much weight as possible ahead of the front wheels. He later conceded: 'This concept requires front-wheel drive but I did not know how to do it at the time'.[5] However, in 1952, just prior to his departure to Alvis, Issigonis had designed an experimental front-wheel-drive Morris Minor in which the entire engine and gearbox unit had been transversely mounted. He revived the engine position for the Mini so that it would leave the maximum amount of space for the car's occupants. But because Lord had specified a

136

small car, Issigonis could not perpetuate the location of its gearbox because it would have resulted in too wide a vehicle. (If Lord had commissioned a larger car, Issigonis could have retained his original concept which would have been considerably cheaper than the ingenious but relatively expensive solution he eventually arrived at.) He did, however experiment with a half of a BMC A Series engine with an end-on gearbox, and although this two-cylinder unit was of a more acceptable width, it was a rough low-powered unit which flew in the face of Lord's original edict.

One of Issigonis's briefs from Sir Leonard was that he could 'use any sort of engine . . . as long as we have it on our present production lines'.[6] Issigonis's masterstroke was to retain the transversely mounted four-cylinder A Series engine, while the gearbox was located underneath it in the sump and connected to the crankshaft by an idler gear. Although Issigonis was the first person to build such a layout, this ingenious configuration had been featured in an article in the 5 September 1952 issue of *The Autocar* as part of a specification for an economy car designed by engineer Alan Lamburn. Issigonis had read the article but, as he rarely reveals his design influences, we can only speculate as to whether he could have recalled the Lamburn design or, like many engineers, could quite independently have reached the same conclusion when confronted by a particular problem.

Once this compact engine-gearbox unit had evolved, Issigonis could press ahead with the bodywork. The basic uncompromising styling resembled a scaled-down version of that executed for XC 9000, and the car measured just 10 feet from bumper to bumper. The revolutionary compact power/transmission unit permitted Issigonis to devote an unprecedented 80 per cent of the remaining space for passenger accommodation and, so as to keep the intrusion of the wheel arches to a minimum, he enlisted Dunlop's co-operation in producing small 10-inch wheels, just as he had pioneered 14-inch ones on the Morris Minor. Suspension was also unconventional. It was all-independent, an unheard-of luxury for a cheap British car, but also rubber was used as the suspension medium.

Two prototypes were on the road by October 1957, and in July 1958, after a run in one of them, Sir Leonard Lord, with characteristic bluntness, told Issigonis to 'make the bloody thing'.[7] Only two major modifications had taken place during the model's evolution. To prevent the exposed carburettor from icing up, the engine was turned 180 degrees so that the unit then faced the bulkhead though this required the introduction of another costly and energy-absorbing transfer gear. It was also found that the suspension units had to be mounted on their own subframes, which were introduced front and rear, and these also added slightly to cost and weight.

The car was announced on 26 August 1959 to a welter of press enthusiasm. For the Mini, with its own utterly distinctive persona, offered not only transport for four but also the road-holding advantages of front-wheel drive, while its appeal straddled the social divide. It was available in Austin Seven and Morris Mini Minor forms and was rightfully hailed as the design triumph it represented: it is a work of true engineering genius. In 1960, the first full year of production, the Mini overtook the Morris Minor as BMC's best-selling car, although it ceded pole position to its 1100 derivative in 1963. Production progressively rose and, in 1965, the millionth Mini was built. It had taken just six years, while Issigonis's Minor had taken fourteen to reach the same figure. A more potent Mini-Cooper derivative had appeared in 1961 and this model was to triumph in the Monte Carlo Rally in 1964, 1965 and 1967, which did wonders for the model's image. Output continued to rise and, in 1970, the Mini shed its Austin and Morris prefixes to become a marque name in its own right. Production peaked in 1971 when 318,475 examples were built. In 1973 the Mini once again became BMC's British Leyland successor's top seller, and was to remain so until 1980. It continues in production at the time of writing (1987), with over five million Minis having been built, and it will remain in production for as long as demand continues.

Internationally the Mini had enormous impact for, after sixty years of Britain effectively building cars to other country's designs, here was a revolutionary idea that was eagerly copied the world over. The first foreign manufacturer to follow the concept was the Italian Fiat Company which, in 1964, introduced its transverse-engined front-wheel-drive Autobianchi Primula. This differed from the Mini in one important respect, for its gearbox was attached to the end of the engine in the manner of Issigonis's experimental Morris Minor. This arrangement was employed in preference to the Mini's gearbox-in-sump layout because, although Fiat's Dante Giacosa, 'admired the constructional simplicity of the Mini's coachwork . . . I was against the high manufacturing costs of the mechanicals'.[8] Therefore, when the Autobianchi was being designed, he specified an end-on gearbox, and when the combined units proved wider than the permitted track, he insisted that the unit be shortened and 'I remember the thrill I got when I was told the problem had been solved.'[9] Fiat engineer Ettore Cordiano had reduced the space taken up by the clutch by hydraulically actuating it via a rod placed inside the gearbox driveshaft. It was then possible to do away with the thrust bearing and lever. This meant that the price of the transversely mounted engine/gearbox unit was not much more than when it was used in the conventional north/south position.

The Fiat 128 of 1967 followed a similar arrangement and although Peugeot, with its 204 of 1965, followed Issigonis, practically all other car makers, including Ford with its 1976 Fiesta and General Motors' X Cars of 1980, endorse, with modifications,[10] the essence of the Fiat formula as did

Leyland's BL successor with its 1983 Austin Maestro. This does nothing to detract from the genius of Alec Issigonis who has altered the design of the motor car in much the same way as Emile Levassor, who transferred the engine from the rear to the front of the 1891 Panhard and in doing so influenced car design world-wide.

The Mini was a perfect expression of Leonard Lord's famous dictum, 'If you build bloody good cars, they'll sell themselves,' and it did exactly that. But when it came to pricing the Mini the corporation made a disastrous error which reflected its lack of marketing expertise. For, at £496 in its cheapest form, it was only £77 more than the archaic Ford Popular and was no less than £93 cheaper than Dagenham's completely new, impeccably costed 105E Anglia, announced at the same time as the Mini. The pricing policy, such as it was, was adopted because BMC 'believed they could not sell it unless it was "the cheapest"'.[11] It all smacks of Lord's deceptively impromptu pricing methods, which went something along these lines: 'What's Nuffield's bloody figure, then? . . . £515 . . . Right, make ours £510.'[12]

'The criterion in a pricing study is always "price against the competition"' explained John Barber, who as Ford's finance director was responsible for the pricing of the Ford Cortina and was to become managing director of British Leyland. 'That was the absolute all the time. We priced at what the market could stand. Then, almost as an afterthought, we would cost it and if it showed a loss, we would have to cost it again. BMC should have said, "Where do we slot into the market? . . . We've got the most sophisticated car in the world. We can afford to charge £100 more than the wretched Ford runabout." Then, having got the Mini into the wrong slot, they did the same with its 1100 successor.'[13] When Barber went to British Leyland, 'we jacked the Mini's price up quite a bit, but it wasn't making any money, apart from its spare parts.'[14] In addition, when Ford's product planning department stripped a Mini down and analysed its cost, they estimated that, at a selling price of £496, BMC was loosing £30 on every one it built. This was endorsed by BMC's financial performance. In 1960 the corporation made a profit of close on £27 million on sales of £346 million. Seven years later, in 1967, its sales had risen to £467 million but it recorded a £3 million loss. Not surprisingly, the aphorism 'Mini cars make mini profits' was born.

In 1962 BMC announced the Mini's successor, which followed in the front-wheel tracks of its distinguished forebear. It was a good-looking family saloon styled by Pininfarina, rather than by Alec Issigonis, for the Turin company had borrowed the lines of the existing rear-drive A40 to great effect. Again the suspension broke new ground and was an all-independent interconnected Hydrolastic system. The 1100 was a roomy, economical vehicle, even if its small boot was considered a drawback. From 1963 until 1971 it was Britain's best-selling car. Yet the lack of forward planning showed because it was also selling against BMC's own Morris Minor and Austin A40 with all three cars powered by the same 1098cc A Series engine.

The arrival of the 1100 crystalized BMC's design philosophy. By adopting a policy of what it termed engineering excellence, the corporation reasoned that if it produced technically advanced cars they would enjoy production runs of ten years or more and thus heavy retooling costs, which would have been required by a model change every four years as practised by Ford, could be avoided. It was an approach that the French Citreon company, which Issigonis much admired, had pursued with some success.

By the time that the 1100 appeared, BMC had a new chairman. In 1961 Sir Leonard Lord stepped down after nine years and became vice president, as Lord Nuffield still held the corporate presidency. In 1962 Sir Leonard became Lord Lambury ('Lord Lord would sound bloody stupid') and he continued to keep in touch with corporate affairs until he died in 1967.

Lord's place as chairman was taken by fifty-three-year-old George Harriman, BMC's managing director since 1956, while Alec Issigonis was promoted to the post of technical director. This duo was to be responsible for directing BMC's model strategy for the next six years. Like Lord, George William Harriman (1908–73) had spent all his working life with the Morris and Austin companies. He was born in Coventry where his father, also George, obtained a job with Morris Engines, and there this 'dynamic, fast-talking, fast-walking, bowler-hatted'[15] man was made works manager. When his son joined him at Gosford Street in 1923 at the age of fifteen and a half, he became 'Old George' and his offspring 'Young George'. The latter recalled starting 'at 23s [£1.15] a week . . . and when I finished my time with 57s 6d [£2.87½], I felt like a millionaire'.[16] He soon struck up a friendship with Leonard Lord and when the latter was transferred to Cowley, he arranged for Harriman to move with him, though George returned to Coventry when Lord fell out with Nuffield. By 1938 Harriman had risen to be assistant works superintendent. In his spare time he had developed a passion for rugby and, as Captain of Coventry and Warwickshire County Club, he was proud of having played for England *versus* The Rest in 1933.

Meanwhile Leonard Lord had moved to Austin and, in 1940, George Harriman followed his mentor there as machine shop superintendent and was responsible for engine production throughout the war. Promotion to production manager followed in 1944 and, in 1945, came an Austin directorship. Harriman became deputy managing director of BMC in 1952, which established him as Lord's 'very right-hand man'.[17] His appointment as managing director in 1956 took many day-to-day responsibilities off

Lord's shoulders and confirmed his position as Sir Leonard's heir apparent. Harriman wore 'an India rubber confidence as consciously as other men assume dignity'.[18] a trait which was greatly enchanced by a natural charm, though 'he had grown up in [Lord's] shadow and the old man continued to exercise a considerable influence upon him; [his] room at Longbridge was left unoccupied and unchanged until the day he died in 1967.'[19] A former colleague of Harriman's summed him up thus: 'George was one of the nicest men you could wish to meet but he did what he was told. That was why Len Lord liked him.'

On a notable occasion, Harriman did disobey. In 1940, during a national scrap-metal drive, Lord seized on the opportunity to permanently disable two of the surviving exquisite 1936 twin overhead camshaft racing cars designed for Austin by brilliant, young Tom Murray Jamieson, who had died in 1938. Leonard Lord hated Jamieson and his cars and ordered Harriman to send their crankshafts, connecting rods, pistons and cylinder liners for scrap. Although one set of components suffered this fate, Harriman took the other home and hid the parts in his garage. There they remained until after his death in 1973, when they were discovered by his widow and returned to British Leyland. This resulted in one of the surviving cars being restored and, in January 1975, it ran again for the first time for 35 years, thanks to Harriman's independence of spirit.

In 1960 Harriman had announced a £49 million expansion plan which was aimed at increasing BMC's productive capacity to a million vehicles a year. Government directives to areas of high unemployment were reflected in its locations: a pressings plant at Llanelli, South Wales, with a new commercial vehicle factory to be established at Bathgate between Edinburgh and Glasgow, following the government's funding the creation of a new steel strip mill at nearby Ravenscraig.

By 1964 the expenditure appeared more than justified because in that year BMC produced a record 730,862 cars, the highest figure it ever attained in its fifteen-year life. Then, in October, the corporation unveiled Issigonis's third front-wheel-drive model, the roomy 1800, though it lacked the flair of the Mini and 1100. Its styling, in particular, was an uneasy combination of his talents and those of Pininfarina: 'I did the centre section of the body . . . and Sergio Farina did the front wings but, unfortunately, he copied . . . Fiat headlamps which were the worst feature of the car.' Despite this, Issigonis maintained, 'I still think [it] was our best car. I loved that car.'[20]

Perhaps the most startling aspect of the 1800's concept was that the company intended to produce it at the rate of 4,000 cars a week, which was about the same as the 1100 and four times the pace of Farina production. The reality was that these ambitious objectives were never achieved and, by 1967, output was running at around only 1,000 a week.

BMC's production dropped, along with the rest of the industry's, to 727,592 in 1965, despite the fact that profits were up slightly to £23.3 million. Although the Mini and 1100 models were still top sellers, giving the corporation 35 per cent of the British market in 1965, the lack of long-term planning was beginning to cause concern to the corporation's financial advisers. At this time Harriman approached Charles Villiers, managing director of Schroder Wagg, BMC's merchant bankers, 'to help the company find a way out of its financial problems'[21] and Villiers investigated the possibility of finding an overseas partner for the firm. On another front, Cooper Brothers, its accountants, had helped Harriman to produce a plan to integrate more closely the corporation that was still operating as three separate companies, Austin, Morris and Fisher and Ludlow, each with their own board of directors and accounts. Until then, BMC had not had a finance director as such, so Harriman asked Ron Lucas, whose service with Austin reached back to 1927 and who was then working for BMC in America, to take over the job of finance director to implement the Cooper proposals.

A director of planning, Geoffrey Rose, was appointed to head a twenty-eight-strong team to establish model prices and ensure that each met its cost and profits targets. A market research department with a staff of thirty was set up, 75 per cent of whom were graduates; and, although its structure did not begin to compare with Ford's, it was at least a start. It issued reports intended to pinpoint corporate shortcomings and, with the 1800 clearly in mind, 'one pointed out that good engineering alone was no longer enough, that the motoring public were becoming increasingly fashion-conscious'.[22] Although Alec Issigonis continued to have overall responsibility for cars, a product planning department, on Ford lines, was established for commercial vehicles late in 1965.

Then, in July 1965, BMC pulled off something of a coup by announcing its own takeover bid for Pressed Steel. At the time the corporation was the only large car-manufacturing company in Europe which did not have its own body plant, for Fisher and Ludlow supplied only about 50 per cent of its needs. Around 40 per cent of Pressed Steel's output went to BMC, while Rootes took another 40 per cent and the balance was made up with bodies for Rover and Jaguar and some of Standard Triumph and Rolls-Royce. Although the move won rare praise from The Economist ('The bid . . . made without the help of a merchant bank – is a brilliantly timed one'), it cautioned that BMC would still be the only major car producer 'to move its bodies any distance. Other parts heavy in weight and unit value per pound weight are easily moved over the country by trainload; but complete bodies are mostly air, and trains are an expensive way to move air. Hence the endless stream of lorries . . . from Pressed Steel's factories to BMC's assembly plants at Oxford and Birmingham.'[23]

One benefit of the takeover, which was referred to and approved by the Monopolies Commission, was that Joe Edwards, so ignominiously sacked by Lord in 1956, was once more in the corporate fold. Harriman had offered him the assistant managing directorship though in 1966, Sir George, as he had become the previous year, suggested a joint managing directorship. Edwards was not interested but indicated that he would like the post of managing director if Harriman became executive chairman, and the latter agreed to this proposition.

Edwards took over in June 1966 and 'when he walked back into the office which he had left ten years before, Lord was waiting for him. "There is only one man in this office today whose hand I want to shake," he said to Edwards. "I should never have done what I did and I'm delighted to see you back" ' When the question of his salary subsequently arose, Edwards told Lord and fellow director Alec Layborn: 'Share it between you.'[24] He had not forgotten Lord's behaviour a decade earlier.

Edwards immediately initiated economies. BMC's workforce was cut by 14,000 in the autumn of 1966 and he began drawing up plans to close some of BMC's factories. In the Midlands he envisaged shutting the Morris Bodies plant in Coventry and the Fisher and Ludlow plant at Castle Bromwich. In the Oxford area the Morris Radiator factory would be closed, along with sections of the MG factory at Abingdon. He estimated that this would reduce the workforce by a further 8,000. In the meantime, Lucas had restructured the corporation, for accounting purposes, into four new divisions: home sales, export sales, engineering and manufacturing. They considered that these reforms would take about eighteen months to take effect although Edwards, in particular, was concerned by a new front-wheel drive 1.5-litre model then under development and intended to slot in between the 1100 and 1800. BMC's profits dropped only slightly, to £21.3 million, in 1966, again thanks to 1100 sales, but Ford's Mark II Cortina was proving particularly threatening.

While Edwards was endeavouring to put BMC's corporate house in order, Harriman had been thinking in terms of a 'big get-together' of Britain's motor manufacturers. There had been talks in 1964 with Leyland Motors, which had taken over Standard-Triumph three years previously, but he and Lucas had considered a merger with Jaguar as the first move. Leyland also had talks with Sir William Lyons in 1965, though these proved abortive, but an approach by Harriman in 1966, with Jaguar's body supplier in BMC's hands, bore fruit. The merger was completed in July 1966 and the combined company took the British Motor Holdings name; however, a condition of the alliance was that sixty-six-year-old Sir William still retained complete control of his Coventry company.

Jaguar's spectacular growth (its output trebled from 6,647 cars in 1950

143

to 20,897 in 1959) meant that by 1960 its Browns Lane plant was, as Lyons put it, 'bursting at the seams'.[25] Sir William did not wish 'to go to a "development" area; [he] was unenthusiastic when he sent teams to different parts of the British Isles to inspect possible sites.'[26] Then, when the firm had reached the point at which it was becoming desperate for space, Lyons heard that 'the Daimler company, which occupied the very fine factory at Radford, within 2 miles of our plant at Browns Lane, was up for sale'.[27] He immediately began talks with BSA's chairman, Jack Sangster, and the result was that Jaguar bought Daimler for £3.5 million. 'I do not recall a more amicable deal with anyone although, when we thought that everything had been settled, a matter of £10,000 [Sangster had overlooked some pension payments] arose between us. Since each of us was honestly convinced that this was in our favour, we decided that the best way to settle the matter was to toss up for it. I am pleased to say that I won.'[28] Jaguar, of all the significant British car makers, had succeeded in expanding without moving away from its Midland heartland.

The Daimler purchase effectively doubled Jaguar's floor space. Car production was concentrated in Browns Lane, while machining and engine production was, in turn, moved to Radford. Jaguar wasted little time in rationalizing the Daimler car line. The recently introduced Majestic Major luxury saloon, powered by a new 4.5-litre V8 engine, lasted until 1968. Jaguar also perpetuated the glassfibre-bodied SP 250 sports car until 1964, and although this was a belated attempt by Daimler to capture American sales, of the 2,645 examples built, more right-hand-drive examples (1,445) than left-hand-drive ones were sold. More successful was the Daimler V8 250, a union of Jaguar's popular Mark II saloon, which arrived in 1959, and the SP 250's 2.5-litre V8 engine. This lasted until 1969 and with it went the V8; thereafter Daimlers became up-market versions of Jaguar's saloon range.

The Daimler takeover gave Jaguar an inadvertent foothold in the commercial vehicle market and, in 1961, this was extended when Lyons secured Guy Motors of Wolverhampton, then in receivership, for a modest £800,000. In 1963 the Coventry-based Coventry Climax company joined the growing Jaguar empire. Founded in 1903, it had built up a sound reputation for its fire pumps and fork-lift trucks and, from 1957 until 1961, successfully diversified into the production of grand prix racing engines, the work of Walter (Wally) Hassan, who was one of the famous team which had designed Jaguar's fabled XK unit. With Hassan once more on the Jaguar payroll, he became, in 1965, chief engineer (power plant). Less successful was Jaguar's purchase, in 1964, of Henry Meadows, which had been building engines and gearboxes since 1919 and was Guy's next-door neighbour. It was to be used to build American Cummins diesel engines in

Britain but the plan had to be abandoned when it was found that they were unsuitable for use in the Daimler Roadliner bus and Big J Guy truck.

The Jaguar car range was, in the meantime, continuing to develop. The big Mark VII had evolved into the Mark IX and, in 1962, it was replaced by the Mark X with independent rear suspension, the largest Jaguar ever built. It was an instance where perhaps Sir William's usual impeccable stylist judgement had deserted him. Its lines quickly dated and this wide, overweight, thirsty model, renamed the 420G in 1966, was discontinued in 1970 and with it went the big Jaguar saloon line. Mark II sales held up but the outstanding Jaguar of the decade was the lovely E-type, the firm's last sports car, which offered sensational looks and 150mph performance for an incredible £1,480 in open form. Lyons, ironically, was not responsible for the E-type's lines; they were the work of Malcolm Sayer, a former aerodynamicist from the Bristol Aeroplane Company, who was also responsible for styling the legendary C- and D-type sports racers.

Jaguar's finances continued to improve. A record £1.6 million after-tax profit was achieved in 1965 and, in the following year, 25,963 cars left Browns Lane, which was the then highest ever total. It was against this background, and with the company's superlative XJ6 saloon in the offing, that Sir William negotiated the merger of his company with the British Motor Corporation. As a union, Sir William maintained, it 'was both necessary and desirable'.[29] An incidental aspect of the merger encapsulated the way in which Sir George Harriman and Sir William Lyons ran their respective businesses: Jaguar's suppliers were almost immediately on the telephone to Arthur Whittaker, pleading with him not to divulge the price that Jaguar was paying for its components to BMC as they were charging the corporation more. Just one instance was a 5-inch-diameter speedometer for which Jaguar paid 30s (£1.50), while the same unit cost BMC 35s (£1.75).

Jaguar's successes in the Le Mans 24-hour race had not escaped the attention of the Ford Motor Company and, in 1966, its Anglo-American GT40 took the chequered flag at Sarthe, so breaking Ferrari's seven-year domination of the race.[30] It represented a shift in emphasis for Ford in America which, from 1962, became actively engaged in promoting a new sports racing profile, marketed under the Total Performance banner. This new approach soon crossed the Atlantic, which was why Ford in Britain's successful Cortina was made available in GT and Cortina Lotus forms.

In many respects Project Archbishop, which became the Ford Cortina in 1962 and was the fastest-selling car in the history of the British motor industry, represented the high point of Sir Patrick Hennessy's eleven-year chairmanship of Ford of Britain. It was the third of a new generation of Ford cars, the first of which had appeared in 1959 in the shape of the 105E

Anglia, with its distinctive inclined rear window. Although this was marketed as a novel feature which permitted more head room for the rear passengers, it had in fact been adopted because it was cheaper for Ford to build it that way. The Anglia, with a 997cc overhead-valve engine, was a completely new model and a highly successful one, of which a record 191,752 examples were built in 1960, the first full year of production. The Anglia was still selling strongly when, in 1961, Ford introduced another new model in the shape of the Classic, a deliberate attempt by the company to move up market to occupy some of the territory then enjoyed by the Hillman Minx.

The Classic was to prove one of Ford's few mistakes. It had initially been intended to introduce it ahead of the 105E Anglia, but then had to give way to it because the side-valve-engined 100E was coming to the end of its production life. Next it was scheduled for 1960 but the success of the new Anglia meant that its launch was again delayed until 1961. However, its first full year of production in 1962 of 58,622 showed that the car, which at £766 was £88 more expensive than the Minx but undercut its Super derivative by the same amount, had not proved a success. In addition, its 1.3-litre engine was considered insufficient for this 18cwt car. Sir Terence Beckett recalls: 'When we looked at the Classic it was a heavy, high-cost car and when viewed in the context of our total strategy we realized that we couldn't go on in this way if we were going to hold on to the image of Ford producing the best value for money on the market.'[31]

That particular slot had been highjacked by BMC's Mini which caused Ford considerable consternation. 'I can remember one month in 1960 the Mini achieving 19 per cent market penetration, that was just *one* model,'[32] says Beckett. Consequently, Ford came under pressure from its dealers, customers and fleet owners but, above all, 'from our colleagues in America. The great thing was that the Mini was a fine piece of innovative engineering and there we were with very conventional cars.'[33] By stripping a Mini down to the last nut and bolt, Ford had proved that BMC was losing money on it, but the model's popularity with the public was not in dispute.

Ford realized that there would have to be a fundamental shift in corporate strategy because the loss-making Mini had outflanked them on one side which meant that Ford could no longer pursue the value-for-money theme in that area. 'We recognized that there was part of the market, and a very important part, which was satisfied by cars such as the Hillman Minx where we could provide a *vehicle of that package at a small-car price.*'[34]

This new strategy was made possible by a chain of events that began in the mid-1950s when the American motor industry started to be concerned by the growth of European imports spearheaded by the Volkswagen

Beetle. Ford's response was the no-frills Falcon of 1960, which was what the Americans called a 'compact' car and a half-way house between the big trans-Atlantic saloon and the small European one; to British eyes, however, this would still have been a large car. Ford then contemplated meeting the European challenge head on by producing what it termed the 'sub-compact', though the small volumes involved in American sales would hardly have justified the tooling costs.

But if the car were produced on a global basis, as the Model T had been, its manufacture might have made more economic sense. In 1957, therefore, Ford asked its British and German subsidiaries to submit designs for the project which was allotted the Cardinal coding. The German concept, which featured the V4-engined front-wheel-drive configuration, was chosen in preference to the more conventional front-engine/rear-drive layout proffered by Dagenham. At this stage it was intended to produce the Cardinal at Ford Germany's Cologne works and at a Ford factory at Louisville, Kentucky. A key aspect of the concept was that Ford engineers in Detroit had developed a new design of body construction which took metal, and therefore cost, out of a car's unitary hull and the Cardinal's body was built according to these principles.

This new initiative was brought back to Ford of Britain by Sir Patrick Hennessy during one of his regular visits to America. Yet another suggestion from Detroit was that Ford of Britain should have some involvement in the Cardinal project. Hennessy's reaction was swift and predictable. Fiercely jealous of Dagenham's independence, he immediately rejected this overture which would have resulted in British Ford's participation in an American/German project. In the spring of 1960 Terence Beckett, head of product planning, and Fred Hart, executive engineer, light cars, who had the mechanical layout of the 105E Anglia to his credit, were summoned to the chairman's office. Hennessy told them that he intended to challenge the Cardinal by producing a rival car at Ford in Britain. The difficulty was that the Cardinal was due to be announced in the autumn of 1962, only two and a half years hence, whereas it normally took three years to develop a new model. Hart immediately pointed out that, with this rigorous schedule, it would only be possible to produce a conventional front-engine/rear drive vehicle.

Yet the attractions were enormous. By adopting the new American body-construction techniques, cost could be taken out of the hull, and if this initial advantage were matched with rigorous costing of the other components, it would be possible to reduce the model's price to the detriment of the opposition and still make a profit. So the concept of the large car at a small car price was born. The project was coded Archbishop by Beckett, even though the Cardinal had no ecclesiastical associations but was a small American bird rather like a robin. 'I knew about this but did it as a bit of a joke. Our American colleagues never stopped pointing out the discrepancy!'[35] says Beckett.

What Ford's body engineers had to do was to develop a monocoque that had enough strength in it for the size and package required and was under 1,700lbs in weight. It was, said chief body engineer Don Ward, 'a matter of removing the unwanted passenger'. He asked Dennis Roberts, a key member of his team, to use the Classic's body as his starting point and remove around 150lbs of metal in the process. Roberts had spent some time in the London office of the Bristol Aeroplane Company: 'I had this background of having been trained as an automobile engineer and aircraft stressman.'[36] He therefore applied these disciplines to the Archbishop's structure and at the same time reduced the number of component parts by around 20 per cent.

Above all, project Archbishop would give Beckett's product planning team an opportunity to prove its worth. As cost was the key factor, the planners developed a policy for pricing the car's principal components. 'You don't attempt to adopt this approach to all the car's parts but pick the crucial 500 as the others tend to be related to them.'[37] Adopting what the planners call the practice of triangulation, the cost objectives were achieved by taking a part from the Anglia and comparing it with those of a competitor's model, in this instance the Hillman Minx and Volkswagen Beetle. The cost and weight of the new part was then considered in relation to the other two. Beckett picked a team of five executives who were each alloted components and had to sign for them in the Red Book, which is an integral part of the product planning process. This meant that each individual was responsible for his parts' specifications and that they were delivered on time. These requirements were then handed over to the engineering department and drawings were not released until the demanding objectives had been achieved. Working in conjunction with the engineers was a team of 200 technical cost estimators who ensured that the financial requirements were met. The Archbishop's steering wheel, for instance, was redesigned four times because it exceeded the planner's estimates by 1d(½p). If this did prove impossible, and the component still breached the rigorous price ceiling, this was accepted but savings had to be made elsewhere to compensate.

In the meantime, the styling requirements were set down on eight pages of typescript and handed to Roy Brown, Ford's head of styling. A Canadian by birth, Brown had joined Ford in America in 1953 and came to Dagenham after being responsible for the lines of the ill-fated Edsel in America. The clay model was approved in November 1960 and 'we blasted through from full clay to finished product in eighteen months'.[38] All the

148

Archbishop now required was a name. By December 1961 it had been decided to call the basic 1.2-litre model the Consul 225, while a 1.5-litre version would carry the Consul 335 name (the suffixes were superficial and had no particular relevance). Consul, an established Ford name, was chosen to convey the impression of a medium-sized car and was accordingly applied to the dummy airscoop on the car's bonnet. Then, early in 1962, Beckett came up with the alliterative Cortina name, after Cortina d'Ampezzo, the Italian Alpine venue of the 1960 Winter Olympics. 'I wanted to give the car a European flavour as Britain was negotiating for membership of the Common Market and the name would also provide a sporting image.'[39]

Job number one, the first Consul Cortina, went down the Dagenham production line in June 1962. The nineteen-month period from approval of the final clay model to the first production car probably constitutes an evolutionary record. Ironically, the rival Cardinal, marketed as the Taunus 12M and only German-built, was to prove nothing like as successful as the Cortina. 'We had the edge on them in terms of reliability and style and it took them a long time to get on top of the front-wheel drive concept, while we already had a proven power train,'[40] says Beckett. But Ford scored an 'own goal' because the Cortina spelt death for the never-robust Classic and it was discontinued in 1964. According to Beckett, 'One of the arts of management is if you recognize that you've done something like this not to endlessly cry about it and try and keep it going but drop it and move on.'[41]

In budgetary terms, Ford had allotted £13 million to the Cortina's development and, aided by the disciples of the Red Book, the planners were £50,000 under the investment target and 16s (80p) below the car's costing. The Cortina, which turned the scales at 15.5cwt and sold for £591 in basic four-door form, compared with the Hillman Minx (19.9cwt) and Vauxhall Victor (19.2cwt) which both cost £616. In price terms the Cortina came closest to BMC's Morris 1100 announced simultaneously, and underpriced like its Mini predecessor which sold for £592, just £1 more than the Ford. The sophisticated Morris contrasted with the Cortina's conventional layout but, although the front-wheel-drive model became the country's most popular car, the Cortina was the faster seller. This apparent discrepancy is explained by the fact that at this time Ford was the country's top exporter and the Cortina was in the forefront of its European and American sales.

Yet because the Morris 1100 was underpriced, and Ford was having to match it, the company initiated a searching enquiry on BMC's finances. This came to the conclusion that the corporation was heading for bankruptcy and Sir Patrick Hennessy promptly telephoned George

Harriman to inform him of the report's findings. But BMC's pricing policy remained unchanged.

This no doubt reflected BMC's attitude to Ford at this time, perfectly illustrated by an incident which occurred when a member of Ford's product planning staff rang George Harriman's Longbridge office to offer a Cortina for appraisal by BMC. (This reciprocal arrangement, operated by manufacturers then and now, gives them an opportunity to evaluate the other's products.) On this occasion the Ford offer was brushed aside with the reply that the BMC chairman was not interested in what Ford was doing . . .

The original Cortina lasted until 1966 and, after 1,010,090 had been built, it was replaced by the Mark II version, which was relatively more expensive than its predecessor because the Ford planners believed that the market would not only grow but also become more affluent. Once established, the impeccably costed Cortina line had become popular as a family saloon and also in the growing fleet market which accounted for around 40 per cent of new car sales. The model, and its successors, were responsible for contributing approximately half Ford's car profits until the line was discontinued in 1982.

Yet Ford did make some mistakes. The Corsair of 1963, which was intended to share the maximum amount of components with the Cortina, got out of control when its development costs soared. Then the massive Mark IV Zephyr/Zodiac, which replaced its Mark III predecessor too soon in 1966 (just 149,247 were built in five years), proved a sales disaster. Its proportions followed American 'bigger and better' thinking and it was unpopular, particularly with women drivers. Significantly, Vauxhall adopted a similar approach with its contemporary Viscount, with even worse results.

Although Ford of Britain was the American parent company's largest foreign subsidiary, Dagenham succumbed to pressure from Detroit for a greater say in its affairs. The first step was in 1961 when Ford's British operations became wholly American-owned, and it cost Ford of America $368 million (£150 million) to buy out its British shareholders. This gave Ford a greater degree of flexibility over its manufacturing operations, just as General Motors had on its overseas companies. Similarly, in the early 1960s the trend was to American managers, and Ford of Britain got Stan Gillen, its first American chief executive, who became managing director in 1965, though Sir Patrick Hennessy continued as chairman.

Ford, like the British Motor Corporation, urgently needed to expand its manufacturing operations but was prevented from doing so at Dagenham by the Conservative government and was directed instead to areas of high unemployment. John Barber was party to many of these negotiations and was able to witness Sir Patrick Hennessy's dealings with the government which culminated, in 1959, in Ford buying a 329-acre site at Halewood on Merseyside. He recalled:

> Hennessy was a very strong, tough character. He fought the government for around a year about Halewood, but although he lost in the end he managed to get far bigger grants than the ones that were originally on offer. I can remember one occasion when I was sitting in a Ford Policy Committee that his PA came in and said, 'The Prime Minister is on the phone,' to which Hennessy responded, 'Tell him I'm in a meeting – I'll call him back.' On another instance he walked out of a meeting with Reginald Maudling when he was Chancellor of the Exchequer. That's the sort of man he was.[42]

Halewood, which extended Ford's capacity by an extra 200,000 cars a year, was opened in 1963, while two years later the company established an axle plant in a former Pressed Steel factory at Swansea, South Wales. Ford's profits had been a respectable £24 million in 1964 but, in the following year, fell to a mere £8.9 million. This, in part, reflected the £275 million that Ford was spending on capital investment in the 1960s and the fact the market did not grow as fast as the firm expected. The company estimated that car sales had fallen 'roughly two years behind their projections.'[43] This left Ford with excess capacity, some of which was absorbed by taking in work from other manufacturers. One of them was making crankshafts for Rootes. After three years, when return on capital was a modest 3.1 per cent, profits revived in 1968 and, at £43 million, were the highest in the company's history.

France's veto of Britain's entry into the European Common Market in 1962 came as a considerable blow to Ford but John Andrews, managing director of Ford of Germany, was beginning to think in terms of a far closer liaison of Ford's German and British companies. In many respects the front-wheel-drive German Taunus 12M and the rear-drive Cortina encapsulated the divergent approaches between the two countries. 'He recognized that producing two lines of cars for what was fast becoming a market for a broad common taste and consumer appetite made no sense.'[44] The answer, believed Andrews, was to consolidate and rationalize the German and British operations, which would be possible if Ford of America first prudently ensured that it owned 100 per cent of both companies. The initial attempt at a common European vehicle came in 1965 with the Transit van, while the first car to be produced in both Britain and Germany was the Escort of 1968.

Ford of Europe came into being in 1967, and in May of the following year, seventy-year-old Sir Patrick Hennessy stepped down as chairman of Ford of Britain. He had fiercely resisted the integration though, from 1966, a former contemporary recalls, 'he was losing out on the battle with the States and in the end the Americans really had to bulldoze him into the ground because they thought he would stop Ford of Europe. It was really rather sad.' So Sir Patrick Hennessy, unquestionably the outstanding British motor industry executive of his generation, retired. He left Ford in 1968 having recorded its highest ever profits and the 30 per cent of British car production that the firm enjoyed that year was also a record. Yet Hennessy's name is barely known outside Ford and he never enjoyed the recognition that his achievements undoubtedly deserve.

For Vauxhall, which represented the other American-owned company in the British motor industry, the years between 1958 and 1967 were the most financially successful in its history and the £17.9 million profit it made in 1964 was to be the highest it ever attained. Philip Copelin, the firm's American chairman, was replaced in 1961 by William Swallow, 'the hard-headed Yorkshireman, who had succeeded Walter Hill as the managing director of General Motors Ltd'.[45]

In 1963 Vauxhall had expanded its British operations, under governmental pressure, by opening a new factory at Ellesmere Port on Merseyside. There, on a former war-time airfield at Hooton, work on the plant began in 1961 and components did not start leaving it until 1963 which were followed, in 1964, by Vauxhall's new small car, the Viva. Until then Vauxhall had ignored that market sector and, despite its apparently characterless styling, the model was to sell well, the first 100,000 examples being built within ten months. By the time this version was discontinued in March 1966, a total of 303,738 had been made.

The Viva was also significant because it marked the first co-operation between Vauxhall and Opel, General Motors' other European subsidiary, on model development. However, this initiative came not from the parent company but from Vauxhall itself. Opel was planning to introduce the Kadett, its own small car, and at Luton, chief engineer Maurice Platt was engaging in 'long and earnest discussions between Philip Copelin, David Jones and Gerald Palmer . . . [when] the idea emerged that much time and money would be saved if we pocketed our pride and proposed a considerable degree of "commonization" between a new Vauxhall and the Kadett, the design of which was already well advanced'.[46] As a result, although the new model, for which William Swallow suggested the Viva name, was styled in Britain, it used the Kadett floor plan, along with its engine. This combining of resources spread the ever-increasing costs of design, development and tooling. After the original HA car of 1963 had been discontinued in 1966, it was replaced by the far more attractive HB version which lasted until 1970 and sold 556,752 examples.

William Swallow left Vauxhall in 1966 and his place was taken by David Hegland, who had previously been managing director of General Motors' Australian Holden plant. In the meantime the big car line continued to evolve. The FB Victor, a great visual improvement on its predecessor, appeared in 1962 and from this grew the enlarged FC model in 1965. It formed the basis of the long-running Cresta line of 1966, though it was powered by a 3.2-litre six-cylinder in-house Chevrolet engine, the first occasion on which an American power unit had been used in a Vauxhall. Yet from 1965 onwards the Victor's fortunes slumped. In 1967 British sales amounted to only 34,722 cars, while the Cresta and its up-market Viscount derivative accounted for a mere 7,287 registrations. The success story, however, was the HB Viva of which 100,200 examples were sold.

Until 1964 Ford and Vauxhall accounted for the sole American representation within the British motor industry, but in that year Chrysler, the smallest member of the American Big Three, took a shareholding in the Rootes Group. Following its deficit in the previous year, Rootes moved back into profit in 1958, and this rose to £4.4 million in the boom year of 1960, the highest ever figure attained by the Group or its Chrysler successors. The downturn of the economy in 1961 saw profits fall across the industry, but Rootes' problems were compounded in September when a strike broke out in its troubled British Light Steel Pressings plant at Acton. The stoppage lasted for thirteen weeks and resulted in the dismissal of individuals identified by the company as trouble makers. Rootes was thus seen to be the first of the motor manufacturers to stand up to the unions, an 'achievement' for which Lord Rootes (he had been made Baron Rootes of Ramsbury in 1959) received congratulations from his fellow car makers. 'Everyone patted Billy on the back,' recalled one company executive, 'but nobody sent a cheque.'[47]

However, the most significant – and, it proved, the most fateful – event of the Group's final years came in October 1960 when Lord Rootes announced that the firm was to build a new car factory at Linwood, 12 miles west of Glasgow, but about 280 miles north of its Ryton factory. It was to be the first Scottish car plant since the demise of the Argyll at Alexandria-by-Glasgow in 1932. Yet, like the other car makers, Rootes had moved away from its traditional Midlands locations because, although it had available land at Ryton, it had been refused an Industrial Development Certificate for expansion there. Pressed Steel had already established a factory at Linwood and the new Rootes facility would be built adjacent to it and have the capacity to produce 150,000 cars a year. The model chosen would be a completely new one for, like Vauxhall,

Rootes, which had hitherto avoided building small cars, had decided to enter that market sector. Yet it is difficult to imagine a greater contrast between the no-frills, ultra-conventional Viva and what was to become the Hillman Imp with its sophisticated overhead-camshaft rear-mounted aluminium engine.

The car's origins reached back to 1955 when Bernard Winter, Rootes' chief engineer, asked Michael Parkes and Tim Fry, two young and enthusiastic members of the company's experimental department, 'to carry out an investigation of existing small cars'. This did not mean that the Group at this stage wanted to build such a vehicle, but the duo were to 'merely look very thoroughly into what the market consisted of'.[48] Their brief was subsequently extended to produce a vehicle that was capable of 60mph, return 60mpg and be capable of carrying two adults and two children. The resulting car was named the Slug and, for reasons of cheapness, a 600cc Villiers-built two-cylinder air-cooled engine was rear mounted. Suspension was by equally frugal swing axles front and rear but, in 1957, the project was turned down by the Rootes board. Sir William Rootes had indicated his dislike of the vehicle by refusing to ride in it. However, although the board felt that the specification was too crude, it suggested that the Slug's engine be replaced by a water-cooled four-cylinder unit. Tim Fry was later to recall: 'We got terribly depressed about this and we said to each other, "We must get on with it quickly otherwise we'll get a great lump of cast iron in the back and the thing will handle like a pig." Then Mike said that he knew just the thing . . . a nice aluminium engine that he thought would go in. So he wrote to Coventry Climax and said he was building a Special, please would they send him installation drawings of the 750cc FWM single-cam engine.'[49]

The enterprising pair obtained the engine and managed to fit it in the space previously occupied by the twin, with the radiator, mounted Fiat 600-style, alongside the power unit. It was running within three weeks of the rejection of the two-cylinder version. This resulted in a much more acceptable vehicle but the project was still not given the go-ahead.

Then, in February 1959, Peter War replaced Bernard Winter as Rootes' chief engineer. A veteran of the war-time rear-engined swing-axle-suspended Fedden car, he had broken his hip when the 1 Ex prototype had turned turtle during tests at Stoke Orchard aerodrome, Gloucestershire. His contribution to the embryo Rootes design was to replace the rear swing-axle layout with more expensive but more acceptable semi-trailing arms. At this time Fry and Parkes both bought Minis and 'we said to each other, if we can make a car that is as good as this but which has a better gearbox and brakes, we won't be doing badly'.[50] By this time the engine capacity had been upped to 800cc, which was in 1960 when the project was given the official go-ahead, but the Mini's 850cc capacity ensured that the Rootes car's engine was again increased – to 875cc.

Development of the Imp then proceeded simultaneously with the construction and equipping of the Linwood factory. When the Rootes baby was introduced in May 1963, it was the most sophisticated car on the British market and, unlike the Mini with its existing BMC A Series engine, the Imp was completely new. The lines were pleasing and resembled those of a scaled-down version of the rear-engined Chevrolet Corvette of 1959. The Imp was a quiet, economical and well-mannered small car with a delightful gear change and its lively engine reflected a top speed nudging 80mph. There were clever features such as an opening rear window and fold-flat rear seats. The all-aluminium Coventry Climax-derived engine ran at a 10:1 compression ratio and, like the Jaguar XK unit, clearance between the single overhead camshaft and valves was maintained by shimming. At £508 in basic form, the Hillman was £61 more expensive than the equivalent Mini, and the projected 150,000-a-year manufacturing target was never realized and the following Imp production figures tell their own story:

1963	23,382
1964	69,420
1965	47,342
1966	43,748
1967	45,240
1968	43,256

So what went wrong? Regrettably, during the first two years of production, the model suffered from a variety of teething troubles which were a reflection of the insuperable twin major problems of producing an unproven design in a brand-new factory. Consequently the car never shook off its reputation for unreliability. The aluminium engine over-heated and garages did not take to it because a torque wrench, rather than straightforward spanners, were required for most jobs related to the power unit. The ingenious but erratic pneumatic throttle was replaced by a conventional cable after a year, while a manual choke took the place of the original automatic one. Some early cars suffered from steering difficulties resulting from seized 'greaseless' kingpins and grease nipples were quickly introduced.

Rootes' Scottish activities were undertaken against a background of two years of losses in 1962 and 1963, and in May of the following year Chrysler announced that it was acquiring 30 per cent of Rootes' voting shares and 50 per cent of non-voting ones. Unlike General Motors and Ford, Chrysler did not have any European subsidiaries, a state of affairs that Lynn

Townsend, who became the corporation's president in 1961, was determined to redress. Its first trans-Atlantic overtures came prior to Townsend's appointment, however, for in 1956 Chrysler had approached Standard to ascertain whether it was interested in developing a small car for the European market. Next, in 1958, the corporation purchased a 25 per cent holding in the French Simca company, though it was 1963 before it acquired a majority 63 per cent stake. In 1961 there were new overtures to the by then vulnerable Standard company and Leyland, the latter firm again being approached in 1962. From that year Chrysler's share of the American market grew from 10 to 18 per cent by 1968, and it was with this improved financial performance that an approach was made to Rootes.

These initial discussions took place in great secrecy at Fountain House, Lord Rootes' Mayfair home, when his servants were given the day off. The Conservative government approved the deal in July 1964, but there was a proviso that if Chrysler wanted to increase its holding it would require governmental approval. In May 1965 Chrysler upped its holding in Rootes to 45 per cent of voting shares and 66 per cent of non-voting ones, which was approved by the new Labour government.

Lord Rootes died, aged seventy, in December 1964, just four months after the Rootes shareholders had approved the deal. Sir Reginald Rootes, two years his brother's junior, assumed the chairmanship, while the new Lord Rootes, who had been managing director since 1962, continued in that capacity. Three Chrysler representatives joined the Rootes board.

The most pressing problem was the ageing Minx range which had also been suffering at the hands of the Ford Cortina. The enlarged Super Minx arrived for 1962, though the basic car, which dated back to 1956, was urgently in need of replacement. Work on a new model, coded the Arrow range, began in 1961 and was confirmed in November 1963. It appeared for 1967 as the Hillman Hunter, with an improved five-bearing crankshaft engine and MacPherson strut independent front suspension. This new shell soon acquired the Humber, Singer and Hillman Minx names.

Yet Rootes continued to make losses and in 1965 and 1966 pre-tax deficits totalled £3.3 million. The only outward evidence of Chrysler's involvement in Rootes came from late 1965 when the corporation's Pentastar (the symbol was yet another Townsend initiative) began appearing in Rootes showrooms. In 1966, following BMC's takeover of Pressed Steel, Rootes had been forced to purchase its Linwood factory for £14 million. By the end of the year Chrysler had spent a total of £27 million on Rootes and the firm was not yet profitable. It was then that the American corporation made it clear that it would not proceed with any further investments until it gained majority control of the company. Of a further £20 million it was prepared to invest in Rootes, £10 million was urgently required in early 1967 for working capital.

Harold Wilson's Labour administration was on the horns of a dilemma, for although Rootes was 'too small to make money, it was always too large to close down'.[51] The government did not want to see the third member of the British Big Five come under American ownership, but neither BMC nor Leyland was interested in taking the firm over. In January 1967 Chrysler was therefore given the go-ahead to acquire a majority holding in Rootes with the government's newly formed Industrial Reorganization Corporation taking a £3 million stake in the company and appointing a representative on the Rootes board.

Losses were running at £4.7 million in the six months prior to 31 January and Chrysler wasted little time in reorganizing the Rootes corporate hierarchy. It effectively marked the end of the family's control of the firm's affairs, and although Lord Rootes took over from his seventy-one-year-old uncle as chairman, he was 'not a member of the eight-man executive committee that runs the company'.[52] His brother, the Hon. Brian Rootes, and his cousin Timothy resigned at this time. The executive floor at the Group's Devonshire House headquarters, hitherto known as 'The Green Belt' because of the leafy hue of the wall-to-wall carpeting, was renamed by a wag 'The Garden of Remembrance'.[53]

The all-important position of managing director went to a newcomer, fifty-two-year-old Gilbert Hunt, formerly chief executive of Massey-Ferguson, who took over the job on the basis that he would have direct access to the Chrysler decision makers in Detroit. Hunt had an unenviable assignment. To the new management it seemed 'that the company had been divided into a number of separate family empires, without close co-ordination between them; and that the autocratic reign of Lord Rootes had been followed by a period of less decisiveness'.[54] It also found that there were no proper financial controls. Rootes had no profit plan, as such; 'instead there was a broad target, say an annual improvement of £2 or £3 million'.[55] It was decided to sell off the seminal sales side of the business, though some family links were maintained when Timothy Rootes subsequently bought up a number of Rootes distributors.

As if this were not enough, capacity was severely underutilized, largely through the failure of the Imp, though the factories in Kew, Acton and Cricklewood were sold off and 2,500 men lost their jobs. On a more positive front, in May 1967 Lord Rootes opened a new factory in Iran which was to assemble £30 million worth of Hillman cars. In 1967 Rootes lost a record £10.5 million.

While the Chrysler men were grappling with the almost intractable problem of returning Rootes to long-term profitability, just that had been achieved by Leyland Motors, which in 1961 bought the loss-making Standard-Triumph company. In doing so it achieved one of the great commercial successes of the post-war years and this impressive turnabout can therefore be seen as the first step along the road that led to the creation of the British Leyland Motor Corporation in 1968.

Back in 1959 Standard-Triumph International, as the firm became that year, had returned a healthy £4 million profit on a record production of 138,762 cars, and the Michelotti-styled Herald made its appearance at the same 1959 Motor Show as the Ford 105E Anglia and the Mini Minor from BMC. It seemed that Alick Dick's gamble was paying off, even though the Herald's unconventional body construction was causing problems. There were complaints by customers of water leaks and criticism that the car was underpowered, yet its arrival marked an effective rebirth of the Triumph name. Standard, by contrast, was allowed to run down as a marque and was discontinued in 1963, a victim of semantics rather than market forces.

Production fell back by 50,000 to 78,735 and profits were halved to £2.2 million in 1960, but there was worse to come. The second half of the year saw a credit squeeze, initiated in the budget, beginning to take effect while the start of a world recession in the middle of the year hit the hitherto buoyant sports car market. The vulnerable Standard-Triumph company was soon in trouble. 'Money poured out like water,' said Dick. 'It was absolutely terrifying. We moved from £6 million in the black to £4 million in the red.'[56] Standard had always run on a heavy overdraft – it had stood at £7 million from 1954 and, in November, Barclays confirmed this figure. However, as luck would have it, that month the Lancashire-based commercial vehicle manufacturers Leyland Motors had made a bid for the firm. The £18 million offer was made public in December, though it was April 1961 before the takeover was approved by the shareholders of the respective firms. In May Lord Tedder was replaced as Standard-Triumph's chairman by Leyland's chairman and managing director, Sir Henry Spurrier.

The Spurrier family's associations with Leyland Motors went back to 1896. The firm's origins can be traced to the early nineteenth century when Elias Sumner was established as the local blacksmith at Leyland, a village 6 miles south of Preston. His descendant, James Sumner, inherited in 1892 what had become a general engineering business and he began to experiment with steam. James first converted a tricycle to steam power and then transferred the unit to an ancient lawn mower that had been presented to him by the head gardener of a local estate. Sumner decided to put the steam-driven lawn mower into production, selling it to the public at £85, and Rugby School bought the first one.

The business prospered and more capital was required, so the Preston engineering firm of T. Coulthard and Company bought a half-share in J. Sumner Ltd. The Spurrier family became involved when the Manchester-based Stott company, run by a George Spurrier, took over the Coulthard interest, leaving that firm as a rival concern as it had begun producing its own steam-powered lorries. Then, on August Bank holiday 1896, George's brother Henry returned from America where he had spent eight years, some of them as a draughtsman with the Florida Central Peninsula Railway. His brother's latest business venture excited Henry's passion for steam and he immediately sought out James Sumner at Leyland. The brothers then descended on their father, also Henry Spurrier, a retired businessman turned Derbyshire farmer, to finance the venture and as a result he became chairman of the Lancashire Steam Motor Company which was established in 1896.

A steam van appeared later in the year and steam lorries followed, and in 1905 the firm introduced its first petrol-driven vehicle, though steam-powered ones continued to be built until 1926. The company produced its first bus in 1906 – for the London General Omnibus Company – and in 1907 the firm merged with Coulthards of Preston and changed its name to Leyland Motors. By 1914 the workforce had grown to 1,500 and 2,092 petrol-engined vehicles had been built.

During the First World War, Leyland-built RAF-type lorries were in considerable demand and no less than 5,932 vehicles of all varieties were produced. The firm decided to buy back and recondition its war-time lorries and the former Sopwith aircraft at Ham, Kingston, Surrey was bought for this purpose. Leyland also decided to enter the car market and the 7.2-litre Leyland Eight of 1920, with a £2,500 chassis price, was Britain's first production straight eight, intended as a Rolls-Royce challenger. Designed by the talented Parry Thomas, who had been made Leyland's chief engineer in 1917, the Eight ceased production in 1922 after about eighteen examples had been built.

Henry Spurrier II took over as chairman and managing director of the company that had been reconstructed in 1919. The post-war slump hit Leyland hard and, by August 1921, losses amounted to £755,515. The firm's bankers were sufficiently concerned to recommend that Henry Spurrier step down as chairman, though he remained as managing director, and he was replaced by John Toulmin, a cheese factor and newspaper proprietor, whose associations with the company reached back to 1896 when he was running Coulthard's.

In 1922 the company began producing another car, and as it was built on a royalty basis, it carried the Trojan rather than the Leyland name. This utilitarian two-stroke four-cylinder solid-tyred vehicle, which only cost £157 on its 1923 introduction, must have gladdened those cost-conscious

Lancastrian hearts. The Trojan – a greater contrast to the Eight is difficult to imagine – has the distinction of being one of the few cars to have been advertised in the *Church Times*. It was built at Leyland's Kingston works until 1928, then production was transferred to the Croydon-based Trojan Ltd, where it continued to be made in van form until 1956.

During the inter-war years Leyland consolidated its position as a front-line manufacturer of buses, of which the first and most significant model was the L type – the Lion, Lioness and Leviathan – with the distinction of having a purpose-built chassis rather than the usual modified goods one. These proved popular and Leyland built fire engines and dust carts as well as lorries. Bus manufacture was further underpinned in 1928 with the arrival of the lowered six-cylinder Tiger and Titan buses, designed by G. J. Rackham, who joined Leyland briefly from its AEC rivals. Leyland had delivered over 2,500 Lions by 1928, the year in which the firm once again began paying dividends. This more prosperous era was marked in 1929 by the company's taking its 3,000 employees on an ambitious works outing to Ostend and the First World War battlefields.

In 1931 Leyland offered its own in-house diesel and from 1933 almost all its vehicles could be so powered. Leyland profits stood at a healthy £636,095 by 1939, a year in which Henry Spurrier II's son, also Henry, became assistant general manager. Born in 1899, Henry Spurrier III was educated at Repton and joined Leyland as an apprentice during the First World War. After war service as an RFC pilot in the Mesopotamian campaign, he returned to Leyland and worked with Parry Thomas, 'the finest automobile engineer I have ever known'[57] on the Leyland Eight, though he never forgot the disastrous early post-war years when his salary was cut from £500 to £400 and the firm flirted with bankruptcy. He continued to work his way through the company and, in 1942, after his father's death, became Leyland's general manager.

The Second World War was again a time of growth and the firm diversified into tank production from a purpose-built factory at nearby Farington. The end of hostilities in 1945 saw Leyland in expansive mood and that year it bought West Yorkshire Foundries of Leeds, the first of nine major takeovers which spanned the next twenty-three years. In 1946 Leyland established British United Traction, for trolley bus manufacture, with its AEC rival. The following year the firm announced its new Comet truck and bus range, intended, as the times dictated, for export markets. That year Leyland built around 3,400 chassis, which made it third in the specialist vehicle league behind AEC with 4,500 and Guy's with 3,750. In 1949 Henry Spurrier became Leyland's managing director and made thirty-five-year-old Donald Stokes, who had been with the firm since he was sixteen, general sales manager.

Donald Gresham Stokes (born in 1914) grew up with a passion for buses while his father was transport manager at Plymouth. By 1935 the city was to have a wholly Leyland fleet! He decided that he wanted to join Leyland when he was eleven and, after education at Blundell's, he fulfilled his ambition when, in 1930, he joined the Lancashire company as an apprentice. Donald Stokes received his technical education at the Harris Institute of Technology in Preston. During the Second World War he served with the Royal and Electrical and Mechanical Engineers and, as a lieutenant-colonel with the army in Italy in 1945, was asked by Henry Spurrier 'to write a brief on the way Leyland should organize its export business when the war was over'.[58] Leyland had exported its products from the very outset and during the 1930s Spurrier, fearing that the firm had saturated the home market, had pursued export ones, so that by the outbreak of the war, one in five Leylands were sold overseas.

In his brief Stokes wrote that European countries with large sterling balances would represent stop-gap markets before they re-established their own industries, 'It was therefore the old Imperial markets, the Middle East and South America, on which Leyland must concentrate.'[59] When Stokes rejoined Leyland in 1946 as export manager, he wasted little time getting to grips with the job, but has subsequently confessed that he had no idea where to start, 'so I did what I've always done when I didn't know what to do. I did something.'[60] In 1948 the small sales team moved to London, and at his office in Hanover House, Hanover Square, Stokes soon propagated a no-nonsense approach to sales coupled with an ebullient, undisguised enthusiasm for the product. In 1950 Leyland introduced its underfloor-engined Royal Tiger and Olympic buses. Stokes secured a $10 million Cuban order for the Royal Tiger and the following year a £4 million contract from the Argentine Ministry of Transport. Such sales, along with further successes in Holland, Scandinavia and Africa, were to set the pattern for the decade. Leyland's output trebled between 1947 and 1952, and the following year Stokes joined the Leyland board. In 1954 the company sales passed the £1 million mark for the first time.

Leyland's Leeds Foundries takeover was followed by a second, in 1951, when the company bought out its Albion competitors. At the time the latter was at the height of its fortunes, which immediately made the combined firm the leading company amongst the specialist vehicle producers. By 1954 Leyland was producing around 10,000 chassis or about double that of AEC, its only significant competitor. Albion was left much to its own devices because its and Leyland's ranges were largely complimentary and it was not until 1955 that some rationalization took place. Then, in 1957, Stanley Markland, Leyland's works director, took over as the Glasgow company's managing director.

Markland was born in Macclesfield in 1903 and, after education at Chorley Grammar School, he maintained, 'I was just kicked out into the world and I had to do the best I could. I just had to shape myself. You don't have to go to Eton or Harrow to do that.'[61] He joined Leyland as an apprentice in 1920 and, in the following year, was awarded the first engineering scholarship to be granted by the company. This resulted in a post as junior assistant in the research department, and Markland became research engineer in 1937 and chief engineer in 1945. A seat on the Leyland board followed in 1946 and Stanley Markland became works director in 1953. By that time Markland had established a formidable reputation as an outstanding production engineer, and was widely seen as Spurrier's heir apparent. He administered his factory in a down-to-earth way: 'I ran it out of the top of my head . . . and that's the cheapest way – if your head works.'[62] On the debit side Markland's blunt approach had upset some of Leyland's customers though his abilities ensured that, by the late 1950s, Leyland's ruling triumvirate consisted of Spurrier, who in 1957 became chairman as well as managing director, Markland and Stokes.

The firm had expanded again in 1955 when it took over Scammell of Watford, a year in which Henry Spurrier received a knighthood. Soon afterwards, his thoughts turned beyond the commercial vehicle world for, in 1957, he received a 'monumental report on the car industry'[63] that he had commissioned from Sir Roy Fedden who was, for a time, Leyland's director of research and development. Not that this represented Spurrier's first post-war interest in the industry. Back in 1949 Leyland had cautiously indicated that it might take 'substantial financial interest' in the troubled Jowett company, 'if, and only if, Briggs [Jowett's body supplier] joined them to an equal extent'.[64] At that time Briggs had no thought of becoming so allied and there the matter rested.

Leyland's finances continued to improve. In 1958 pre-tax profits stood at £6.4 million and in 1960, the year the firm made its bid for Standard-Triumph, they had spiralled to a record £9.4 million. Today Lord Stokes is emphatic that the Standard bid was not the first step in a master plan for Leyland to take over the British motor industry in the same way that it had swallowed up its commercial vehicle competitors. He said:

I would like to say that there was such a plan but I don't think that there was one. We were first attracted to Standard because we thought we might co-operate with them on some of their overseas interests [in New Zealand]. This applied to most of our takeovers because we were good on the export side. Back in the 1950s we found in Africa, Australia and various other countries that we were running into headlong competition with Albion and it seemed stupid for two relatively small British companies to be competing against each other so we merged with them. Later when we found we needed heavy vehicles for the oil fields and so on, we either had to develop them ourselves or acquire Scammell which is what we did.[65]

With Leyland's bid for Standard-Triumph confirmed in 1961 the commercial vehicle manufacturer once again joined the ranks of the car makers yet, Stokes points out, 'we weren't motor car people. I think that we were much more down-to-earth and less flamboyant. We switched lights off and counted pennies.'[66]

In addition to Sir Henry Spurrier becoming Standard's chairman in May 1961, Stanley Markland and Donald Stokes, along with Sidney Baybutt. Leyland's chief accountant, joined the board, though Alick Dick remained as managing director. That was until just before the firm's summer holidays in August when, Harry Webster recalled, 'Sir Henry Spurrier and Stanley Markland asked whether they could have the use of my office in the engineering section which was some distance from the central office block.'[67] For the rest of the day members of the original Standard board, from Alick Dick downwards, were summoned and sacked. In all, seven lost their jobs, the exception being Frank Dixon who had only recently joined the board from Hall Engineering where he had been managing director.

Alick Dick's place as managing director was taken by Stanley Markland, who immediately initiated a programme of sweeping economies. Eight hundred staff were sacked, which saved £1 million, a paint plant was bought by Jaguar and the firm's in-house pattern-making business was sold off. In December, Spurrier asked Markland to devote most of his time to Standard-Triumph (he was still managing director of Albion) in addition to his Leyland duties. Only 78,383 cars had been built in 1961, the lowest figure since 1957, and with a break-even figure of 95,000, Standard made a pre-tax loss of £1.5 million.

From December, Markland scrapped the customary board meetings ('we just ran it . . .'[68]), and with the firm's overdraft standing at £9 million, he was seeing the bank manager every fortnight. He decided to risk increasing production from March in the interests of dealer confidence which paid off when the budget, in April, reduced purchase tax on cars from 55 to 45 per cent. In May the firm was moving towards the 1,800-car-a-week break-even point and in June the overdraft had fallen to below £5 million. Output for the year rose to 100,764, though the firm was still losing £10 on every Herald it built, despite the arrival of a 1200 version in 1961, improved quality and greater market penetration. Work was also proceeding apace on project Barb, a replacement for the Standard

Vanguard, initiated by Markland and Stokes, which was approved by the Standard board in July 1961. 'It was one of Markland's great contributions to the Standard revival that when other Leyland men were having doubts about the 2000, his faith remained unshaken; it was largely at his insistence that the project went ahead in that form.'[69]

Meanwhile the Standard board had been strengthened, from May 1962, with the arrival of Harry Webster and George Turnbull. The latter had joined Standard as an apprentice in 1941 and won the Sir John Black Scholarship to Birmingham University, where he took a BSc engineering degree, and although he left Standard briefly to work for Petters, he returned to Canley in 1956 as divisional manager, car production. His 1962 appointment as general manager was an endorsement of the abilities and tough-minded approach of this thirty-five-year-old man.

Nineteen sixty-two also saw the arrival of the Spitfire sports car. One day during the previous year Harry Webster and Stanley Markland had been walking through the Banner Lane styling studio when Markland spotted the outline of a car concealed under a dust sheet. Webster recalls, 'He immediately wanted to know what it was. It didn't have a name at that stage, so I said it was a sports car on the Herald chassis. Markland asked that it be wheeled out and asked me, "why aren't we making it?" I told him that at the time that it had been produced [1960], we had no money. "Ridiculous," he said. "I'll take responsibility. It's a winner." '[70]

The highly acclaimed 2000 appeared in 1963 and its Triumph badging was the final nail in the coffin of the Standard name. Aimed, along with the rival Rover 2000, at the growing executive market, it was well priced at £1,094, and its Michelotti styling and all-independent suspension (it was the first British car to employ the subsequently popular rear semi-trailing arms) helped ensure that Standard-Triumph never again made a loss in its pre-British Leyland Motor Corporation days. In addition, by 1965, Triumph's Herald was enjoying the highest resale price of any British small car, and with the arrival of the 1300 version in 1966, the firm could barely keep pace with demand. Leyland, and more particularly Stanley Markland, had successfully taken Triumph up market as a producer of quality cars: the company returned record profits of £6 million in 1967/8. Yet, at the end of 1963, Markland stepped down, not only as managing director of Standard-Triumph but also as deputy managing director of Leyland Motors, retired to his Chorley farm and followed his father into the laundry business.

'He was just about the best boss I ever had,' remembered Webster, 'and he was an engineer to his finger tips.'[71] To begin to ascertain the reasons for the grievous loss to Triumph, and to the British motor industry, we must briefly retrace our steps to 1962. That year Leyland took over AEC, its competitor in the bus market from pre-First World War days, giving it complete dominance in the specialist commercial vehicle market. Then, in September, in his hour of triumph, Sir Henry Spurrier, the engine of Leyland's stupendous post-war growth, fell ill and immediately asked Donald Stokes to take over as managing director. In Sir Henry's absence, Markland chaired the next Leyland board meeting. But afterwards Spurrier offered a surprised Sir William Black, chairman of AEC, the deputy chairmanship of Leyland Motors. When Markland heard of this in February 1963 for the first time, he responded, 'What, at Seventy?'[72] He himself was fifty-nine at the time. At a subsequent meeting, Spurrier told Markland of his decision. 'Markland said he would have to resign but was quite prepared to word his resignation as a retirement if he could go with full pension rights.'[73] Spurrier departed for a trip to South Africa in the hope that it would restore his health, but was taken ill on board and in May was told that he had six months to live. Sir William Black had become Leyland's chairman and in July ironically, just as Standard-Triumph moved into credit, Markland addressed a special board meeting when he bitterly pointed out 'that he had been used to solve one of the company's most difficult problems, namely the rehabilitation of Standard-Triumph, and that Sir Henry's action in failing to honour the promises made to him . . . was a serious breach of good faith.'[74] When Markland resigned in December 1963, Donald Stokes replaced the ailing Spurrier as Standard-Triumph's chairman. The managing directorship was left vacant but George Turnbull assumed greater responsibilities.

Sir Henry Spurrier died from a brain tumour on 17 July 1965, the day after his sixty-sixth birthday. Why had he not wished Stanley Markland to succeed him? An undoubted factor was that his manner was against him. One industry commentator described Markland as looking 'so Dickensian that it is almost a surprise not to find him in a wing collar'.[75] In Lord Stokes's opinion: 'Stanley Markland was a clever engineer and shrewd businessman. But he was a rather blunt Lancastrian and did not always flatter people enough. I know that Sir Henry Spurrier, and the board, were worried that Stanley wasn't quite in the mould to carry that responsibility. It was a task that called for a lot of diplomacy.'[76] Stokes confirms that he told Spurrier he would have been quite prepared to work with Markland and he appreciated that he was eleven years older than he was. 'I wasn't trying to jump over his head but he just wasn't quite smooth enough.'[77] But when Markland departed, Leyland lost one of the ablest members of its already seriously stretched management team.

When the Leyland Motor Corporation was formed in February 1963, seventy-year-old Sir William Black was appointed chairman and although Stokes, as deputy chairman and managing director, was forty-nine, his other colleagues, Lord Brabazon (who also came from AEC) and Leyland's own Walter West were seventy-nine and seventy respectively. However, the Corporation's growing stature was reflected in its move into prestigious new offices at Berkeley Square House in London.

Leyland's profits continued to grow and achieved an all-time pre-tax high of £20.4 million in 1965 but it suffered, along with the rest of the industry, from the Labour government's deflationary policies from 1966 onwards. In that year the surplus dropped to £16.4 million, though it rose again to £18.2 million in 1967. As the company's fortunes rose again, Sir Donald Stokes (he had been knighted in 1965) replaced Sir William Black as chairman of the Leyland Motor Corporation and, while he continued as managing director, Dr Albert Fogg, who had been the first director of the Motor Industry Research Association, became deputy managing director. George Turnbull also joined the Leyland board.

Stokes had, in the meantime, become a founder member of the Industrial Reorganization Corporation set up by the Labour government in 1966 with the aim of using 'every means available to improve the competitiveness of British industry'.[78] The IRC was also concerned that the growing number of mergers taking place during the decade 'were motivated by either mainly financial or defensive considerations'.[79] It would play an increasingly significant role in the negotiations between Leyland and BMC that had been intermittently under way since 1964.

In addition to these discussions, Leyland had also held talks with Jaguar. When Sir William Lyons agreed to merge with BMC in 1966, Leyland turned to Rover, which like Jaguar had become vulnerable when BMC took over Pressed Steel, its body supplier, in 1965. Rover had dramatically changed its image during the 1960s. Spencer Wilks had retired as the company's chairman in 1962 and Maurice Wilks stepped down as managing director in 1963. George Farmer, who had joined Rover in 1940, shared the Rover managing directorship with Maurice Wilks from 1960 and, as a one-time colleague put it, 'George's expertise stopped short of engineering [he is a chartered accountant] and Maurice's stopped short of finance – it was an ideal arrangement.'[80] George Farmer took over Rover's chairmanship from Spencer Wilks in 1963 and William Martin-Hurst, who was Maurice Wilks's brother-in-law and had joined the company from Teddington Aircraft Controls in 1960, became managing director. A younger, talented generation was also taking over at Solihull. In 1960, Spencer and Maurice Wilks nephew, Malvern College-educated Peter Wilks, who had joined Rover in 1946, was appointed chief engineer and became Rover's technical director in 1964. Then there was his cousin, Spen King, thirty-five years old in 1960, who after education at Haileybury and a Rolls-Royce apprenticeship had come to Solihull at about the same time.

They, along with stylist David Bache and heavyweights Robert Boyle and Gordon Bashford, were responsible for the company's all-new four-cylinder 2000, which appeared in 1963. Like its Triumph contemporary, the new four-cylinder Rover was aimed at a young, prosperous clientèle who would never have contemplated buying one of the dignified but old-fashioned P4 'Auntie' Rovers. The 2000, designated P6, was soon outselling its distinguished predecessor, but if it did have a shortcoming it was that its performance was a little disappointing. As predecent demanded, there was a six-cylinder P7 derivative waiting in the wings, though this was discontinued following a visit William Martin-Hurst made to America in the winter of 1963/4.

It was while visiting Carl Keikhaefer of General Motors' Mercury Marine division's experimental workshop at Fond du Lac, Wisconsin, in the hope of obtaining a Rover gas turbine order, that Martin-Hurst spied a small alloy V8 engine, destined for a boat, which Keikhaefer had just removed from a Buick Skylark. On enquiry it proved to be a 215 cu. in. (3523cc) unit which Buick had just discontinued because it was too expensive for the low-price Special range, of which the Skylark was a version. The company had designed a cast-iron 198 cu. in. (3244cc) V6 derivative to take its place. Martin-Hurst was extremely interested in the V8 as he was convinced that it would fit in the Rover 2000's engine compartment. This was spacious because when the P6 had been conceived there had been thoughts about a gas turbine-powered version. Rover was a pioneer in the field, which followed on from its war-time work, but the concept had been abandoned.

Martin-Hurst returned to Britain, full of enthusiasm for the V8, and after he had overcome initial in-house opposition at Solihull, negotiations with General Motors were opened in 1964 for Rover to take over its manufacture. The licence was granted in January 1965 and although Joe Turlay, the engine's designer, was only eighteen months from retirement, he was whisked over to Solihull to supervise the V8's anglicization. Its first appearance, in 1967, was in the slow-selling 3-litre Rover, introduced back in 1958 and confusingly renamed the 3.5-litre, whereas the 1968 V8-engined 2000 was called the 3500! Even more exciting was the P6BS, an experimental mid-engined sports car conceived by Spen King and Gordon Bashford. The V8 has since powered the 2000's SD1 successor, the Land-Rover, the Range Rover, the MGB GT V8 and the low-production Morgan sports car. Rover and, later British Leyland, were to have every reason to be grateful for Martin-Hurst's chance encounter in Wisconsin.

Like all the car makers, Rover was urgently in need of more factory space by the late 1950s when it estimated that it required a further 250,000 square feet. Inevitably there was room at Solihull but government policy forbade expansion there. Rover was insistent 'that for the long term good of the company, private car assembly must remain at Solihull'.[81] In 1960 came a compromise. Rover received approval to build a new North Block at Solihull but it also established a new factory at Pengam Moors, near Cardiff, on the site of the city's former airport, and this was used for P6 gearbox manufacture. Meanwhile Land-Rover production was continuing unabated and the half-millionth example was built in April 1966.

In July 1965 Rover had bought Alvis. Sands were running out on the latter's lovely 3-litre, and the firm wanted to concentrate on aero engines and military vehicle production, but Rover was keen to see a new generation of Alvis cars. Then, in the autumn of 1966, Leyland made its approach and the deal was swiftly and amicably concluded on 11 December, though was not confirmed until March 1967. The agreement had only just been finalized in late 1966 when Stokes received an approach from the Minister of Technology, Anthony Wedgwood Benn, following Chrysler's intimation that it wished to take a controlling interest in Rootes. While Stokes agrees that the government was impressed by the success that Leyland had made of Triumph, 'it was as much the amount of trouble that Rootes had got itself into' that prompted the approach. 'I remember spending a lot of time at Wedgwood Benn's house in Notting Hill Gate when he tried to get us to take an interest in Rootes. We found that the terms and conditions were too difficult and the opportunities too limited for us to get involved with Chrysler. Thank goodness we didn't.'[82]

One area where governmental influence had greater success was with the Leyland British Motor Holdings merger. While the Rootes talks were under way, Benn had informed the newly established Industrial Reorganization Corporation 'that the government favoured a merger between Leyland and BMH'. In February 1967 he made a statement in the House of Commons to the effect that Leyland and BMH were holding exploratory discussions and the IRC would be an ideal intermediary. Also early in 1967 came an independent confirmation of BMH's parlous state when the Department of Economic Affairs identified Britain's motor industry as one of the 'problem industries of the 1970s'.

The negotiations were becoming protracted as the two firms strove to arrive at a mutually acceptable 'match'. In October, in an attempt to improve the negotiating atmosphere, prime minister Harold Wilson invited Benn, Stokes and Harriman to dinner at Chequers. At the Motor Show later the same month, the exhibits on BMH's Austin stand starkly encapsulated the need for a merger. There the 1100, after five years, finally got an enlarged 1300 engine to counter the growing challenge of the Ford Cortina, but there was also the new 3-litre, a big ungainly 1800-based rear-drive saloon, powered by a redesigned version of the BMC C Series engine, which was thirsty, lacked power and refused to rev. When it finally staggered into production in 1968 only 9,992 examples were built over three years and MG's hitherto impeccable track record was marred by the arrival of the shortlived MGC which shared the same power unit. In November BMH announced that it had made a pre-tax loss of £3.2 million. Leyland, by contrast, had made an £18 million profit.

That month Leyland decided to make an outright bid for BMH though, just before Christmas, Stokes and Harriman met with Benn when he suggested Sir Frank Kearton, chairman of the IRC, as an intermediary. His negotiating skill helped to bring about an agreement which was made public on Wednesday 17 January. The new company would be called the British Leyland Motor Corporation and would be the fifth largest car company in the world, in sales terms, after the American Big Three and Volkswagen. Sir George Harriman was to be chairman, Sir Donald Stokes managing director and there would be ten other directors, drawn equally from BMH and Leyland. The IRC would provide a £25 million loan.

There were problems almost from the outset because it was then found that BMH was unlikely to make a profit in 1967/8. 'We very nearly backed out at the last minute,' says Stokes, 'but we were persuaded very strongly by the government to go ahead. We were given lots of assurances that there would be help and support which, of course, never materialized.'[83] When the British Leyland Motor Corporation came formally into being on 14 May 1968, Sir George Harriman had agreed to retire after six months and Joe Edwards resigned in April, Harriman having unsuccessfully tried to protect his status. Sir Donald Stokes had, arguably, taken on the toughest job in British industry.

7

The Leyland Years

1968–75

'The British Leyland Motor Corporation today forms a major driving force throughout the world in marketing a unique range of automotive and allied products. These include sports, saloons and prestige cars, trucks, buses, engine and transmission units, and extend into the field of fork-lift trucks, road-rollers, construction and contractors' equipment, commercial refrigerators, and heavy-duty auto-electrical equipment.'

British Leyland Motor Corporation: Growth Constitution
Factories Products, 1968

The British Leyland Motor Corporation lasted just seven years and during this period its market share fell a full 10 points from a record 40 per cent in 1968 to 30 per cent in 1975. This decline was a reflection of the many problems that plagued the Corporation from the very outset. Some were historical ones and the result of the deep-seated malaise that had infected the British Motor Corporation, though they were compounded when the first generation of Leyland cars appeared, some of which were markedly inferior to those of their BMC predecessors. This, coupled with an apparent continual succession of strikes, resulted in the public, for the first time, perceiving that the British-owned sector of the car industry might follow in the wheeltracks of the motor-cycle makers that had been all but extinguished by Japanese competition in the 1960s. Then, in the wake of the world depression triggered by the oil crisis, British Leyland ran out of money in 1974 and, in the following year, was nationalized by a new government, some members of which had actively encouraged its birth back in 1968.

These were also difficult years for the rest of the industry. Chrysler strove to revive the remnants of the Rootes Group, but its troubles also boiled over in 1975 and it too turned to the British government for help. Vauxhall toppled into deficit in 1969 and, apart from a modest profit in 1971, it remained in the red throughout this period. Of all the Big Batallions, only Ford made substantial and consistent profits during these seven years though, in 1971, the firm recorded a £30.7 million loss, its first since 1933, and the result of its factories being paralysed by a ten-week strike.

Yet although the British motor industry produced a record 1.9 million cars in 1972, its highest-ever figure, output fell for the next three years and, in 1975, Italy overtook Britain's third place in the European production league. Exports also took a tumble. In 1968 they stood at 676,571 cars but, by 1975, had slumped to 516,219. More significantly, imports, which accounted for an 8.3 per cent market share in 1968, increased every year from then on until 1975 when they quadrupled to over 33 per cent. This was in part due to Britain's joining the Common Market in 1973 when European import duties were reduced and by 1975 they stood at 4.4 per cent, while most of the rest of the world, notably Japan, paid 10 per cent. In 1973, for the first time since 1913, Britain's car imports exceeded those of exports, and although these briefly moved ahead in 1974, imports again surged forward in 1975 and the automotive trade balance has remained in deficit ever since. Although sales of European cars continued to grow, by 1975 it was the Japanese Datsun that headed the imports lists, followed by the French Renault and Volkswagen from Germany.

But back in 1968, British Leyland's prospects looked bright. Sir Donald Stokes, an effective communicator, was already established as one of the outstanding salesmen of his generation. His audacious sale of £9 millions' worth of Leyland Olympic buses to Communist Cuba in 1964 had, in particular, done much to enhance his reputation in the public eye. Already British Leyland's managing director, in September 1968, by prior arrangement, he took over the chairmanship from Sir George Harriman, who became the corporation's president, and thereafter took no part in Leyland's day-to-day running. He did, however, continue to work for the company until he died in 1973 at the age of sixty-five. Stokes had appointed two deputy chairmen, Sir William Lyons, who protected Jaguar's interests with a vigour and determination that belied his sixty-seven years, and Lewis Whyte, chairman of the London and Manchester Assurance Company, who had been a director of ACV (which owned AEC) and had joined the Leyland board in 1964.

There were three deputy managing directors. Jack Plane, from South Africa, was one whose company, J.H.Plane South Africa Ltd, had merged with Leyland in 1963 to form the Leyland Motor Corporation of South Africa. He had become a Leyland director in 1965 and was given responsibilities for British Leyland's overseas operations. The others were Dr Albert Fogg, who became director of engineering, and George Turnbull, who was given the demanding job of managing director of the Austin Morris division. The important post of director of planning and finance went to John Barber – with ten years' experience at Ford behind him, he joined Leyland in December 1967. Rover's interests were represented by Sir George Farmer, knighted in 1968, though the only surviving BMC presences on the board were Ronald Lucas and stock-broker Robin Stormonth-Darling, who had been a BMC director since 1960. Stokes also recruited Jim Slater to the British Leyland board. Slater had joined AEC in 1956 and worked briefly for Leyland after it took the firm over, leaving in 1963 when the city lights beckoned.

Perhaps the most striking feature of the British Leyland board was its lack of experience in running a large car-manufacturing company; Joe Edwards, who had, was no longer with the firm. Only one board member, John Barber, had been directly involved with the management of a major vehicle producer. Leyland had built at most around 23,000 vehicles a year, while Jaguar and Rover were specialist producers and Triumph's best year had been 1967 when it built about 140,000 cars, whereas BMC had the capacity to manufacture a million vehicles per annum. Today Lord Stokes is the first to recognize this deficiency:

> I wasn't, none of us were, trained to run a company of 190,000 or so people. I think I was probably good at selling. I was not and I have never pretended to be a manufacturing expert, ever. I have no pretensions as to that. I am an engineer by training but I think that my strength lies in selling and I think that it is worth recalling that we did sell, until the oil crisis, everything that BMC could make.[1]

In addition, Stokes found that

> The management of BMC was not as strong as one would have hoped. It was much worse than we could have imagined because it was overmanned in practically every area, it was short of manage-ment skills in lots of areas, its model programme, particularly its model replacement programme, was almost non-existent. Profitability on cars like the Mini was infinitely small. After Sir Leonard Lord departed there was no proper line of succession and I doubt whether they had a policy. The commercial vehicle side up in Bathgate was a disaster because practically every truck they made broke down.[2]

Stokes was also alarmed to discover what he found at the BMC factories.

Cowley itself was deplorable and although Longbridge wasn't so bad, it always seemed to be half-finished. I'll give you an example. They had a foundry there, half of it had been modernized and the other half hadn't . . . and it shouldn't have been there anyway.

When we got into BMC we did realize that we had bitten off a pretty large morsel, and that was a bit disheartening actually. It was not going to be easy, but we never thought it was . . . but we were young in those days and we hoped that we were going to make a success of it.[3]

Despite his apprehension, Stokes and the British Leyland board wasted little time in producing their restructured plan for the Corporation. It was split into seven divisions: Austin Morris, comprising Austin, Morris and MG; Specialist Cars, consisting of Jaguar, Rover and Triumph; Foundry and General Engineering; Pressed Steel Fisher; Overseas; Truck and Bus and Construction Equipment, which included Aveling-Barford, acquired by Leyland just prior to the BMH take over.

All this amounted to a total of forty-eight factories, which included BMH's twenty-three major plants. In taking over BMH, Leyland had absorbed a business that had never been merged properly in the first place and was clearly crying out for rationalization. The firm's rate of productivity, at 5.6 vehicles per employee in 1968, was about half that of Ford. In the light of these statistics, John Barber prepared a report which recognized that there would have to be about 30,000 redundancies within two years and some Midlands plants would have to be closed. This was picked up, in April 1968, by that perceptive motor industry watcher, BBC television's economics correspondent Graham Turner. 'I said that quite innocently and I got dreadful stick internally for having said it,' recalls Barber. 'Even Stokes said, "You shouldn't have said that. I am going to have trouble now from Scanlan and Jones." '[4] (Jack Jones, assistant secretary, Transport and General Workers Union, and Hugh Scanlan, president, Amalgamated Union of Engineering and Foundry Workers.) Stokes immediately countered the report by stating, 'It is going to take quite some time to interpret the studies and talking about closing factories and sacking people before we have even done that is stupid.'[5]

Lord Stokes well recalls the occasion:

Unfortunately, purely by coincidence, GEC (having taken over AEI) had closed down its Woolwich works with huge redundancies and created an absolute core of resistance amongst the trade unions to any job losses whatsoever and we just couldn't face a strike because it would have resulted in an all-out one. We had shareholders and we couldn't take that strong a stand. You couldn't go on forever with a public company resisting unions that were hell bent on confrontation in those days.[6]

In this approach Stokes came into a disagreement with John Barber.

Donald Stokes is a nice chap. He was, I think, too kind, and if you're running a business like British Leyland you must expect to knock a few heads together but he wasn't willing to do that. He decided to do it gradually, but if you decide to do something gradually it never happens. Arnold Weinstock [of GEC] was just the opposite – he used to say 'ruthless in decision generous in execution'. He would decide to get rid of people and then pay them off generously. Very different from gradualism which meant that you never took a ruthless decision.[7]

Lord Stokes, in retrospect, maintains: 'I don't think we could have been tougher and even if they had brought in a genius to run the place, I don't think anyone could have been tougher. George Turnbull, who was running Longbridge, and he ran it very well, was as tough as anybody. We went to the brink as often as we could but we always had to pull back in the end for fear of going bust.'[8] In many ways Stokes was reflecting the paternalistic Leyland approach of his youth. A 1971 appraisal described him as 'essentially a soft-hearted man who finds it difficult to fire people'.[9] Lord Stokes agrees: 'I don't like firing people. I hate it. I didn't agree to the merger of the British motor industry to get rid of people. I thought that we were going to create jobs.'[10]

In November 1969, the IRC, which had made British Leyland a £25 million loan, held the first of two full-scale meetings with the Corporation's management. The IRC executive 'was particularly concerned about British Leyland's industrial relations problems and about the group's low productivity as compared with those of its international competitors. They estimated that to reach the level of sales per employee of Volkswagen, British Leyland would need to cut as many as 47,000 from its workforce of 188,000.'[11] Yet in the previous year the Corporation had taken on 8,000 more workers. 'One IRC executive complained that the presentation was nothing more than a public relations exercise with no chance for detailed questions, let alone a more positive IRC role.'[12] Stokes had hoped that production would expand sufficiently to absorb the extra numbers. 'I think that with his sales background he believed that sales would go up rather than down,' says Barber.[13]

Was there any political pressure on Stokes not to cut the workforce from the Labour government, which had so encouraged British Leyland's creation? 'No, to be fair to the government, no, though I don't think that they would have been exactly overjoyed if I had. When we were running the business, we had very little pressure from the government.'[14]

Prime minister Harold Wilson had few illusions about overmanning levels. He recalled that when BMC shop stewards descended on the 1966 Labour Party conference to protest at redundancies initiated by BMC's Joe Edwards, and they asked whether a deputation of six could address Wilson at his Brighton hotel, 'I agreed – and *twelve* [Wilson's italics] of them entered the hotel . . . "That's what's wrong with BMC," I told them, "always needing twelve men to do what six should be doing." '[15] Even after the redundancies had been effected, Wilson still believed that BMC was overmanned.

Meanwhile Stokes had to decide what to do about the car programme, such as it was, that he had inherited from BMC. The only model in a sufficiently advanced state of development was a 1.5-litre car which emerged in 1969 as the Austin Maxi, though 'it was unusable when we took it over'.[16] He thought that the styling left much to be desired and considered the interior 'ridiculously stark – like a hen coop'. The model had initially been delayed because BMC had decided to produce a brand-new E Series engine for the car and a new £20 million factory had been built to produce it at Longbridge. 'Maybe we should have taken the decision and scrapped it,' says Barber, 'but they'd invested a lot of money in the Coften Hackett engine plant, so we soldiered on, made some improvements, but the car wasn't any good.'[17]

The creation of the British Leyland management effectively spelled the end of Alec Issigonis's reign at Longbridge, though he was made director of research and development for the Corporation. Lord Stokes considers 'Alec a brilliant innovator but innovators aren't always good as chief engineers and putting models into production'. Issigonis had been given far too much rein at BMC and 'when he decided on something, *nothing could be changed*. He had some odd ideas, as well as some brilliant ones, but as far as the individual aspects of a car were concerned, he was completely dogmatic. It was only when we came in that the Mini got its winding windows. He said they should be sliding and that was that.'[18]

Issigonis's place as technical supremo at Longbridge was taken by Harry Webster from Triumph and his job at Canley went to Rover's Spen King, who recalled: 'One day I was called into George Farmer's office, to find Donald Stokes already there. It was just after the British Leyland merger had been announced and I was told that Harry Webster was moving to Longbridge and would I be interested in his old job. I was dumbfounded!'[19] He had five minutes to make up his mind and accepted.

Soon after Harry Webster arrived at Longbridge, he was asked to draw up plans for the Austin Morris division. Webster's strategy was submitted to the Corporation's production control committee in August 1968. There would be no more badge engineering. Instead of the Austin and Morris names being applied to the same models, as in the case of the Mini, 1100 and 1800, two quite separate policies were to be developed for the respective makes. Austin would perpetuate the existing BMC front-wheel drive philosophy, though the styling would be 'more durable'. The intention was to sell in the existing BMC markets and against those continental makes (such as Volkswagen, Citroen and Renault) that offered a similar high technological profile. Morris, on the other hand, would be conventionally engineered but with more adventurous styling and a sporting ingredient would be introduced.

The first car to incorporate this new strategy was the rear-wheel-drive Morris Marina, which appeared in 1971 and was intended as Longbridge's long-awaited challenge to the Ford Cortina and Vauxhall Viva. The concept reached back to May 1968, when Harry Webster proposed giving the once-popular but by then ageing Morris Minor a new enlarged body shell. It could then be offered with Minor's 1100cc engine but also 1300 and 1500 options. The price would be about £20 above that of the Vauxhall Viva and he considered Fiat's conventional but lively 124 as an example.

The opposing view was that resources might have been better diverted to the all-important 1100/1300 front-wheel-drive replacement. Yet another strand of opinion came from John Barber, who, along with Stokes, was based at British Leyland's Berkeley Square headquarters. He disagreed with the idea of a car to challenge the Cortina.

That was stupid in the first place, because it challenged Ford, a very strong company. My advice at the time, and all the way through, was that we ought to go a bit up market of Ford, and if we had deliberately pitched it a bit beyond the Cortina in quality, image and so on, we might have done something. But we really ought to have capitalized more on Rover, Jaguar and Triumph.

If you look at what we were good at in those days, our volume-car management and engineers were not up to world standards. Jaguar and Rover and a few people at Triumph were. If we had capitalized on the wonderful engineering we had at Jaguar, we could have done something. We could have moved Austin and Morris gradually up market: that would have automatically kept the volumes down. It wouldn't have been a sudden change but each successive car would have been more expensive than its predecessor. The trouble was that the government had the idea of us producing more and more cars and, later, when Ryder came in, he had even grander ideas.

I kept reminding Donald Stokes that, apart from the Americans, there were six other companies that were bigger than us. We decided, in due course, that we would adopt the BMW/Mercedes–Benz approach rather than the Ford one. But we didn't have a hope in hell. We had too many different models made in too many different places.[20]

One early casualty of the merger had been Riley. The marque was discontinued in 1969; only 8,348 examples had been sold in the previous year.

One of Barber's contributions to the Marina project, then coded ADO 28, was the principle of the Ford Red Book he had co-authored with Terry Beckett back in the early 1960s. British Leyland called theirs the Blue Book but, says Barber, 'it was nowhere as successful as when it was used at Ford because we didn't have the all-important detailed financial structure.'[21] It highlighted yet another weakness that British Leyland inherited from BMC which was its purchasing activity. During the 1960s BMC's purchasing policy was a cause for some amusement at Ford, which bought its components cheaper, even though BMC believed that it was paying the same price as its competitors!

Despite all the problems that the incoming British Leyland management experienced when it took over BMH, the Corporation managed to make a respectable £37.9 million profit in its first 1968/9 financial year, which was a reflection of car sales running at near-record levels in 1968. Rover contributed £7 million and Triumph achieved a record £9 million, which compensated for poor figures from Jaguar which was getting its new XJ6 saloon into production. Even Austin Morris managed £2 million, while the Bus and Truck Division made £8 million. The profits were the best in the industry, apart from those of Ford, which stood at £43 million.

British Leyland, having decided that it could no longer postpone the five-door Maxi, announced it in April 1971 and, while a 1750cc version was in the offing, it was estimated that it would cost another £1 million, and a further year's development, before it was ready. So the model was introduced with its 1.5-litre engine. The Maxi's styling, despite some last-minute attention to its front end, could at best be described as restrained, though dull might have been a more appropriate epithet, and its appearance was not helped by the fact that for economic reasons it had been designed with doors from the 1800. As a result the model possessed none of the vitality of Renault's R16 that had done so much to popularize the hatchback concept. Its mechanics were equally unhappy. The new overhead-camshaft E Series engine had been designed with no water jacketing between the cylinders, a not uncommon feature at the end of a power unit's life but not at the beginning of it. This was adopted because it was the first BMC engine to have been specifically designed for a transverse location where the unit's width was constrained by its location, particularly as there was a six-cylinder derivative in the offing. This prohibited an increase of the 76mm bore size which remains inviolate. The result was a noisy power unit that lacked low-speed torque. Matters were made worse by the five-speed gearbox's imprecise cable control which one motoring journalist accurately likened to 'stirring a knitting needle in a bag of marbles'.[22]

Although sales forecasts had spoken of 6,000 Maxi sales a week, by the winter of 1969 demand was running at around 400 when plans for a cheaper four-door derivative were sidelined. All Leyland could do was to soldier on until October 1970 when a much improved version of the Maxi appeared. It was instantly identifiable by a new radiator grille, and Stokes's criticisms of the original interior had resulted in a much improved one with a pleasing wood-grained dashboard and reshaped and upholstered seats. The engine was enlarged to 1748cc by increasing the stroke from 81 to 95mm, while the gear lever's ghastly cables were replaced by rods. This modification was also extended to the 1500 version, which continued in production. These changes greatly improved the car and it settled down to selling around 30,000 a year from the mid-1970s. By the time it was discontinued in 1981, 472,098 had been built.

Finances also held up well in 1969 when British Leyland made a £40 million profit. Of this Austin Morris contributed a better-than-hoped-for £6 million surplus. Rover and Triumph also had good years and Bus and Truck contributed a greatly improved £8 million. However, the Austin Morris division's biggest seller was the seven-year-old 1100/1300 range which was still a good 17,000 sales ahead of the Ford Cortina. Although the evergreen 1100/1300 continued to sell strongly, in 1970 the Austin Morris division made a loss of close to £16 million as labour troubles increased in frequency and size. George Turnbull, as the division's managing director, was in the eye of that particular storm. 'Stokes was besides himself . . . he just didn't know what to do. I said, "We'll have to see it through; we just can't abandon it." Then, after making my feelings known, I began to get some original thinking from the management and the troops. I had a period of two weeks without any industrial action – which was quite exceptional when the norm was several strikes per *day*.'[23] As luck would have it, the rest of the Corporation was profitable and contributed £20 million, though the Austin Morris deficit had reduced overall profitability to a mere £4 million in 1970.

The labour problem was one nettle which had to be grasped. In the early days at British Leyland, its management adopted what it called a policy of mutuality. This meant that it had to get mutual agreement with the unions on all works practices. Whereas Ford paid a fixed day rate and laid down specific times for a particular job, at British Leyland piecework rates had to be negotiated with the shop stewards. 'We had the ludicrous situation, when we brought out the Mini Clubman in 1969 with its redesigned front, that the shop stewards wanted to renegotiate the piecework rates for the entire car,' recalls John Barber. 'Any sensible person would have just negotiated on the new pieces of sheet metal and it really illustrates the inequity of the piecework system.'[24]

Paradoxically, piecework did have an attraction for some factions within Austin Morris 'because it enabled management to abdicate, in effect. Once a man is paid piecework he is going to earn enough money to live on, so you don't have to "manage" him, it's sort of self-managing but, inevitably, if he'd finished his quota by three o'clock in the afternoon, he would go home,'[25] says Barber.

In 1970 British Leyland appointed its first director of industrial relations in the shape of Pat Lowry, who had twenty-four years of industrial relations experience with the Engineering Employers' Federation, and in 1972 he joined the Leyland board. The Corporation introduced measured daywork to its 134,000 employees still on piecework in 1971. It was phased in over a three-year period, though its arrival coincided with that of the incoming Conservative government's Industrial Relations Bill and the three million working days the motor industry lost in 1971 was the worst year for labour relations since the general strike. But the start of measured daywork, important as it was, did little to stem the industrial disputes plaguing British Leyland. In the 1969/70 financial year, ending in September, the Corporation lost 5 million man hours in strikes and this doubled to 10 million in 1971/2. It briefly fell back to 7.4 million in 1972/3 though rose again to 9.6 million man hours lost in 1973/4.

The reason that the switch from piecework to measured daywork had so little effect on British Leyland's labour problems lay, maintains John Barber, in the quality of its first-line management.

The crucial thing about piecework is that, effectively, you don't have foremen. But, under daywork, a foreman is absolutely crucial because he's the one who keeps the men at work for, without the incentive of piecework, you've got to have your manager on the spot. In British Leyland, for the first time in their lives, the foremen became front-line managers. Up until then they had been nothing and BMC and Triumph just didn't have the supply of front-line managers. So, for the first few years, we operated measured daywork with inadequate managers and it took some time to catch up. It was this deficiency that was probably the biggest single factor in making our productivity so low.[26]

The benefits of measured daywork were eventually reaped by the Corporation's management, but that was not until British Leyland had passed into state ownership.

Nineteen seventy-one was also significant for the arrival of the Morris Marina, the first car to have been designed under the direction of the new British Leyland management. It represented a corporate bid for a share in the all-important fleet market which was dominated by the Ford Cortina. Harry Webster's original idea for rebodying the Morris Minor had run into trouble when it was found that, although its engine was suitable, the gearbox lacked synchromesh on first gear. Webster immediately thought about the gearbox being developed for the rear-drive derivative of the front-wheel-drive Triumph 1300 which was so equipped. He calculated that it would be cheaper to produce that in quantity than to modify the Minor one. A Triumph rear axle was used for the same reason. So £7 million was spent converting the former Flight Shed complex at the eastern end of the Longbridge works as the corporate gearbox plant. A further modification to the original concept came when it was decided to modify the engine compartment so that it could accept the 1.8-litre B Series engine.

The car itself was to be built at Cowley, which Stokes was acutely aware was in urgent need of modernization. It was partially gutted, a more up-to-date production line was introduced and, with an eye to improved quality, a ¼-mile-long enclosed conveyor was built from Pressed Steel plant on the south side of the Oxford Eastern Bypass, which snaked over factory roofs to the Marina assembly line on the other side. This meant that bodies 'in white' (hulls that had yet to be painted) would not have to be exposed to the elements to the detriment of their subsequent paintwork.

The Morris Marina was launched in April 1971 after such options as Monaco, Machete (!) and Mamba had been considered. It was available in two body styles, a four-door saloon and fastback coupé. The 1800 version was intended to challenge the Ford Cortina and Vauxhall Viva, while the 1300 was aimed at the Ford Escort, Chrysler's new Hillman Avenger and the smaller Vivas.

Sales targets, this time of 5,000 cars a week, were again not met, but although the model got off to a slow start, in 1973 and 1974 the Marina was British Leyland's best-selling car. Styling was the work of Roy Haynes, recruited in 1966 to BMC from Ford, where he had been responsible for the lines of the best-selling Mark II Cortina, and although the Marina's appearance was in no sense extravagant, the car was well proportioned and did not offend. The model was to endure until 1983, having been updated as the Ital after 1.2 million had been built, making it the most numerically successful car of the Stokes era. It was also the last purpose-designed Morris.

Despite the labour troubles which arrived with measured daywork, British Leyland managed to build a record 886,721 cars and achieved pre-tax profits of £32.4 million in 1971. During the first quarter of the year when the Corporation began to make money, George Turnbull can still vividly recall 'ringing Donald Stokes in South Africa to tell him'.[27] But hopes of a £50 million profit were dashed by a strike of delivery drivers mid-way through the year.

Another new car appeared in March 1972, though the six-cylinder 2200 was, in essence, the last of the BMC-initiated designs. It was, in effect, the 1800 body with a six-cylinder version of the Maxi's E Series engine. If Harry Webster's 1968 marque profile had been adopted, the six would have been an only Austin, but because Morris dealers could not live by Marina alone, the model was also badged as Morris. In addition it was available in more luxurious Wolseley Six form. Badge engineering was back! The 2227cc engine inherited many of the constraints of the original Maxi unit in that it was a six-cylinder version of the 1.5-litre engine and consequently was not able to avail itself of the 1750's cylinder head with its improved breathing. Why was this so? The answer is that a 2622cc six based on the 1750 was found to suffer from unacceptable torsional vibrations and, because of the narrowness of the unit, with its small bores and no water jacketing between, there was no room to design a stronger crankshaft that would have made the large-capacity engine a practical proposition. Because of the width of the power unit, part of the 2200's engine compartment had to be restructured otherwise the car would have had an unacceptably wide turning circle. This also meant that there was not room for the customary side-located radiator, so a forward-mounted one with an electric fan was fitted, the first front-wheel-drive car from Longbridge to be so equipped. It also had the advantage that it kept rain off the engine, thus rectifying a shortcoming of the original arrangement. This 100mph car was, in truth, a stop-gap model and the engine was transferred to the new Princess range in 1975. It relied on the not particularly attractive eight-year-old 1800 shape and sales also suffered from the effects of the oil crisis. Only 20,865 were built.

In March 1972, the month of the 2200's launch, British Leyland announced a restructuring of its Specialist Car Division. This meant an integration of the Rover and Triumph companies, though Jaguar continued on its separate way as the Corporation recognized its special and unique position within the industry. Seventy-year-old Sir William Lyons retired in the same March after fifty years with Jaguar and its SS predecessor. F.R.W. 'Lofty' England, who had joined Lyons in 1946, took over as chairman and chief executive at Browns Lane but, unlike Sir William, he did not have a place on the British Leyland board.

The perpetuation of Triumph and Rover as separate entities, prior to their 1972 integration, was in line with what Lord Stokes had told the IRC in 1970 when he maintained that if a plant was operating profitably, he preferred to leave it alone. John Barber, by contrast, had been pressing for several years for a Rover/Triumph amalgamation and 'we wasted an awful lot of money by running them separately'.[28] Disillusioned with the cars being produced by the Austin Morris division, Barber turned his attention to Rover, which was complementary to his aim of taking British Leyland products more up market.

> Rover was easily the best controlled company in British Leyland. It had much more information about its costs than any of the others. Everything about Rover was well done. I had a high regard for George Farmer: he ran the company well and was a wise business-man. But he was an ultra-cautious manager and although we wanted him to put in extra Land-Rover capacity, he put some in but nothing like what was needed. Spen King was a super engineer. One of his great strengths was that he could visualize a total motor car and not all engineers can do that. Then William Martin-Hurst was a visionary sort of chap and David Bache a marvellous stylist.[29]

When Leyland had merged with Rover in 1967, prior to the BMH takeover, Stokes and Barber had been informed of the existence of the P8 project which was a big expensive five/six-seater 'Mercedes-eater' saloon powered by the ex-Buick V8. At that stage it would have been a potential Leyland flagship though, with the 1968 creation of the British Leyland Motor Corporation, it would have represented a challenge to Jaguar's new XJ6 saloon. Despite this, it was scheduled for the 1972 model year but was cancelled in March 1971, just six months before it was due to enter production but not before it had absorbed many millions of pounds.

Sir William Lyons was responsible for vetoing Rover's exciting P6BS mid-V8-engined sports car, which would have acquired the P9 designation had it entered production. Barber remembers it as 'a super car. I took the prototype to Brands Hatch once and, apart from the rear suspension coming unhitched, it was fine. But it was pressure from Lyons that cooked it. Bill was a very nice man but he only thought Jaguar. He wasn't very interested in British Leyland and he was afraid that the Rover would damage Jaguar. He kept on and on about it, so it was dropped.'[30]

(*Left*) Alec Issigonis (born 1906), FRS 1967, knighted 1969, was responsible for the world famous Mini, and he was the architect of the British Motor Corporation's front-wheel-drive strategy of the 1960s. He is pictured here in 1948.

(*Right*) The creation of the British Leyland Motor Corporation is announced on 17 January 1968. Sir George Harriman (*left*), chairman of British Motor Holdings, tries to put a brave face on what was a takeover of his firm by Leyland, headed by the dynamic Sir Donald Stokes (*right*).

(*Below*) John Barber, Ford's former finance director, who became managing director and deputy chairman of the British Leyland Motor Corporation. A consistent advocate of moving the firm's model range up market, he is pictured with a Jaguar XJ6-based Daimler Sovereign.

Rover's much vaunted 2000 of 1962 which lasted until 1977. Aimed foursquare at the executive market, it featured a base frame body structure and de Dion rear axle.

(*Above*) Stanley Markland initiated the Michelotti-styled Triumph 2000 of 1962, engineered under Harry Webster's direction. This is the Mark 2 version, introduced in 1969, which endured until 1975.

(*Below*) The Austin/Morris 1800, BMC's first demonstrable stumble of the 1960s. Introduced in 1965, it lasted until 1975 and never sold in the expected numbers.

The Marina was the first British Leyland Motor Corporation designed car and the last Morris. Introduced in 1971, it remained in production until 1983, having been updated as the Ital in 1980.

(*Above*) British ingenuity 2: Spen King and Gordon Bashford were responsible for the four-wheel-drive 3.5-litre V8 engined Range Rover, introduced in 1970. This is the current Vogue version.

(*Below*) British Leyland's Austin Allegro of 1973 was markedly inferior to the 1100/1300 range it replaced. This is a 1981 car.

CONTINENTAL CONTRASTS

The front-wheel-drive Traction Avant Citroen, introduced in 1934, with unitary body, overhead valve engine, torsion bar suspension, hydraulic brakes and, from 1936, rack and pinion steering. This is a 1938 15/6 version.

(*Above*) The German KdF-Wagen of 1938 was reborn as the Volkswagen in 1945. This 1950 version has a rear-mounted 1131cc four-cylinder, air-cooled engine and all independent torsion bar suspension.

(*Below*) Gallic vitality: the front-wheel-drive Renault R16 of 1965 which did so much to popularise the hatchback concept. Powered by a 1.5-litre four-cylinder alloy engine, it remained in production until 1979.

British conservatism: 1937 Standard 14, with chassis frame, half elliptic spring front and rear, rod brakes and 1.7-litre side valve four-cylinder engine.

(*Above*) The 1950 Mark III Hillman Minx, unitary construction, 1.2-litre side valve engine, it was built in this form until 1953.

(*Below*) A BMC inheritance for British Leyland, the front-wheel-drive Austin Maxi hatchback with 1.5-litre overhead camshaft engine, appeared in 1969. Production lasted until 1981.

The 3-litre V8-engined Triumph Stag of 1970, the British Leyland Motor Corporation's flagship. Plagued by reliability problems, only 25,877 were built. It survived until 1977.

(*Above*) The all-important but flawed Rover SD1 of 1976, pictured at Solihull. Alas, the final finishing and valeting being undertaken here failed to rectify poor build quality.

(*Below*) British Leyland's Ugly Duckling, the Speke-built 1.9-litre Triumph TR7 sports car. Introduced to America in 1975, it only lasted until 1981. The Michelotti-styled Spitfire in the background appeared in 1963 and endured until 1980.

The BL/Honda-designed front-wheel-drive 800 Series Rover of 1986. This is the top line Sterling version with 2.5-litre Honda V6 engine.

(*Above*) The Austin Metro of 1980, the most successful Longbridge-designed car since the best-selling 1100/1300 range of 18 years before. This is the Mayfair version introduced in 1986.

(*Below*) Demand for Jaguar's highly acclaimed new XJ6 of 1986 helped the firm's Browns Lane factory to produce 47,000 cars in 1987: an all-time record for the Coventry company.

(*Left*) Terence Beckett headed Ford's pioneering product planning department from 1955 until 1963 and was chairman of Ford of Britain in 1976/80. He was knighted in 1978, and became director-general of the Confederation of British Industry. He is pictured here in 1970.

(*Right*) Opening rounds: BL's new chairman, Michael Edwardes, knighted 1979, addresses the company's 700 union officials and shop stewards at Chesford Grange Hotel, Kenilworth, on 1 February 1978, when he spelt out the firm's parlous state and his future plans. He is flanked by managing directors Ray Horrocks of Austin Morris (*left*), and David Andrews, Bl International. Industrial relations director Pat Lowry is seated extreme right.

(*Below*) John Egan (*left*), knighted in 1986, with Sir William Lyons, founder of the SS and Jaguar companies, at the latter's Wappenbury Hall home, with a Series 3 XJ6 Jaguar and 1937 SS in 1982, on the occasion of the firm's 60th anniversary.

The P8, however, was not intended as a succesor to the 2000/3500 range. Gordon Bashford, Rover's chief engineer, had begun work on that, which was allotted the P10 designation, in March 1969. Then, in 1970, Triumph was informed by the British Leyland board that it could not proceed with a replacement for its 2000/2500 saloon, rebodied in 1969. At Rover, Peter Wilks was instructed to co-operate with his cousin, Spen King, by then established at Canley. Consequently, in February 1971, the P10 became the RT1 ('RT' standing for Rover Triumph) but in April was renamed, for the third and final time, the SD1 ('SD' indicating Specialist Division) which had to replace the P6 Rover and the big Triumph. Then, in July, Peter Wilks, Rover's respected technical director, retired aged only fifty-one suffering from heart disease, and his death in the following year represented a loss to both Rover and the British motor industry. Spen King thereafter took sole charge of engineering and the integration of the two companies was completed by the spring of 1975.

As far as the shape of the SD1 was concerned, since the late 1960s David Bache had been thinking in terms of a big four-door saloon with a hatchback, though at that time the medium-sized Maxi and Renault R16 were the largest examples on the market. The SD1 would be much bigger as it was aimed foursquare at BMW and Mercedes-Benz opposition. In concept the SD1 was as mechanically straightforward as the 2000 had been complicated, with strut suspension front and rear and a live back axle. The proven V8 was to be carried over, but Triumph would be responsible for developing alternative six-cylinder engines and the gearbox, the latter to be used across the British Leyland car range. The rear axle would also be developed at Canley.

As Solihull hardly had enough room to produce its existing products, the SD1 would require a new plant. In 1971 the Rover management had proposed a new factory adjoining its Solihull works with capacity for producing 1,500 cars a week. But the British Leyland board, committed to its move up market, encouraged Rover to double the size of the plant so that it would be capable of producing 3,000 cars a week. Originally it was intended to build a two-storey assembly hall; however because of objections from local residents, its height was reduced by 28 feet to a single storey. This meant doubling the width of the plant, though the paintshop remained as a two-storey structure. The plan received an Industrial Development Certificate in January 1973 which marked a demonstrable end of governmental pressure to establish car factories in areas of high unemployment. At a total cost of £26.8 million, £14.8 million for the assembly hall and £12 million for the paintshop, the half-million-square -foot factory represented the largest investment in the British motor industry since Ford had established its Halewood factory on Merseyside in 1963.

While the SD1 was continuing to evolve, Rover had initiated another product line in 1970 which had much the same impact as the Land-Rover twenty-two years previously. Rover had been toying with the concept of a more luxurious version of the Land-Rover since 1952 when the firm experimented with a two-wheel-drive station wagon built on the P4 chassis. A Series 2 version of this Road-Rover was created in 1956, but the idea was abandoned in 1959, probably because the firm was fully committed to other projects.

It was not until 1966 that Spen King's thoughts once again turned to the concept of a luxury Land-Rover. Even before this, Gordon Bashford had been working on what he called the 100-inch Station Wagon 'because when I finished sketching up the first package, the wheelbase turned out to be 99.9 inches!'[31] The dimensions were accordingly rounded up and the project gained momentum with the arrival of the ex-Buick aluminium V8, which was much lighter than the 3-litre P5 unit then under consideration. As for the styling, King and Bashford undertook this themselves, with some unofficial help from Geoff Crompton of the Styling Department. The result was a well-proportioned station wagon which perpetuated the Land-Rover's two-door layout, had a split tailgate and possessed those uncompromising and functional lines that had made its forebear such a success though, unlike that vehicle, four-wheel drive was permanently engaged. The prototype was completed in August 1967, having been approved by the Rover board in February just prior to the Leyland Motors merger. Developed under the Concept Oyster coding, it was announced as the Range Rover in June 1970. Demand for this unique vehicle concept was immediate and waiting lists soon built up. It was the Land-Rover story all over again but the single Solihull production line was unable to build more than 250 examples a week.

If the years between 1968 and 1975 represented an era of investment and expansion for Rover, 10 miles away at Canley, Triumph was coming to terms with playing second fiddle in the merged Rover-Triumph combine. With George Turnbull's and Harry Webster's departure for Longbridge in 1968, Andrew Swindle, formerly Triumph's works director, took over the day-to-day running of Canley, though Lord Stokes remained as chairman. In 1970, however, Swindle became British Leyland's director of facilities planning and William (Bill) Davis moved from Longbridge, where he had been deputy managing director of Austin Morris, to become Triumph's chairman and chief executive. But when Triumph and Rover merged in March 1972 under Sir George Farmer, *Autocar*, for one, pointed out that 'Rover men fill seven of the twelve posts announced'.[32] When Farmer stepped down a year later, at the age of sixty-five, Rover's managing director, A. B. Smith, took over as Rover-Triumph's chairman, with Bill

Davis as managing director. In the management reshuffle of September 1973, Davis became British Leyland's director of manufacturing and Bernard Jackman, whose family association with Rover went back sixty-eight years, became managing director.

A new Triumph, with no carry overs from previous models, arrived in 1970 in the shape of the Stag, intended as a prestigious grand tourer to take on the best of the European opposition in Britain and, it was also hoped, to build up a useful American export market. The project had begun way back in 1964 and its protracted birth in many ways encapsulated the difficulties in integrating so many divergent car-manufacturing companies, with the inevitable model overlaps and changes of personnel. The project began when stylist Giovanni Michelotti, having successfully completed the Triumph 2000, wanted to produce a open sporting derivative. The model, for no particular reason, was coded Stag and is a rare instance of an internal factory designation being perpetuated as a model name. It was to be powered by a 2498cc version of the 2000's six-cylinder engine then under development, though was subsequently fitted with a purpose-designed 2.5-litre V8. Its origins are to be found in 1963 when Triumph engineers began thinking in terms of a new generation of engines and had already decided on a V8 with single overhead camshafts and a related four-cylinder derivative. Then, in late 1963, Triumph was approached by the Swedish Saab company which wanted a new four-cylinder four-stroke engine to replace the two-strokes on which it had hitherto relied. There were considerable financial incentives to such an association and it was decided that Saab could have its Canley-built engine first. It appeared in the 1969 front-wheel-drive 99 model, to be followed by Triumph's V8 and, finally, Canley also used the single-overhead-camshaft four itself.

Although it was intended that the Stag would share as many parts as possible with the 2000, it eventually developed its own set of unique components and the car was scheduled for production in 1968. Then complications set in. Leyland's merger with Rover in 1967 meant that two Leyland Motor Corporation divisions had V8s. The Rover unit was due for production that year, and when attempts were made to fit it in the Stag, it was found to be too large. Perhaps understandably, the Canley engineers did not try too hard, but it was unfortunate because when the Triumph unit subsequently proved troublesome, private conversions were offered with the Rover unit fitted in its place. So the Stag retained its own power unit, and there were further delays caused by the impending American safety regulations and the fact that the all-important 2000 facelift of 1969 had predecence. When Spen King arrived at Canley from Solihull in 1968, he was concerned at the fuel-injected 2.5-litre V8's lack of low-speed torque, the idea of fitting the 2.5-litre six having been sidelined by this time. The

V8's capacity was therefore increased to 3 litres and carburettors replaced fuel injection, but this, in turn, meant a stronger gearbox, rear axle, brakes and larger wheels.

When the Stag finally entered production in 1970, its production embraced no less than three Triumph – or, more correctly, British Leyland – factories. The original tooling derived from the former Hall Engineering plant at Speke, which became Liverpool factory number 1. Body assembly, plus painting and trimming were undertaken at number 2 Liverpool plant about a mile away and also Speke-based. This location dated back to the pre-Leyland management when, in 1960, Alick Dick had ceremoniously bulldozed the first sod, though building proper had not begun until 1966 and was not finished until 1969. Once the bodywork had been completed there, the bodies were transported to Canley for final assembly.

Tragically, the Stag never lived up to its impressive specifications. On paper it was a good-looking, 115mph grand tourer and would have been an undoubted money spinner had it sold in sufficient numbers. Unfortunately it was plagued with a variety of problems, mostly associated with its engine, the cylinder heads of which tended to warp, causing the gaskets to blow, followed by loss of coolant. An even more serious problem was experienced with the single-link timing chain which stretched with use. The timing would jump and the valves then collided with the pistons which could wreck the engine. Most of these failures were experienced by British buyers and, in these circumstances, it was perhaps just as well that of the 25,877 Stags built between 1970 and 1977, only 6,780 went to overseas customers. A major blow to the export programme came when three quarters of the supplies sent to America suffered from valve problems and had to be withdrawn.

The Stag's tarnished reputation was a severe setback for Triumph and also British Leyland as the model had been widely regarded as the corporate flagship, and today it is still Lord Stokes's favourite car. In addition, the problems it experienced coincided with mechanical maladies in two other Triumph models, which dealt the marque's reputation a further blow. In 1967 the TR5 sports car appeared with Lucas indirect fuel injection and its six-cylinder engine was fitted, in detuned form, in the Triumph 2.5-litre P1 saloon of 1968. Regrettably, both models suffered from problems with the injection system, which was particularly sad for the big saloon as it also experienced a spate of under-bonnet fires. Although this shortcoming was subsequently cured, it did little to enhance the reputation of a car that had hitherto enjoyed a good record for reliability. It was not until 1975 that the fuel injection was finally abandoned and the system replaced by carburettors, by which time the ageing model had only a further two years to run.

Like the big 2500, Triumph's medium-car line also had its origins in the

1960s. With the Herald in urgent need of replacement, in 1967 Harry Webster had decided to use the 1300 front-wheel-drive saloon of 1965 as the principal building block of Triumph's medium-car line for the following decade. It was decided to improve the front-wheel-drive model's specifications and increase its capacity to 1493cc. The same hull would also form the basis of a new rear-drive model and Herald replacement which would retain the 1300 power unit. Michelotti lengthened the front and back of the front-drive model, which was called the 1500, while the rear-drive car became the Toledo and retained the original 1300 tail but benefited from a new front end. Both models were announced in 1970, the 1500 being Canley-built while complete Toledos were the first product of the Liverpool number 2 factory at Speke.

By this time, Triumph had emerged as the up-market builder of medium-sized cars within the British Leyland corporate family and, in 1972, Canley produced yet another variation on the 1500/Toledo theme. The Dolomite used the 1500's new front end in conjunction with the Toledo's rear-drive transmission but, significantly, it was to be the first recipient of the new Triumph-designed 1.8-litre overhead-camshaft slant four, which had been used by Saab since 1969. Labour problems delayed the launch of this urgently needed model, which was due for release in the summer of 1971 but was postponed to 'November, and finally it made it to the showrooms at the begining of 1972. . . . Production cars had been built and stored by summer 1971, but would not be delivered until 1972.'[33] When it reached the public, the Dolomite proved a steady seller and was second only to the Toledo in popularity.

With the Dolomite at last in production, Spen King came up with an exciting variant, the 115mph Sprint, with a sixteen-valve engine enlarged to 2 litres, which arrived in 1973. This clever and potent conversion was first detailed by Triumph's Lewis Dawtrey, with input from King and Jaguar. Aimed foursquare at the BMW market, the Dolomite Sprint never realized its full potential, one factor being the combination of a potent engine installed in an ageing body shell that was already looking high and narrow when compared with its contemporaries. In addition, it was plagued with the unreliability that was becoming synonymous with the Triumph name. When John Barber drove one, 'I used it fairly hard and it had to go back regularly to Triumph for them to sort the troubles out. The head castings were made so badly that water flow would be impeded, the heads used to distort and the head gasket would go. They never got it right.'[34] Eventually only 22,941 Dolomite Sprints were built.

In 1973, the same year in which the Sprint was announced, Triumph discontinued its front-wheel-drive 1500 so that the marque became completely rear-drive. The 1500's unit parts were then reshuffled and the

187

result was the rear-wheel-drive 1500TC. This, along with the Toledo, Stag, TR6 and evergreen Spitfire, constituted the Triumph range up until 1975. All these models were firmly rooted in the 1960s, and although the fragile Stag was the most recent creation, as a 3-litre car its sales were suffering in the wake of the oil crisis. In 1975 only 1,751 were registered in Britain. For Triumph the buoyancy and profitability of the 1960s were replaced by falling sales and deficit in the following decade.

The company's only new major project was the TR7 sports car, whose creation highlighted the plight of the MG marque. This car is dealt with in detail in the next chapter. The MGB had made its appearance back in 1962 and, in reality, was less of a sports car than its MGA predecessor and more of a high-speed tourer, but a very good one at that. In 1966 came a closed GT derivative and both cars proved immensely successful, far outstripping the MGA in popularity. A replacement, coded EX 234, was accordingly put in hand: it was a rationalized design styled by Pininfarina, intended to take a variety of engines, and replacing both the MGB and the Midget. But its 1968 completion coincided with the creation of British Leyland. MG became part of the Austin Morris division and the concept was sidelined, while the Abingdon management and workforce began to believe that they were playing second fiddle to Triumph which had, after all, been the first jewel in the Leyland corporate crown. The MGB was left successfully to uphold the MG name into the 1970s, though its appearance was marred from 1975 by the introduction of energy-absorbing bumpers, demanded by the increasingly stringent safety regulations of the all-important American market.

Austin Healey, BMC's other sports-car line, had come to the end of the road in 1970. The Austin Healey Sprite continued until then, although the Big Healey had ceased production in 1967, but the MG Midget endured until 1980. British Leyland had decided to cease royalty payments to firms outside the corporate orbit and the Cooper Car Company's Mini-Cooper suffered a similar fate.

If 1968 represented a watershed year in the affairs of the industry, with the creation of the British Leyland Motor Corporation, it also marked the pinnacle in the career of Sir William Lyons as, in September, Jaguar unveiled its supreme creation, the XJ6 saloon which replaced both the big 420 and smaller Mark II line. Superlatives are rightly used in this case without reservation. For Sir William it was the model that he held in the highest esteem. 'Without hesitation the XJ6, a car which we took six years to develop, has pleased me most.'[35] As a model it perfectly reflected Lyons stylistic philosophy, which he summed up thus: 'I believe that a car should be attractive to the eye, well balanced and free from unnecessary embellishment. It should be capable of giving pleasure to the owner for a long period of time. Totally new concepts in styling, like fashion, can often prove shortlived in terms of satisfaction and pleasure.'[36] Although the XJ6 boasted a new body shell, it incorporated well-proven components which were developed to a high degree of refinement. Its 4.2-litre version of the XK engine had first appeared in 1964, though a 2.8-litre long-stroke 2.4 derivative was developed for it, while the independent rear suspension arrived with the Mark X of 1961. Being a Jaguar, the XJ6 was destined for a long production run, but there were few who viewed this £2,254 car at the 1968 Motor Show who could have predicted that it was to last eighteen years and so help the company to survive the most traumatic years in its history.

Work on what was to become the XJ6 had begun in earnest in 1964 under the direction of chief vehicle engineer Robert (Bob) J. Knight, who had joined Jaguar in 1945, having been a power unit engineer with Armstrong Siddeley and the Bristol Aeroplane Company. Using experience gained on the unitary-construction 2.4, Knight's team took Lyons's low, sleek lines and produced a model which achieved new standards of road holding and silence, helping Jaguar to build a record 32,589 cars in 1971, an achievement that would not be surpassed until 1984. One of the XJ6's few shortcomings was lack of room for the rear passengers and, in 1972, the model's wheelbase was increased by 4 inches. The same year Jaguar's long-awaited 5.3-litre V12 engine was fitted under the XJ6's bonnet, it having first appeared in the Series 3 E-type of 1971. This long-standing project had been occupying Jaguar thinking since 1955 when chief engineer William Heynes had recognized that the six-cylinder XK engine's racing days were numbered against the V12-powered Ferrari opposition. The configuration was therefore originally conceived as a Le Mans winner, but when Jaguar withdrew from the competitive fray in 1956, the concept was sidelined. It was revived in the 1960s and a V12 power unit ran for the first time in 1964, with twin-overhead-camshafts per cylinder bank, and in this form it powered the mid-engined XJ13 sports racer which Jaguar might have fielded at Le Mans in 1967 had it not merged with BMC. By the time that the V12 appeared in production form, the bulky and expensive twin-overhead-camshafts had been replaced by single-cam units. Even so, fuel consumption was around the 13/14mpg mark and the model ran straight into the energy crisis. Only 584 XJ12s were built before the Series 2 version of the XJ series appeared in September 1973.

Another reason for the XJ12's poor production figures was that its launch coincided with a strike at Browns Lane, which began in June 1972 over the changeover from piecework to measured daywork and paralyzed the Jaguar production line for ten weeks. It was the worst industrial dispute to hit the firm since a five-week stoppage in 1965. This represented a baptism of fire for F.R.W. 'Lofty' England who took over as Jaguar's managing director and chief executive following Lyons's departure in March, though the position of chairman lapsed. Yet England was sixty in 1972 and he recognized that if Jaguar was going to retain its autonomy it was essential that a younger successor be found. Then, in the summer of 1973, 'Stokes rang England at rather short notice and asked him to be chairman of Jaguar and for his agreement to bring in Geoffrey Robinson as managing director, although no date was fixed.'[37]

The appointment of thirty-four-year-old Robinson was a recognition by the British Leyland management of the necessity for Jaguar to retain its separate identity. He arrived at Browns Lane with impressive credentials, having read Russian and German at Cambridge prior to obtaining an economics degree at Yale. After returning from America in 1963, he became a Labour Party research assistant and was recruited from Transport House to the board of the Industrial Reorganization Corporation by Lord Stokes. When the incoming Conservative government disbanded the IRC in 1971, Robinson joined British Leyland as financial controller before moving, in May 1972, to take charge of the corporation's newly acquired Innocenti business in Milan. This meant his learning another language! But after fourteen months in Italy he was called back to Britain to run Jaguar. On his arrival at Browns Lane in September, England became executive chairman and, in January 1974, announced his retirement. While he departed on a final tour of Jaguar's overseas agencies, Robinson set up a seven-man management committee at Browns Lane, though it only contained two Jaguar names: engineering supremo Bob Knight and sales director Alan Currie.

Geoffrey Robinson was pushing for expansion of Jaguar's Allesley manufacturing facilities. In December 1973 he had addressed a public meeting in Coventry and spoke optimistically of a £60 million investment plan which would double the firm's output from 30,000 to 60,000 cars a year by the end of 1975. There would also be 'flexibility' to up this figure of 90,000 cars per annum 'if necessary'.[38]

Despite the three-day week and first effects of the oil crisis, Jaguar's 1974 production figure of 32,565 cars approached that of the record year of 1971, yet 'it was achieved without the promised improvement in quality'.[39] A team of fitters was subsequently despatched to America to 'update' stocks there. It was the manifestation of a problem that was to be exacerbated in the latter half of the decade, though even during the 1968/75 era unreliability was beginning to infect the Jaguar marque. John Barber ran several XJ6s 'and in the first few months I logged up fifty faults in one when ten was about average'.[40]

If reliability problems were plaguing the top end of the British Leyland range, they were soon to manifest themselves on the Austin Allegro, which was the corporation's all-important 1100/1300 replacement. If it is possible to define the moment when the British Leyland Motor Corporation's decline became outwardly apparent, it was on the introduction of the Allegro in May 1973. Until then, it had been possible to find reasons for a shortfall in the public's expectations of British Leyland's cars. The Maxi and 2200 had been BMC inheritances; the Marina had, by its very nature, been something of a rushed job and was selling reasonably well. The Allegro, by contrast, had enjoyed a five-year gestation period. Yet it never achieved the market penetration of its long-running predecessor, which even in 1971 was Britain's best-selling car, and its failure to sell in sufficient numbers demonstrably marked the start of a decline in the fortunes of the Austin Morris division.

Work on the Allegro, coded ADO 67, had begun in 1968, the year of the British Leyland Motor Corporation's foundation, and its all-important body lines followed Harry Webster's brief, set down that April, that the front-wheel-drive Austin range would have 'more durable' styling than its rear-drive Morris stablemates. Prior to the creation of a styling department at Longbridge, Harris Mann and Paul Hughes produced rival designs at Cowley and Mann's was accordingly chosen. A clay model was produced from it and 'one afternoon in December 1968 Harry Webster and George Turnbull went down to Cowley . . . liked what they saw and the go-ahead was given to continue with the work'.[41] Further refinement was undertaken, though it was not until 19 September 1969 that the model was signed off as acceptable by the British Leyland management.

At that stage, and in an effort to prevent road mud and rain water entering the engine compartment to the detriment of the power unit, which was a continual bugbear on transverse-engined front-wheel-drive cars, the Allegro had a solid front end with an air intake below the front bumper. This would have meant retaining the usual side-mounted radiator but noise levels on the left-hand side of the car, where it was mounted, became so high that they would have breached the Common Market's regulations on noise emissions. The radiator was therefore moved to the front and a conventional grille introduced, though this meant lengthening the car's nose. The new radiator's location, in conjunction with a thermostatically controlled electric fan, cut down the interior noise and protected the engine from the elements.

From the very outset it had been intended to offer a wider range of engines on the new model than the 1100/1300 capacities available to its predecessor. So the Allegro was also designed to receive the 1500 and 1750 E Series Maxi engines which would, in addition, help the underutilized Coften Hackett engine plant. The earlier car's Hydrolastic interconnected

191

independent suspension was replaced by more compact Hydragas units, which obviated the need for subframes. This saved weight and cost, though the body structure, thanks to computer assistance, would be more efficient.

As a replacement for the 1100/1300, the Allegro was over 3 inches wider and 5 inches longer than its predecessor. Responding to criticisms about the small boot on the 1100/1300, the Allegro's petrol tank had been moved forward and the tail extended by 6 inches, so that its capacity was upped by 60 per cent. The car's interior was initially less happy. At a formative stage it had 4 inches *less* room than its predecessor, and although this was subsequently rectified, 'even then it was a bit of a problem to get into the rear seat and we had to cut off a bit of a corner of the cushion', Barber recalls; 'it was very much a bodged job.'[42] Thirty different types of facia were considered and the one chosen was approved on 29 May 1970. Then the Allegro had a conventional steering wheel though, by December 1971, designs for a new so-called quartic wheel had been submitted for approval.

This went back to a day earlier in the year when 'George Turnbull . . . after attending a corporate styling presentation by David Bache at the Rover-Triumph studio in Solihull . . . returned clutching one of Bache's more way-out doodles consisting of four gentle arcs joined together'. Turnbull 'insisted [it] would be right for the high-technology image and must go on the Allegro'.[43] The wheel was sanctioned for use on the car in January 1971.

By mid-1972, modifications were still being made to the design and the car was subsequently tested on a cold-weather proving run in Finland and on Automotive Products' Shennington testing ground as, at this stage, British Leyland did not possess its own test track. Several months before the Allegro was due to be announced, a handful of selected technical journalists were invited to Longbridge to view the design. 'About the best compliment that they could pay the car was that at least it looked different enough not to be confused with anything else. They entered several strong pleas, not least that the nose should be given more character and that the "quartic" wheel should be done away with. They were assured that, while time was short, due weight would be given to everything they had said.' When the car made its debut in May 1973, 'the Allegro was announced in a form almost exactly as they had seen it, and even the quartic wheel was still in its place'.[44]

Although the unconventional steering wheel gave the headline writers plenty of scope, the Allegro's 'durable' styling fell badly short of expectations. While the intention had been to produce a clean design, uncluttered by unnecessary decoration, which would not date and so enjoy a long production run, the barrel-shaped profile resulted in a blob of car, particularly in its two-door form.

The truth was that the Allegro's looks did not compare with those of the Pininfarina-styled 1100/1300 it was replacing. That enjoyed 59,198 British sales even in 1973, which was its last year of production. The Allegro's best sales year was 1975 when 63,339 were registered in Britain, which was about half the rate that the 1100/1300 had been selling. By 1974 flat-out production was running at about 4,500 to 5,000 cars a week, which compared with 8,000 Cortinas leaving Ford's Dagenham plant. The Allegro lingered on until 1983, by which time 642,350 had been built, compared with 1.1 million examples of its forbear produced over a similar production span. Actually the Allegro was both stylistically and mechanically inferior to the 1100/1300 series it had been created to replace, shortcomings that were compounded by a deterioration in corporate build quality.

When *Autocar* staff came to test the Allegro, they voiced an instant dislike for the quartic wheel. 'It took quite a while before one stopped going round corners in quarter-turn-bites and got used to the jerky way it spun back through one's hands after a tight turn. It is hard to understand why this gimmick was thought necessary, especially as it is bound to introduce some initial sales resistance.'[45] They subsequently predicted strong sales of conventional replacement wheels on the accessory market.

Yet when David Bache's 'doodle' finally emerged on the 1976 SDI Rover, 'the profile was so carefully shaped that most observers did not notice', which compared with Austin Morris's interpretation which 'was angular and crude'.[46] British Leyland persevered with it for a while, but when the hideous Vanden Plas Princess 1500 version of the Allegro appeared in 1974, the quartic had been replaced by a conventional wheel and the feature was phased out on the mainstream model from May 1975.

The Allegro's unusual steering wheel was, in essence, a cosmetic miscalculation with some practical shortcomings. But when *Autocar* came to evaluate the 1.3-litre Allegro's 0-60mph acceleration, it was in for a shock: 'We could not reach 60mph in less than eighteen seconds, which is about one second slower than the manufacturer's claim and nearly two seconds slower than the 0-60mph time we recorded with the Austin 1300 of 1971.' This the magazine charitably put down to having to test the Allegro in 'rather unsuitable weather' because of 'some troubles with the test car'.[47] But its 82mph top speed was also found to be inferior to that of the Austin 1300 and the Morris Marina, which shared the same A Series engine, tested by *Autocar* in the same year.

In May 1973, in the same month that the Austin Allegro was announced and on the fifth anniversary of British Leyland's formation, fifty-nine-year-old Lord Stokes, declared that although he would be continuing as chairman until the age of sixty-five, John Barber would move up from finance director to become deputy chairman, while the managing directorship would go to George Turnbull who would continue to head Austin Morris. With this appointment, John Barber clearly emerged as Lord Stokes's heir apparent.

Almost from the Corporation's creation in 1968, the International Reorganization Corporation felt that it would be a mistake for one man to attempt to carry out the role of chairman and chief executive in such a large and complex company as British Leyland. So 'in the summer of 1968 [the IRC] began to make enquiries aimed at discovering whether there was anyone available with the right experience and ability, since it was felt that outsiders should be considered, in addition to anyone within the company who might be thought to be capable of taking on the role'.[48]

These criticisms were to some extent alleviated when Stokes announced his management changes in September 1968 and some of his duties were devolved to George Turnbull, but he continued to be involved in the minutiae of the Corporation's business. 'Nobody in the company is allowed to spend anything, even £25 for a new typewriter, unless it has been authorized by him. He checks every item personally, from investments costing £1 million to batteries for fork-lift trucks, arguing that it took little of his time.'[49] That was Stokes in 1968, but he subsequently became rather more liberal in delegating authority, and on the plus side 'he deals with day-to-day problems with great deftness and skill . . . he is absolutely dedicated; he has the knack of saying precisely the right thing, whether to shop stewards or managers; and he uses newspapers and television more effectively than any other British industrialist.'[50]

John Barber endorses this appraisal.

Donald Stokes was very much a 'people person', he was extremely good at dealing with them, he would get around and talk to them and in doing so he appeared to be managing in a 'hands-on' way. But he wasn't managing in the sense of planning, setting out targets, measuring performances and so on. When I first became finance director I said to him, 'Look, we haven't got any budget or control system.' He responded, slightly tongue in cheek, 'I'm a bit doubtful about budgets. I don't know what is going to happen next week, let alone next year. . .'[51]

By 1970 Stokes recognized that 'he had to learn new tricks. For an old dog that takes time.'[52]

Today Lord Stokes conceded that, in some respects, it was 'probably true' that he should have delegated more, though it should be remembered that he came from Leyland Motors which he is the first to identify as very much a 'hands-on operation'. He also maintains that at British Leyland 'a lot more delegation went on than might have been apparent. I got blamed for everything that went wrong and somebody else down the line got the credit for anything that went right. That's the normal situation. If a fire started you had to put it out yourself but John Barber, George Turnbull, Bill Lyons and George Farmer all had tremendous authority delegated to them. I couldn't have run a thing like that by myself.'[53]

When, in 1973, it came to appointing a deputy, Stokes recalls, 'It was either George Turnbull or John Barber and, by a very narrow margin, the board appointed John Barber. I was carrying too much load and you can't have joint managing directors.'[54] Five months later, in September, British Leyland announced forty-seven-year-old Turnbull's resignation and, in the following year, he joined the South Korea-based Hyundi Motor Company to establish a car-manufacturing facility at Ulsan, 250 miles south of the capital, Seoul.

Turnbull's departure represented the first significant resignation from the British Leyland board. 'It was five years of extremely hard work,' he later recalled. 'I will never work as hard again, nor wish to. To run the operation while planning the reorganization and all the time having to handle all the labour problems involved in an organization of 80,000 was a superhuman task. It was only through having very good people around me that I was able to cope.'[55]

David Andrews, who joined British Leyland as controller from Ford in 1969 and became finance director of Austin Morris in 1970, remembers that Turnbull 'got to grips with a number of things, he was ahead of his time on communications, internally to managers and employees, which was all the rage then, and he was good at it'.[56] In June 1972 George Turnbull had consolidated his position within the corporation when he took over responsibility for the Bus and Truck Division, in addition to his Austin Morris duties, which many industry pundits believed signified his emergence as a possible successor to Lord Stokes.

But behind the scenes there was a 'basic conflict' being enacted between Turnbull and Barber which the latter sums up thus: 'We had a complete difference in philosophy. He was more of a "doer" and I was more of a planner. Coming from Ford it was inevitable. I was pushing Stokes towards moving up market; George wanted to be a high-volume producer.'[57]

In addition to this, Turnbull was opposed to a plan for the restructuring of British Leyland which meant that the truck and car operations would report to a central operating point. When this had been first proposed in 1971, 'Turnbull had told Stokes that he, George, was trying to bring about this type of reorganization at Longbridge and it had been a long uphill battle. Stokes, in reply, said that if Turnbull wasn't in favour of the scheme he had better resign.'[58] Matters came to a head with Barber's appointment. 'There was an argument partly over structure and partly who came out on top,'[59] remembers Andrews. For Turnbull the reorganization 'looked like another Ford but in practical terms it wasn't. At British Leyland the management structure was threadbare, although we were building it up, and to suddenly decimate it and change all the heads of departments around was counter-productive and totally demoralizing.'[60]

After Turnbull resigned, David Andrews, who became managing director of the new Power and Transmission Division, recalls that 'the Austin Morris group was broken up and divided into engineering, manufacturing, sales and marketing. It was run from the centre, which did not prove to be terribly effective, though they did not have all that much time because British Leyland got overtaken by events. But it wasn't a universal view that that was the best way to go.'[61]

With Turnbull's departure, John Barber, in addition to being British Leyland's deputy chairman, also took over the managing directorship. There was good news for the corporation in 1973 when it recorded pre-tax profits of £51 million, the highest ever achieved, although Barber acknowledges that 'it wasn't enough money, the profits just weren't big enough. We had made progress over six years which we ought to have made in two, perhaps. If we had continued, we would have achieved in ten years what we ought to have done in three or four.'[62] Yet there was a note of optimism in the air when the Corporation moved from its London offices in Berkeley Square to the fourteen-storey former Burmah-Castrol building at 174 Marylebone Road, renamed Leyland House following the oil company's move to new headquarters in Swindon. This would contain 'the top management team together with all the corporate central staffs'.

One of Barber's first actions as managing director was to introduce a complete ban on recruitment. 'We just insisted on saying "No hiring" with one or two exceptions like specialist people. I got rid of 30,000 people and I did it quietly too, without hitting the headlines.'[63]

In October 1973, just as British Leyland's fortunes appeared to be brightening and only two months before the Corporation announced its 1973 profit figures, the Arab-Israeli War broke out. The Arab oil-exporting countries, for the first time using oil as a political weapon, reduced Britain's oil supplies (which represented half the country's energy requirements) by 15 per cent and quadrupled the price. Edward Heath's Conservative government responded by introducing a three-day working week from 1 January 1974, and a 50mph speed limit to conserve fuel supplies. These difficulties were compounded by trade-union opposition to the administration's Phase Three counter-inflation measures which erupted into a miners' strike in February. That month, against a turbulent industrial background, the government called a general election, which it lost, and Labour and Harold Wilson were back in power.

These upheavals had a devastating effect on British Leyland's fragile finances. Lord Stokes recalls: 'We were stretched financially, and were on a pretty tight rope. With the oil crisis, export and domestic markets collapsed; it was a disastrous situation.'[64] To add to these problems, the economical but loss-making Mini overtook the Marina as the Corporation's best-selling car. The firm had projected a £68 million profit in 1974, though in the six months to the end of March it lost £16.6 million but had hopes of returning to profitability in the latter half of the year. Then, in June, Austin Morris's technical director, Harry Webster, left the Corporation to join Automotive Products, having been offered a job as group engineering director. In his place John Barber brought in Spen King.

By the summer of 1974 the Corporation recognized that it would have to scale down expansion plans announced the previous year, and that it would not be possible to finance them from its own resources. In July it met Barclays, Lloyds, Midland and the National Westminster, its principal bankers, seeking medium-term finance of £150 million (of which £50 million was to be used to reduce its overdraft) to execute a modified version of the plan. Simultaneously the Corporation began talks with the Department of Trade and Industry which was concerned by the long-term effects of the cutback. The Corporation responded that it could proceed with its plans but would need an extra £100 million 'from external sources'.[65]

By September a cash-conservation programme had been instituted and restrictions placed on capital expenditure. British Leyland was predicting an unaudited loss of £9.9 million, which together with an £11.8 million deficit following the closure of its Australian subsidiary, suggested an overall loss of £21.7 million. In fact, the eventual figure proved to be £23.9 million. At that time the company's overdraft at home and overseas stood at £148 million, which was offset by bank deposits of £105 million.

The clearing banks were becoming increasingly concerned and, in November, instructed accountants Thomson McLintock and Company 'to examine the validity of the cash projections made available to them the previous July'. The situation continued to deteriorate and, on Wednesday 27 November, tripartite talks were held at the Department of Trade and Industry between the company, the department and the banks. British Leyland estimated that it would reach the limit of its British overdraft facilities in December and cash payments of £30 million were due in January 1975. 'It became clear that, in these circumstances, the banks were most unlikely to grant BL further facilities.'[66]

Further talks culminated in the secretary of state for industry, Tony Benn, making an all-important statement about British Leyland's future to the House of Commons on 6 December. Because of the company's importance to the economy and as a leading exporter, parliamentary approval would be sought to guarantee working capital. In addition the company had asked for support for its investment programme and 'the Government also intends to introduce longer-term arrangements, including a measure of public ownership'. Benn informed the house that they proposed to appoint a 'high-level team', lead by Sir Don Ryder, the government's industrial adviser, 'to advise on the company's situation and prospects, and the team will consult with the company and the trade unions in the course of its work'.[67] Ryder's assignment was confirmed on 18 December and approval was obtained for a £50 million guarantee of bank lending.

While the public was awaiting the findings of the Ryder Report, British Leyland introduced, in March 1975, what was to be its last model, intended to replace the ageing 1800 and 2200 range. Work on the project had begun in 1971 and the Longbridge design team this time offered an adventurous wedge shape, the work of Harris Mann. It was available with a choice of two engines, the heavy and long-running B Series unit carried over from the 1800 or the E Series overhead-camshaft six which came from its 2200 derivative. Here, at last, was a roomy, comfortable car with a better driving position than its predecessor's, though sales prospects for such a model looked bleak as the effects of the oil crisis continued to bite. The car was named the 18-22, to reflect its engine options, and if the original 1968 marque brief had been followed it would have been marketed only as an Austin. But the requirements of the Morris dealership demanded a badge-engineered version and there was also an up-market 2.2-litre Wolseley version, though it was to prove the last of the line: in September the 18-22 range became the Princess.

Sir Don Ryder presented his report, 'British Leyland: the next decade', to Tony Benn on 26 March, fourteen weeks after it had been commissioned. It was first considered by a ministerial committee and then by the cabinet on 22 April. Barbara Castle noted in her diary that the discussion on it was led by chancellor of the exchequer Denis Healey, who spoke on behalf of the committee. He warned that the massive commitment of investment, which amounted to £2,800 million over seven years, would determine the government's industrial policy for its lifetime. It would be a 'tricky gamble'. Ministers were recommending it unanimously. 'Ryder's report was ruthlessly thorough.' Leyland suffered from poor management, Stokes would have to go, there was grotty machinery and bad industrial relations. The alternative was nearly a million unemployed and the end of the British motor industry. 'And so, with very little opposition, it was agreed.' Harold Wilson 'added wistfully that Donald

198

Stokes had been a long-standing friend. This would hurt him terribly and he hoped that he might be used in the sort of job he excelled at: as a travelling export promoter for the company.' Only the chancellor of the Duchy of Lancaster, Harold Lever, cautioned that they were 'rushing into a grandiose folly . . . it was like "a bad Pharaoh's dream" in which we weren't even promised seven fat years after the seven lean ones,'[68] but his words had little impact. Wilson informed the House of Commons the following day that the government accepted Ryder's recommendations and would take a substantial holding in the new company through the National Enterprise Board which was soon to be set up.

In essence Ryder recommended that British Leyland should remain as both a volume and specialist car producer and that the entire car-manufacturing operation be grouped together under the Leyland Cars umbrella. This prompted the departures of John Barber, Rover-Triumph's Bernard Jackman and Jaguar's chief executive Geoffrey Robinson. Lord Stokes was to become president.

The British Leyland Motor Corporation ceased to exist on 27 June 1975 when it was renamed British Leyland Ltd. Its production, British market share and financial performance are set down below:

Year	Car Production	British Market share (%)	Pre-Tax Profits (£ millions)
1968	719,477	40.6	38
1969	830,874	40.2	41
1970	788,737	38.1	4
1971	886,721	40.2	32
1972	916,218	33.1	32
1973	875,839	31.9	51
1974	738,503	32.7	2
1975	605,141	30.9	(23.6)

If the years between 1968 and 1975 were traumatic ones for British Leyland, they were a time of growth and consolidation for Ford which, by 1972, had completed the integration of its British and German operations under the Ford of Europe umbrella. Its headquarters were British-based, at Warley, Essex. The void left by the retirement of Sir Patrick Hennessy was filled by Sir Leonard Crossland (knighted in 1969) who, like his predecessor, had spent much of his career, from 1937 until 1954, in the company's purchasing department and had been purchasing manager from 1960 until 1962. He was replaced in 1972 by Sir William Batty (knighted in 1973), who had joined Ford in 1930 and came to the chairmanship via its tractor division.

During this era, Ford alone amongst its British contemporaries was profitable with the exception of the year 1971 when it recorded a £30.7 million loss, the result of a ten-week strike which paralysed all its British plants. It was the longest strike in the company's history and its objective had been to secure parity for Ford workers with the highest-paid labour in the Midlands. That would have meant rises of up to £15 a week or 50 per cent on basic rates. It finally ended when Ford offered 'a first payment of 16.2 per cent, with later instalments bringing the offer up to an inflationary 33 per cent over two years'.[69] Ford was back in the black the following year and, in 1975, was the only British car company to make a profit, a respectable £43.8 million, which, maintains Sir Terence Beckett who succeeded Batty as chairman of Ford of Britain in 1976, was when 'the careful planning of many years before, providing the essential profit return, paid off when many of Ford's rivals were left in real trouble'.[70]

Ford planned to launch the Escort, its long-awaited Anglia replacement, in 1968, though Ford of Europe, well aware of its impending arrival, decided that the car should also be tooled up for production at Ford of Germany's Ghenk plant. That is what occurred, though in the face of some scepticism from the German product planners who believed that its ultra-conventional front-engine/rear-drive mechanicals might not be sufficiently innovative. Their fears were ill-founded. By 1969 the Escort had helped Ford of Germany to recover 2.2 percentage points of the German market and contributed to lifting production from 207,763 cars in 1968 to 300,856 in the following year. In Britain the Escort, after the Ford Cortina, was Britain's second best-selling car from 1972 when it overtook the long-running Austin 1100/1300. When this Mark I Escort ceased production in 1975, it had established itself as the best-selling British-designed Ford ever, for its dual manufacture had resulted in a record 2,155,301 being built.

The Escort had proved the validity of the European concept, though the next model that Ford of Britain announced, in 1969, had been conceived, some way into its development, as a European project. What became the Capri started as a British response to the success in America of the Ford Mustang of 1964. Lee Iacocca, who had replaced Robert McNamara as head of the Ford division in 1960, initiated market research which showed that the twenty to twenty-four-year-old age group would grow by 50 per cent during the decade as the post-war 'baby boom' reached maturity. The result was the sporty Mustang, a small car by American standards and created specifically for the youth market. No less than 680,992 Mustangs had been sold by the end of 1965 which was 'an all-time industry record for first-year sales'[71] and the millionth Mustang was built in March 1966, only twenty-three months after the car had been launched.

With such an impressive track record it was not surprising to find Ford of Britain studying the feasibility of such a car from late 1964 which was, in truth, a rather un-Fordlike product and appropriately coded Colt. From the very outset the intention was to offer across-the-board engine options as with its American cousin. The project was approved by Ford of Britain in 1966, but by the time that Ford of Europe was created in 1967, its analysts considered that the European market had become sufficiently affluent to respond to what was, in truth, a speciality car. This meant dual production, like the Escort, but they looked upon it not so much as an Anglo-German model as a European one and product clinics, where consumer reaction is gauged *prior* to a model's announcement, were held in Brussels, Amsterdam and Milan as well as London and Cologne. When the Capri, with its distinctive fastback styling and its 1.3- to 3-litre engine options, appeared in January 1969, it was soon being built simultaneously in Hailwood and Ford's new plant at Saarlouis in south-west Germany, opened in 1969. With the Capri, Ford built on its performance image honed in the 1960s, offering the family man the looks and panache of a pukka Grand Tourer but without its cost or complication. The Capri exceeded the Ford planners' targets, for it soon attained 2.5 to 3 per cent of the British market and more than 3.5 per cent of the German one. 'It also captured a greater number of customers from competing makes than any other Ford model.'[72] Germany took over complete production in 1976 and the Capri endured for a record seventeen years, finally being discontinued in 1987.

The Cortina Mark II was replaced for 1971 by its Mark III successor, which was the same length, but 2.1 inches wider and 2.7 inches lower than its forebear, and embodied an integration of Ford's British and German engineering facilities. It was accordingly the first 'all metric' Ford car. The body had been developed at the company's new body and chassis engineering centre in Merkenich, Germany, opened in 1967, though the design was sufficiently flexible for the Cortina to incorporate its distinctive 'Coke bottle' lines while the Taunus 17M was a straight-sided affair. Engine development was a British responsibility and was undertaken at a new £10.5 million research and engineering facility, also opened in 1967, at Dunton, Essex. Although initially the British and German cars had different engines, a common denominator was a new 1.6-litre overhead-camshaft unit which had first appeared in Ford of America's 1970 sub-compact Pinto model. Although the Cortina was outsold by the Austin 1100/1300 range in its first production year of 1971, in 1972 it became Britain's best-selling car and, with the exception of 1976 when the Ford Escort moved ahead, the Cortina line was, until 1981, the country's most popular model.

In 1972 Ford replaced its slow-selling Mark IV Zephyr Zodiac range and the German 20M with the four-cylinder Consul, reviving a model name that had been in abeyance since 1965, and the V6-engined Granada which shared the same body shell and was built in both countries. In view of the criticisms of the dimensions of its predecessor, the new range was 5 inches shorter than the Mark IV, and although the usual front-engine/rear-drive layout was perpetuated, both models were fitted with independent rear suspension which was an innovation on a European Ford car. The Consul name was dropped in 1975; thereafter the Granada name prevailed. Production ceased in 1977 after 833,302 examples of these big Fords had been built, which favourably compared with 149,247 Mark IVs, particularly in the post-1973 energy crisis years. This hit Ford along with the rest of the British motor industry. The 329,648 cars it built in 1975 was its lowest production figure since 1961.

Ford's success during the eight years between 1968 and 1975 almost exactly coincided with a fall in the fortunes of General Motors' Vauxhall subsidiary which, over this period, lost £40.6 million and recorded only modest profits in 1968 and 1971. David G. Hegland, who had been Vauxhall's chairman and managing director since 1966, was, in September 1970, reported to be 'on special leave of absence'[73] and was replaced by Alexander D. Rhea who, like his predecessor, came to Luton from General Motors' Australian Holden subsidiary.

The reason for Vauxhall's disastrous performance was, in the main, the failure of the new generation of FD Victor models to match, or even surpass, sales of the earlier FC range. Yet the FD was an all-new car with a 2-litre engine, featuring an overhead-camshaft driven by a neoprene toothed belt, and was the first British-built car to offer this facility. But it proved a poor seller. British registrations were only 34,772 in 1968 which was down on 1967, the last year of its FC predecessor, when 38,517 found customers. Sales fell back even further in 1969 and 1970, though subsequently peaked at 36,651 in 1972 with the arrival of a more powerful FE version, a year in which Ford sold 187,159 Cortinas. The FD-based six-cylinder Ventora of 1968, which perpetuated the Cresta theme, was even more disappointing and, in 1970, a mere 3,597 were registered. The reasons for this dramatic decline in Vauxhall's fortunes were a combination of poor looks and bad road holding. They appeared big and unwiedly; the American 'bigger and better' approach had not successfully crossed the Atlantic. The cars' interiors looked cheap and nasty and suffered from an excess of plastic. These visual shortcomings, along with disappointing ride and cramped rear passenger accommodation, kept the customers away.

The Viva continued to be the only bright spot on the Vauxhall sales chart. The pretty HB continued to sell strongly. In 1968 it achieved record sales of 101,067 and, on 20 July 1971, the millionth example left Vauxhall's Luton works while number 1,000,001 was built at Ellesmere Port on the same day. The model entered its HC series in 1972 and, as the car market boomed, sales once again approached the 100,000 mark. Less happy was the Firenza, introduced in 1971 and Vauxhall's answer to the Ford Capri, though this failed to have much impact. In its introduction year of 1971 only 5,988 were sold in Britain. In 1974 Vauxhall lost a record £18.1 million.

Then, in March 1975, Vauxhall introduced 'its' Chevette, which was effectively an Opel Kadett C, launched in Germany in 1973. Luton designs were to be progressively phased out and, with the 1979 demise of the Viva, the Vauxhall range became exclusively rebadged Opel. It had been in 1974 that Vauxhall's General Motors parent decided to upgrade Opel, its German subsidiary, and that country's number 2 car manufacturer, and make it responsible for the design and engineering of its European passenger cars. This followed Opel's having successfully executed what the Corporation called Project 1865. Initiated in the summer of 1970, it was, in effect, a world car with a body that could be built by General Motors' subsidiaries in plants as far afield as Germany, Japan, Brazil, America itself and Britain. Engines would differ, according to locations, so 1865 was designed to accommodate locally sourced power units. Although the Viva-engined Chevette and Kadett C were sisters under the skin, their first cousins were scattered the world over. In 1976 this three-door hatchback, with a Vauxhall front end, became the make's best-selling car.

Yet, in 1968, General Motors had begun building a brand-new 700-acre vehicle proving ground at Millbrook, 22 miles north of the firm's Luton factories. This work was completed in 1970 at a cost of £3.6 million, only four years before Vauxhall lost its engineering and design status.

Chrysler, the third member of the American Big Three was, in the meanwhile, having a tough time with what had been Rootes Motors and which, in 1970, became Chrysler United Kingdom. In 1973 the final connection with the previous administration was severed when Lord Rootes stepped down as chairman to be replaced by Gilbert Hunt, who had been managing director since 1968. His place was taken by the deputy managing director, American Don Lander. During these eight years, the losses of Chrysler's British company totalled £65.3 million, the highest in the industry. It was profitable only in the three years between 1971 and 1973 and its best performance was in the last year of the three when it managed a £3.7 million surplus.

These problems were a reflection of the fact that Chrysler was constrained by a limited and ageing product range. Then, in 1970, the firm filled the massive gap between the slow-selling Imp and the staid Minx with the Hillman Avenger. As might be expected from an American company, and with the presence of the controversial rear-engined Imp as an uncomfortable reminder, the all-new model was a conventional front-engine/rear-drive design and represented Chrylser's first major contribution to the former Rootes model range. It was available in two- and four-door forms, its distinctive short tail with upswept rear dictating the use of coil springs and trailing arms as the cheaper and simpler half-elliptics would have been untidily revealed by the distinctive profile! The Avenger, with 1.2- and 1.5-engine options, was built at Chrysler's Ryton factory, while its body was inconveniently produced at Linwood at the other end of the country and had to be expensively transported to Coventry by train. Its engines came from the firm's nearby Stoke plant.

The Avenger got off to a fairly good start. The 50,000th example was built in August 1970 and 50,133 were sold in Britain that year, compared with a mere 14,023 Hillman Minxes. Demand peaked in 1973 when 78,644 Avengers were sold, but thereafter sales fell away, no doubted affected by Chrysler's much-publicized financial troubles (these are considered in the next chapter). However, the Avenger's relative success helped Chrysler to overtake Vauxhall in the British production league in 1970, though Luton redressed the balance in 1975.

The Humber name continued to appear on the up-market Minx-related Sceptre, while the Roy Axe-styled sporty Sunbeam Rapier of 1968, resembling a scaled-down in-house Plymouth Barracuda, was an adventurous concept marred by its dated Rootes pushrod engine. In 1970 Chrysler discontinued Singer as a marque name; that year only 1,357 Vogues had been registered and the only other model was the low-production Imp-derived Chamois. So after sixty-five years, Singer, which in 1929 had been the third largest car maker in Britain, was no more.

Chrysler's British operations continued to be plagued by industrial disputes, though 'without question 1973 was the worst year of stoppages ... in terms of available production lost'.[74] There was a five-week strike at Ryton in May and June, and it was during this stoppage that the management announced that plans to build its new Alpine model in Britain would be shelved with production being switched to its French Simca subsidiary. A further electricans' dispute at Ryton that began in Coventry on 2 August, spread to its loss-making Linwood factory, and dragged on until 9 November. By the end of the year the firm had lost a record 91,129 vehicles through internal and external disputes.

The effects of the oil price rise wrought havoc with Chrysler UK's always-precarious finances. In 1974 it lost £17.7 million and British banks, concerned by the state of the motor industry, 'began to refuse to renew short-term loans and, in addition for Chrysler UK specifically, the banks were requiring Chrysler Corporation guarantees on any loans that were made'.[75] In December 1974 the parent company made a $12 million injection while, in January and February 1975, Chrysler's British operations were kept alive by subsidies of $13 million each month which were made against a background of escalating Chrysler losses in America. These were the opening rounds in a crisis that would culminate in Chrysler withdrawing completely from Britain in 1978.

8

Ryder and After

1975–87

'In all areas [the Metro] approaches those standards set by the best cars of its class so that as a whole it represents a formidable challenger indeed to established superminis. Like the Mini before it, I can see it becoming a cult car. It looks chic, it is chic – but above all it is very good.'

Motor, on the occasion of the launch of the Austin Metro,
11 October 1980

The twelve years between 1975 and 1987 saw Britain slip to fifth place in the European production league, having been overtaken by Spain in 1980. This was largely due to the decline in production from the state-owned sector which, since 1975, has been variously known as British Leyland, BL Cars and, more recently, the Rover Group.

The Ryder Report had optimistically spoken of British Leyland retaining around 33 per cent of the home market, which, it opined, should reach 1.6 million cars in 1980; however, the 923,744 actually built represented the lowest British production figure since 1957. The reality was that the world had been pitched into a financial trough caused by the effects of the second – and more serious – oil crisis in 1979. More damaging was the Report's main-line recommendation which was that British Leyland's car divisions be amalgamated into a single business, though this proved unworkable and was abandoned after only two years. Mounting labour problems almost brought the company to its knees in 1977, but the appointment that year of Michael Edwardes as British Leyland's chairman marked a turning point in the firm's affairs. Sir Michael, as he became in 1979, met the union militants head on, rebuilt the model programme, initiated long-overdue plant closures and cut the workforce. The Metro of 1980 was the best-received model from Austin Morris since the arrival of the top-selling 1100 range in 1962. But the company tumbled into deficit in 1979, and losses continued to mount until 1983 when the firm was briefly back in the black. It slid into the red again and this spiralled into a record deficit of £892 million in 1986. With profitability once more on the horizon, the return of this state-owned industry to the private sector by 1992 seems a possibility.

In 1975 British Leyland still retained 30 per cent of the British market, with Ford some way behind with 21 per cent. Then, in 1977, the inevitable happened and Ford replaced Leyland as the country's market leader, a position it has maintained ever since. That was despite the fact that British Leyland built more cars – 651,069 compared with Ford's 406,633 – the difference being made by Ford imports from Germany, Belgium and, for the first time, Spain. The renamed Rover Group's market share stood at 15 per cent by 1987, a year in which imports accounted for 50 per cent of the market. The remaining members of the slimmed-down Big Four continued to enjoy varying fortunes. The Chrysler Corporation, in deep trouble in America, disposed of its loss-making British subsidiary to the French Peugeot company in 1978. Vauxhall, after more than a decade in the doldrums, experienced a sales revival from 1982 onwards, which caught the market off balance. But Jaguar, nearly obliterated in the chaos of the post-Ryder years, returned to profitability and subsequently rejoined the private sector in 1984, having found in Sir John Egan a worthy successor to Sir William Lyons.

These were years that saw the demise of some of the country's most famous marque names: Hillman, Humber, Triumph and Morris. During this period, the British sports car also came to the end of the road. The last MGB was built in 1980, while the Triumph TR line was extinguished when production of the TR7 stopped in 1981. Canley's life as a car-manufacturing plant came to an end, after sixty-one years, in 1980, though it still remains within the Rover Group. Similarly Solihull, home of the Rover car since 1945, ceased to be so in 1982 when production was transferred to Cowley, though Land-Rover and Range Rover manufacture continues at the site.

Yet, ironically, the Ryder Report had made no recommendations of plant closures, though it did specify 'changes in BL's top management'.[1] When Lord Stokes became company president, a non-executive chairman, in line with the report's recommendations, was appointed in October 1975 in the shape of Sir Ronald Edwards, president of the Beecham Group, though he was destined to hold the post for only four months before his sudden death, aged only sixty-four, in January 1976. British Leyland's new chief executive was Alex Park, who had taken John Barber's job as finance director in 1974 after the latter had become managing director. Park, who had previously held a similar appointment with Rank Xerox, subsequently acknowledged that he was just as surprised as the public when he was offered the position. 'You must be joking,'[2] he had told Lord Stokes.

Ryder had recommended that British Leyland 'should continue in both the "volume" and the "specialist" sectors of the car market', and the report set down that the company be split into four divisions: Cars, Trucks and Bus, International and Special Products. Four scenarios had been considered for the structure of the all-important car division. It could be: recast as a single business; divided into three (Austin Morris, Triumph and Rover); re-organized into two (Volume and Specialist Cars); or re-aligned on the basis of product groupings (Austin Morris, Rover Triumph and Jaguar). While Ryder recognized that there was a need to preserve the distinctive product identity of the specialist cars and the loyalty of employees, the report maintained that 'BL cannot, however, compete successfully as a producer of cars unless it can make the most effective use of all its design, engineering, manufacturing and marketing resources'.[3] It therefore concluded that a 'single integrated car business . . . would serve the best interests of BL in the future'.[4] The man given the unenviable job of putting these recommendations into effect as managing director of the newly titled Leyland Cars division was Derrick Whittaker, formerly managing director of the Corporation's body and assembly division.

But even as the new appointments were being announced in August 1975, the all-party House of Common's Expenditure Committee issued its own critical comments on Ryder's report following evidence taken by its Trade and Industry subcommittee for its report *The Motor Vehicle Industry*. It had decided to undertake this assignment after the British Leyland collapse of December 1974, and the nine-member subcommittee, under the chairmanship of Labour MP Patrick Duffy and consisting of five Labour members, three Conservatives and one Scottish Nationalist, began work in January 1975. What followed was one of the most detailed investigations ever undertaken by a parliamentary committee into the British motor industry, with evidence taken from top managers, trade union officials and civil servants.

The committee was particularly critical of how the report had costed its programme. These estimates were based on a concept study made by British Leyland on the basis of 'a fairly free availability of cash'. But it was 'unlikely to have rigid economy as its central theme and it is rigid economy and high cost effectiveness which should be two of the criteria for the expenditure of public money, not to mention commercial survival'.[5]

'What Ryder did (I was there at the same time),' recalls Barber, 'was to say to Alex Park, the finance director, and controller Gerry Wright, "In an ideal world, give me a projection if you had unlimited money, where you think that British Leyland can go." They did a plan for him on that basis. They produced this "what if" study and gave it to Ryder and then Stokes and I and others had great difficulty in curbing him from using it.'[6]

Another cause for concern was Ryder's estimates of British Leyland's 33 per cent share of home market and that BL's penetration of the European one would rise by a quarter to 3.9 per cent by 1985. In the words of *The Motor Vehicle Industry* report:

> We are not satisfied that the [Ryder] report's marketing forecasts were carried out sufficiently objectively or, indeed, sufficiently thoroughly . . . if there were overcapacity in the European industry, or if the strong possibility of a price war in the European market were realized, or if an increase in the price of cars relative to incomes were to damage the UK market, then BLMC's increased sales would be placed in jeopardy.[7]

The relationship between the chief executive and managing director of the car division was also highlighted by the committee. 'Commenting on the disproportionate power of the managing director of the Car Division, Sir Don said, "This is going to be a matter where great care on chemistry has got to be exercised." ' On this the committee stated, 'We are of the opinion that Ryder has put too much onus on personalities rather than the correctness of the structure. This is inherently dangerous.'[8] This could have been avoided by 'organizing mass-produced and quantity cars in separate divisions'.

In addition, Ryder was criticised by the committee for his recommendation that funds could be geared to industrial relations: 'We cannot believe that this is a practical possibility.' It also grasped the nettle of the labour problem. Referring to the poor productivity levels then operating at British Leyland, it maintained that 'unless the Corporation achieves a very much higher level of output, and related sales, than Ryder forecasts, it must shed labour.'[9]

Although the committee had revealed many of the flaws of Ryder's report, the reality was that the latter's recommendations had been accepted by the cabinet three months previously. When the National Enterprise Board, whose role was to oversee the implementation of Ryder's findings, came into being in November 1975, Ryder himself (who had just been made a life peer) was its first chairman. The Board's terms of reference had been set down in a government White Paper of August 1974, *The Regeneration of British Industry*. Its role would be similar to that of the old

Industrial Reorganization Corporation and its function to encourage industrial efficiency and profitability. In addition, the scope of the former Conservative government's 1972 Industry Act was widened to permit the NEB to purchase share captial in a company in return for financial assistance. 'We need,' proclaimed the White Paper, 'both efficient publicly owned industries and a vigorous, alert, responsible and profitable public sector.' Yet, in truth, the affairs of British Leyland were to dominate the NEB's activities and those of its chairman, Lord Ryder of Eaton Hastings.

Sydney Thomas Franklin (Don) Ryder, born in 1916 is a former editor of the *Stock Exchange Gazette* who rose to become managing director of the Reed Paper Group in 1963, and when it merged with or, more correctly, took over the International Publishing Corporation in 1970, Ryder became chairman and chief executive of the renamed Reed International. Ryder's appetite for work became legendary, as did his much-publicized eighteen-hour day, and following the election of the Labour government in 1974, Sir Don (knighted in 1972) became its industrial adviser. He was attached to the cabinet office with direct access to the prime minister and had produced his report on British Leyland in that capacity.

When Michael Edwardes, chairman of the Chloride Corporation, joined the NEB in 1975, he soon became aware that any 'suggestions and comments' made to Lord Ryder on the report 'were dismissed on the grounds that his industrial adviser role was insulted from his NEB role – a quite bizarre situation'.[10] While the central theme of his report had been expansion, it had ignored the questionable appeal of the company's model range and the fact that British Leyland's market share had fallen a full 10 points since 1968. Lord Ryder visited British Leyland's factories where he addressed employees and unions, exhorting them to help solve the company's problems; though, in Edwardes's opinion, 'this undermined the company's management, and it made no impact on the disillusioned workforce'.[11]

In the meantime, the model programme conceived during the Stokes era continued to be seen through. In May 1976 the Triumph TR7 sports car, introduced in America in the previous year, made its appearance on the British market, to be followed in June by the all-important Rover SD1. The Triumph's arrival effectively spelled death to MG as the long-running MGB, fourteen years old in 1976, could not remain in production indefinitely. The Triumph became British Leyland's corporate sports car and was the outcome of an in-house competition between MG and Triumph. MG had submitted an advanced wedge-shaped mid-engined concept, coded ADO 21, styled at Longbridge by Harris Mann but detailed at Abingdon. Triumph's contribution, produced under the Bullet name, was by contrast a conventional front-engined design. What British Leyland did was to combine these two concepts. The distinctive wedge-shaped coupe, styled by Mann at Longbridge, became a front-engined model which was engineered at Canley under Spen King's direction. A special variation of the 2-litre overhead-camshaft slant four was conceived for the car which shared the bore and stroke of the Dolomite Sprint engine, though with an eight-valve cylinder head. It was decided to build the new car at the Liverpool number 2 factory at Speke, from sheet metal pressings produced at the number 1 factory. Engines were delivered from Coventry and the TR7 was the first British Leyland car from 1976, to be produced with the corporate '77mm' gearbox, so named after the spacing between the mainshaft and layshaft centres. Available in four- and five-speed forms, it was subsequently fitted to the Rover SD1 and, from 1978, on the Jaguar XJ6.

British Leyland had high hopes for the Rover SD1, introduced the month after the TR7, from its brand-new Solihull factory. Here was a roomy, stylish 120mph saloon, which was intended to replace Rover's 2200/3500 and Triumph 2500, though both models continued until 1977 when smaller-engined versions of the new Rover arrived. Criticism of the 2000's carrying capacity had been met with the distinctive hatchback styling, while Rover's former Buick V8 had been uprated so that the SD1 was a 120mph car. The Rover became Car of the Year in 1977 but, above all, big cars meant big profits. For once, British Leyland, or more particularly Rover, had produced a car which looked all set to take on the best of the continental opposition.

As British Leyland drifted, industrial unrest increased. Strikes during 1976 included stoppages at SU Carburettors, Canley, Rover factories at Solihull and Wales, the Llanelli pressings plant, Drews Lane, Birmingham, Jaguar and Longbridge. At the end of 1976 Eric Varley, who had taken over from Tony Benn as industry secretary in 1975, declared that the government's commitment to British Leyland was 'not, of course, open-ended. The government will insist on positive progress from management, unions and all employees.'[12]

But how was Jaguar coping with the effects of the Ryder recommendations? When the report was published in April 1975 it caused 'stark dismay' at Browns Lane. It fell to engineering director Bob Knight to keep the Jaguar flame alight during those dark days and he has subsequently recalled, in Philip Porter's *Jaguar Project XJ40* (Haynes, 1987), that he 'used to fight with cars'[13] in his efforts to maintain an all-important degree of independence. While Ryder and his team were deliberating in the spring of 1975 prior to the publication of their report, Sir Don's Rolls-Royce had burnt out and he thought it appropriate to have a Jaguar replacement. Although he had ordered a 4.2-litre six-cylinder XJ6, Knight cannily prepared a pre-production fuel-injected V12 'which was clearly a very good car, especially by the standards of the day',[14] and this was duly delivered to Ryder. He subsequently telephoned Geoffrey Robinson, enthusing about the V12, and told him to forget about the 4.2-litre, which was exactly what Knight had hoped would happen. It was this experience, he believes, 'which caused Ryder to keep Jaguar Engineering as an entity . . . it was the only part of the Ryder Report not to be implemented'.[15]

Knight needed something to restore plummeting morale at the factory and an appeal to Derrick Whittaker, managing director of Leyland Cars, produced the Jaguar Operating Committee 'which was a bit like a board'.[16] Chaired by Tony Thompson from Cowley, who had replaced Robinson, the committee experienced problems preventing it from operating effectively. The difficulty was that Jaguar was part of Leyland Cars while its Radford engine plant came under the direction of another part of the company. These difficult times were perhaps typified by the fact that, from 1975, for the first time Jaguar no longer had its own Motor show stand and had to share space with the rest of Leyland's products. Yet plant director Peter Craig tried to keep morale up by introducing *Jaguar Topics*, a modest newspaper. Alas, he died suddenly in February 1977, aged only fifty-six, after what was thought to be a simple operation.

The big event on the car front had been the launch, in September 1975, of Jaguar's long-awaited grand tourer, the V12-engined XJ-S. Styled by Malcolm Sayer, it lacked some of the flair that had made the XJ6 such a success, and inside the traditional walnut facia was absent, though the treatment was in line with that offered on sports Jaguars from 1957 onwards. Unfortunately, the model's timing could not have been worse because this 150mph GT arrived during the after-effects of the first oil crisis. *Autocar* averaged 15.4mpg on its example, though this figure was recorded on a car fitted with a manual gearbox. With an automatic unit, consumption could drop as low as 10mpg. At £8,900 the XJ-S was also the most expensive Jaguar ever.

The XJ6 was inevitably the main line product though, during these years, 'quality control at Browns Lane was probably worse than it had ever been in the company's history'.[17] Few of the faults could be put down to poor component design but to 'a lack of concern by outside suppliers, coupled with Jaguar's apparent inability to enforce standards with these and its own workforce [which] led to a fairly widespread loss of confidence in the product by dealers and customers alike'. Output was suffering too. In 1976 31,903 Jaguars had left Browns Lane, but in 1977 the figure slumped to 23,688.

Nineteen seventy-seven was to prove a watershed year in British

Leyland's affairs and was probably then that parts of the company came closest to closure. In March *The Economist* bluntly declared: 'The Ryder plan to save and reconstruct British Leyland is now officially a lame duck. The company is next to being a dying one.'[18] This followed a declaration by the firm's toolmakers that they were intending to strike from 21 February, which they did and remained out for a month. It was to prove the most damaging strike in the company's history. 'For the first time since the rescue operation, the National Enterprise Board and the company's management are seriously considering the possibility of eventually shutting part of the troubled car division.'[19]

Varley responded by freezing government funding and the British Leyland board stated that it would not ask for finance through the NEB until the strike was resolved. It also took a firm hand on the stoppage and stated that it was prepared to dismiss those who were on unofficial strike. When the strike was over, the NEB undertook yet another review of British Leyland's future and the firm enjoyed a more or less strike-free three months. It was on that basis that the board asked for a further £100 million of government funding to be released.

Then, in August, Lord Ryder resigned as chairman of the National Enterprise Board, Harold Wilson, who had appointed him, had stepped down in March of the previous year and was replaced by James Callaghan. Ryder's deputy, Leslie Murphy, 'a tougher character',[20] who had been deputy chairman of Schroders merchant bank, took over the NEB chairmanship. During the Ryder regime, debate about British Leyland had been discouraged, but now it was possible for members to voice their feelings and it soon emerged that 'changes at the top' were essential for the firm's survival.

Murphy soon held a meeting with British Leyland's chief executive, Alex Park, and Murphy reports their conversation as follows: ' "Well, Alex, I really don't know an awful lot about the motor industry. Tell me, which models make profits and which make losses?" . . . He said, "I don't know." I was slightly surprised but, "Never mind, it's our first meeting," I said. "We can talk about it next time." "No, no," he said, "that's not what I mean – I can't find out. The accounting system at BL is such as not to produce an answer." '[21]

His successor was to experience a similar problem, for in October Murphy telephoned NEB member Michael Edwardes at his office, asking to see him. 'Then came the bombshell.' Murphy asked the Chloride chairman, 'Are you willing to take on British Leyland?' Edwardes later recorded that he was 'momentarily taken aback, but within half a minute I realized that there was a certain logic to the proposition'.[22] At that stage Murphy saw the job as a dual purpose one with Ian MacGregor, already a non-executive director of British Leyland, as chairman and Edwardes as chief executive.

Then, in October, British Leyland's chairman, Sir Richard Dobson, resigned. A former chairman of British American Tobacco, he had been appointed in March 1976, following the sudden death of Sir Ronald Edwards two months before. His resignation followed some incautious remarks made at a private dinner party, which had been subversively recorded, about the ' "perfectly respectable fact" that BL was "bribing wogs" ',[23] though at the time of the incident a successor was being sought.

Michael Edwardes's appointment as British Leyland's chairman *and* chief executive was announced on 25 October; he took over the dual task on the three-year secondment from Chloride, on 1 November. He had, by this time, considered it essential that he undertake both roles: 'I want a free hand,'[24] he had told Murphy. In retrospect, Edwardes's appointment marked a turning point in British Leyland's turbulent history, but before considering how he tackled his seemingly impossible task, we must briefly retrace our steps to see how that other troubled British car maker, Chrysler UK, was faring.

It will be recalled that, in 1974, Chrysler's British subsidiary had recorded a £17.7 million loss and was being subsidized by its faltering American parent. In January 1975, secretary of state for industry Tony Benn wrote to Chrysler Corporation chairman John Riccardo to ask the firm of its intentions for the future of its British operations. On 18 February Riccardo responded and 'hinted at further production cuts, painted a fairly gloom picture for investment and gave no definite commitment to stay in the United Kingdom'.[25] Prime Minister Harold Wilson publicly took this as a 'clear understanding that Chrysler would continue its operations in the United Kingdom'.[26] Nevertheless he asked Sir Don Ryder, then in the throes of his report into British Leyland's affairs, to turn his attention also to Chrysler's British operations.

On 18 March the Chrysler Corporation made an application for a £35 million loan from Finance for Industry to restructure its debts, but the results proved inconclusive. Then, in May, it began talks with the Department of Trade and Industry with a view to being granted financial assistance under the terms of the 1972 Finance Act. It required £25 million to help it replace the ageing Arrow range with a Linwood-built successor. In the same month what was to prove a three-and-a-half-week unofficial strike broke out at its Stoke engine plant. The request was formalized in July, following the failure of its discussions with FFI, and the Chrysler Corporation's own parlous state was underlined by its recording a six-month loss of $153 million. September and October saw the Department of Trade and Industry completing its assessment of Chrysler's application. But then the Corporation ominously asked that this be deferred, pending 'a reassessment of the figures'[27] of its British operations. The pace quickened when Chrysler UK's Gilbert Hunt and Don Lander, chairman and managing director respectively, flew to America to attend a corporate board meeting on 30 October.

However, the day before, John Riccardo, by then Chrysler's chairman, held a press conference at which he pinpointed the disposal of its British operations as its 'biggest single problem'.[28] This was the first public declaration by the Corporation that it wanted to rid itself of its UK subsidiary. Chrysler had lost $232 million in the nine months to the end of September, but Riccardo's statement was made without prior consultation with the British government, which immediately requested his presence in Britain. On 3 November Riccardo and his team attended a meeting with Wilson and his ministers at Chequers which had just begun when the lights were symbolically blacked out by a local power cut. Riccardo wasted little time in putting forward his three possible options: Chrysler could either liquidate its British operations in the three months from the end of November; it could give its subsidiary to the British government; or it could transfer a majority interest of over 80 per cent to the government and itself retain 20 per cent. As Wilson later recalled: 'When I used the word "blackmail", and the accusation that he had held a pistol at the heads of the government, understatements though they were, they were thoroughly justified; the already unpopular tribe of multi-nationals had done anything but improve its image.'[29]

The Chrysler ultimatum put the Labour administration in a tight spot. It was possible that Chrysler UK could be operated by the National Enterprise Board, alongside British Leyland, or it could be integrated with Leyland. The reality was that, while this second option was a possibility, 'the view of all parties was that Leyland's reorganization problems were so large on their own as to preclude any possibility of taking Chrysler on board'.[30] Discussions were also held between the Department of Trade and Industry and Ford, and also Vauxhall, to see whether they might be interested in taking over all or part of Chrysler's operations, but neither firm responded positively to these overtures.

With industry secretary Eric Varley firmly against any of Chrysler's proposals, and after some agonizing discussions and re-appraisals of the situation, the government decided, against a background of rising jobless figures, that it could not let Chrysler UK go to the wall. If that had happened, it would have meant an immediate loss of 25,000 jobs with a further 20,000 indirectly at risk. Yet another factor was the loss of the important Iranian contract with Chrysler, and the firm's bankruptcy might affect the country's balance of payments negatively to the tune of £200 million. Harold Lever was dispatched to Iran, but the Shah and his officials rejected the alternative of assembling Morris Marinas there instead. There was also the problem of the serious unemployment which would have resulted in Scotland from the closure of Linwood, while the rise in the popularity of the Scottish Nationalist Party was an additional complication for a government with a five-seat majority.

Then came a change in Chrysler's stance. On 26 November, Riccardo made it clear that if the government would take the firm over completely, it would make a £35 million payment, though if it retained its 20 per cent it would contribute £13 million. However, on 5 December, there was another change in its position. The final agreement resulted in Chrysler continuing to operate its subsidiary but the British government would bear the first £50 million of its expected 1976 loss. It was similarly committed, up to £10 million, for 1977 and to a maximum of £12.5 million in 1978 and 1979. There was a £55 million loan for capital development, guaranteed by Chrysler. The government would also provide a £35 million loan, which was guaranteed by both parties. Its total potential commitment stood at £162.5 million.

For its part, Chrysler agreed to contribute £10 million to its 1976 and 1977 losses, £12.5 million to any 1978 and 1979 deficits, and £10 to £12 million to produce the new Alpine in Britain, while it waived £19.7 million on interests and loans made to Chrysler UK. Avenger production would be switched from Ryton to Linwood. Ryton, for its part, would also be used for the production of the British-designed Chrysler Alpine, Car of the Year in 1976, which was then being built only by the Corporation's French subsidiary as the Simca 1307/1308. Chrysler was forbidden to make 'any substantial alterations to the nature of its business . . . and from disposing of any subsidiary companies without the agreement of the secretary of state'.[31] The agreement was signed on 5 January and the all-party report on the crisis summed up the affair thus: 'By no stretch of the imagination can the events leading up to this agreement with Chrysler be said to form a glorious chapter in the history of the government's industrial relations.'

This much-publicized corporate agonizing did little for Chrysler's British sales. In 1974 it had built 261,801 cars and had a 8.9 per cent share of the market but, in the following year, the entire industry took a tumble and Chrysler's output and share fell to to 226,612 and 6.5 per cent respectively, its subsidiary sustaining a record £35.5 million loss. During 1976 the firm dropped its Hillman and Humber marque names; all cars were thereafter badged as Chryslers. Losses stood at £31.9 million in 1976, though this fell to £8.2 million in 1977. In July of that year the firm introduced the Linwood-built rear-drive Sunbeam, based on a cut-down Avenger floor-plan, a roomy two-door hatchback with three engine options: a 903cc

Imp-derived unit and 1.3- and 1.6-litre versions of the Avenger engine. But the firm's share of the British market had fallen again to 6.2 per cent which represented 79,730 cars sold, and was less than half its 1973 figure of 159,357.

Across the Atlantic in America, Chrysler's position continued to deteriorate. It lost $49.7 million in the final quarter of 1977 and further losses were expected in the first three months of 1978. Then, in August, the news that Chrysler was selling its European operation to the French Peugeot group came as a complete surprise to the British government. The first overture had come from the French government back in October 1976 with Renault as the original possible purchaser, though Chrysler was later advised that private rather than public money should be involved. As Renault was nationalized, this meant PSA Peugeot, recently revitalized under the direction of Jean-Paul Parayre. But Chrysler wanted $1 billion for its European operations, a price which Peugeot considered too high, and in any case it was interested in Simca, not the American company's troubled loss-making British subsidiary. Then the deal went cold but was re-activated in January 1978 and the news finally broke on 10 August.

For tax reasons the agreement was signed on British soil, and the ceremony took place in the unlikely surroundings of Heathrow Airport with passengers bustling around. Parayre signed for Peugeot and, in doing so, his firm became Europe's leading car company and the Gallic motor industry wholly French-owned. It had paid Chrysler $230 million in cash and the American company had a 15 per cent share of Peugeot stock. In addition, it inherited Chrysler's $400 million debts and its British subsidiary. Only the month before the signing of the agreement, Linwood had been on strike with losses running at £1.2 million a week and of the £162.5 million alloted to Chrysler by the British government, only £7.5 million remained. The British part of the deal was subject to governmental approval, duly given in September. So a sector of the British motor industry switched from American to French control, which came as a surprise, not only to the Labour administration but also to British Leyland, which was just completing its first year of Michael Edwardes's chairmanship and had been talking to Chrysler UK about a possible merger.

What was the state of the company Edwardes had taken over on 1 November 1977? That year it had built 651,069 cars which, although slightly up on 1975, the year of Ryder's report, coincided with a slump in the firm's share of the British market by six points, so that it now stood at 24 per cent. Ford had also taken over that year as market leader. Exports had continued to hold up well. The 293,316 cars sold by British Leyland in 1977 represented 45 per cent of output and the figure was an improvement on 1975's of 256,672.

David Andrews ran the International Division for two and a half years after Ryder and prior to Edwardes's arrival. He recalls:

> It actually made money. One year I think we made over £70 million, though we had the pound in our favour. But in the early 1970s, British Leyland had made three overseas commitments that turned out to be disasters. One was the Australian subsidiary which was selling the P70, a great tank of a thing. Our Spanish business had closed, and I got the job of liquidating it. It was the same story at Innocenti in Italy which we sold to de Tomaso. They had gone off and developed their own car but it was the same story as Australia. If you do low-production quite expensively tooled cars in a narrow market, you are going to lose your shirt. The Innocenti Mini was a case in point. It looked smart, but was a rushed job – it had no real package. It cost a fortune and didn't meet its cost objectives. These three projects had probably cost British Leyland well over £100 million.[32]

In terms of overall profitability, British Leyland's record was a chequered one. In 1975 it had made a £23.6 million loss, and in the fifteen months to 31 December 1976, when the company's financial year was changed from the end of September, it made a pre-tax profit of £112 million. Although British Leyland made a £72.5 million profit in 1977, the post-tax figure represented a £5 million loss when Edwardes joined British Leyland, and the company was once again on the point of running out of money following the effects of the toolmakers' strike earlier in the year. The workforce of 195,000 was about 4,000 greater than the 1975 figure. Productivity had reached an all-time low with each employee building four vehicles a year, whereas in 1968, the year of the British Leyland Motor Corporation's creation, the figure had been 5.6 vehicles. The factory structure was almost exactly as it had been in 1975, with fifty-five manufacturing plants. Since the Ryder Report, British Leyland had drawn on only £150 million of government money.

The diminutive forty-seven-year-old South African-born Michael Edwardes had read law at Grahamstown University and joined Chloride in Britain as a management trainee in 1951. He became a company board member in 1969, was appointed its chief executive in 1972 and executive chairman in 1974. In 1975 Edwardes had been named as *The Guardian*'s Young Businessman of the Year. Although Chloride's pre-tax profits had tripled under Edwardes to £26.4 million in 1977, it was a relatively small company with about 20,000 employees and *The Economist* cautioned that 'when faced with a nine-week strike at Chloride earlier this year . . . Mr Edwardes backed down'.[33]

217

Edwardes's first task, begun on 25 October on the afternoon of the announcement that he was joining BL, was to restructure that company's board. Only three members of the previous administration remained: Ian MacGregor, who became deputy chairman, Sir Robert Clark, chairman of Hill Samuel merchant bankers, and Alex Park, though he resigned in December when he was replaced by David Andrews. The new directors were Sir Austin Bide, chairman of Glaxo, who became deputy chairman in 1980 following Ian MacGregor's move to the chair of British Steel, and Albert Frost, former finance director of ICI who resigned at about the same time.

There was considerable support within the company for retaining the existing centralized Leyland Cars, though Edwardes felt that 'the cars structure was claustrophobic and its philosophy was a disincentive, in that it provided little, if any, scope for people down the line . . . to exercise initiative. Great names like Rover, Austin, Morris, Jaguar and Land-Rover were being subordinated to a Leyland uniformity that was stifling enthusiasm and local pride.'[34] Edwardes was dismayed to find that Jaguar engines were being built at Radford Engines and Transmission Plant, while the cars were produced at Browns Lane Plant Large/Specialist Vehicle Operations with no trace of the famous Jaguar name in evidence. After years of being known as 'the Austin" the Birmingham plant went under the title of Longbridge Body and Assembly Plant, Small/Medium Vehicle Operations. It was the same story at Rover and MG. Yet a further dilution of identity occurred because the engines for the respective cars were the responsibility of a separate management function. 'So as well as erasing the marque names, the organization divided management responsibility for individual products. In short, the worst type of corporate centralism was at work; I found it stifling.'[35]

When Edwardes had been appointed, the National Enterprise Board 'was determined to improve British management in the sector that it could influence'.[36] A trade union member of the NEB later recalled that it was a 'priority from the beginning [to] grasp the nettle of management. We weren't just concerned to put money in and take up new ventures. We were concerned to put in good management as well.'[37] At British Leyland, when Michael Edwardes came to evaluate its top managers, he considered that he had a classic case of faulty executive appointments: 'the wrong people in simply hundreds of key jobs, and only a change in organization would provide the fluidity in which personnel changes would be the norm'.[38] Edwardes introduced psychological assessment, which he had used to effect at Chloride, for British Leyland's top 300 managers and a further 60 were recruited. Of the remaining 240, no less than 150 were found new positions, while 'many more were asked to leave' and were allowed to resign: 'in short, we pushed good young men into top jobs.'

In February 1978, just four months after he had taken office, Edwardes unveiled the essence of his 1978 Corporate Plan in an address to union members and shop stewards when he told them that 12,000 jobs would have to go that year, mostly through natural wastage which, at that stage, was running at about 5 to 6 per cent a year. The centralized corporate approach would end and the firm would be split into five divisions: Austin Morris; Jaguar Rover Triumph; BL Components, which would consist of body-making facilities, foundries and parts; the Bus and Truck Division which would become Leyland Vehicles; while the remaining ragbag of companies, ranging from Coventry Climax fork-lift trucks to Aveling Barford earth-moving equipment, would be combined to form a special products division to be named SP Industries. Edwardes was keen to dispense with the Leyland name 'and bury British Leyland Ltd', though it remained on commercial vehicles which was where it belonged. British Leyland Ltd was replaced by the low-key BL Ltd, which was officially born on 1 July 1978, so allowing the marque names to flourish.

The all-important post of managing director of the Austin Morris division went to forty-eight-year-old Ray Horrocks, who after nine years with Ford which included a spell as head of its Advanced Vehicle Operations, had joined the American Eaton Corporation. He says: 'They wanted me to go and work in the 'States but I didn't want a permanent assignment and the notion of becoming an American didn't appeal. Berry Wilson of British Leyland's recruitment knew I was available and I found myself, in November 1977, working with Michael [Edwardes].'[39] On a more personal level, when Horrocks told one of his daughters that he was going to join the company, 'she was absolutely appalled because her sixth form had been doing an appraisal of British Leyland and had concluded unanimously that the thing was dead!'[40] His first job was as assistant managing director of Leyland Cars, though Derrick Whittaker, the managing director, was on the point of departure. Horrocks's own choice had been to run Jaguar Rover Triumph, because he thought that 'it had a greater chance of survival', but he was given the demanding Austin Morris post.

The Jaguar Rover Triumph managing directorship went to an industry outsider, William Pratt Thompson, an American who joined BL from Bowthorne Holding Electronics, where he had been deputy managing director. He established himself at Browns Lane, though 'without getting to know Jaguar people at all'[41] during his two years in the job.

Michael Edwardes, Ray Horrocks and David Andrews soon emerged as the executive triumvirate running the company. Andrews, who had been in charge of the International Division up to this point, became vice chairman of BL. A crucial nettle that had to be grasped was the labour troubles that were plaguing the firm. 'The difficulties we had with the labour force, and the unions in particular at that time, meant that there had to be an over-investment in capacity; you had to invest 150 per cent to get 100,' recalls Horrocks. 'The saddest part of it was the general mistrust of management.'[42]

The first factory to feel the effects of Michael Edwardes's new tougher approach to labour relations was the Speke number 2 factory on Merseyside, which had been building the Triumph TR7 sports car since 1974. It has to be made clear, however, that the plant's poor labour record was not the sole reason for its closure, for the reality was that it could never be profitable building only one model. In 1976 the factory, which had been capable of building 100,000 cars a year, had produced only 27,657 Triumphs, though in the autumn of 1977 Speke was gripped by a seven-week stoppage as a result of strikes in other parts of the Leyland group. On 1 November, the day Michael Edwardes took over at British Leyland, the Speke workforce returned to work, only to be called out on strike over a manning dispute which was to drag on for the next four months. It was to prove a fatal stoppage which prevented urgently needed examples of the improved 1978 model TR7 reaching America. For what had been conceived as the British Leyland Motor Corporation's sports car had acquired a controversial reputation from the very outset. Initially it was available only in coupe form, and the adventurous wedge shape failed as a styling concept because many people considered the car plain ugly. The model was also plagued with mechanical problems. While he was running the Internationl Division, David Andrews felt the full force of the TR7's failure on the American market:

> The car was not being well built and the overall quality was bad. It had been originally designed with a four-speed derivative of the Marina '55mm' gearbox but it wasn't up to the job. In a hilly place like San Francisco it just couldn't cope and it reached the stage when I refused to take TR7s with the four-speed unit and insisted on a five-speed one which was fitted from 1976. But the whole car was unreliable and we were getting terrible warranty problems.[43]

British Leyland took the decision to close Speke, though the announcement, made on 15 February, was greeted with scepticism from the press and the Speke management. Ray Horrocks recalls: 'I was talking to the guy who was running Speke and when I told him what was planned he responded, "I've had that said to me three or four times, and at the eleventh hour there's always been a call from central office saying, 'It's all off . . . don't do it.'" I said, "Well, yes, the only way to convince you is to do it," and we did.'[44]

In March the factory was re-opened and TR7s once again began leaving Speke, but further arguments broke out about severance terms and BL 'got wind of rumours of a factory occupation plan . . . and the doors were locked abruptly [on 26 May] several days ahead of the publicly announced closure date'.[45] When Speke number 2 was shut, it represented the first closure of a major British car factory since the Nuffield Organization's 1948 rationalization and had been made with the full knowledge of Labour Prime Minister James Callaghan. 'The Conservatives were a darn sight more interventionist than the Labour government,' Ray Horrocks recalls, but on the occasion of the Speke closure, he remembers that BL did receive a telephone call from industry secretary Eric Varley 'to ask, "Are you going to do it?" as it coincided with some political happening. It was a low-key approach and the only occasion on which it occurred with the Labour administration.'[46]

With Speke's closure, TR7 production was transferred to the Triumph factory at Canley, Coventry, and in the five-month hiatus between output ceasing in May and restarting again in October, the company took the opportunity to make over 200 modifications to the design, with the result that the Coventry-built cars were markedly superior to their Liverpool-sourced predecessors. The end of TR7 production on Merseyside did not affect Speke number 1 plant which continued to provide Canley with its pressings, along with Dolomite hulls.

A casualty of the Speke closure was the Lynx, intended as a replacement for the Stag and due to enter production there in 1978, which was now scrapped. The project dated back to John Barber's bid to move Leyland's products more up market and the car, engineered by Rover, would have been badged a Triumph and was effectively a long-wheelbase version of the TR7; a stylish 2+2 with an opening hatchback, powered by the Rover 3.5-litreV8. An earlier casualty had been its SD2 contemporary, in essence a scaled-down Rover SD1, intended to take over from the ageing Triumph Dolomite range and also based on TR7 running gear. When it was found that the SD2 and ADO 77, conceived at Longbridge to replace the Morris Marina, were aimed at much the same market, both concepts were killed off and replaced by a shortlived TM1 (Triumph Morris 1) project, intended to replace both the Triumph Dolomite and Morris Marina, although this rear-drive concept never moved beyond the paper stage.

Austin Morris itself continued to soldier on with a range of models, the origins of which reached back to BMC and the Stokes era. In 1977, as the effects of the first oil price rise began to fade, the Marina took over from the

Mini as the top-selling Austin Morris car, but the figure of 66,083 examples sold in Britain was around half that of the Ford Cortina market leader, which in the same period found 120,601 new owners. In 1979, with petrol prices once again soaring following the Iranian revolution, the barely profitable Mini was back on top, with the Marina next and the Allegro a poor third. Ray Horrocks recognizes that the Allegro 'wasn't an attractive product. It looked like an egg, was expensive to make, and although the 1750 version with a five-speed gearbox was very quick, it did not have the charisma of the big cars.'[47] Clearly new models were desperately needed.

Jaguar Rover Triumph represented an equally unhappy prospect. At Jaguar, the XJ6 continued to be plagued by reliability problems which were perpetuated on the new Series 3 version, introduced in March 1979, with cleaner, sleeker lines, the update having been skillfully executed by Pininfarina with input from the ever-vigilant Sir William Lyons, although officially in retirement! Output was devastated by severe teething troubles experienced at a new paintshop at the Castle Bromwich body plant which served both the Rover and Jaguar factories. Difficulties were experienced applying new thermoplastic paint to the Jaguar hulls which also suffered on the short journey to Allesley. For that reason most early Series 3 XJ6s were available only in white, yellow and red. In the year since the Series 3's launch, Jaguar achieved only 40 per cent of its required production as a result of Castle Bromwich's difficulties, while the effects of the 1979 oil crisis only compounded the problem. In 1978, the year of Michael Edwardes's arrival at BL, 27,346 Jaguars had left Browns Lane. But 1979's figure of 13,988 was the lowest since 1957 and, in the following year, Jaguar was to lose £47 million. When Michael Edwardes had proposed his Jaguar Rover Triumph combination, he asked Jaguar's Bob Knight whether he would be interested in taking over engineering for the division, but this 'sent a fair old chill down my spine', said Knight, because he recognized that what was proposed 'could easily become a smaller version of Leyland Cars'. Knight suggested to Edwardes that he favoured separate company organizations, reporting to a Jaguar Rover Triumph administrator. 'This apparently carried the day and it was decided that there would be a managing director of three companies. Almost inevitably [in January 1978] I was one of them.'[48]

The situation was perhaps even worse at Rover. The universally acclaimed SD1 was, from the very outset, in short supply, and when examples were available, poor build quality was readily apparent. A Rover director subsequently admitted, 'It was a nightmare of a debut for a car which had received rave reviews and for which we had such high hopes. It was two years before it recovered.'[49] In 1976, the year of its introduction, a mere 6,816 SD1s were sold in Britain, with 12,374 finding buyers in 1977.

Only in 1978 did the SD1 begin to take off when home sales amounted to 31,669 cars, about the same as the figure achieved by its Rover 2000/3500 predecessor back in 1971. The model's entry into the European market at the 1977 Geneva Motor Show proved a shambles because of a shortage of cars following the toolmakers' strike and a dispute at the Castle Bromwich body plant. 'Leyland International only managed to extract dealer demonstrator stock,' reported *Autocar*, and consequently 'there are no cars in dealer hands to meet any flood of eager German, Swiss or French who want to buy cars from Swiss dealers at the Show.'[50] As in Britain, none of the country's main distributors was prepared to quote delivery dates.

The SD1's most obvious fault was rusting around the front and, more particularly, the rear wheel arches and along the lower edge of the hatchback. Inside, the end caps on the instrument binnacle had a habit of falling off and the electric windows and central locking gave trouble. Fortunately, the proven V8 was reliable enough, though the same could not be said of the 2300 and 2600 variants of the SD1 which appeared in 1977. These six-cylinder cars employed Triumph-designed power units that had started life as engines for the long-running 2000/2500's replacement which had been cancelled in favour of the big Rover. Both models suffered from the body problems which had marred the V8 but these early sixes soon became notorious for excessive oil consumption, burned-out pistons, oil leakages and gasket failure. So why was it that the big Rover, which had been conceived as the locomotive of the British Leyland Motor Corporation's recovery, proved such a disaster?

The Castle Bromwich paintshop was one reason. Another was that, at the time of the car's 1976 launch, Rover was being pressured to get the model into production as quickly as possible. Peter Grant was production manager at Solihull at this time. He recalled: 'I was at a dance at the Civic Centre in Solihull and a senior director of British Leyland came up to me and said, "You Rover people are all the same. You worry about quality. We want quantity. We've got to get this SD1 turned out in quantity." '[51]

But there were more fundamental reasons for the Rover's difficulties. According to Ray Horrocks:

When the SD1 was designed back in the early 1970s there were not enough production engineers alongside the design engineers. It was built by engineers for engineers so the car was productionized as it went down the line. There wasn't enough development done of the car which reflected the lack of testing facilities then available to the company. When you launch a new model, there are a number of things you aim to avoid. They are putting it into production at a new

223

plant, with a new paintshop and with a new engine and transmission. The SD1, particularly in its six-cylinder form, suffered from all these shortcomings.[52]

Although the Triumph factory at Canley was still producing cars, the reality was that its products, with the exception of the TR7, were all rooted in the 1960s. The front-wheel-drive 1500 had been transformed into the rear-drive 1500TC for 1974, while the Toledo was discontinued in 1976 and the surviving 1300, 1500, 1850 and Sprint were all badged as Dolomite. These Michelotti-styled saloons were running on borrowed time, as was the attractive but similarly ageing Spitfire which was still being produced.

These were just some of the problems that faced Michael Edwardes and his team when they started to plan a new generation of models. The project that was most advanced on Edwardes's arrival was the long-awaited Mini replacement, coded ADO 88. Only eight weeks after he took up the BL chairmanship, Edwardes and his advisory board scrapped it after £300 million had been expended on its development. It had been a difficult decision to take but Edwardes recognized that the car 'looked like turning into national disaster'[53] if it had been built. Customer clinics were held in Britain and Europe, and at one, only 3 per cent of the 500 participants made ADO 88 their first choice, compared with 39 per cent who opted for the Ford Fiesta. So, late in 1977, it was decided to upgrade the product, to compete in the so called Super Mini class where it would rival such models as the Ford Fiesta, Volkswagen Polo and Fiat 127.

The trouble was that this area of the market offered the lowest profit margains, while what was really needed was a replacement for the ailing Allegro. But no amount of juggling could advance the all-important LC10 – what we know now as the Maestro – from its 1983 launch date. Edwardes recognized that 'we didn't have the engineering resources to alter the order . . . switching [it] would have meant that *neither* could have been launched in 1980'.[54]

What became the Austin Metro, at that time coded LC8, was scheduled for production in October 1980, having been approved by the BL board in July 1978. The project was then handed over to Ray Horrocks and his team at Austin Morris. The demanding development period was only possible because the design team had the aborted ADO 88 project as its starting point. The car itself was only half the programme, however; the other was a new 725,000-square-foot factory at the Longbridge West works to produce the model, which was built as the car was being developed. Work also began on LC10 which became the Maestro in 1983, and LM11 which was to emerge as the Montego in 1984. But how was the yawning two-and-a-half-year gap between the arrival of the Metro in 1980 and Maestro in 1983 to be filled? The answer was a collaboration with another manufacturer.

From the outset of his tenure at British Leyland, Michael Edwardes found himself in full agreement with Sir Leslie Murphy (knighted in 1978) and the National Enterprise Board that parts of BL could only survive if there were such an alliance. But it was essential that the firm was of a comparable size to BL or the British company would have ended up the junior partner. Product planner Mark Snowden and Ray Horrocks 'sat down and made a list of competitors whom we thought had a suitable car coming through. Chrysler UK was number one and Honda number two.' Horrocks recalls the discussions with Chrysler which were held during 1978, 'just before they pulled out of Britain. They were actually in worse shape than we were, though we weren't to know it.'[55] The dialogue was centred on BL's co-operating with the production of the Horizon model, though the talks foundered with the surprise takeover of Chrysler's British subsidiary by Peugeot.

There was a further strand to the BL/Chrysler dialogue which could have led to outright merger. What particularly attracted BL in July/August 1978 was that at the time it was suffering from an acute shortage of engineering facilities and the engineering centre that the American company had established at Whitley, Coventry, was particularly attractive. However, such an alliance would have probably spelled the end of Chrysler's Linwood and Ryton plants. 'We would have quite liked to have got hold of Whitley,' remembers David Andrews. 'It would have saved us making the investment at Gaydon. This would have meant that BL Technology would just have had the test track there rather than the facilities that we eventually had to build.'[56]

In the meantime, there had been discussions with European manufacturers such as Renault, BMW and Fiat. 'We talked to about everyone there, we pretty well covered the waterfront,' remembers Andrews. 'Then of all the studies we had done we liked Honda the best, as it was more internationally minded.'[57] Honda, third in the Japanese manufacturing league behind Toyota and Nissan, had only diversified from motorcycle to car production in 1962 and, above all, was roughly the same size as BL. In 1977 Honda had built 576,631 cars compared with the British company's 651,069.

'We used an intermediary in Tokyo to sound them out in principle if they were interested in co-operating, though without saying who we were so if the overtures came to nothing there would be no loss of face by either side. When we got a positive response, we identified who we were,' says Andrews. These began in August 1978 and, in October, came the first meeting between the two parties in San Franciso. Andrews recalls: 'It was a very successful meeting. In principle they were obviously ready to receive us.'[58] This paved the way for a memorandum of understanding between the two companies of 15 May 1979. The outcome of the discussions was that the Honda's Ballade model, then under development, would also be badged a Triumph, built at Canley, and introduced in October 1981, a year after the Metro. The project received BL board approval in October 1979 and a draft agreement between the two firms was prepared, awaiting the approval of the 1980 Corporate Plan. As far as Honda was concerned, 'the attraction for them was a way through into Europe, later an exposure of the executive car market, and it provided for us a good challenge for our people and gave them an insight of how things worked in Japan and the foundations of what they were achieving, which up until then had been a bit of a closed book,' says Andrews. This initial project was followed by what became the Rover 200 series of 1984, a mildly reworked and rebadged Honda Ballade, and the all-important 1986 Rover 800, jointly developed by Honda and BL.

None of these plans would have been possible without Michael Edwardes having received NEB and ultimately governmental approval of his strategy. When he joined British Leyland, it had been on the point of once again running out of money following the effects of the disastrous toolmakers' dispute earlier in 1977. At the insistence of the NEB he had negotiated standby credit with city banks in the hope that his plan would be approved by the parliamentary Easter recess. It was not, so a £275 million bridging loan was arranged by the department of industry. In April approval for the corporate plan was given which provided a life-giving £450 million to the company. But a year later, in May 1979, there was a change of government with a victory by a markedly non-interventionist Conservative administration and Margaret Thatcher replaced James Callaghan as prime minister while Sir Keith Joseph was the new secretary for trade and industry.

In 1979 a rise in the value of the pound, which had begun in January, gained momentum following the Conservatives' election victory, and this, coupled with a downturn in the market prompted by the Iranian oil crisis, meant drastic action was required by the BL board. It informed Sir Keith Joseph in July that 'the whole of the LC programme . . . will go by the board unless the government provides additional funds *and* we take very drastic action'.[59] A few weeks after this meeting, the BL advisory board met at the Ye Olde Bell inn at Hurley, Berkshire, to put together a Recovery Plan. There it was recognized that a further 25,000 jobs would have to be shed. Triumph production at Canley would have to cease and the MG factory at Abingdon would have to close. At this point BL was losing £900 on every MGB it sold in America. The plan was published on 10 September 1979 and Edwardes was convinced of the need to place it before the workforce. On 1 November 80 per cent voted and of those 87 per cent (over 106,000 employees) gave their approval to the plan.

It was this ballot that culminated in BL's taking one of its best-remembered actions of the Edwardes era: the sacking of communist Derek Robinson, chairman of the Leyland Combine Trade Union Committee and senior conveyor at Longbridge, dubbed 'Red Robbo' by the popular press. The first occasion on which Ray Horrocks had met Robinson was at a meeting of the Cars Council, the joint management/senior shop stewards committee set up following the Ryder recommendations. 'I found myself teaching basic economics to many of them,' recalls Horrocks. 'Afterwards I had lunch with him and I said, "What do you think of all this?" He said, "I'm here to learn . . . how to do your job when we take over the outfit." '[60]

Then, in February 1979, Robinson's actions had become widely publicized when he made the claim that production targets had been missed only by a 'gnat's whisker' and that management had reneged over a productivity deal. A strike of 20,000 of the workforce had followed almost immediately. After the BL employees had voted in November by an overwhelming majority in favour of the Recovery Plan, Robinson was signatory to a pamphlet voicing its opposition to the plan. This, entitled *The Edwardes Plan and Your Job*, was published by the Leyland Combine Trade Union Committee and was distributed to the Longbridge work-force. It drew attention to the fact that, 'in other industries, such as Upper Clyde Shipbuilders, work-ins and occupations have been necessary to prevent closure. If necessary, we shall have to do the same.'

The BL board wasted little time in responding. Ray Horrocks remembers:

> I went up to Longbridge and Harold Musgrove, who was then the manufacturing director, and I met Derek Robinson and Jack Adams, who was the secretary of the committee. They came into the office and I said to Derek, 'If you create such a confrontation you are going to lose.' After he'd gone, I said to Harold, 'If he publicly rails against the plan, that's an act of gross misconduct.' Back in London that evening I said to Michael, 'You will probably have to fire Robinson,' and he thought for a moment, as anyone would, and then said, 'Yes, you're right.'[61]

Edwardes and the BL board had no hesitation in endorsing Horrocks's recommendation as 'Robinson had kept Longbridge in ferment and up-heaval for thirty months', which had resulted in 523 disputes, the loss of 62,000 cars and 113,000 engines worth £200 million.[62]

Consequently, on 19 November, Robinson was asked by Longbridge plant director Stan Mullet, in the presence of the AUEW district secretary, to withdraw his name from the pamphlet. This he refused to do and made it clear that, ballot or no ballot, he was opposed to the plan. He was then dismissed, which produced a partial walk-out at Longbridge and some other plants. The BL board responded by insisting on a return to work. A meeting with the unions involved resulted in an AUEW committee of inquiry which, although critical of Robinson, recording his 'serious failings' as an AUEW convenor, said that he should be reinstated because the company had not followed the correct disciplinary procedure. With strike action looming, Horrocks suggested that a ballot be held, but on 8 February there came a spontaneous 2,000-name petition protesting against the proposed stoppage. As a result, the AUEW suspended the strike call in order to sound opinion. The matter was decided at a mass meeting at Cofton Park on 20 February 1980 which overwhelmingly rejected Robinson's re-instatement.

'Red Robbo's' dismissal was followed by a further victory for Edwardes and his team when they introduced new work practices, which allowed men to be moved from job to job and also abolished cash buy-outs for 'practices and customs' which had been negotiated on a factory-to-factory basis. The new work practices were introduced after lengthy but fruitless discussions, over the heads of shop stewards after the Easter holidays on 8 and 9 April, and 'thirty years of management concessions were thrown out of the window . . . our car factories found themselves with a fighting chance of being competitive'[63] recalled Edwardes.

The essence of the proposals had been communicated to the BL workforce in the 'Blue Newspaper' and the acceptance of its conditions by the post-Easter return to work was, for Ray Horrocks, 'the day in which you could feel that the country was changing'.[64] Even though the company's labour troubles were far from over – a pay dispute in November 1981 nearly brought BL to the verge of disaster – for at least one member of the firm's front-line management, April 1980 was when the corner was turned.

The inexorable rise in the value of the pound continued to play havoc with BL's finances. In December 1979 the government had provided the firm with a further £205 million in addition to the funding pledged by Ryder. However, in July 1980 Edwardes and his top managers met at the Compleat Angler hotel at Marlow, Buckinghamshire, for another crisis meeting. What emerged was what Edwardes dubbed the 'Marlow Concept', a development of the Recovery Plan of the previous year, which resulted in a cutback of manufacturing facilities to 600,000 cars a year while still leaving surplus capacity. Perhaps the most devastating decision taken was that the showpiece four-year-old factory at Solihull would have to close along with Speke number 1 plant, though in the event Rover SD1 production was transferred to Cowley and Land-Rover and Range Rover output expanded at Solihull. When Jaguar Rover Triumph had been created in July 1978, Land-Rover Ltd was established for the first time as a separate company and was soon to benefit from a £280 million expansion plan which was a welcome bonus for a division that had been perpetually starved of funds, a state of affairs which Ryder had also ignored. This allowed the long-running six-cylinder Land-Rover to be replaced by the V8-powered model in 1979 and permitted a much-needed increase in Land-Rover capacity, while Range Rover production facilities were improved so that output could be increased by half as much again. It also allowed a four-door Range Rover, waiting in the wings since 1971, to enter production in 1981, *ten years* after Solihull had produced its first prototype. The future for both models was therefore underpinned, though the same, alas, could not be said for the SD1.

Although the Rover's quality had improved somewhat since its disastrous launch, as a large car it had been hit by the effects of the second oil crisis and at Solihull production fell back from 46,540 in 1979 to 26,106 in 1980 in a factory that had been conceived to produce 3,000 cars a week. The model's failure highlighted the plight of the Jaguar Rover Triumph division which was dissolved in mid-1980. 'If the SD1 had been a success, even an average one, and it had therefore had been a good enough car to put into the 'States (they tried and failed miserably), then we might today be looking at at a combined Land-Rover, Rover, Jaguar, rather than just Jaguar,'[65] says Horrocks, who in 1980 was made chairman of BL Cars. One of his first actions was to establish Land-Rover and Jaguar as separate, self-contained entities within the BL Cars organization.

Jaguar, in the meantime, was facing mounting losses. Pratt Thompson moved on to BL International in London and in the winter of 1979/80 Horrocks appointed Percy Plant to hold the fort pending the new appointment. In April 1980 there was a strike over grading and Edwardes issued the workforce with an ultimatum: return to work or lose your jobs. 'With rumours of Jaguar assembly being moved to Solihull or even stopping, morale at Jaguar over Easter 1980 was as low as it had been when Ryder published his plan five years before.'[66]

Horrocks 'went to see Bill Lyons, who was still going into the factory two or three days a week. I said to him, "We've got to get this right." '[67] Late in 1979 Edwardes had suggested to Ray Horrocks that John Egan might be worth trying again. Horrocks recalls:

Funnily enough, John Egan had been approached by Michael as early as 1978 to run Jaguar Rover Triumph and John had said no. We asked

him again and when he started at Jaguar we were in the middle of a
fairly serious problem there. The guys were insisting that they were
skilled, and that they had a higher element of skill in general terms
than any other company. The other unions were crying 'elitism' and
we therefore had a very explosive situation.[68]

It was against this background that, in April 1980, forty-year-old John
Egan became, significantly, chairman of Jaguar Cars, the first full-time
holder of the office for five years. No stranger to Coventry, he had spent
his last two years of schooling at the city's famous Bablake School, and
then went to Imperial College, London University. In 1962 he joined Shell
with a BSc in petroleum engineering, which involved time in the Middle
East, and his switch to the motor industry occurred almost by chance.
'After a few years with Shell I decided to do a masters course in business
studies at the London Business School. I remember giving a lecture to a
group of businessmen on the use of business graduates in industry. A
director of General Motors was there and he invited me along to talk about
employment and I ended up taking a job with General Motors.'[69] This
1968 appointment was as general manager of AC Delco's replacement
parts division, which paved the way for Egan joining what was then the
British Leyland Motor Corporation in 1971 and Unipart, followed by a
spell in Italy with Massey-Ferguson where he became corporate parts
director.

When the approach came to run Jaguar, Egan thought that 'it was still
possible', though 'I estimated that the chances of recovery were no more
than 50-50.'[70] Another significant factor in Egan's decision to take the job
was the election of a Conservative government in 1979. 'I thought in
Jaguar's case it just might be done, especially as the prime minister had
made a point of saying that an enterprise culture was to be one of the main
platforms of her new administration. There was another feature and that –
remember that I had worked abroad – was that I hated the thought of 83 per
cent of my salary disappearing in tax. I saw people who owned their own
businesses, or were speculating in anything, usually making more money
than I did.'[71]

On arrival at Browns Lane, John Egan spent his first weekend, of 26/27
April, in consultation with union officials and managers in an attempt to
resolve the strike. 'They were in the middle of a shoot-out with Michael
Edwardes. He said that unless they accepted the standard terms and
conditions of BL, then he would definitely close Jaguar down. The
workforce said, "Well, you've done everything else to us, you might as
well do just that," so I thought that I was going to be the only chairman of a
car company who never made a single car.' It took Egan three days of 'very,

very hard talking. I had nothing to offer except myself. I said, "Well, I'm new, I'll do my best." Strangely enough, they agreed that they would have a go.'[72]

By a small majority vote the production lines were running again and Egan set about the awesome task of rebuilding Jaguar's badly tarnished image. He recognized that he possessed three potential assets, the first two of which were the cars themselves and the workforce, for 'despite all attempts to superimpose the Leyland Cars organization on them, there was still a flicker of Jaguar pride and identification in their hearts'.[73] One of Egan's first actions was to put the famous Jaguar mascot back on to the factory gate. 'I thought that there used to be two or three big Jaguars on the gate and a friend of mine believed that he knew where to find them. We never did and we initially ended up with a fairly small one. But I wanted a big ceremony of the Jaguar flag being raised and the mascot being put back. The workforce did have a lot of affection for their company and I thought I might as well harness it.'[74]

The third asset that Egan identified was the Jaguar image: 'built up over the fifty years of Sir William Lyons's stewardship, it had only recently become tarnished.'[75] Within weeks of his arrival he met Sir William and continued to do so regularly until the latter's death in 1985, though initially Jaguar's founder was somewhat wary of the new chairman. 'Don't forget that six or seven people had been sent to run Jaguar since he had retired in 1972. He had seen some which he had thought were wrong 'uns, you know.' After a while Sir William intimated to Egan that 'any help I asked of him, of which he was capable, would be freely given and he was extremely useful during our privatization process. His family told me how relieved and happy he was when he could see that something was coming out of what he had created.'[76]

The most pressing need was one of quality. A market research programme was immediately instituted and the experience of Jaguar owners was compared with those of Mercedes-Benz and BMW customers. This identified 150 key problems. Egan then appointed a task force to diagnose and cure the problems, while the twelve worst received the attention of the Jaguar board. One of the patterns that soon emerged was that '60 per cent of faults on our cars resulted from bought-in component failures', which was an area in which Egan had particular experience. 'So we hauled in our suppliers and told them we would all lose business unless they improved. We also made them liable for full warranty costs following failure of their components.' This soon began to show itself on production cars and 'within a year we were making saleable cars again'.[77]

In addition, 'we started to phase in productivity improvements in the middle of 1981 when we were still losing money at the rate we had done right from the start'. Then there was the £100 million XJ40 programme, which included a new body in white shop at Castle Bromwich. In addition there was a commitment to re-equip Radford for the impending AJ6 engine, both investments being intended as much-needed updates of the company's manufacturing facilities. 'We put together the programme, which looked like a winner. Then some woolly thinking began to emerge that the XJ40 in some sense could be the saviour of the company. I have never thought that. I always thought it would be far too late. I believed that we always had to turn ourselves round with our existing products.'[78]

This was a very difficult period for Jaguar and Egan because, for about six months, 'I had to report every month to the BL board on our progress and I felt that if there had been a couple of months of going backwards, we would have been actually finished.'[79] Today Ray Horrocks maintains 'that there was never any question of us closing Jaguar. I think that only the workforce was capable of doing that.'[80] In his relations with the BL board, Egan recalls that Sir Michael Edwardes 'never ran out of patience; he always believed'. During Sir Austin Bide's chairmanship, Norman Tebbit, who became trade and industry secretary in 1983, 'also helped us. For some strange reason he took a bit of a shine to us which helped enormously.'

The £47 million loss in 1980 was cut to £32 million in 1981 and output rose marginally from 13,360 to 14,677. Then 'in September 1981 we launched the improved 1982 model year Jaguars. There had been big registrations in August, volumes started to pick up . . . and we weren't too far away from break-even. By the following January, we actually made our first profits and we've been profitable ever since.'

A key element in Jaguar's return to viability was the all-important American sales which had been the firm's principal export market since the early 1950s. 'I remember trying to persuade the BL people that we could sell 6,000 cars in America in 1982 rather than the 3,000 they were proposing. In the end our arguments were accepted, but it was terrifying.'[81] Aware that the trans-Atlantic order could make the difference between profit and loss in 1982, Egan recalls:

We had the US dealers over here. Their confidence was mounting and we were trying very hard. They'd been round the factory and we ended up with a big party at the Hilton and I wanted them to agree with the 6,000 figure.

I gave a little speech, saying how delighted we had been to have all the American dealers over with us, and I said, 'Gentlemen. After you'd been to Browns Lane, many of the Jaguar workers came into my office and said, "Did the Americans like what we are doing?" and

I said, "Oh, you can't tell with Americans, they're very shy and reserved people," ' and there was a big hoot. 'Oh,' I said, 'I can't tell whether the Americans think we're doing any good or not.' Then there was a big roar at the back of the room: 'Yes, you're doing your best, we're with you, John,' and I responded, 'Gosh, they think that we can only sell 6,000 cars in the United States, and I want to sell more.' At that stage one of the dealers, Robby Robinson, an ex-Londoner who had a dealership to San José in California, stood up and said, 'John, I speak for all South Californians who are round here, all Californian dealers, I think that we can sell more than six. I think we can agree with you. We can sell 9,000.' At that moment I gave a signal and in walked the band of Grenadier Guards, to big roars and cheers. We ended up selling 10,500, so by the end of 1982 we had got the business under control in that we were doing what we said we could do.[82]

Jaguar made a profit of £9.6 million in 1982. In the following year it rose to £50 million.

Soon after Egan's arrival, a question mark was hanging over the future of the XJ-S, sales of which had been drastically affected by the effects of the 1979 oil crisis, though as Ray Horrocks points out, 'As far as I can recall, it was never policy to discontinue the XJ-S though it was touch and go at times.' Egan remembers: 'When I came here they had already stopped making it. OK, we once opened the lines up to make a few for Canada but in the main it was a very hit-and-miss, stop-and-start process.' But Egan then had an informal approach from the Jaguar product planning director who 'told me in 1980 to can the product. He told me that we would never sell it. So I never bothered to invite him here, though he did come. If he was going to chop one of the only two cars I'd got, there was no point in listening to him any more. I'm afraid that I was very rude to him every time he came to Browns Lane. I told him, "If we were a German car company we would be selling 10,000 XJ-Ss a year." '

Fortunately for Egan, an HE (for High Efficiency) version of the V12 engine had been under development, intended to make the 5.3-litre unit more economical, and this arrived for 1982. It improved fuel consumption by around 22 per cent, which made the psychological 20 mpg consumption a reality in the XJ-S. In 1983 the XJ-S became the first recipient of Jaguar's new AJ 6 (Advanced Jaguar) six-cylinder twin-overhead-camshaft replacement for the long-running XK series engine, which was destined for the new XJ6. 'Last year [1986] we damn near sold 10,000 – we did about 9,000 of them. In a way the XJ-S's growth of sales has been the most spectacular of the lot,'[83] says Egan.

If 1980 marked the start of Jaguar's renaissance, the same, alas, could not be said for the eighteen-year-old MGB sports-car line that came to the end of the road that year after over half a million had been built. The model had effectively been served its death warrant during the Stokes era when the Triumph TR7 was chosen as the corporate sports car. Despite this, sales had held up remarkably well and it had not been until 1976 that roadster production had peaked when 25,860 left the Abingdon factory. But the rising value of the pound had wrought havoc with the all-important American market, and the closure of the MG factory and the end of the MGB had been an element in Edwardes's 1979 Recovery Plan. Ironically, MG was celebrating the fiftieth anniversary of the Abingdon plant in 1979 which included celebrations at the factory and a visit from a party of about 100 American dealers and their wives. The events culminated with a dinner at the Connaught Rooms and it fell to BL vice chairman David Andrews to break the news that the company was to stop making MG sports cars. 'It really was one of the worst things I've ever had to do, and I've had plenty, to stand up and tell them. So, instead of making an after dinner speech, I decided on a before-dinner one.'[84] The announcement, in September 1979, resulted in a massive public outcry which was a reflection of the enormous world-wide loyalty the MG marque enjoyed. The go-ahead MG Owners' Club staged a public protest of MGBs in London, and in April 1980 came news of a rescue bid from a consortium headed by Alan Curtis of Aston Martin, though this subsequently foundered. Sir Michael Edwardes later recognized that the MG affair 'created more public fuss and misunderstanding than anything in the whole five years, even greater than whole-scale factory closures and massive job losses'.[85] When the last MGB was built at the end of 1980, the MG name went into abeyance for the first time since 1924. But within eighteen months the MG octagon was back on a sporty version of the Mini Metro which had appeared in 1980.

This was a car that *had* to be right. Production began in June to ensure that 6,000 cars were in dealers' hands by the October 1980 launch date, which was timed to coincide with that year's Motor Show at the Birmingham National Exhibition Centre. The reception it received – the Metro name had been chosen following a ballot of the workforce – rivalled that which had greeted the original Mini of twenty-one years previously which, in 1980, was still BL's top-selling car. 'Had the Metro been delayed beyond October 1980, I am convinced that the government's marginal decision to provide £990 million for 1981 and 1982 would have gone against us, for the euphoric success of the Metro made a big impression on the cabinet,'[86] Edwardes was later to recall. In 1981 the car became BL's best-selling model and remains so at the time of writing (1987).

The Triumph factory at Canley, Coventry, ceased to be a car-manufacturing plant in 1980. The last Spitfire was built in August and Dolomite output was also halted. Although it had originally been intended to build the Honda Ballade-based Triumph Acclaim at Canley, because of the factory's closure what was to be the last ever Triumph went into production at Cowley in 1981, and with its 1984 demise the Triumph name was extinguished after sixty-one years. TR7 production had been progressively transferred from Canley to the Rover factory at Solihull during the spring and summer of 1980. But, in May 1981, BL announced that production would cease and it did so later in the year. The strength of the pound and the model's poor reputation had combined to render production uneconomical. Rover SD1 output ceased at Solihull and was transferred to Cowley early in 1982.

Sir Michael Edwardes stepped down from the BL chairmanship in September 1982, his original three-year secondment from Chloride having been extended, at the government's request, by a further two. The company he left was very different from the one he had joined five years previously. Its workforce had been reduced by 75,000 to 108,000 world-wide, while there were 83,000 British employees compared with 130,000 in 1977. Factory closures meant that Longbridge and Cowley, which had been extensively modernized, became the company's sole car-manufacturing plants and a much-needed proving ground and technology centre had been established at Gaydon, Warwickshire. Industrial disputes, which had been gripping the company when Edwardes joined it, had been dramatically reduced. In 1977, strikes had accounted for 5.9 per cent of total hours worked; by 1982 this had fallen to 1.6 per cent. Productivity rates, particularly on the highly automated Metro line, were beginning to rival the best in Europe. Above all, management, not the shop floor, was demonstrably seen to be in control of the business and the firm was heading for profit in 1983, though there was clearly still a long way to go.

On the debit side, losses totalled £575 million, before redundancy and interest payments. Government financing stood at £1.4 billion and there had been substantial private funding. Although the Metro had provided the company, and the country, with a considerable psychological fillip, the more profitable Maestro and Montego models had yet to come and the joint Honda/BL Rover 800, theoretically the firm's biggest money spinner, was still four years away. Exports had slumped from 293,316 in 1977 to 118,615 cars five years later. With the demise of the BL sports cars, the company had all but withdrawn from the vast potential of the American market, with only Jaguar fast rebuilding its tarnished reputation there. BL's share of the British market, as the following figures show, had fallen 6.5 points to 17.8 per cent.

Year	Car Production	British Market Share(%)	Pre-tax Profit/Loss (£ millions)
1977	651,069	24.3	72.5
1978	611,625	23.5	77
1979	503,767	19.6	(30.3)
1980	395,820	18.2	(282.4)
1981	413,440	19.2	(236.6)
1982	383,074	17.8	(101.7)

While Sir Michael Edwardes had been wrestling with BL's problems, how was Peugeot, which had bought Chrysler Europe in 1978, faring? The French company had appointed George Turnbull to run its British operations. After completing his Hyundai contract in 1977, Turnbull had moved to Tehran where he joined the Iran National Motor Company which imported Chrysler UK's Hillman Hunter kits into that country. In 1979 Turnbull returned to Britain as chairman of Talbot UK, as Peugeot had decided to rename its British subsidiary. He was to experience a tough job in wooing customers to a company with a limited model range and which had suffered so much adverse publicity during the Chrysler years. He also had to wrestle with the problem of a new name. 'It seemed a good idea because it had both British and French connotations. But I think we underestimated the allegiance to the Chrysler name.' Peugeot had the rights to sell Chrysler-designed products under the Chrysler name but elected to rebadge them as Talbots. 'My own advice at that time was that we should change the company name to Chrysler Talbot.'[87] This harked back to his experience with Standard, which became Standard-Triumph and, finally, Triumph.

'Undoubtedly we lost a lot of traditional Chrysler business and it was very hard to replace. It was almost impossible to recover from the market share we sustained because we had no products with which to do it.'[88] Talbot's sales figures speak for themselves. From 7.7 per cent of British sales in 1978, its fortunes progressively slumped in a market shattered by the effects of the world depression triggered by the second oil crisis. The firm's home sales reached an all-time low of 3.6 per cent in 1981 and have not risen above 5 per cent since.

The Sunbeam, hastily introduced by Chrysler in 1978, was another headache. Turnbull considered it poorly engineered which, in its turn, produced reliability problems. Customers' complaints caused him to take a closer look at the Sunbeam and 'I found that there had been very little development engineering.'[89] Just one of the improvements made to the model was a complete change of its electrics. Turnbull immediately set out to improve management/staff relations, an approach which harked back to his Austin Morris days, and introduced team briefings.

Initially the Horizon, Chrysler's front-wheel-drive Simca 1100-based compact of 1978, proved Talbot's best seller, but this disappeared from Britain's top twenty best-selling cars in 1981. The Solara, a notchback version of the Alpine, appeared in 1980 and, in the following year, came the 2.1-litre Tagora, a big car at the wrong time, which made little impact and lasted only until 1984.

In 1981 Peugeot decided to close the loss-making Linwood factory, the Scottish car plant opened by Rootes in 1962. 'I didn't want to close Linwood, nor for that matter did Jean-Paul Parayre, head of Peugeot. It wasn't anything to with labour relations: they were coming along fine. It was mainly that we had no new investment to make at that point.'[90] Turnbull considers Linwood's demise as his 'blackest day', though he believes that improved labour relations were a factor in its relatively non-acrimonious closure. This left Talbot with just two plants, the Stoke works in Coventry, which produced Hillman Hunter kits under the Arrow coding for Iran, and the former Rootes Shadow Factory at Ryton-on-Dunsmore. The Talbot workforce had fallen accordingly. In 1978 the firm had employed 22,800 people; by 1983 this had been cut by two thirds to 7,109. Inevitably, Talbot recorded losses between 1978 and 1982 – in 1981 alone they had totalled £61.9 million. In 1984 came a return to viability and profits of £24.8 million, the year in which Turnbull completed his five-year contract with Peugeot.

Geoffrey Whalen, who had joined Talbot in 1980, became managing director and in 1986 the parent Peugeot company completed a £30 million modernization of its Ryton facilities. In 1985 this factory began building its Horizon replacement, the Peugeot 309, and in the following year the works produced its first left-hand-drive 309s for export to West Germany, Holland and Belgium. Following the completion of its sometimes-precarious Iranian contract, Peugeot closed part of its Stoke factory in 1987, leaving Ryton as its sole British car-manufacturing plant. But all the British-built cars are now French-designed. In 1986 Peugeot sold its engineering centre at Whitley, Coventry, once coveted by British Leyland, to Jaguar.

It was much the same story at Luton. Since 1979 all Vauxhalls have been German-designed rebadged Opels. In 1976 Vauxhall introduced the Cavalier, in reality an Opel Ascona, and the following year production began at Luton; hitherto cars had been imported from General Motors' Belgian subsidiary. The British models were progressively phased out. The Victor name disappeared in 1976, to be replaced by the VX label, though this had gone by 1978 and the Viva ceased production in 1979. In 1978 came the Carlton, sold in Germany as the Opel Rekord.

All these cars were front-engine/rear-drive models, but in 1980, a year in which Luton lost £53.4 million and had an 8 per cent share of the British market, came the first of a new generation of front-wheel-drive designs; the Vauxhall Astra and Opel Kadett D in Germany. The next arrived in August 1981 in the shape of the Cavalier which was Vauxhall's version of the Opel Ascona C. Available in both hatchback and notchback forms, it immediately became a fast seller. In 1982 it was the fifth best-selling car in Britain and helped Vauxhall to achieve a record 16.5 per cent market share in 1985, a revival which caught Ford and, more seriously, BL severely off balance. The international nature of General Motors' operations is reflected by the fact that Vauxhalls are imported from corporate plants in Germany, Spain and Belgium, in addition to those produced at Luton and Ellesmere Port. But Vauxhall's secondary role in General Motors' European operations was further underlined in 1987 when the corporation was selling its 700-acre Bedfordshire proving ground at Millbrook, opened only in 1968 at a cost of £3.5 million.

Ford of Britain, operating within the Ford of Europe umbrella and the market leader since 1977, has remained consistently profitable throughout the past twelve years. Indeed, in 1979 profits reached an all-time high of £425 million. In 1976 Terence Beckett, by then dubbed 'Mr Cortina' within the corporate hierarchy, became Ford of Britain's chairman. Knighted in 1978, he left the company in 1980 to become director general of the Confederation of British Industry. His place as chairman was taken by Sam Toy, who joined Ford in 1948 as one of its first graduate recruits.

The car programme continued to evolve. The successful and ultra-conventional Escort was uprated in 1975, and in the following year appeared the final version of the Cortina which remained Britain's best-selling car until 1981. In 1977 came a big event for the corporation: the launch of the Fiesta, its first ever front-wheel-drive model. It was built at a new Spanish plant, and a factor in its creation had been the company's relative weakness in the south of the continent. 'You might as well call us Ford of northern Europe,' Henry Ford II had barked. In 1980 Fiesta's British sales overtook those of BL's long-running Mini for the first time on the British market.

The Cortina line was finally discontinued in 1982 after twenty years. The most significant post-war Ford model line was replaced by a very different product: the Sierra, the first Ford to be obviously influenced by aerodynamic considerations. Development was divided between Britain and Germany with the former responsible for the car's interior and the latter for the exterior, even though German-born Uwe Bahnsen, Ford's vice president of design, who is credited with the Sierra's lines, was Dunton-based! Ford management was apprehensive that customers might be frightened away by the car's adventurous appearance, a fear which was confirmed when the radical shape 'caused some consternation at customer clinics . . . [though] Bahnsen explained to his peers that this was because an anonymous member of the public, selected at random, who had just spent all his savings on a traditional-looking three-box car, was hardly likely to make himself look a fool by energetically announcing his approval for a car that immediately made his own possession look out of date.' Bahnsen won the day and at the final clinic 'no one guessed that the unnamed new car, which was judged by its appearance to be $2,000 more expensive than its competitors, was a Ford'.[90]

The Sierra perpetuated the Cortina rear-drive layout, though with a Dunton-designed independent rear suspension, because the model was to be offered with a huge engine range from a 1.3 four to a 3-litre V6 and a transverse location could have meant altering the bonnet contours to the detriment of the car's aerodynamics. The first Sierra went down Ford's Ghenk production line in June 1982 and in 1983, the first full year of production, output was extended to Britain.

Yet the Sierra has never achieved the same success as its Cortina predecessor. Although it was second in the list of top-selling cars in 1983, it had dropped to fifth place in 1984 and 1985, the second slot being taken in both instances by Vauxhall's Cavalier, and in 1984 Ford began to speak of its production forecasts having been 'wildly over-optimistic'. However, modifications, particularly to the front end for 1985, helped put the Sierra back in the number three spot in 1986, just 386 cars behind the Cavalier!

The Ford that did replace the Cortina as Britain's best-selling car in 1982 was the Escort, which has been in pole position ever since. A completely new front-wheel-drive model, sold not only in Europe but the world over, it was endowed by Uwe Bahnsen with a rear-end 'bustle' which suggested that what was in fact a hatchback had retained the more traditional boot. In 1981 the Escort became the best-selling car in the world, so following in the wheeltracks of its distinguished Model T forebear. Like General Motors, today Ford imports a substantial amount of its cars from its plants in Germany, Belgium and Spain.

Meanwhile, what was happening at BL in this increasingly competitive climate? With Sir Michael Edwardes's 1982 departure, the post of chairman became a part-time non-executive one and was taken by Glaxo chairman Sir Austin Bide. BL was then run by two executive officers, Ray Horrocks, responsible for cars and the Unipart spares business, and David Andrews, whose remit was Land-Rover and Leyland Vehicles. The firm's car division was renamed Austin Rover and the post of its chairman and chief executive went to Harold Musgrove, who had joined Austin as an apprentice in 1945 and, as managing director of Austin Morris, had played a key role in seeing the Metro through to a successful fruition.

In March 1983 the LM10 project, initiated during the Edwardes era, reached the showrooms. The Austin Maestro, styled in house by Ian Beech, was a roomy five-door hatchback, though it did differ in some important respects from its front-wheel-drive predecessors. For the first time the Issigonis formula of the gearbox being located beneath the engine was replaced by an end-on unit, which had become the norm, but that fitted to the Maestro was a five-speed unit from the Volkswagen Golf. 'The reason why Austin Morris had to buy in lots of its transmission was that the only in-line gearboxes available to it were to be found with Rover and that was mainly concerned with transfer and heavy-duty boxes. The guys at BMC knew about transmissions, but at a time when they should have been concentrating on looking at end-on gearbox location, they weren't, they were busy on the Marina range,' says Horrocks.[91] The Maestro has had a tough time in establishing itself in a highly competitive market and its 1986 British sales of 51,465 were behind both the Metro and Montego.

The Montego, effectively a booted version of the Maestro, even though the only common exterior panels are the front doors and the lower section of the rear ones, appeared in April 1984, and represented BL's all-important bid for the fleet market.

The launch of the Montego saw the long-running Marina, updated as the Ital in 1980, cease production in 1983. With it went the Morris name, in its seventieth year, and the final irony was that the model had been latterly been built at Longbridge, home of the Austin which was Morris's arch rival of the inter-war years. Ital production had been moved from Cowley to make way for the Triumph Acclaim, and when that model was discontinued in 1984, its Japanese replacement was the Honda Ballade-based Rover 200 series soon to establish itself as a useful seller.

The big corporate event of 1984 was the privatization of Jaguar in August. John Egan says:

> For us it was very much a matter of survival, we also knew that we had to pour far bigger resources into our capital investment than we would have been allowed to do by BL. It is just that they wanted the money, as it were, more than they perceived we did. In the last year they were taking it off us in hatfuls. I think in total we paid £65 million in dividends to them. That's a hell of a payback. In fact I believe that the balance sheet, vis à vis BL, was clean. All the money that we had been lent to build the XJ40 and AJ6 engine had been paid back by that time.[92]

Horrocks points out that 'at that time BL was anxious that Jaguar be floated with a realistically geared balance sheet. In order to achieve that, Jaguar's existing debt in BL was transferred to that balance sheet and the result was that £50 to £60 million came out of Jaguar. In the event it was obvious that Jaguar had been given the benefit of the doubt by £20 to £30 million at least.'

When it came to privatization, Horrocks initiated the idea of BL retaining a 25 per cent holding in Jaguar, 'to avoid anybody acquiring it, as we'd had Ford and General Motors sniffing around. Also I felt that it would prove a good trade investment for us anyway.' In fact the idea was vetoed by the prime minister and then the government came up with the 'golden share' idea, so insulating Jaguar from takeover bids until the end of 1990. In 1985, the first year after privatization, the firm's profits rose to £121 million.

BL's share of the British market had remained fairly stable in 1984 and 1985, standing at 17.8 and 17.9 per cent respectively. In 1986, however, it took a nosedive and slumped a full 2 points to 15.8 per cent. This Horrocks puts down to 'incessant government carping about privatization and performance resulting in people not buying our products, whereas the same year our European sales rose 20/25 per cent'. During his eight years with BL, Horrocks found 'that Conservatives were much more interventionist than Labour politicians. I think that is because many Tories consider themselves businessmen just because they've run a small company, though the two secretaries of state most in tune with industry were Cecil Parkinson [1983] and Norman Tebbit [1983/5].' Horrocks witnessed direct Conservative government intervention when BL wanted to close its Scottish Bathgate truck factory. 'Because there was a by-election, the closure was delayed which frankly cost the company money and prolonged uncertainty as far as the workforce was concerned.'

Then, on 2 February 1986, Roy Hattersley, deputy leader of the Labour Party, revealed that General Motors was negotiating to buy Leyland Trucks and Land-Rover. 'This was government initiated, as opposed to the Honda tie-up which we did ourselves,' says David Andrews. 'They were worried about the truck industry in the UK because Ford was losing money, GM was losing money and so were we. We had initial discussions with GM and also Ford. GM took it up and it seemed that there were areas in which we could collaborate. Anyway, they came up with a proposition to take the lot, apart from buses.' To General Motors the attractions of merging its loss-making Bedford truck operations at Luton with Leyland's business were considerable. Andrews recalls:

BL's truck management believed, somewhat optimistically, that they would come out on top, but GM never committed themselves to that, they simply said that this would have to be the subject of studies. In the case of Land-Rover/Freight Rover, they wanted it because of its profitability and its cash flow to fund their losses on the truck side. The real risk at the time was that they would have run the cash out of Land-Rover as they had done over Bedford. They were quite explicit over that. So the long-term future of the business was rather bleak.[94]

It was the Land-Rover part of the deal that prompted a public outcry and one from members of parliament on both sides of the House of Commons. Then, the following day, news broke that the government had been negotiating with Ford about the possibility of its buying Austin Rover. The news had come as a complete surprise to Ray Horrocks:

I had a phone call early in December 1985 from a colleague who had been asked by the chairman to call me. They had just been to see secretary of state for industry Leon Brittan to talk about trucks. They were talking about the GM situation and at the end, I am told, Leon said, 'Oh, by the way, there's another matter I want to bring up. We've been approached by Ford, who want to study the proposition of acquiring Austin Rover and we want you to pursue this with speed and enthusiasm.' I just couldn't believe it. I called Austin [Bide] and he said . . . that's how it went. That's how I got to know.[95]

In January Horrocks was instructed by Brittan 'to permit Ford access to all costings. We had the same information from them, but if you give a guy who is 7 feet tall a big stick and you give a little guy who is 4 feet tall an equally big stick, who's going to win? They knew, for instance, exactly how much profit we had to play with on the Metro.'[96]

If the Ford takeover had been approved, Ray Horrocks would have offered his resignation. 'To make any sense of it, there would have to have been some massive reductions in the workforce, and then if you go downstream to the distribution network, you would have lost dealers as well and you could end up losing upwards of 100,000 people.'[97]

Had the approach come from Ford or the government? Ministers at the time were insisting that the first approach came from Ford after the collapse of its negotiations to merge its European operations with Fiat, but 'there is some evidence that Mr Norman Tebbit was having discussions with Ford about collaboration when he was trade and industry secretary".[98]

On 6 February, only three days after the news had broken, the cabinet's economic affairs committee, which had first considered the matter on 28 January, insisted on the talks ending, following a lead taken by social services secretary Norman Fowler, MP for Sutton Coldfield, with support from energy secretary Peter Walker and paymaster general Kenneth

Clarke; chancellor of the exchequer Nigel Lawson was the prime minister's principal ally. At that stage the General Motors takeover of Leyland Trucks and Land-Rover was continuing, but Lonrho subsequently announced that it was submitting a bid, followed by a management buy-out by five of Land-Rover's senior managers led by David Andrews, though it had submitted its proposal to Downing Street prior to the news breaking. On 2 March owners of more than 1,000 Land-Rovers from all over Britain drove in them to Downing Street, as part of their campaign to keep Land-Rover British. Renewed cabinet opposition from Lord White-law, Norman Tebbit, Peter Walker and Norman Fowler culminated in General Motors' withdrawal from the deal on 24 March, though exactly a month later, on 24 April, secretary of state for industry Paul Channon announced that Land-Rover and Freight Rover, which had also been included in the deal, would remain part of BL, 'while preparations for future privatization are made'.[99]

Then, on 1 May 1986, the firm got a new chairman in the shape of Canadian lawyer Graham Day, a man with an impressive track record for improving the viability and efficiency of nationalized industries, who had just completed a thirty-eight month contract as chairman and chief executive of British Shipbuilders. Day is very much of a 'hands-on' manager and, by September, Ray Horrocks, David Andrews and Harold Musgrove had all departed.

In July the all-important Project XX, the joint BL/Honda replacement for the SD1, emerged as the front-wheel-drive Rover 800 series four-door saloon. Offered with alternative Honda 2.5-litre V6 and BL's 2-litre twin-overhead-camshaft four-cylinder engines, it is also being built by Honda in Japan, so giving Rover access to Far East sales. In 1987 Rover returned to the vital American market, though it was selling the specially badged 800 under the Sterling name. The Legend, the Honda version of the project, had appeared earlier in 1986 and is also built in Britain at Cowley along with, from 1987, the Ballade, which also forms the basis of the Rover 200 series. Cars are first delivered to a new factory Honda has built at Swindon, prior to distribution. In 1987 the Japanese company announced plans to build a new engine plant, adjoining its existing facility, to produce 75,000 power units a year for Austin Rover though, unlike the Nissan factory at Washington, Cumberland, opened in 1986, it does not manufacture complete cars. That plant aims to be building 100,000 cars a year by 1991, so introducing a further element to Britain's multi-national-based motor industry.

Jaguar's long-awaited and highly acclaimed new XJ6 was launched three months after the Rover, in October 1986. Its 3.6-litre twin-overhead-camshaft six-cylinder engine had been available in the XJ-S since 1983, though with the valve gear quietened and refined. There was also a new single-overhead-camshaft 2.9-litre six, derived from the V12. But in international terms Jaguar is still a relatively small company. In 1987 it built a record 47,000 cars while Mercedes-Benz produced about 600,000, of which approximately 111,000 were comparable S-class cars.

Privatization of other parts of the Rover Group, as Day renamed BL in July 1986, continues apace. In January 1987 came a management buy-out of Unipart and the same month Leyland Buses was sold in a similar way. In May the loss-making Leyland Trucks, along with Freight Rover, was merged with the Dutch DAF Trucks. What of the future of the Group's car-manufacturing rump? Austin Rover employs 39,000 people in its twelve principal factories and its Longbridge and Cowley facilities have a joint capacity to produce 750,000 cars. In 1986 its share of the British market dropped to 15.5 per cent and losses soared to a record £892 million. However, the greatly slimmed-down Group was back in the black in 1987, and the production figure was about 450,000, yet the firm has to build 600,000 cars a year to cover development costs for its new models. It has, in effect, the output of a specialist manufacturer but the products of a quantity one. In European terms, Rover is easily at the bottom of the production league in a market place where overcapacity is in the order of 20 per cent. On his arrival, Day spoke of less importance being attached to market share, which suggests moves up market with echoes of John Barber's strategy of nearly 20 years before.

By the turn of the century the Rover model line-up will probably feature a restyled Metro, the 800 saloon and 600 hatchback derivative, while the AR8, another joint Rover/Honda project, is due to replace the Rover 200, Maestro and possibly Montego models. Sporting versions will retain the MG badge, but the Austin name will probably follow Morris into oblivion.

Privatization plans are coming to fruition this year, and the government is committed to returning the company to the private sector by 1992. Ford, Chrysler and Honda have all been mooted as possible takeover candidates – or will Rover still be in British ownership when the centenary of the industry's birth is celebrated in 1996?

9

Some Reasons Why

'The world of Ford and that type of British company [Leyland] is so utterly and completely different, we are not talking about Ford versus BMC or Ford versus Standard-Triumph, we are really dealing with the difference between earth and the planet Mars.'[1]
Hamish Orr-Ewing, light car planning manager, Ford Motor Company (1959–63) and Leyland Motor Corporation (1963–5)

Although the British Leyland Motor Company collapsed at the end of 1974, the reality is that the British motor industry, by which I mean BMC, had been heading for disaster a good decade before that. For if it is possible to identify the era in which the industry went into decline, it was during the twenty years that followed the ending of the Second World War, though the Corporation's shortcomings were masked by the seller's market of the 1950s. With the arrival of the more competitive 1960s, BMC failings became all too apparent. Managed by the talented, dictatorial and dangerous Sir Leonard Lord, the British Motor Corporation, during these two decades, remained a bastion of pre-war thinking and prejudices. Lord was the blunt, straight-talking, sometimes foul-mouthed leader of industry that some of his more memorable aphorisms suggest. Yet he could also be capable of great kindness and good humour, and a paradox of his personality is that he courageously abandoned a generation of motor industry traditions when he commissioned Alec Issigonis to create the front-wheel-drive Mini.

But the arbitrary way in which it was initiated, during a short-lived period of petrol rationing, placed too great a corporate reliance on small, low-profit cars and reveals the limits of Lord's marketing horizons. Even then the Mini could have heralded a new era for BMC, had it been priced correctly. While Ford was pursuing a carefully orchestrated policy of product planning, BMC was still relying on a combination of hunch and whim to plan and price its products, which, in retrospect, appears naive and amateurish. Lord was in turn replaced by the genial but ineffectual George Harriman, who owed his entire motor industry career to his predecessor and, like him, had only ever worked for the Austin and Morris companies. Yet in the 1960s the Corporation, as the market leader, was outwardly riding high with an apparently unshakeable belief in its marketing strategy, or lack of it. One motor industry critic described BMC at this time to me as 'an arrogant company but one with no pride in itself'.

The Economist put its finger on the problem back in 1962, a year after Harriman assumed office, when it wrote:

> BMC has stayed right out of fashion by virtually ignoring the arts graduate – and, indeed, the engineering graduate as well. It has stuck firmly to the motor industry's tradition that managers and engineers should work their way up, preferably from apprentice . . . it has cut itself off from the mainstream of able young men – something that no large company can afford to do. Compared with Ford, its lacks the bright young graduates in their thirties which now form the nucleus of that company's middle – and sometimes its top – management.[2]

When John Barber was at British Leyland, he recalls:

> I tried to set an example by driving other cars. I drove fifty competitors' models in the first year, and I used to flaunt them. But they were very loath to follow my example. They couldn't see beyond the walls of Longbridge. When we were developing the Allegro, we were having some problems with the suspension and at that time the Alfasud had an excellent reputation for handling. I kept on and on to the people at Longbridge to get hold of one to make some comparisons and they didn't do anything for months. In the end I bought one and got them to test it, and they came back to me and said, 'We see what you mean.' It was a terrible make-do-and-mend company.
>
> The intellectual calibre was very low. But they were good at getting out of difficulties. If they had a major problem in production, they could get out of it, but they weren't any good at planning on how not to get into it.

Barber found a great resistance to introducing any changes that had been initiated at Ford. 'When we were doing the Marina, we made them strip down several cars and pin the pieces up on the wall, just as we'd done at Ford. The attitude was still: "We are Longbridge, we are Austin. We can do it better."'[3]

The British Motor Corporation was not alone in its attitude to Ford at this time. Hamish Orr-Ewing had been light car planning manager on the Ford Cortina project, 'a marvellous example of what can be done in this country when we set our mind to it and are properly led'.[4] In 1963 he joined the newly formed Leyland Motor Corporation, which had taken over Standard-Triumph two years previously, as a product planner. There he found that the cost of manufacturing a Leyland diesel engine was something like 350 per cent more than the equivalent Ford unit. But the attitude to Ford was not 'How do they manage to be so cost effective?' but 'We don't do it that way. We don't have Ford's resources.' This was, in part, due to the fact that the Leyland Corporation itself had not been properly integrated. 'It was all over the place in penny pieces. Each factory had its chief engineer and drawing office. But there was a lack of real muscle where it was needed.' This became all too apparent when Orr-Ewing spent some time at the Corporation's Leyland factory. 'I regarded it as a tragedy. Some of the people there were absolutely superb. They were loyal, tough Lancastrians who were capable of enormous amounts of hard work and would have done anything they were asked. All they needed was good leadership and modern management.'[5]

Its absence was in part a result of the fact that, in the post-war years, Sir Henry Spurrier, who never forgot the early 1920s, when Leyland nearly went to the wall, 'cheerfully [loaded] more and more work and responsibility on a small circle of executives, and these people "doubled up" on an astonishing range of jobs'.[6] With such a background it is little wonder that Lord Stokes 'viewed with some apprehension getting involved in this huge mammoth' when Leyland was faced with taking over BMC. Yet he had been 'supremely happy at Leyland. It was a super job. I'd been there since leaving school and I much admired Henry Spurrier. He was a dedicated manager, was extremely self-sacrificing and took practically nothing out of the business. It was his life. They were nice people and I knew them all. But I was absolutely convinced that BMC would have gone bust if we had not stepped in and I felt that there was no option.' In retrospect, Lord Stokes believes that it might have been 'much more sensible to let it go broke and then bought some of the pieces'.[7]

When Leyland took over BMC, 'we weren't exactly flooded with management skills'. As a result British Leyland recruited executives from Ford, but 'whether that was a success or not, I don't know. Ford's management philosophy was so different from the sort of philosophy we had, and I don't think that it ever proved compatible.'[8] David Andrews had been assistant controller, Ford of Europe, when he was recruited by John Barber to join British Leyland in 1969. His first impressions of the corporation were that there was 'no rapport, or a limited rapport, certainly no common ethos or culture, no common system, multiplicity of style, multiplicity of technology, multiplicity of everything'.[9]

This was, alas, the BMC inheritance of a group of companies that had grown piecemeal, a process that had begun in 1923 when the Cowley-based William Morris bought the Coventry firm of Hollick and Pratt which was 50 miles away. He defended his acquisitive policy in 1924 against the accusation that 'with our large output, we could do the thing cheaper ourselves; that we are piling up transport costs and so on'. In fact, claimed Morris, 'it costs only a fraction more to send steel from Sheffield or Birmingham to be machined and afterwards to transport the finished unit here, than to pay the full weight of the raw material, direct from Sheffield to our works.'[10] The inheritance of this strategy was that when British Leyland took over BMC in 1968, it was spending over £2 million a year transporting components around the group.

Again Ford had an enormous advantage over its rival, with its highly integrated Dagenham factory, though government policy in the 1950s and 1960s had the effect of fragmenting the industry even more by refusing Industrial Development Certificates to car companies which wanted to expand their manufacturing facilities adjacent to their existing factories.

Government direction was more relevant when, in 1945, Sir Stafford Cripps asked the industry to provide 'a cheap, tough, good-looking car ... produced in sufficient quantities to get the benefits of mass production'.[11] Examples of the Volkswagen Beetle were sent to practically every British car company for inspection. Rootes' appraisal, that 'we do not consider that the design represents any special brilliance . . . [and] is not to be regarded as an example of first-class modern design to be copied by the British industry',[12] has echoed down the years. But in Alec Issigonis's Morris Minor, Britain had an equivalent product. All that was lacking were the will and imagination to develop and export it in those car-hungry early post-war years. Rover came closest to the spirit of Cripps's exhortations by producing the Land-Rover which, like the Volkswagen, is still in production.

With the creation of British Leyland, Stokes says:

> I naively thought two things. One was that government would have given us support. Whether it was reasonable to expect that, I don't know. We were expected to buy from British Steel. But we never got it any cheaper and anyway it was bloody awful steel, the sheet in particular was very bad. We also had tremendous trouble in getting the government to purchase British vehicles.
>
> Secondly, I certainly thought that the trade unions would have given us a lot more support because, after all, we were trying to save their jobs.

It was union intransigence that prevented Stokes from making the all-important rationalization of British Leyland's manufacturing facilities that he knew was so essential.

There were a number of factories that, for historical reasons, were absolutely redundant in the Birmingham area and which could have been closed. Two were quite close together. We closed one down and everyone went on strike. We didn't even sack anyone in that instance. We just wanted them to move but they wouldn't even travel 2 more miles to work in another place. Things are different now.

We were grossly undercapitalized for what we were expected to achieve, but our trouble was that we hardly had any greenfield sites; almost everything we had was in old, uneconomic factories, and trying to get production costs down where labour would not be made redundant proved an impossible task.

[Before measured daywork was introduced], there were different rates of pay and different rewards, and you couldn't cost anything. Once the piecework rate was agreed, you couldn't change anything, it was custom and practice, and if you did you had to retime the whole car. If someone wrote to me and complained, 'This car is marvellous but why don't you put the cigarette lighter where you can reach it?' I'd say, 'I couldn't agree with you more,' but I couldn't change it.[13]

John Barber recalls:

When we came in 1968, the shop stewards practically ran Standard-Triumph. This all went back to Sir John Black's day. He destroyed labour relations, because to stop the workforce going to someone big, like Austin, he paid them more, relaxed discipline and made the factory a nice place to work in. The unions certainly had more control there than at Longbridge. The Triumph assembly plant was certainly the worst in that respect that I've ever seen in the world by a long way, far worse than anything at BMC. It was dreadful.[14]

Yet another difficulty was components supply. 'Most of our troubles were caused by electrical equipment. Paint was always a problem but electrics gave us most trouble,' Stokes remembers. 'We could not get our suppliers to come into line because their products were in such demand and, when we complained, they just said, "Well, all right, we won't supply you, we'll go and supply someone else."' A further headache that the incoming Leyland team experienced was that some of the cars of the BMC era had been designed with insufficient attention to the manufacturing process. 'Some were very nearly impossible to make. The number of body pressings in a BMC car was about three times the amount that there should have been,' says Stokes.

Of all the cars produced during his time in the motor industry, Lord

Stokes believes that 'the best one was the Triumph 2000. I think that was an extremely good car. Harry Webster and Stanley Markland were responsible for that. I think that the Triumph Stag was becoming good, but they went and scrapped it.' He does, however, recognize that the Longbridge-designed cars were 'always sort of mediocre, really'.

With the coming of the oil crisis, 'everyone stopped buying expensive cars in order to buy the ruddy Mini again'. Then, in 1975, came nationalization following the Ryder Report. Lord Stokes considers it 'a disaster, and I don't say that with any personal ill-feeling. It was an uninformed document which seemed to be made by people with very little knowledge of our basic problems and they did not consult with the British Leyland board regarding their conclusions. At least we had learned our lessons. We knew our mistakes. Events have proved that its findings were absolute rubbish. History has been the judge.'[15]

When Ryder's recommendations proved unworkable, Michael Edwardes arrived in 1977. The last word goes to Harold Musgrove and an incident that encapsulates the problems of the British-owned motor industry in which neither management nor workforce emerge with credit. Musgrove had started his career with Austin in 1945 and in 1963 moved to BMC's Bathgate factory, where he was subsequently made production director. In 1978 he returned to Longbridge to become director of manufacturing. He recalls:

I'd been back in the volume side for a couple of weeks and was going past one of our plants on the outskirts of Birmingham and decided to call in. I hadn't been there for many years. It was approximately two o'clock in the afternoon. I called into the plant director's office and said that I'd like to look around to see what was happening. When we walked the shop floor, I think 90 per cent of the employees had actually gone home. When I asked, 'What happened?' [I was told] 'Well, they've finished their stint.' In fact, some had finished by one o'clock. I pointed out that we paid them until 4.30. 'How do you explain it?' [The response was] 'They've been doing it for years.'

We'd been establishing targets, establishing line rates and achieving 60 per cent of the target which meant that the track stopped for 40 per cent of the day. That was not the responsibility of the employees, that was not the responsibility of the workforce. That had to be the responsibility of management.[16]

References

1. M. R. Argles, *South Kensington to Robbins* (Longmans, 1964), p. 137.

Chapter 1
From Tricycles to Tin Lizzies

2. H. O. Duncan, *The World on Wheels* (Duncan, Paris, 1926), p. 690.
3. *The Times*, 21 February 1986.
4. H. B. Light, *Rover and Alvis News*, 1968.
5. 'Sir Herbert Austin, His Life Story', *The Autocar*, 23 August 1929 p. 370.
6. Ibid., p. 371.
7. *Motoring Annual* (Motoring Illustrated, 1903), p. 39.
8. Anthony Bird and Francis Hutton-Stott, *The Veteran Motor Car Pocketbook* (Batsford, 1963), pp. 29–30.
9. Maurice Hendry, 'Cadillac' *Automobile Quarterly*, 1977, p. 15.
10. Ruth Brandon, *Isaac Singer* (Lippincott, 1977), p. 91.
11. Hendry, op. cit., p. 18.
12. *The Times*, 5 June 1899.
13. Duncan, op. cit., p. 899.
14. David Thoms and Tom Donnelly, *The Motor Car Industry in Coventry since the 1890s* (Croom Helm, 1985), p. 44.
15. *The Economist*, 9 December 1911, p. 1202.
16. Ibid.
17. Dudley Noble, *Milestones in a Motoring Life* (Queen Anne Press, 1969), p. 29.
18. Ibid.
19. A. F. C. Hillstead, *Fifty Years with Motor Cars* (Faber and Faber, 1960), p. 76.
20. Ian Nickols and Kent Karslake, *Motoring Entente* (Cassell, 1956), p. 8.
21. Ibid.
22. Ibid., p. 9.

23. Ibid., p. 18.
24. Bird and Hutton-Stott, *The Veteran Motor Car Pocketbook*, p. 221.
25. *The Economist*, 9 December 1911, p. 1202.
26. S. B. Saul, *The Motor Industry in Britain to 1914*, Business History V, 1962, p. 28.
27. *Motor Sport*, November 1977.
28. Nickols and Karslake, op. cit., p. 48.
29. Brian Smith, *Royal Daimlers* (Transport Bookman, 1976), p. 29.
30. Kenneth Richardson, *The British Motor Industry 1896–1939* (Macmillan, 1977) p. 31.
31. Anthony Bird and Francis Hutton-Stott, *Lanchester Motor Cars* (Cassell, 1965), p. 126.
32. P. W. Kingsford, *F. W. Lanchester, Life of an Engineer* (Edward Arnold, 1960), p. 74.
33. Bird and Hutton-Stott, *The Veteran Motor Car Pocketbook*, pp. 213–14.
34. Anthony Bird, *The Motor Car 1765–1914* (Batsford, 1960), pp. 213–14.
35. Bird and Hutton-Stott, *The Veteran Motor Car Pocketbook*, p. 81.
36. R. P. T. Davenport-Hines, *Dudley Docker* (Cambridge University Press, 1984), p. 50.
37. Hendry, op. cit., p. 77.
38. Allan Nevins and Frank Ernest Hill, *Ford: Decline and Rebirth 1933–1962* (Charles Scribner's Son, 1963), p. 80.
39. C. F. Caunter, *The History and Development of Light Cars* (Her Majesty's Stationery Office, 1957), p. 33.
40. Ibid.
41. Kent Karslake, *Racing Voiturettes* (Motor Racing Publications, 1950), pp. 133–4.
42. Ibid., p. 134.
43. James M. Laux, *In First Gear, The French Automobile Industry to 1914* (Liverpool University Press, 1976), p. 120.
44. Bird and Hutton-Stott, *The Veteran Motor Car Pocketbook*, p. 213.
45. W. R. Morris, 'How We Made a £6,000,000 Turnover Last Year', *System*, March 1923, p. 150.
46. W. R. Morris, 'Policies That Have Built the Morris Motor Business', *System*, February 1924, p. 73.
47. Cecil Bayliss, interview.
48. *The Economist*, 22 November 1913, p. 1120.

Chapter 2

Wheels of Fortune

1. Morris, 'How We Made a £6,000,000 Turnover Last Year', *System*, March 1924, p. 150.
2. 'Sir Herbert Austin, His Life Story', *The Autocar*, 23 August 1929, p. 491.
3. P. W. S. Andrews and Elizabeth Brunner, *The Life of Lord Nuffield* (Basil Blackwell, 1955).

REFERENCES

4. Morris, 'How We Made a £6,000,000 Turnover Last Year', *System*, March 1924, p. 148.
5. Ibid.
6. Ian Lloyd, *Rolls-Royce, The Years of Endeavour* (Macmillan, 1978), p. 125.
7. A. J. P. Taylor, *English History, 1914–1945* (Oxford University Press, 1965), p. 145.
8. Harry Edwards, *The Morris Motor Car* (Moorland, 1983), p. 81.
9. Morris, 'Policies That Have Built the Morris Motor Business', *System*, February 1924, p. 73.
10. Ibid.
11. Jonathan Wood, 'MG insignia', *Thoroughbred and Classic Cars*, March 1982, p. 68.
12. St John Nixon, *Wolseley* (Foulis, 1949), p. 99.
13. Roy Church, *Herbert Austin, The British Motor Car Industry to 1941* (Europa Publications, 1979), p. 185.
14. Davenport-Hines, *Dudley Docker* (Cambridge University Press, 1984), p. 173.
15. J. D. Scott, *Vickers* (Weidenfeld and Nicolson, 1962), p. 167.
16. Andrews and Brunner, op. cit., p. 156.
17. *RAC Handbook*, 1924.
18. Ibid.
19. Mira Wilkins and Frank Ernest Hill, *American Business Abroad, Ford on Six Continents* (Wayne State University Press, 1964), p. 142.
20. Jonathan Wood, 'The Birth of the Austin Seven', *Thoroughbred and Classic Cars*, July 1977, p. 17.
21. Ibid., p. 19.
22. Church, op. cit., p. 65.
23. Ibid., p. 105.
24. Alfred Sloan Jnr, *My Years with General Motors* (Sidgwick and Jackson, 1965), p. 319.
25. Dudley Noble, *Milestones in a Motoring Life* (Queen Anne Press, 1969), p. 91.
26. Kenneth Richardson, *The British Motor Industry, 1896–1939* (Macmillan, 1977), p. 112.
27. G. S. Davidson, *At the Wheel* (Industrial Transport Publications, 1931), p. 40.
28. Noble, op. cit., p. 71.
29. Ibid., p. 79.
30. Graham Robson, *Motoring in the 1930s* (Patrick Stephens, 1979), p. 129.
31. Ibid., p. 131.
32. Maurice Platt, *An Addiction to Automobiles* (Frederick Warne, 1980), p. 39.
33. Ibid., p. 40.
34. Noble, op. cit., p. 111.
35. Platt, op. cit., p. 40.
36. Ibid.
37. A. C. Armstrong, *Bouverie Street to Bowling Green Lane* (Hodder and Stoughton, 1946), pp. 133–4.

38. Ian Nickols and Kent Karslake, *Motoring Entente*, (Cassell, 1956), p. 249.
39. Robert Jackson, *The Nuffield Story* (Frederick Muller, 1964), p. 18.
40. Sloan, op. cit., p. 320.
41. Michael Sedgwick, *Vauxhall* (Beaulieu Books, 1981), p. 16.
42. Platt, op. cit., p. 90.
43. Ibid.
44. Ibid., p. 91.
45. Ibid.

Chapter 3

Six of the Best?

1. H. G. Castle, *Britain's Motor Industry* (Clerk and Cockeran, 1950), p. 179.
2. P. W. S. Andrews and Elizabeth Brunner, *Life of Lord Nuffield* (Basil Blackwell, 1955), p. 195.
3. Sir Miles Thomas, *Out on a Wing* (Michael Joseph, 1964), p. 142.
4. Ibid.
5. Ibid., p. 172.
6. Ibid., p. 179.
7. Ibid., p. 171.
8. Ibid., p. 140.
9. Ibid., p. 180.
10. Frank Woollard, 'Sir Leonard Lord', *The Motor*, 6 July 1955, p. 883.
11. Thomas, op. cit., p. 165.
12. Ibid., p. 171.
13. Ibid., p. 173.
14. Paul Skilleter, *Jaguar Saloon Cars* (Haynes, 1980), p. 157.
15. Thomas, op. cit., p. 174.
16. Ibid., p. 177.
17. Bill Gunston, *By Jupiter! The Life of Sir Roy Fedden* (Royal Aeronautical Society, 1978), p. 39.
18. Thomas, op. cit., p. 181.
19. Roy Church, *Herbert Austin, The British Motor Car Industry to 1941* (Europa Publications, 1979), p. 161.
20. Ibid.
21. Mira Wilkins and Frank Ernest Hill, *American Business Abroad, Ford on Six Continents* (Wayne State University Press, 1964), p. 134.
22. Ibid., p. 239.
23. Ibid., p. 288.
24. Alfred Sloan Jnr, *My Years with General Motors* (Sidgwick and Jackson, 1965), pp. 327–8.
25. Maurice Platt, *An Addiction to Automobiles*, (Frederick Warne, 1980), p. 93.
26. *Who's Who in the Motor Trade* (Motor Commerce, 1934), p. 9
27. Platt, op. cit., p. 93.

28. Ibid., p. 96.
29. J. B. Butterworth, 'William Edward Rootes', *The Dictionary of National Biography 1961–70*, (Oxford University Press, 1981), p. 894.
30. Dudley Noble, *Milestones in a Motoring Life* (Queen Anne Press, 1969), p. 92.
31. Ibid., p. 96.
32. *The Motor* 28 September 1926, p. 322.
33. Platt, op. cit., p. 322.
34. Michael Sedgwick, *Cars of the 1930s* (Batsford, 1970), p. 314.
35. Platt, op. cit., p. 42.
36. Butterworth, op. cit., p. 894.
37. *By Jupiter!*, p. 82.
38. Ibid.
39. Ibid. p. 83.
40. David Thoms and Tom Donnelly, *The Motor Car Industry in Coventry since the 1890s* (Croom Helm, 1985), p. 97.
41. Graham Robson, *Motoring in the 1930s*, (Patrick Stephens, 1979), p. 129.
42. Thoms and Donnelly, op. cit., p. 103.
43. Noble, op. cit., p. 198.
44. John Barber, interview.
45. Harry Webster, interview.
46. J. Foreman-Peck, *Exit, Voice and Loyalty as Responses to Decline: The Rover Company in the Inter-War Years* (Business History, XIII, 1981), p. 202.
47. Ibid.
48. Sir William Lyons, 'The History of the Jaguar and the Future of the Specialist Car in the British Motor Industry', Lord Wakefield Gold Medal Paper, 28 April 1969, p. 1.
49. Ibid.
50. Ibid., p. 2.
51. Ibid., p. 3.
52. Ibid.
53. Ibid.
54. Skilleter, op. cit., p. 64.
55. Ibid.
56. Lyons, op. cit., p. 3.
57. W. M. Heynes, 'Milestones in the Life of an Automobile Engineer', *Proceedings of the Institution of Automobile Engineers*, October 1960. p. 1.
58. Lyons, op. cit., p. 5.
59. Ibid., p. 4.
60. Sedgwick, op. cit., p. 290.
61. Richard Langworth and Graham Robson, *Triumph Cars, The Complete 75-year History* (Motor Racing Publications, 1979), p. 77.
62. R. P. T. Davenport-Hines, *Dudley Docker* (Cambridge University Press, 1984), p. 225.
63. Ibid., pp. 225–6.
64. Anthony Bird and Francis Hutton-Stott, *Lanchester Motor Cars* (Cassell, 1965), p. 179.

65. Davenport-Hines, op. cit., p. 226.
66. Noble, op. cit., p. 74.
67. Davison, *At the Wheel*, p. 105.

Chapter 4
A Backward Business

1. Laurence Pomeroy, *The Mini Story* (Temple Press, 1964), p. 66.
2. L. T. C. Rolt, *Victorian Engineering* (Pelican Books, 1974), p. 162.
3. David S. Landes, *The Unbound Prometheus* (Cambridge University Press, 1969), p. 345.
4. Sir Alexander Fleck, *Technology and its Social Consequences, A History of Technology, The late Nineteenth Century, c. 1850-c. 1900* (Oxford University Press, 1958), p. 821.
5. Bill Gunston, *By Jupiter! The Life of Sir Roy Fedden* (Royal Aeronautical Society, 1978), p. 6.
6. Ibid.
7. Ibid.
8. Ibid.
9. Sir Miles Thomas, *Out on a Wing* (Michael Joseph, 1964), p. 29.
10. Hugh Tours, *Parry Thomas* (Batsford, 1959), p. 15.
11. Ibid.
12. Lord Brabazon of Tara, *The Brabazon Story* (Heinemann, 1956), p. 170.
13. S. B. Saul, *The Engineering Industry, The Development of British Industry and Foreign Competition 1875–1914* (George Allen and Unwin, 1968), p. 226.
14. Kent Karslake and Laurence Pomeroy, *From Veteran to Vintage* (Temple Press, 1956), pp. 85–6.
15. Ibid., p. 89.
16. Ibid.
17. Sir Harry Ricardo, FRS, *Memories and Machines: The Pattern of My Life* (Constable, 1968), p. 168.
18. R. P. T. Davenport-Hines, *Dudley Docker* (Cambridge University Press 1984), p. 226.
19. Thomas, op. cit., p. 123.
20. Brabazon, op. cit., p. 24.
21. Michael Sanderson, *The Universities and British Industries 1850–1970*, (Routledge and Kegan Paul, 1972), p. 287.
22. Robert Jackson, *The Nuffield Story* (Frederick Muller, 1964), p. 38.

Chapter 5
Two into One Won't Go

1. *Financial Times*, 28 September 1954, in Peter J. S. Dunnett, *The Decline of the British Motor Industry* (Croom Helm, 1980), p. 57.
2. Kenneth O. Morgan, *Labour in Power 1945–1951* (Oxford University Press, 1985), p. 144.

REFERENCES

3. Ian Mikardo, MP, *The Second Five Years* (Fabian Publications, 1948), p. 14.
4. William Plowden, *The Motor Car and Politics* (Bodley Head, 1971), p. 314.
5. Ibid.
6. *The Autocar*, 23 November 1945, p. 851.
7. Plowden, op. cit., p. 312.
8. Michael Sedgwick, *The Motor Car 1946–1956* (Batsford, 1979), p. 192.
9. *The Economist*, October 1949, p. 627, in Dunnett, op. cit., p. 37.
10. Sir Miles Thomas, *Out on a Wing* (Michael Joseph, 1964), p. 204.
11. Desmond Donnelly, *David Brown's, The Story of a Family Business 1860–1960* (David Brown, 1960), p. 68.
12. Thomas, op. cit., p. 239.
13. Ibid., p. 248.
14. Ibid., p. 250.
15. Ibid.
16. Ibid.
17. Ibid., p. 251.
18. Ibid.
19. Ibid., pp. 237–8.
20. *The Autocar*, 15 October 1948, p. 987.
21. Ibid., 15 July 1949, p. 694.
22. Thomas, op. cit., p. 221.
23. Philip Turner and Tony Curtis, 'The Man who Made the Mini', *Motor*, 14 October 1978, p. 93.
24. Paul Skilleter, *Morris Minor* (Osprey, 1981), p. 33.
25. Ibid., p. 41.
26. Turner and Curtis, op. cit., p. 94.
27. Graham Turner, *The Leyland Papers* (Eyre and Spottiswoode, 1971), p. 96.
28. Ibid.
29. Ibid., p. 96.
30. Jonathan Wood, 'Healey', *Thoroughbred and Classic Cars*, August 1983, p. xi.
31. Ibid.
32. Ibid.
33. Donald Healey, interview.
34. Wood, op. cit., p. xii.
35. *The Economist*, 5 September 1959, p. 754.
36. Allan Nevins and Frank Hill, *Ford: Decline and Rebirth 1933–1962* (Charles Scribners Sons, 1963), p. 392.
37. Mira Wilkins and Frank Ernest Hill, *American Business Abroad, Ford on Six Continents* (Wayne State University Press, 1964), p. 157.
38. Ibid.
39. Ibid., p. 316.
40. Jonathan Wood, 'Captivating Cortina', *Thoroughbred and Classic Cars*, July 1983, p. 44.
41. Ibid.
42. Ibid.
43. Graham Turner, *Cars* (Zenith Books, 1965), p. 19.

44. John Barber, interview.
45. Wilkins and Hill, op. cit., p. 386.
46. Ibid., p. 387.
47. Ibid.
48. Sir William Lyons, 'The History of the Jaguar, and the Future of the Specialist Car in the Motor Industry', Lord Wakefield Gold Medal Paper, 28 April 1969, pp. 5–6.
49. Ibid., p. 6.
50. Richard Langworth and Graham Robson, *Triumph Cars, The Complete 75-year-History* (Motor Racing Publications, 1979), p. 138.
51. Peter Pagnamenta and Richard Overy, *All Our Working Lives* (British Broadcasting Corporation, 1984), p. 229.
52. Turner, The Leyland Papers (Eyre and Spottiswoode, 1971), p. 38.
53. Dudley Noble, *Milestones in a Motoring Life*, (Queen Anne Press, 1969), pp. 197–8.
54. Harold Nockolds, *Lucas The First Hundred Years* (David and Charles, 1978), p. 90.
55. David Thoms and Tom Donnelly, *The Motor Car Industry in Coventry since the 1890s* (Croom Helm, 1985), p. 157.
56. *The Autocar,* 13 November 1953, p. 789.
57. Turner, op. cit., p. 40.
58. Langworth and Robson, op. cit., p. 179.
59. Turner, op. cit., pp. 40–1.
60. *The Autocar*, 13 November, 1953, p. 789.
61. Jonathan Wood, 'Enter the Herald', *Thoroughbred and Classic Cars*, May 1983, p. 90.
62. Ibid.
63. Ibid., p. 91.
64. Jonathan Wood, 'Herald Triumph', *Thoroughbred and Classic Cars*, June 1983, p. 79.
65. Ibid.
66. Ibid., p. 80.
67. Thoms and Donnelly, op. cit., p. 165
68. Graham Robson, 'The Fall of Singer', *Thoroughbred and Classic Cars*, December 1981, p. 72.
69. Maurice Platt, *An Addiction to Automobiles* (Frederick Warne, 1980), p. 164.
70. Ibid., p. 171.
71. Ibid.
72. Ibid., p. 184.
73. D. G. Rhys, *The Motor Industry, An Economic Survey* (Butterworth, 1972), p. 164.
74. K. and J. Slavin and G. N. Mackie, *Land-Rover, The Unbeatable 4 × 4* (Haynes, 1984), p. 11.
75. Ibid., p. 13.
76. Graham Robson, *The Rover Story* (Patrick Stephens, 1977), p. 86.
77. Ibid., p. 85.

78. Paul Addison, *Now the War is Over* (Jonathan Cape and the British Broadcasting Corporation, 1985), p. 191.

79. Lyons, op. cit., p. 5.

80. W. M. Heynes, 'The Jaguar Engine', *Proceedings of the Institution of Automobile Engineers*, February 1953, p. 11.

81. Ibid.

82. Lyons, op. cit., p. 7.

83. Ibid.

84. R. P. T. Davenport-Hines, *Dudley Docker* (Cambridge University Press, 1984), p. 231.

85. Ibid.

86. Ibid., p. 232.

Chapter 6
Mini Cars Make Mini Profits

1. Ronald Barker, 'Alec Issigonis', *Automobile Design, Great Designers and their Work* (David and Charles, 1970), p. 310.

2. Philip Turner and Tony Curtis, 'The Man who Made the Mini', *Motor*, 14 October 1978, p. 95.

3. Barker, op. cit., p. 310.

4. Alec Issigonis, Introduction, in Laurence Pomeroy, *The Mini Story* (Temple Press, 1964), p xiii.

5. Ibid., p. xiv,

6. Laurence Pomeroy, *The Mini Story* (Temple Press, 1964), p. 29.

7. Christy Campbell, 'The Making of the Mini', *Thoroughbred and Classic Cars*, September 1979, p. 18.

8. Dante Giacosa, *Forty Years of Design with Fiat* (Automobilia, 1979), p. 248.

9. Ibid., p. 250.

10. Purpose designed end-on gearboxes are now smaller than their in-line predecessors and cars wider.

11. Graham Turner, *The Car Makers* (Eyre and Spottiswoode, 1963), pp. 179–80.

12. Graham Turner, *The Leyland Papers* (Eyre and Spottiswoode, 1971), p. 94.

13. John Barber, interview.

14. Ibid.

15. Sir Miles Thomas, *Out on a Wing*, p. 140.

16. Turner, *The Car Makers*, p. 179.

17. Thomas, op. cit., p. 341.

18. Turner, *The Car Makers*, p. 178.

19. Graham Turner, *Business in Britain* (Eyre and Spottiswoode, 1969), p. 380.

20. Turner and Curtis, op. cit., p. 95.

21. Douglas Hague and Geoffrey Wilkinson, *The IRC – An Experiment in Industrial Intervention* (George Allen and Unwin, 1983), p. 133.

22. Turner, *Business in Britain*, pp. 382–3.

23. *The Economist*, 31 July 1965, p. 458.

24. Turner, *The Leyland Papers*, p. 100.

25. Sir William Lyons, 'The History of the Jaguar, and the Future of the Specialist Car in the British Motor Industry', Lord Wakefield Gold Medal Paper, 28 April 1969, p. 8.

26. Andrew Whyte, *Jaguar: The History of a Great British Car* (Patrick Stephens, 1980), p. 153.

27. Lyons, op. cit., p. 8.

28. Ibid.

29. Ibid., p. 29.

30. Ford also won in 1967, 1968 and 1969.

31. Jonathan Wood, 'Archbishop to Cortina', *Thoroughbred and Classic Cars*, August 1983, p. 11.

32. Jonathan Wood, 'Captivating Cortina', *Thoroughbred and Classic Cars*, July, 1983, p. 45.

33. Ibid.

34. Ibid., p. 46.

35. Ibid.

36. Jonathan Wood, *The Ford Cortina Mk I* (Osprey, 1984), p. 40.

37. Wood, 'Archbishop to Cortina', p. 10.

38. Ibid.

39. Ibid.

40. Ibid., p. 11.

41. Wood, *The Ford Cortina MK I*, p. 94.

42. John Barber, interview.

43. Turner, *Business in Britain*, p. 390.

44. Dennis Hackett, *The Big Idea* (Ford Motor Company, 1978), p. 46.

45. Platt, *An Addiction to Automobiles*, p. 183.

46. Ibid., p. 181.

47. Turner, *Business in Britain*, p. 305.

48. Mike Parkes and Tim Fry, 'The Devil We Know', *Motor*, 9 March 1968, p. 17.

49. Ibid., p. 20.

50. Ibid., p. 21.

51. Stephen Young and Neil Hood, *Chrysler UK: A Corporation in Transition* (Praeger Publishers, 1977), p. 85.

52. Turner, *Business in Britain*, p. 395.

53. Ibid.

54. Ibid., p. 396.

55. Ibid.

56. Turner, *The Leyland Papers*, p. 54.

57. Sir Henry Spurrier, Foreword, in *Parry Thomas by Tours*, p. 8.

58. Turner, *The Leyland Papers*, p. 21.

59. Ibid., p. 22.

60. Ibid., p. 24.

61. Turner, *The Car Makers*, p. 194.

62. Turner, *The Leyland Papers*, p. 35.

63. Bill Gunston, *By Jupiter! The Life of Sir Roy Fedden* (Roy Aeronautical Society, 1978), pp. 141–2.

64. Jonathan Wood, 'Jowett: The Inside Story'. *Thoroughbred and Classic Cars*, February 1980, p. 33.
65. Lord Stokes, interview.
66. Ibid.
67. Harry Webster, interview.
68. Turner, *The Leyland Papers*, p. 65.
69. Ibid., p. 66.
70. Jonathan Wood, 'Herald Triumph', *Thoroughbred and Classic Cars*, June 1983, p. 80.
71. Harry Webster, interview.
72. Turner, *The Leyland Papers*, p. 76.
73. Ibid.
74. Ibid., p. 77.
75. Turner, *The Car Makers*, p. 144.
76. Lord Stokes, interview.
77. Ibid.
78. Hague and Wilkinson, op. cit., p. 3.
79. Ibid.
80. Graham Robson, *The Rover Story* (Patrick Stephens, 1977), p. 95.
81. Ibid., p. 97.
82. Lord Stokes, interview.
83. Ibid.

Chapter 7
The Leyland Years

1. Lord Stokes, interview.
2. Ibid.
3. Ibid.
4. John Barber, interview.
5. *Motor*, 13 April 1968, p. 60.
6. Lord Stokes, interview.
7. John Barber, interview.
8. Lord Stokes, interview.
9. Graham Turner, *The Leyland Papers* (Eyre and Spottiswoode, 1971), p. 180.
10. Lord Stokes, interview.
11. Douglas Hague and Geoffrey Wilkinson, *The IRC – An Experiment in Industrial Intervention* (George Allen and Unwin, 1983), p. 129.
12. Ibid., p. 130.
13. John Barber, interview.
14. Lord Stokes, interview.
15. Harold Wilson, *The Labour Government 1964–1970* (Weidenfeld and Nicolson and Michael Joseph, 1971), p. 289.
16. Lord Stokes, interview.
17. Turner, *The Leyland Papers*, p. 182.
18. Lord Stokes, interview.

19. Graham Robson, *The Rover Story* (Patrick Stephens, 1977), p. 154.
20. John Barber, interview.
21. Ibid.
22. Jeff Daniels, *British Leyland: The Truth about the Cars* (Osprey, 1980), p. 95.
23. Mike Taylor, 'Troubled Times', *Classic Cars*, May 1987, p. 70.
24. John Barber, interview.
25. Ibid.
26. Ibid.
27. Taylor, op. cit., p. 70.
28. John Barber, interview.
29. Ibid.
30. Ibid.
31. Robson, *The Rover Story*, p. 138.
32. *Autocar*, 16 March 1972, p. 2.
33. Richard Langworth and Graham Robson, *Triumph Cars* (Motor Racing Publications, 1979), p. 267.
34. John Barber, interview.
35. Peter Garnier, 'Pride of Lyons', *Autocar*, 16 March 1972, p. 9.
36. Courtenay Edwards, 'Sir William Lyons', *Motor Industry*, October 1971, p. 8.
37. Andrew Whyte, *Jaguar: The History of a Great British Car* (Patrick Stephens, 1980), pp. 168–9.
38. Ibid., p. 170.
39. Ibid., p. 172.
40. John Barber, interview.
41. Geoffrey Howard, 'Allegro Background to Styling', *Autocar*, 17 May 1973, p. 46.
42. John Barber, interview.
43. Daniels, op. cit., p. 122.
44. Ibid., pp. 122–3.
45. *Autocar*, 17 May 1973, p. 4.
46. Robson, *The Rover Story*, p. 158.
47. *Autocar*, 17 May 1973, p. 4.
48. Hague and Wilkinson, op. cit., p. 130.
49. Graham Turner, *Business in Britain* (Eyre and Spottiswoode, 1969), pp. 386–7.
50. Ibid., p. 388.
51. John Barber, interview.
52. Turner, *The Leyland Papers*, p. 211.
53. Lord Stokes, interview.
54. Ibid.
55. Mike Taylor, 'Troubled Times', *Classic Cars*, May 1987, p. 70.
56. David Andrews, interview.
57. John Barber, interview.
58. Taylor, op. cit., p. 70.
59. David Andrews, interview.
60. Taylor, op. cit., p. 70.
61. David Andrews, interview.

62. John Barber, interview.
63. Ibid., June 1974; UK 176,000 Overseas 35,000: Total 211,000. September 1975, UK 155,000, Overseas 25,000: Total 180,000. Source: BLMC Accounts.
64. Lord Stokes, interview.
65. *British Leyland: The Next Decade* (Her Majesty's Stationery Office, April 1975), p. 12.
66. Ibid.
67. Ibid., pp. 12–13.
68. Barbara Castle, *The Castle Diaries 1970–74* (Weidenfeld and Nicolson, 1980), p. 374.
69. Peter Paterson, 'Ford Strike in Retrospect', *Motor Industry* 1971, p. 33.
70. Sir Terence Beckett, Foreword, in Jonathan Wood, *Ford Cortina Mk I* (Osprey, 1984), pp. 6–7.
71. Richard Langworth, *The Mustangs* (Motor Racing Publications, 1984), p. 34.
72. Dennis Hackett, *The Big Idea: The Story of Ford in Europe* (Ford Motor Company, 1978), pp. 49–50.
73. *Autocar* 17 September 1970, p. 31.
74. Stephen Young and Neil Hood, *Chrysler UK: A Corporation in Transition* (Praeger Publishing, 1977), p. 233.
75. Ibid., p. 279.

Chapter 8
Ryder and After

1. *British Leyland: The Next Decade*, (Her Majesty's Stationery Office, 1975), p. 7.
2. Edouard Seidler, 'Alex Park', *Autocar*, 8 November 1975, p. 6.
3. *British Leyland: The Next Decade*, p. 47.
4. Ibid.
5. *Fourteenth Report from the Expenditure Committee, The Motor Vehicle Industry* (Her Majesty's Stationery Office, 1975), summary of recommendations, para. 9.
6. John Barber, interview.
7. *The Motor Vehicle Industry*, para, 232.
8. Ibid., para. 238.
9. Ibid., para. 227.
10. Sir Michael Edwardes, *Back from the Brink* (Collins, 1983), p. 36.
11. Ibid., 37.
12. *The Economist*, 12 February 1977, p. 107.
13. Philip Porter, *Jaguar Project XJ40* (Haynes, 1987), p. 47.
14. Ibid.
15. Ibid.
16. Ibid., p. 48.
17. Paul Skilleter, *The XJ-Series Jaguars* (Motoring Racing Publications, 1984), p. 58.
18. *The Economist*, 5 March 1977, p. 88.

19. *The Economist*, 26 February 1977, p. 101.
20. *The Economist*, 22 October 1977, p. 86.
21. Phillip Whitehead, *The Writing on the Wall: Britain in the Seventies* (Michael Joseph, 1985), p. 264.
22. Edwardes, op. cit., p. 40.
23. *The Economist*, 29 October 1977, p. 86.
24. Edwardes, op. cit., p. 42.
25. Stephen Young and Neil Hood, *Chrysler UK: A Corporation in Transition* (Praeger Publishing, 1977), p. 279.
26. Ibid.
27. Ibid., p. 281.
28. Ibid.
29. Harold Wilson, *Final Term* (Weidenfeld and Nicolson and Michael Joseph, 1979), p. 197.
30. Young and Hood, op. cit., p. 283.
31. Ibid., p. 290.
32. David Andrews, interview.
33. *The Economist*, 29 October 1977, p. 86.
34. Edwardes, op. cit., pp. 53–4.
35. Ibid. p. 54.
36. Whitehead, op. cit., p. 264.
37. Ibid.
38. Edwardes, op. cit., pp. 54–5.
39. Ray Horrocks, interview.
40. Ibid.
41. Andrew Whyte, *Jaguar: The History of a Great British Car* (Patrick Stephens, 1980), p. 174.
42. Ray Horrocks, interview.
43. David Andrews, interview.
44. Ray Horrocks, interview.
45. Richard Langworth and Graham Robson, *Triumph Cars*, (Motor Racing Publications, 1979), p. 282.
46. Ray Horrocks, interview.
47. Ibid.
48. Porter, op. cit., p. 54.
49. *The Times*, 10 July 1986.
50. *Autocar*, 19 March 1977, p. 14.
51. Pagnamenta and Overy, *All Their Working Lives*, p. 241.
52. Ray Horrocks, interview.
53. Edwardes, op. cit., p. 175.
54. Ibid., p. 174.
55. Ray Horrocks, interview.
56. David Andrews, interview.
57. Ibid.
58. Ibid.
59. Edwardes, op. cit., p. 117.

60. Ray Horrocks, interview.
61. Ibid.
62. Edwardes, op. cit., p. 109.
63. Ibid., p. 127.
64. Ray Horrocks, interview.
65. Ibid.
66. Whyte, op. cit., p. 175.
67. Ray Horrocks, interview.
68. Ibid.
69. Sir John Egan, interview.
70. Sir John Egan, 'Winning with a growl', *Sunday Times*, 27 May 1984.
71. Sir John Egan, interview.
72. Ibid.
73. Egan, op. cit.
74. Sir John Egan, interview.
75. Egan, op. cit.
76. Sir John Egan, interview.
77. Egan, op. cit.
78. Sir John Egan, interview.
79. Ibid.
80. Ray Horrocks, interview.
81. Sir John Egan, interview.
82. Ibid.
83. Ibid.
84. David Andrews, interview.
85. Edwardes, op. cit., p. 266.
86. Ibid., p. 186.
87. Alan Brinton, 'George Turnbull', *Motor Industry Managment*, March 1987, p. 12.
88. Ibid.
89. Mike Taylor, 'Troubled Times', *Classic Cars*, May 1987, p. 70.
90. Ibid., p. 70.
91. Stephen Bayley, *The Car Programme* (Boilerhouse Project, 1982), pp. 41–2.
92. Sir John Egan, interview.
93. Ray Horrocks, interview.
94. David Andrews, interview.
95. Ray Horrocks, interview.
96. Ibid.
97. Ibid.
98. *Sunday Telegraph*, 9 February 1986.
99. *The Times*, 25 April 1986.

Chapter 9
Some Reasons Why

1. Hamish Orr-Ewing, interview.

2. *The Economist*, 11 August 1962, pp. 546–7.
3. John Barber, interview.
4. Jonathan Wood, *The Ford Cortina Mk I* (Osprey, 1984), p. 9.
5. Hamish Orr-Ewing, interview.
6. 'A New Force in the Car Industry', *Sunday Times*, 3 September 1961.
7. Lord Stokes, interview.
8. Ibid.
9. David Andrews, interview.
10. W. R. Morris, 'Policies That Have Built the Morris Motor Business', *System*, February 1924, p. 74.
11. William Plowden, *The Motor Car and Politics* (Bodley Head, 1971), p. 314.
12. Jonathan Wood, *The Volkswagen Beetle* (Motor Racing Publications, 1984), p. 37.
13. Lord Stokes, interview.
14. John Barber, interview.
15. Lord Stokes, interview.
16. Harold Musgrove, *All Their Working Lives, The Motor Industry* (BBC Television, 1984).

Bibliography

Magazines and Newspapers

The Autocar (now *Autocar*)
Car
Classic and Sportscar
The Economist
The Motor (now *Motor*)
Motor Industry (now *Motor Industry Management*)
The Sunday Times
The Times
Thoroughbred and Classic Cars (now *Classic Cars*)

Government Publications and Annuals

British Leyland: The Next Decade (Her Majesty's Stationery Office, 1975)
Fourteenth Report from the Expenditure Committee, The Motor Vehicle Industry (Her Majesty's Stationery Office, 1975)
The Motor Industry of Great Britain, 1926–1986 (Society of Motor Manufacturers and Traders)

Articles

'Sir Herbert Austin, His Life Story', *The Autocar*, 23 August and 13 September 1929
Christy Campbell, 'The Making of the Mini', *Thoroughbred and Classic Cars*, September 1979
John Egan, 'Winning With a Growl', *Sunday Times*, 27 May 1984
J. Foreman-Peck, 'Exit, Voice and Loyalty as Responses to Decline: The Rover Company in the Inter-war Years', *Business History XIII*, 1963
Sir William Lyons, 'The History of the Jaguar and the Future of the Specialist Car in the British Motor Industry', Lord Wakefield Gold Medal Paper, 28 April 1969

W. R. Morris, 'Policies That Have Built the Morris Motor Business', *System*, February 1924

W. R. Morris, 'How we made a £6,000,000 Turnover Last Year', *System*, March 1924

Graham Robson, 'The Fall of Singer', *Thoroughbred and Classic Cars*, December 1981

S. B. Saul, 'The Motor Industry in Britain to 1914', *Business History V*, 1962

Mike Taylor, 'Troubled Times', *Classic Cars*, May 1987

Philip Turner and Tony Curtis, 'The Man who Made the Mini, *Motor*, 14 October 1978

Jonathan Wood, 'Archbishop to Cortina', *Thoroughbred and Classic Cars*, August 1983

Jonathan Wood, 'The Birth of the Austin Seven', *Thoroughbred and Classic Cars*, June, July and August, 1977

Jonathan Wood, 'Captivating Cortina', *Thoroughbred and Classic Cars*, July 1983

Jonathan Wood, 'Enter the Herald', *Thoroughbred and Classic Cars*, May 1983

Jonathan Wood, 'Healey', *Thoroughbred and Classic Cars*, August 1983

Jonathan Wood, 'Herald Triumph', *Thoroughbred and Classic Cars*, June 1983

Frank Woollard, 'Sir Leonard Lord', *The Motor*, 6 July 1955

Books

P. W. S. Andrews and Elizabeth Brunner, *The Life of Lord Nuffield* (Basil Blackwell, 1955)

Ronald Barker and Anthony Harding, *Automobile Design* (David and Charles, 1970)

Anthony Bird, *The Motor Car 1765–1914* (Batsford, 1960)

Anthony Bird and Francis Hutton-Stott, *Lanchester Motor Cars* (Cassell, 1965)

Anthony Bird and Francis Hutton-Stott, *The Veteran Motor Car Pocketbook* (Batsford 1963)

Roy Church, *Herbert Austin* (Europa Publications, 1979)

Jeff Daniels, *British Leyland: The Truth about the Cars* (Osprey, 1980)

R. P. T. Davenport-Hines, *Dudley Docker* (Cambridge University Press, 1984)

H. O. Duncan, *The World of Wheels* (Duncan, 1926)

Peter J. S. Dunnett, *The Decline of the British Motor Industry* (Croom Helm, 1980)

Harry Edwards, *The Morris Car 1913–1983* (Moorland Publishing, 1983)

Michael Edwardes, *Back from the Brink* (Collins, 1983)

Colin Fraser, *Harry Ferguson: Inventor and Pioneer* (John Murray, 1972)

G. N. Georgano, *The Complete Encyclopedia of Motorcars* (Ebury Press, 1982)

Bill Gunston, *By Jupiter! The Life of Sir Roy Fedden* (Royal Aeronautical Society, 1978)

Dennis Hackett, *The Big Idea: The Story of Ford in Europe* (Ford Motor Company, 1978)

Douglas Hague and Geoffrey Wilkinson, *The IRC – An Experiment in Industrial Intervention* (George Allen and Unwin, 1983)

BIBLIOGRAPHY

Robert Jackson, *The Nuffield Story* (Muller, 1964)

Lytton P. Jarman and Robin Barraclough, *The Bullnose Morris* (Macdonald, 1965)

Kent Karslake and Laurence Pomeroy, *From Veteran to Vintage* (Temple Press, 1956)

Richard Langworth and Graham Robson, *Triumph Cars* (Motor Racing Publications, 1979)

Seventy Years of Progress, (Leyland Motor Corporation, 1966)

George Maxcy and Aubrey Silberston, *The Motor Industry* (George Allen and Unwin, 1959)

Michael Moritz and Barrett Seaman, *Going for Broke: The Chrysler Story* (Doubleday, 1981)

Allan Nevins, *Ford: The Times, The Man, The Company* (Charles Scribners Sons, 1954)

Allan Nevins and Frank Hill, *Ford: Expansion and Challenge 1915–1933* (Charles Scribners Sons, 1963)

Allan Nevins and Frank Hill, *Ford: Decline and Rebirth 1933–1962* (Charles Scribners Sons, 1963)

Ian Nickols and Kent Karslake, *Motoring Entente* (Cassell, 1956)

St John Nixon, *Daimler 1896–1946* (Foulis, 1947)

St John Nixon, *Wolseley* (Foulis, 1949)

Dudley Noble, *Milestones in a Motoring Life* (Queen Anne Press, 1969)

R. J. Overy, *William Morris* (Europa Publications, 1976)

Maurice Platt, *An Addiction to Automobiles* (Frederick Warne, 1980)

William Plowden, *The Motor Car and Politics* (Bodley Head, 1971)

Laurence Pomeroy, *The Mini Story* (Temple Press, 1964)

Philip Porter, *Jaguar Project XJ40* (Haynes, 1987)

John Rae, *The American Automobile* (University of Chicago Press, 1965)

D. G. Rhys, *The Motor Industry: An Economic Survey* (Butterworth, 1972)

Sir Harry Ricardo, *Memories and Machines* (Constable, 1968)

Kenneth Richardson, *The British Motor Industry 1896–1939* (Macmillan, 1977)

Graham Robson, *Motoring in the 30s* (Patrick Stephens, 1979)

Graham Robson, *The Rover Story* (Patrick Stephens, 1977)

Michael Sedgwick, *Cars of the 1930s* (Batsford, 1970)

Michael Sedgwick, *The Motor Car 1945–1956* (Batsford, 1979)

Michael Sedgwick, *Passenger Cars 1924–1942* (Blandford, 1975)

Michael Sedgwick, *Vauxhall* (Beaulieu Books, 1981)

Paul Skilleter, *Jaguar Saloons* (Haynes, 1980)

Paul Skilleter, *Morris Minor* (Osprey, 1981)

K. and J. Slavin and G. N. Mackie, *Land-Rover: The Unbeatable 4 × 4* (Foulis, 1986)

Alfred P. Sloan, *My Years with General Motors* (Sidgwick and Jackson, 1959)

David Thomas and Tom Donnelly, *The Motor Car Industry in Coventry Since the 1890s* (Croom Helm, 1985)

James Taylor, *The Range Rover* (Motor Racing Publications, 1986)

Miles Thomas, *Out on a Wing* (Michael Joseph, 1964)

Graham Turner, *Business in Britain* (Eyre and Spottiswoode, 1969)

BIBLIOGRAPHY

Graham Turner, *Cars* (Zenith Books, 1965)

Graham Turner, *The Car Makers* (Eyre and Spottiswood, 1963)

Graham Turner, *The Leyland Papers* (Eyre and Spottiswood, 1971)

Stephen Young and Neil Hood, *Chrysler UK: A Coporation in Transition* (Praeger Publishing, 1977)

Mira Wilkins and Frank Hill, *American Business Abroad: Ford on Six Continents* (Wayne State University Press, 1964)

Andrew Whyte, *Jaguar: The History of a Great British Car* (Patrick Stephens, 1980)

Jonathan Wood, *The Ford Cortina* (Osprey, 1984)

R. J. Wyatt, *The Austin 1905–1952* (David and Charles, 1981)

Index